D0142028

HUMAN NATURE AFTER DARWIN

JONES LEARNING RESOURCE LIBRARY
MIAMI-DADE COMMUNITY COLLEGE

'Janet Radcliffe Richards has scored yet another success. *Human Nature after Darwin* is simply the clearest and most accurate introduction that there is to the current controversies about evolution, about Darwinian evolution in particular, and about how these do or do not apply to our own species. This is a book that will prove invaluable to students of all ages. Highly recommended.'

Michael Ruse, University of Guelph, Ontario.

'. . . a superb book . . . Written with real verve and large doses of humour, *Human Nature after Darwin* provides insights with relevance to many issues in public policy and to numerous fields, including philosophy, political science, sociology, and law.'

Cass R. Sunstein, Law School and Department of Political Science, University of Chicago.

'A really excellent text. Richards uses the controversy over sociobiology as a way to discuss a whole series of traditional philosophical problems . . .'

David Hull, Northwestern University

'This book provides a valuable introduction to philosophical methods of thinking . . . always clear, well-informed and challenging.'

Roger Trigg, Warwick University

'Janet Radcliffe Richards reveals the real 'implications' of Darwinism for our view of ourselves. If you knew that the anti-Darwinians must be wrong but you lacked ammunition – here it is.'

Helena Cronin, London School of Economics

'What evolutionary psychology needs most is clear thinking. Richards provides it. . . . This book has long been needed, and will be much appreciated.'

Randolph M. Nesse, University of Michigan

Human Nature after Darwin: A Philosophical Introduction is an original investigation of the implications of Darwinism for our understanding of ourselves and our situation. It casts new light on current Darwinian controversies, and in doing so provides an introduction to philosophical reasoning and a range of philosophical problems.

Janet Radcliffe Richards is Reader in Bioethics at University College London. She was formerly lecturer in philosophy at the Open University and is the author of the acclaimed book *The Sceptical Feminist*.

HUMAN NATURE AFTER DARWIN
A philosophical introduction

Janet Radcliffe Richards

London and New York

EDV

First published 2000
by Routledge
11 New Fetter Lane, London EC4P 4EE

Simultaneously published in the USA and Canada
by Routledge
29 West 35th Street, New York, NY 10001

Routledge is an imprint of the Taylor & Francis Group

© 2000 The Open University

This updated and revised version is based on a coursebook
previously published by the Open University.

Typeset in Aldus by Taylor & Francis Books Ltd
Printed and bound in Great Britain by TJ International Ltd, Padstow, Cornwall

All rights reserved. No part of this book may be reprinted or
reproduced or utilized in any form or by any electronic,
mechanical or other means, now known or hereafter invented,
including photocopying and recording, or in any information
storage or retrieval system, without permission in writing
from the publishers.

British Library Cataloguing in Publication Data
A catalogue record for this book is available from the British Library

Library of Congress Cataloging in Publication Data
Richards, Janet Radcliffe.
Human nature after Darwin: a philosophical introduction/Janet Radcliffe Richards.
Includes bibliographical references and index.
1. Philosophical anthropology. 2. Philosophy–introductions. 3. Darwin, Charles,
1809–1882. 4. Evolution (Biology)–Philosophy. I. Title.
BD450 .R4683 2000   00–042460
128–dc21

ISBN 0–415–21243–X (hbk)
ISBN 0–415–21244–8 (pbk)

75.00   AVH – 8658   6/24/03

Contents

Acknowledgements

This book started life as an Open University text, and I am grateful to the members of the OU philosophy department, and particularly to the course's external assessor, Michael Clark of the University of Nottingham, for all their comments on earlier drafts. I am also grateful to Shirley Coulson, the course manager, and to Peter Wright, the editor, for a great deal of help and support in the writing and production of the text, as well as for their advice about the content.

During the writing of this version I was considerably helped by discussions with the members of the Darwin@LSE group, and I am particularly grateful to Helena Cronin for her detailed comments on the penultimate draft.

Grateful acknowledgement is made to the following sources for permission to reproduce material in this book: D. C. Dennett (1995) *Darwin's Dangerous Idea: Evolution and the Meanings of Life*, Touchstone, by permission of Simon & Schuster; S. J. Gould (1985) 'Adam's Navel', from *The Flamingo's Smile: Reflections in Natural History*, copyright © 1985 by Stephen Jay Gould, reprinted by permission of W. W. Norton & Company, Inc. and Penguin Books Ltd; R. Dawkins (1976) *The Selfish Gene*, Oxford University Press; R. Wright (1994) *The Moral Animal*, copyright © 1994 by Robert Wright, reprinted by permission of Pantheon Books, a division of Random House, Inc., and Little, Brown and Company (UK); R. Dawkins (1982) *The Extended Phenotype*, copyright © 1982 by W. H. Freeman and Company, used with permission; P. Kitcher (1985) *Vaulting Ambition: Sociobiology and the Quest for Human Nature*, The MIT Press.

Introduction

One of the charms of coming with a Darwinian eye to the study of organisms is recognizing the mixture they display of astonishing adaptive sophistication and botched improvisation. For a long time one of the most persuasive arguments for the existence of God was the so-called Argument from Design: the idea that the finely tuned structures of organisms simply could not have come into existence by chance, and must therefore be evidence for the existence of an unimaginably powerful and intelligent creator. Once Darwin's theory of evolution by natural selection had proposed a mechanism by which such structures might result from purely natural and unplanned processes, what increasingly impressed biologists was the extent to which organisms turned out – despite being miracles of coordination and functioning – to be riddled with absurdities that no self-respecting designer would have allowed as far as the drawing board. Darwinian evolution does not work by planning from scratch with some end in view. The organisms produced by natural selection are merely the ones that happen to keep reproducing in the environments where they happen to be, and selection has nothing to work on but chance variations in structures that have previously been selected, often for quite different purposes. The result is that organisms carry with them fossils of their design history – which is why there has been so much success in tracing that history.

This fact provides a rather pleasing coincidence between this book and the Darwinian organisms that are its starting point. This is not, I hasten to say, in its being unplanned or the kind of thing any self-respecting designer would disown (an analogy need not work on all fronts), but in being rather different from what it would have been if it had been planned from scratch as an argument for its main thesis. And it is worth mentioning this because, as again Darwinians know very well, what looks odd or inexplicable if you approach it with one set of presuppositions may not only make perfect sense if you start from a different point, but also reveal elements that might otherwise have been invisible.

The book is, as its title implies, a contribution to the current Darwinian debate, whose main focus is the implications of the Darwinian revolution for our understanding of what we are and where we fit into the scheme of things. Everybody knows, because it is part of the legend, that Darwin's theory came as a horrible shock to the respectable Victorians on whom it was let loose, because this radically new account of their origins was so totally at odds with their own self-image. Everybody also knows – if only because of the recurring headlines about American schools that try to banish evolution from the curriculum, or insist that it is taught as 'only a theory' along with 'creation science' – that there are places where this horror is still felt, and where the Darwinian account of human origins is as strenuously resisted as ever. But it may be less clear, because there is such confusion in the public debate, that even where evolutionary theory is not resisted in its entirety, a modified version of the same controversy still continues. Many people who are by now resigned to the idea of our biological relationship with apes and fruit flies, and even yeast, are nevertheless alarmed by the way Darwinism seems increasingly to be getting ideas above its station, and encroaching on territory that at first looked as though it could be kept sacrosanct. Darwinian thinking is seeping through the intellectual landscape; and there is a general anxiety that the further it penetrates, the more we lose in the way of traditional ideas about the kind of thing we are or can hope to achieve. This anxiety about ourselves and our situation seems still to be, just as it always was, a large part of the reason why the battles over Darwinism are so fierce.

This book is about the extent to which these fears are justified, and it deals with topics that are familiar subjects of anxiety: free will and responsibility, the possibilities for change and improvement, ethics, altruism, and personal and political ideals and aspirations. It approaches the matter, however, not by joining in the battles about the extent to which our origins and nature can be understood in Darwinian terms, but by taking on the more fundamental – and relatively neglected – question of how much is really at stake in these battles. Its purpose is to work out the extent to which the more radical forms of Darwinism really do have the alarming implications they are alleged to have. Different problems appear in different places, but the overall conclusion is that for a variety of reasons – many connected with an insufficient appreciation of how radical Darwinian thinking is, and a failure to recognize philosophical problems for what they are – much less turns on the outcome of the battles than often seems to be assumed.

However – to return to the matter of design history – although the main purpose of the book is to investigate the implications of different degrees of Darwinian thinking, it started life with that as only its secondary purpose. It was originally written as part of an Open University course – *Philosophy and the Human Situation* – which was intended primarily to teach philosophy, and philosophical techniques, at an introductory level. Darwinism was chosen as the subject of this book partly for its intrinsic interest and its appropriateness for the course as a whole, but largely because it raised a wide range of relevant philosophical problems. A good deal of the original chalk has been dusted off this version of the book, but there is still no mistaking its origins as a teaching text. The design fossils, once you recognize them for what they are, are apparent everywhere, to the extent that the book is as much a Darwinian introduction to philosophical analysis as a philosophical analysis of problems raised by Darwinism.

I am not, however, intending this as an apology. For one thing, the fact that so much of the original teaching material remains means that the book can still be used as an introduction to philosophy by anyone who likes the idea of approaching the subject by way of this flourishing area of modern science and controversy. But also, and of direct relevance to the book as a contribution to current Darwinian debate, it probably does the job of explaining and defending its substantive thesis better in this form than it could otherwise have done. Much of the smoke of the Darwin wars is generated by widespread unfamiliarity with fairly basic techniques of philosophical argument and analysis, and making them explicit is just what is needed for clearing the air. This direction of approach, furthermore, also turns out to have given the book what amounts to a secondary thesis – a methodological one running in parallel with the substantial case – because the attempt to devise teaching techniques turned out (as it so often does) to be immensely helpful for getting to grips with the issues themselves. There were several points at which an obdurately amorphous tangle of problems actually began to cooperate when I tried to keep to the order of analysis and argument construction I had been trying to work out for students; and I think a good deal more progress could be made by means of this approach, given time, even with the subjects dealt with here. The detailed setting out of arguments also has the advantage of allowing anyone who disagrees with the conclusions reached – as many inevitably will, in an area as controversial as this – to be able to see exactly which part of the supporting argument they need to challenge.

All in all, it is difficult to know whether to count the book as a substantive thesis about the implications of Darwinism with a subsidiary methodological thesis, or a philosophical introduction to Darwinism, or a Darwinian introduction to philosophy. Still, that should not bother anyone except pre-Darwinians who are uncomfortable with anomalous forms that cannot be readily classified as existing species (though I wish this category did not include the proprietors of certain large bookshops who insist that any book can be classified under only one subject heading). It is all of those things, and readers with different interests can adjust their dosage of the different elements accordingly. If you know the biology, you will immediately recognize the sections you do not need to read; if you want the overall thesis without too much introductory philosophy, you will quickly see which explanations of techniques and discussions of texts can be skimmed or omitted. And, conversely, if you do want the book as an introduction to philosophy and its techniques, you will find that in many places the arguments are accumulated in ways that make the text easy to treat as a workbook, in which you pause to work out the next stage of the argument before reading on.

Anyway, I hope that for everyone who is – or is ripe for becoming – enchanted by the Darwinian view of life, or by philosophy, or ideally both, its being of no clear species will not matter. It can be counted as one of those Hopeful Monsters, setting out to find, in this vast and expanding subject, its own ecological niche. That, too, sounds appropriately Darwinian.

1   The theory

To understand the implications of the Darwinian revolution, it is necessary to understand the world view it replaced. This chapter provides a brief introduction to Darwin's
theory of evolution by natural selection by presenting it as a successor to the scientific
revolution of the sixteenth and seventeenth centuries, and as having the potential to
complete the overthrow of the traditional ways of thinking that the earlier revolution
had begun.

In particular, it distinguishes between teleological and non-teleological explanation, and shows Darwin's theory as relying on non-teleological explanation in contexts
where teleological explanation had previously seemed essential.

The first scientific revolution

When *The Origin of Species* was published in 1859, it not only offered a radically
different account of animal origins from anything there had been before, but also
carried the unmistakable implication that most traditional beliefs about our own
nature and our destiny would need equally radical reconsideration. The zoologist
G. G. Simpson, writing in 1966, said that all attempts to answer questions about the
nature of human beings and the meaning of life before 1859 had been worthless,
and that we should be better off if we ignored them completely (Simpson (1966)).

This book is about the implications of the Darwinian revolution for our
understanding of ourselves and our situation, and in particular about the extent
to which it demands changes in traditional ideas about the kind of thing we are.
But to understand the extent of any such changes it is necessary to know what
they are changes from; and since many of the most deeply rooted ideas of
human nature are of ancient origin, it will be useful to go back not just to the
world into which *The Origin of Species* exploded, but further still, to the time
before the first scientific revolution of the sixteenth and seventeenth centuries,
and consider how the world seemed to Western people then.

This will also be useful for another reason. The scientific revolution that
began in 1543 with the publication of Copernicus's idea that the earth was a
planet in orbit around the sun, and reached its watershed with the publication of
Newton's *Principia* in 1687, is now far enough in the past to allow us to see
clearly what kind of change it involved and how much difference it made to
people's understanding of themselves and their position. Since we are still in the
thick of the Darwinian revolution the situation is much less clear, and the earlier
revolution will provide some useful illustrations and analogies.

So, bearing in mind that this can be nothing more than the sketchiest of
sketches, start by considering the situation before Copernicus (1473–1543),
Galileo (1564–1642) and Newton (1643–1727).

Until this time, by far the most powerful and unified theory of the universe was that of Aristotle (384–322 BC). He thought of the cosmos as a series of concentric spheres, with the earth – itself spherical – at the centre. Enclosing the earth was a series of rotating solid, transparent ('crystalline') spheres which carried the sun, the moon, the planets and the fixed stars in their orbits, and, beyond them, the Empyreum, which enclosed them all.

These concentric layers differed in substance and nature, and there was, in particular, a radical difference between the heavens and the earth. The earth with its immediate surroundings – everything 'sublunary', below the moon – was made of the four earthly elements of earth, water, air and fire. Each of these had its own distinctive characteristics, and also its own natural position in the scheme of things, towards which it would move unless forcibly prevented and where it would remain until moved by external forces. Earth's natural position was at the centre of the universe, followed by a layer of water, then air, and then, just below the moon, fire. This was why stones fell and flames rose: they were trying to get back to their natural positions. The sublunary elements were, however, mixed together and kept in a perpetual state of turmoil by the power of the heavens, and things made of them were subject to generation, corruption and decay as the various elements came together and separated.

The heavens – the crystalline spheres, and the heavenly bodies they carried – were quite different. They were composed of a fifth element – the 'quintessence' – and because they were pure, rather than composed of separate elements that could mix and scatter, they were not corruptible. The only change they were capable of was that of position, and their natural motion was not up or down, but circular – constant and unending. They were also more powerful than anything in the sublunary sphere, with strong influences over the earth and everything on it. Then, finally, beyond the heavens, there lay the Empyreum. This was the purest and most powerful region of all, and unsusceptible to change of any kind.

Aristotle's universe became the basis of most intellectual ideas about cosmology after its reintroduction to the West through the Muslim world in the twelfth century, and it remained so until the scientific revolution of the seventeenth, for reasons that are not difficult to understand.

The first of these was that most of its foundations were intuitively plausible. If you think about the way things would seem to someone with no modern understanding of science, standing on the surface of the earth and watching what was going on around, you can easily see how this general view of things accorded with observation. The heavenly bodies do appear to move in circles round the earth; earth and water do appear to move naturally downwards unless prevented, and fire and air to move upwards. The heavens do seem far more powerful than the earth, and the main influence on what happens: people have always been at the mercy of climate and weather. Winds can devastate the land and churn up the seas; too much sun will burn you and shrivel your crops, too little will leave you and your plants to freeze. The only part of the scheme that does not look immediately plausible is the idea of a spherical earth, but this had also been recognized as in accordance with observation before the time of Aristotle. The curved shadow of the earth during lunar eclipses, the disappearance of ships over the horizon, and the extending of the horizon with altitude, were well-known phenomena.

Second, Aristotle fitted the elements of his scheme together into an impressive intellectual whole. The basis of the idea that the earth was a sphere at the centre of the universe, for instance, was not just that it was known to be spherical, and that everything else seemed to go round it; it also fitted the idea that the elements of which it was principally made – earth and water – naturally moved downwards unless positively prevented. This meant that matter would inevitably accumulate in the centre of the universe: if parts became separated from the centre, they would try to find their way back again. There could, therefore, be only one earth, and that must take the form of a sphere in the centre of things.

Of course the scheme was by no means complete or flawless, and the eventual development of modern science came about through persistent and determined attempts to deal with the many anomalies that appeared. The planets, for instance, always presented a problem, since they did not move in smooth circles ('planet' comes from the Greek for 'wanderer'): they kept interrupting their progress round the earth with little backward movements known as retrogressions. But no other scheme offered anything like such a systematic account of observation, and the Aristotelian cosmology became even more established when it was systematized further in the second century AD by the Greek astronomer Ptolemy, in his *Almagest*. The Ptolemaic system explained the retrograde movements of the planets without giving up the fundamental Aristotelian idea that it was the nature of heavenly bodies to move in circles. This involved a good deal of contrivance, with complicated sets of epicycles (circles revolving round moving points on the circumferences of other circles) and various other *ad hoc* devices for 'saving the appearances' (making the theory fit the observations); but the system gave good predictions of the positions of the planets into the indefinite future, and its success helped to entrench the Aristotelian view of the cosmos.

Finally, the basic Aristotelian idea became further entrenched – most strikingly in the work of Dante – by an overlay of Christian theology which integrated the universe of concentric spheres with a theological and moral order. Hell – Dante's inferno – was literally underground, at the centre of the universe, with Dante's nine circles of Hell reflecting deeper and deeper turpitude. Above the earth rose the spheres of the heavens of increasing power and purity, kept in their motions by 'intelligences', and the nine orders of angels. And finally, beyond them all, lay the throne of God in the unchanging Empyreum. Mankind was in the middle of this scheme of things: the only being that combined heavenly and earthly natures. Human beings consisted of immaterial souls, whose substance was that of the heavens, and material bodies that were animated by those souls. The souls were striving to reach their natural position among other heavenly things; their earthly bodies were bent on pulling them downwards, to

Hell. The cosmology both reflected and entrenched the Christian rejection of the material, and its conception of the bodily as sinful. It is one of the most striking ways in which these traditional ideas still linger.

This is only an impressionistic sketch, of course; and although it is useful in giving a sense of how the universe was regarded before the scientific revolution, and why it seemed so generally plausible, it must not be mistaken for a scheme that was uniform in detail, or accepted by everyone without much question. Most educated people took the fundamentals for granted, but everyone who considered the details was aware of problems. The crystalline spheres, for instance, raised problems both mechanical and theological. They needed to be solid, if they were to fulfil their purpose of pushing the planets around. But then how could the epicycles work? How could the planets move through the solid crystal? Similar problems arose for ascensions, which were the literal taking up of earthly bodies into the heavens. There were also persistent discrepancies between the geometrical models devised by astronomers and the observed motions of the heavenly bodies. The *ad hoc* contrivances for saving the appearances gradually proliferated into mechanisms of baroque complexity, in which epicycles were added to epicycles and joined by a menagerie of devices with names like 'equants' and 'hippopedes', in a never-quite-succeeding attempt to make the elements fit together. By the time of Copernicus, astronomy was widely recognized as being in a scandalous state; and it was the continuing failure to solve the problems of the Ptolemaic system that eventually led Copernicus to look for a more radical solution, and to suggest that the earth was itself a planet circling the sun.

We tend to think of the Copernican revolution as though it was Copernicus himself who gave us our present view of the solar system; and of course that is to some extent true. But Copernicus's original proposal, although obviously radical in one way, was still conservative in most others. Like his contemporaries, Copernicus still accepted as background much of the Aristotelian system. He still took it for granted that the motions of the heavenly bodies must be explained in terms of perfect circles and crystalline spheres, and by the time his scheme had been worked out in detail his arrangement of circles turned out to be about as convoluted with epicycles as the system he was trying to replace. He also still accepted Aristotle's ideas of mechanics, according to which things remained in their natural places unless there was a positive force moving them, and against this background the idea of a moving earth seemed simply incredible. If the earth was hurtling round the sun at high speed, why was there not a ferocious gale all the time? Why did loose objects not fly off into space? What force could possibly keep the earth moving? Some people were quickly persuaded by Copernicus's scheme, but those who resisted, or treated it simply as a geometrical device, had good reason to be sceptical.

What changed things was the revolution in mechanics that came first with Galileo – who also was the first person to use a telescope for astronomy and discover changes and imperfections in the perfect and unchanging heavens – and finally with the work of 'the incomparable Mr Newton' (as Locke called him).

The Aristotelian theory of distinct elements, each with its own natural motion and its own proper place in the universe, was replaced by Newton's theory of universal gravitation, which regarded matter as the same kind of thing throughout the universe; and Newton's laws of motion – according to which things remained at rest or continued in a straight line unless acted on by other forces – replaced the Aristotelian idea that force was needed to keep things moving. This removed the idea that it was the nature of the heavenly bodies to move in circles: the planets would (as it were) move in straight lines if they could, but were pulled into ellipses by the gravitational attraction of the sun. It also removed the need for a force to keep the earth moving, and accounted for our not being able to perceive its movements. The anomalies vanished, and the Copernican scheme – shorn of its encrustation of epicycles and unconstrained by requirements for circular motion – fell triumphantly into place.

All this was bound to make a considerable difference to people's understanding of their place in the universe, though this did not take quite the form that is commonly believed. It is often said that when the Copernican revolution began to unfold, making the earth only one planet among others, part of the reason for people's resistance was their losing a place of special privilege at the centre of things. But this mistakes the point. The earth was indeed at the centre of the Aristotelian universe, but human beings themselves were not; they were on the surface of the earth, which was some distance from the centre. And anyway, the Aristotelian view was that everything became *less* worthy, and less good, and less in every way, towards the centre – the lowest circle of Dante's Hell was utterly frozen and immobile – so there was nothing cosmically impressive about being in the middle. The good, powerful, important things were (as our traditional thinking leaves no doubt) above. The real change came in the disappearance of the orderly, layered, cosmos, in which everything had its proper place, and in which the moral and theological order corresponded with the physical. With the Newtonian revolution the universe suddenly became infinite, and therefore without any centre at all – not even the sun. And, most important of all, the laws of nature became in this conception the same throughout the universe. The earth was the same sort of thing as the heavenly bodies, and not radically different in kind. Newton had broken down the distinction between the heavens and the earth.

This change in conception is, incidentally, particularly strikingly shown in the rapid and complete abandonment of astrology by astronomers. Astrology had been a respectable (though not very successful) science for most of the history of astronomy, and most astronomers had also been astrologers; belief in astrology had, indeed, provided much of the original motivation for the study of astronomy. Since the heavens were quite reasonably thought to be very different in kind from the earth and to have powerful effects on it, and since the seasons do change with the movement of planets across the background of the fixed stars, it was plausible to try to find connections between what went on in the heavens and what happened on earth – just as it was plausible to wonder about the significance of comets and (what we now know as) supernovae. It was natural, therefore, that enquiring people should take to watching the planets closely, with a view to predicting their movements and influences. But the whole basis of astrology had been the idea of a radical difference in kind and in power between the heavens and the earth; and if the earth is just one planet among the others, the heavens have no more influence on it than it has on them. There is no reason to think of celestial happenings as having any particular significance for events on earth, and certainly not of the kind that formed the basis of astrology. All the reasons for thinking astrology plausible had vanished.

So the change brought about by Copernicus and Newton was indeed a revolution, and obviously made a considerable difference to people's conception of their place in the scheme of things. Spinning around in an infinite universe is decidedly less comfortable than being enclosed by spheres and angels and God; and if you disrupt the physics of a universe that also incorporates the moral and religious order, you are bound to cause some anxiety. Where, if there was no Empyreum, was the throne of God? Where was Hell? What if there were other inhabited planets in the universe; had it been necessary for them to have incarnations and salvations as well? If the Bible was not literally true in its account of heaven and earth, what did that imply for the rest of it? Obviously religious scepticism – which had always existed – found itself newly fuelled.

On the other hand, although the view of the world had radically and irrevocably changed, there was still a sense in which, from the point of view of people's understanding of their own nature, all this could be seen as detail. Although the earth and heavens had been pulled together into a single scheme, and so could no longer be seen as characterizing the two essential aspects of human beings, this did not as such threaten the traditional distinction between the material and the spiritual. The idea of an immaterial soul put into human bodies by God, and of human distinctness from animals, who had no soul (or at least, only 'souls of sense', not rational souls), could still be kept intact. And although the advance of science led more and more to the study of the human body as a kind of machine, that in itself did not raise any direct problems. The body had always been thought of as material.

Furthermore, in spite of problems about the location of God now that there was no Empyreum, the change did not seem to most people to make the slightest dent in the idea of God as creator and sustainer of the universe. It was still regarded as obvious that intelligence must lie at the root of things. Inanimate matter could not possibly fill that position, since matter could only transmit, not initiate, motion and change, and had no intelligence at all – let alone the amazing intelligence that seemed necessary for the complexity of design manifested in all aspects of the world, and for the creation of minds. For the world to be as it was, it still seemed essential to have mind, will and intention at its foundation.

This again is something that looks intuitively obvious from everyday experience. Here is John Locke (1632–1704) – who was himself in the thick of the scientific revolution, and caught up in its excitement – on the subject of what seemed obvious to everyone at the time, and probably still does to many people:

If, then, there must be something eternal, let us see what sort of Being it must be. And to that it is very obvious to Reason, that it must necessarily be a cogitative Being. For it is as impossible to conceive that ever bare incogitative Matter should produce a thinking intelligent Being, as that nothing should of itself produce Matter.

(Locke (1964 edn), p. 221)

This passage is quoted by Daniel Dennett in *Darwin's Dangerous Idea* (Dennett (1995), p. 26), as exemplifying what he calls the 'Mind First' view: the idea that intelligence must lie at the root of everything. A cogitative being is a thinking being: a being that has, or perhaps is, mind. Locke regards it as simply inconceivable that mind should emerge from 'bare, incogitative Matter'. This is a deeply rooted idea, and there was nothing in the Newtonian revolution to undermine it.

So although the first scientific revolution broke down the geographical distinction between the heavens and the earth, it still left unaffected the traditional belief that mind and matter were two distinct substances, and that it was mind that had the real power. The change called for greater sophistication in the interpretation of religious doctrine, but not for the abandonment of any essentials. God, as pure mind, or spirit, could still be seen as the creator and sustainer of the material universe, even though not occupying the heavens in the literal way that had been believed. And even though human beings could not be understood as combining heavenly and earthly substance in quite the way that had been thought in the pre-Newtonian era, they could still be regarded as of dual nature, with the spiritual aspect more powerful, and more worthy, than the material. The soul could still be thought of as giving us the capacities that distinguished us from 'bare incogitative matter'. The duty of people could still be understood as pressing the spiritual side of their nature towards God, even though no longer in the literal sense of trying to rise upwards.

So although the Newtonian revolution undermined many traditional ideas about people and their place in the universe, the most deeply rooted elements remained unaffected.

Exercise 1.1

1   Aristarchus of Samos, in the fifth century BC, had put forward the theory that the earth was a planet circling the sun. This was one of many early ideas about the nature of the cosmos, and indeed it was Copernicus's study of ancient ideas about the universe that led to his own proposal. On the basis of what has been said in this section, why do you think its truth was not accepted until more than two thousand years later?

2   Even Newton practised astrology early in his life. Why, on the basis of the account given, did scientists abandon it later?

3   To what extent did the Newtonian revolution leave intact the previous view of human nature?

(Answers on p. 273)

The Darwinian revolution

This is a useful vantage point from which to approach the Darwinian revolution, because the best way of understanding its significance is in terms of its apparent potential for completing the synthesizing process. Newton had broken down the distinction between the heavens and the earth, and brought them into a single explanatory scheme. Darwin's theory of evolution by natural selection has seemed to many people to hold out the threat (or promise) of breaking down the other distinction, and showing that it is, after all, possible for the workings of 'bare incogitative matter' to lie at the root of all complexity and consciousness, and for traditional dualism (the idea that there are two distinct substances, spirit and matter) to be replaced with monism (the idea that there is only one). Monism comes in two main forms: it may regard spirit as fundamental (as did the philosopher George Berkeley (1685–1753)), and see matter as explainable in terms of spirit, or it may regard matter as fundamental, and try to explain mind and consciousness in terms of matter. The Darwinian threat was to make plausible the idea of material monism, or materialism,[1] and in doing so to cast doubt on the Mind First view of the world. And if this threat could be fulfilled, its implications for our understanding of ourselves and our situation would presumably be far more radical than those of the Copernican/Newtonian revolution had been.

I say that the Darwinian revolution held out the *threat* of providing a justification for materialism, because from the point of view of a historical account it is important to realize how far some of Darwin's successors have moved from Darwin's own (at least published) position, and also how controversial some of these extensions and developments still are. We are still in the middle of the Darwinian revolution, arguing about how much of a revolution it really is and what its significance is. To understand this threat, and be in a position to reach some judgement about whether or not it can be fulfilled, it is necessary to see what the Darwinian theory is.

The next three sections try to explain this. The first gives an outline of the theory, the second explains what was significant about it, and the third shows why some people think it has the potential to complete the Newtonian synthesis and bring mind and matter together in a single explanatory scheme.

Natural selection

Everyone knows that Darwin's theory was about evolution. Ideas of evolution, however, go back to the ancient world, and cropped up many times, and in many forms, before Darwin. They were certainly current in Darwin's own time. Several other people – including Darwin's grandfather, Erasmus Darwin – were interested in the possibility of evolution, and the idea became more and more plausible with the advance of geology. Geological exploration was not only revealing large numbers of fossils, but also showing that particular kinds of fossil appeared in particular strata, and that the simpler forms appeared in the older rocks. It was beginning to seem likely that life forms had originally been simple and had gradually become more complex, rather than that all had been brought into existence at once, and also that the earth was very much older than had traditionally been thought. And, of course, this accumulating evidence was also beginning to undermine confidence in the biblical account of things, and open the way for the development of alternatives.

So the ideas were there; but there was a considerable stumbling block in the fact that nobody had any real idea of how evolution could possibly have worked. The situation just before Darwin was rather like the situation when Copernicus put forward the idea of an earth that moved round the sun. Even though Copernicus's idea did offer a solution to many astronomical puzzles, it was difficult for most people to take seriously because the earth showed no signs of movement, and there seemed to be no force to make it move or keep it moving. The early ideas of evolution had foundered in the same way as the early ideas of a heliocentric universe: they offered solutions to serious problems, but there seemed to be no real evidence for them, and a good deal against. But change came about in the same kind of way in both cases. Investigation revealed more and more problems in the traditional ways of thinking, which in turn led to attempts to generate new ones. And then, as with so many scientific advances, the real breakthrough came not in the idea itself – of evolution or a heliocentric system – but in the idea for a mechanism that would make it possible. The early evolutionists were like the astronomers who thought that Copernicus's account of the universe was interesting and promising, but could not see how to overcome the objections raised by Aristotelian mechanics. Darwin was like Newton, in proposing a mechanism that made the idea seem feasible.

The idea was in its essentials very simple, as revolutionary ideas often are. It was of evolution by natural selection. Here is Dennett's account of the matter.

> The idea of natural selection was not itself a miraculously novel creation of Darwin's but, rather, the offspring of earlier ideas that had been vigorously discussed for years and even generations … Chief among these parent ideas was an insight Darwin gained from reflection on the 1798 *Essay on the Principle of Population* by Thomas Malthus, which argued that population explosion and famine were inevitable, given the excess fertility of human beings, unless drastic measures were taken. The grim Malthusian vision of the social and political forces that could act to check human overpopulation may have strongly flavoured Darwin's thinking … but the idea Darwin needed from Malthus is purely logical. It has nothing at all to do with political ideology, and can be expressed in very abstract and general terms.
>
> Suppose a world in which organisms have many offspring. Since the offspring themselves will have many offspring, the population will grow and grow ('geometrically') until inevitably, sooner or later – surprisingly soon, in fact – it must grow too large for the available resources (of food, of space, of whatever the organisms need to survive long enough to reproduce). At that point, whenever it happens, not all organisms will have offspring. Many will die childless. It was Malthus who pointed out the mathematical inevitability of such a crunch in any

population of long-term reproducers – people, animals, plants (or, for that matter, Martian clone-machines, not that such fanciful possibilities were discussed by Malthus). Those populations that reproduce at less than the replacement rate are headed for extinction unless they reverse the trend. Populations that maintain a stable population over long periods of time will do so by settling on a rate of overproduction of offspring that is balanced by the vicissitudes encountered. This is obvious, perhaps, for houseflies and other prodigious breeders, but Darwin drove the point home with a calculation of his own: 'The elephant is reckoned to be the slowest breeder of all known animals, and I have taken some pains to estimate its probable minimum rate of natural increase … at the end of the fifth century there would be alive fifteen million elephants, descended from the first pair' [Darwin (1859), p. 64]. Since elephants have been around for millions of years, we can be sure that only a fraction of the elephants born in any period have progeny of their own.

So the normal state of affairs for any sort of reproducers is one in which more offspring are produced in any one generation than will in turn reproduce in the next. In other words, it is almost always crunch time. At such a crunch, which prospective parents will 'win'? Will it be a fair lottery, in which every organism has an equal chance of being among the few that reproduce? In a political context, this is where invidious themes enter, about power, privilege, injustice, treachery, class warfare, and the like, but we can elevate the observation from its political birthplace and consider in the abstract, as Darwin did, what would – must – happen in nature. Darwin added two further logical points to the insight he had found in Malthus: the first was that at crunch time, if there was significant variation among the contestants, then any advantages enjoyed by any of the contestants would inevitably bias the sample that reproduced. However tiny the advantage in question, if it was actually an advantage (and thus not absolutely invisible to nature), it would tip the scales in favour of those who held it. The second was that if there was a 'strong principle of inheritance' – if offspring tended to be more like their parents than like their parents' contemporaries – the biases created by advantages, however small, would become amplified over time, creating trends that could grow indefinitely. 'More individuals are born than can possibly survive. A grain in the balance will determine which individual shall live and which shall die, which variety or species shall increase in number, and which shall decrease, or finally become extinct' [ibid., p. 467].

What Darwin saw was that if one merely supposed these few general conditions to apply at crunch time – conditions for which he could supply ample evidence – the resulting process would necessarily lead in the direction of individuals in future generations who tended to be better equipped to deal with the problems of resource limitation that had been faced by the individuals of their parents' generation. This fundamental idea – Darwin's dangerous idea, the idea that generates so much insight, turmoil, confusion, anxiety – is thus actually quite simple. Darwin summarizes it in two long sentences at the end of chapter 4 of *Origin*:

> If during the long course of ages and under varying conditions of life, organic beings vary at all in the several parts of their organization, and I think this

cannot be disputed; if there be, owing to the high geometric powers of increase of each species, at some age, season, or year, a severe struggle for life, and this certainly cannot be disputed; then, considering the infinite complexity of the relations of all organic beings to each other and to their conditions of exis-tence, causing an infinite diversity in structure, constitution, and habits, to be advantageous to them, I think it would be a most extraordinary fact if no vari-ation ever had occurred useful to each being's own welfare, in the same way as so many variations have occurred useful to man. But if variations useful to any organic being do occur, assuredly individuals thus characterized will have the best chance of being preserved in the struggle for life; and from the strong principle of inheritance they will tend to produce offspring similarly charac-terized. This principle of preservation, I have called, for the sake of brevity, Natural Selection.

[Ibid., p. 127]

This was Darwin's great idea, not the idea of evolution, but the idea of evolution by natural selection, an idea he himself could never formulate with sufficient rigour and detail to prove, though he presented a brilliant case for it.

(Dennett (1995), pp. 40–2)

Here is a more succinct account of the same idea, from Stephen Jay Gould:

1   All organisms tend to produce more offspring than can possibly survive (Darwin's generation gave this principle the lovely name of 'superfecundity').
2   Offspring vary among themselves, and are not carbon copies of an immutable type.
3   At least some of this variation is passed down by inheritance to future genera-tions. (Darwin did not know the mechanism of heredity, for Mendel's principles did not gain acceptance until early in our century. However, this third fact requires no knowledge of how heredity works, but only an acknowl-edgement that heredity exists. And its mere existence is undeniable folk wisdom. We know that black folks have black kids; white folks, white kids; tall parents tend to have tall children; and so on.)

The principle of natural selection then emerges as a necessary inference from these facts:

4   If many offspring must die (for not all can be accommodated in nature's limited ecology), and individuals in all species vary among themselves, then on average (as a statistical statement, and not in every case), survivors will tend to be those individuals with variations that are fortuitously best suited to changing local environments. Since heredity exists, the offspring of survivors will tend to resemble their successful parents. The accumulation of these favourable variants through time will produce evolutionary change.

(Gould (1997), p. 138)

This is the essence of Darwin's theory. Organisms produce more offspring than can survive. Offspring resemble their parents to some extent. If there are even slight differences between the organisms that do and the ones that do not reproduce successfully, the characteristics of the successful will persist while those of others die out. This is how evolutionary change comes about.

The most popular illustration of this idea comes from Darwin's own observations of finches in the Galapagos Islands. (As so often in the history of science, the popular version misrepresents and oversimplifies the historical truth, but since it catches the essential point it will do for this purpose.) Each of the various islands had its own species of finch, differing in various ways, and in particular in beak shape. Darwin's idea was that these finches were all descendants of a single kind of ancestral finch, but that the different environments of the different islands had given advantages to different characteristics in its finch population. If one island had an abundance of insect food, for instance, but relatively few seeds and nuts, finches that happened to be born with fine beaks that could pick out insects from small crevices would do better than birds with large, hard beaks. The fine-beaked birds would succeed in rearing more young than their coarse-beaked relatives, and as the offspring would tend to inherit their parents' characteristics, that beak shape would gradually spread through the finch population of the island. The reverse would happen on islands where there were more seeds than insects, and where the birds whose beaks were better adapted to seed-crushing would flourish. Eventually the separated populations would become too different to interbreed, and would be separate species.

Exercise 1.2

1   What was Malthus's main claim?
2   What was the significance of Darwin's adding to this the observation that organisms varied, and offspring tended to resemble their parents?

(Answers on p. 273)

Cranes and skyhooks

That is the essence of Darwin's theory; but what makes it so potentially radical? What is it about the idea of evolution by natural selection that threatens to break down the distinction between mind and matter, in the way that Newton broke down the distinction between the earth and the heavens?

The question of whether the theory can actually fulfil this potential is a matter of its scope: the question of *how much* can be explained in Darwinian terms. That will be discussed in the next section. But to understand the radical potential of the theory and the significance of questions about scope, it is necessary to consider in more detail the kind of theory it is. And the most important point is that it reverses the traditional order of explanation, by accounting for the higher in terms of the lower, rather than the other way round.

You can get a sense of what this means by thinking of what is often known as the Great Chain of Being. This is the traditional idea of the contents of the world as forming a natural hierarchy, ranging from inanimate matter at the bottom, through plants (which are living organisms), animals (which are sentient as well as living), and human beings (possessed of rationality as well as life and sentience), until finally, at the top, is God, who is pure reason.

This is an idea that began with Aristotle, and is obviously closely connected with the Aristotelian idea of a layered cosmos, where the physical layering reflected to a considerable extent the order of natural merit. The idea was modified and extended in the Christian interpretation, where nine orders of angels continued the chain of increasing perfection from the human soul to God, but it did not change the essential idea that mind, or spirit, was higher than matter, in natural position as well as in power and moral worth. Humans, although on earth like other material beings and partly material themselves, were superior to the others in their possession of a rational soul; other living creatures (according to Aristotle and some, but not all, later thinkers) had lesser kinds of soul. And, in the Christian way of thinking about these things, order in the material world must be explained in terms of the purposes of minds, and ultimately of God. Power worked hierarchically, from higher minds to lower minds and from lower minds to matter. It could not work the other way round.

Once again, as with Aristotle's account of the nature of mechanics and the cosmos, this traditional direction of explanation is the one that accords with common sense and familiar observation. We have experience of inanimate matter, and this experience suggests that there are some things it can do, but many that it cannot. Material objects can interact with each other in a limited, mechanical way: stones can fall and shatter, seas can wash away sand, wind can blow down branches. What emerges from these natural processes, however, is always random, and shows no signs of design. Stones do not naturally shatter into perfect shapes for building, or get swept by rivers into the shapes of palaces or cottages. Matter can transmit motion to other matter, but it can, as it were, only pass on what it has received: it cannot initiate motion from rest, or design itself into complex structures. The only beings capable of doing such things are ones with minds, like us. We can decide to put ourselves into motion without being pushed; we can plan designs and shape inanimate matter into them. You cannot see minds, but you can infer their existence because something is needed to account for the difference between animate and inanimate matter, and the otherwise inexplicable difference between a newly-dead body and a living one. Our own capacity for initiating movement, however, cannot account for the world's having got going in the first place: we are nothing like powerful enough, and anyway the world was here before we were. And, furthermore, we are not capable even of understanding the intricate designs and perfect adaptations of organic nature, let alone of creating them. It seemed obvious, therefore, that all the order of nature must result from the work of something like us in being mind or spirit, but unimaginably greater. There must be a supremely powerful Mind to bring about the marvels of the natural world.

It was this direction of explanation, from the higher to the lower, that

Darwin's idea began to upset. His concern was specifically with organic evolution – evolution from lower to higher organisms – and he did not venture, at least in public, beyond this limited territory. His theory did not extend to the development of life from inanimate matter, and he did not venture directly on to theological ground. But it was startling nevertheless, because he proposed a mechanism by which mindless processes might produce the kind of complexity that had previously seemed explicable only in terms of the intentions and power of what Locke called a cogitative Being. Darwin explained organic complexity as something that just happened over vast periods of time, when simple creatures with no aspirations at all, influenced by nothing but unconscious natural forces, reproduced more of their kind than could survive. Darwin's direction of explanation was from the bottom upwards, rather than from the top downwards. It began to explain the more powerful in terms of the less powerful.

Another way of putting this is that Darwin was offering a *non-teleological* explanation in a context where teleological explanation had always been presumed essential. 'Teleology' comes from the Greek *telos*, meaning 'end', or 'goal', or 'purpose', and teleological explanations are ones that explain what is happening in terms of something to be achieved, rather than in terms of mechanical causes. They pull from in front, rather than pushing from behind. If you say that you moved the car because you wanted to make space for your neighbour, you are giving a teleological explanation, in the sense that is relevant here, because it is in terms of what you are trying to bring about. Your intentions – what you want to achieve – as it were pull the course of events from in front. If you say that your car disappeared from outside your house because its brakes failed and it ran down the hill, you are giving a non-teleological explanation. Your explanation is in terms of existing states of affairs' pushing things into the future.

We tend naturally to think in terms of teleological explanations whenever we encounter complexity and the appearance of design. In our ordinary lives we are always drawing distinctions between things that seem just to have happened without any plan (accidents and coincidences), and things that people have intentionally done or brought about. Unplanned, natural happenings result in disorder (if a pile of rocks falls it remains a pile of rocks); human intentions can bring about order (piling the rocks into specific designs, for boundaries and shelters). When we find in the natural world an appearance of order and design that seems impossible to explain in terms of random configurations of inanimate matter, therefore, it is not surprising that we automatically think in the same terms.

This idea, that whenever there is any complexity or any appearance of design you need conscious intentions to explain it, is the intuitive basis of Dennett's Mind First view (Dennett (1995), pp. 26–8). It accounts for creation stories like the one in Genesis, where elements that were originally confused together in a primeval chaos were separated and made orderly by the power and intentions of God. It also accounts, incidentally, for the familiar allegation that science explains how but never why. The 'why' part is about reason and purpose, and to imply that science is missing something in leaving out this element is to *presuppose* that there must be a purpose at the root of things. What Darwin was proposing, in contrast, was a non-teleological account of how, among organisms, order and complexity could come about without any conscious planning at all.

The way Dennett expresses the difference between Darwinian and traditional explanations is to contrast those that involve only *cranes* (cranes being things that are rooted to the ground but are capable of lifting things above themselves from there), with those that invoke *skyhooks* (things that descend from above to pull up what cannot lift itself) (ibid., pp. 73ff.). What Darwin provided, within the range of organisms, was a wonderfully simple mechanism for bringing the higher out of the lower by means of nothing but cranes.

Dennett's terminology, it must be said, is decidedly tendentious, since 'skyhook' has connotations of illusoriness and pie in the sky, which is no doubt what he intends. Dennett thinks of skyhooks as an ancient mistake, which Darwinism has rightly shown us how to get rid of. Obviously, anyone who believed – or was anxious to believe – in what Dennett calls skyhooks would not use such a derogatory term. Still, the crane/skyhook contrast is so striking, and so effectively catches the essence of the difference between traditional and Darwinian kinds of explanation, that I shall keep to it.

Exercise 1.3

1   What is presupposed by the claim 'Science explains how, but never why', when this is intended as a criticism of science?

2   Which of the following explanations are entirely non-teleological, and which involve teleological elements? (Consider each statement in exactly the form given. In many of these cases it would be easy to rewrite the teleological claim in a non-teleological form, and vice versa.)

(a)   She became a vegetarian because she wanted to help to stop the suffering of farm animals.

(b)   She became a vegetarian because after a visit to an abattoir meat made her sick.

(c)   She became a vegetarian because her brain operation caused a personality change.

(d)   He painted the room green because psychologists had shown that it was soothing.

(e)   He painted the room green because that was the only colour he had.

(f)   She fell off the ladder because the rung broke.

(g)   She fell off the ladder because she wanted some time off work.

(h)   She fell off the ladder because someone shouted and interrupted her concentration.

(i)   She fell off the ladder because someone had deliberately weakened one of the rungs.

(j)   Trees in rain forests grow tall because they are struggling to reach the light.

(k)   Trees in rain forests grow tall because the top parts get the most light, and this causes their development.

(l)   Trees in rain forests grow tall because there are no grazing animals to stunt their growth.

3   (This part of the exercise goes beyond the text. It is intended to give further practice with teleological and non-teleological explanations, and at the same time to illustrate a general point that will be of particular relevance later.)

Different explanations of a phenomenon are often rivals, and cannot both be true. However, this is not necessarily the case. Sometimes different explanations of the same phenomenon are compatible. In the following pairs of explanations, the first is teleological and the second non-teleological. For each pair, say whether the two are compatible or competing explanations.

(a)   She fainted because she wanted to cause a diversion.
She fainted because the room was stuffy.

(b)   The ladder broke because a workmate had sawn halfway through the rung for revenge.
The ladder broke because he was heavy and the rung had been weakened.

(c)   He stole the car because he wanted to impress his latest girlfriend.
He stole the car because he had had a deprived childhood.

(d)   She failed the exam because she didn't want to seem cleverer than her friend.
She failed the exam because she wasn't clever enough to pass.

(e)   He looked after his elderly mother because he cared about her happiness.
He looked after his elderly mother because he had been brought up to care about other people's happiness.

4   Even Darwinians frequently use teleological forms of explanation as shorthand in contexts where they are well aware that the real Darwinian explanation should be non-teleological. For example:
Teleological shorthand:

Stoats used to moult and grow a white coat in winter, to be less conspicuous in the snow, and then change back to brown in the spring. Now there isn't so much snow it is safer for them to stay brown all year. That is why ermine is even rarer than it used to be.

Non-teleological Darwinian explanation:

Stoats that happened to grow a white coat after their autumn moult were less conspicuous in the snow than the ones that stayed brown, and were less easily seen by predators. More of them therefore survived the winter, and produced offspring which also turned white in winter. But as the climate changed and winters were no longer snowy, the white stoats were more easily picked off by predators than the brown, and the brown ones became the ones that survived the winter and produced offspring afterwards. This is why white stoats are now rare, and ermine is even rarer than it used to be.

The teleological shorthand is convenient but potentially misleading, because it gives the impression that the stoats, or the designer of the stoats, planned this as a way of making sure that stoats kept going. Darwinian evolution has no plans at all, and it is important to remember what the full Darwinian form should be. Rewrite the following teleological explanations in Darwinian terms. (Do not bother about whether they are correct in detail, or indeed at all; this exercise concerns only the form of the explanation, and not its content.)

(a)   The finches on the islands where there were lots of seeds developed strong, blunt beaks to crush them; the ones on the islands where there were more insects needed pointed beaks to get them out of cracks.

(b)   The peppered moth used to be light brown, to conceal itself against the trunks of trees. But since industrial pollution has blackened the trees, the moth has changed its colouring to match.

(c)   Some flowers mimic insects, to cheat insects into coming to pollinate them.

(Answers on p. 273–4)

Scope and potential

It is common knowledge – almost folklore – that Darwin's theory was horrifying to most of his contemporaries because, like Copernicus's, it presented a direct threat to received religious belief.

In early Victorian Britain most people – at least according to censuses and on Sundays – were Christian; and since their Christianity tended to fundamentalism, most would probably have claimed to believe in the literal truth of the Genesis creation story. According to this account, God had made the world in six days, and created animals as distinct species in (it was taken for granted) their modern forms. And although the Bible did not say anything directly about the age of the earth, Archbishop James Ussher in 1654 had done calculations on the basis of Old Testament genealogies, and his conclusion that the earth was created in 4004 BC – on 23 October – was generally accepted. By the nineteenth century these beliefs were already under threat from the work of geologists who were beginning to have ideas of evolution and of a much older earth. But nobody had any real idea how evolution could have occurred, and fundamentalists resisted the new ideas with explanations of their own – such as that fossils could be the remains of creatures who had died in Noah's Flood, or that there had been a series of creations and annihilations. The reason why Darwin's theory presented a serious threat to fundamentalism was that it made the heretical idea of evolution seem plausible and comprehensible for the first time.

Even so, there was a limit to how serious the theory was (and is) for established religion as a whole, because theology has always been ready to increase its sophistication in response to new problems. It had already coped with the collapse of the Aristotelian universe, and by Darwin's time many theologians were themselves already questioning literal interpretations of the Bible. Not much doctrinal upheaval was needed for a shift to the view (which many people hold now) that God could have arranged animal creation by the method Darwin described, and intended the Genesis account only as a metaphor for the unsophisticated. The idea of animal evolution did not, on its own, affect the fundamental conviction that only spirit could initiate change. It seemed to leave intact the need for God to create the world in the first place, to bring life from inanimate matter, and to make individual human souls.

But although the immediate effects of Darwin's theory were in some ways not all that radical, the fact remains that the intrusion of a theory of this type, with its inversion of the familiar pattern of explanation, was radical in itself, and made a profound difference to ways of thinking. The appearance of design in the animal world – the adaptation of creatures to their surroundings – had always been regarded as part of the evidence for the existence of God. The theory of evolution by natural selection did not in itself remove the apparent necessity for Mind to get life going in the first place – Darwin himself probably thought something of the kind was necessary – but God had traditionally been thought essential to explain not only the existence of life, but also the details of organic design. If Darwin's theory could explain the appearance of design without direct appeal to God for the details, might it not be able to do a great deal more? The real danger lay not in the immediate challenge to Genesis, but in the radical nature of Darwinian explanation, and its reliance on cranes in a context where skyhooks had previously seemed indispensable. It was this that was revolutionary; and revolutionary ideas have a habit of spreading.

Once again, Dennett's characteristically colourful account of the matter is too good to resist:

> Did you ever hear of universal acid? This fantasy used to amuse me and some of my schoolboy friends … Universal acid is a liquid so corrosive that it will eat through anything! The problem is: what do you keep it in? It dissolves glass bottles and stainless-steel canisters as readily as paper bags. What would happen if you somehow came upon or created a dollop of universal acid? Would the whole planet eventually be destroyed? What would it leave in its wake? After everything had been transformed by its encounter with universal acid, what would the world look like? Little did I realize that in a few years I would encounter an idea – Darwin's idea – bearing an unmistakable likeness to universal acid: it eats through just about every traditional concept, and leaves in its wake a revolutionized world view, with most of the old landmarks still recognizable, but transformed in fundamental ways.
>
> Darwin's idea had been born as an answer to questions in biology, but it threatened to leak out, offering answers – welcome or not – to questions in cosmology

(going in one direction) and psychology (going in the other direction). If redesign could be a mindless, algorithmic process of evolution, why couldn't that whole process itself be the product of evolution, and so forth, all the way down? And if mindless evolution could account for the breathtakingly clever artefacts of the biosphere, how could the products of our own 'real' minds be exempt from an evolutionary explanation? Darwin's idea thus also threatened to spread all the way up, dissolving the illusion of our own authorship, our own divine spark of creativity and understanding.

(Ibid., p. 63)

You can see what he means by this by thinking again in terms of the Great Chain of Being. What Darwin did was to take some links in the middle of this chain – the links containing the various levels of organism – and invert the traditional order of explanation for those links. The range of animals was to be explained not by a skyhook's coming down and creating it all at once, but by the development of the higher animals through natural, unplanned processes among simpler ones. But once this kind of bottom-up rather than top-down explanation starts to seem feasible at all – once the acid has begun its work of dissolving traditional assumptions – why should it stay comfortably in the middle, confined to change among animals? Might it not work just as effectively on other parts of the chain?

Nobody could miss the potential for Darwin's own next step, which was to extend the account of evolution to include human beings, in *The Descent of Man* (1871). This was much more serious, as everyone knew. Tradition had presented animals as created specifically for us to have dominion over, and not as, literally, our relations. It had also explained our nature by our possession of a rational soul, directly created by God. People could still resist the most radical implications of this extension of the theory – again, as many now do – by claiming that even if human *bodies* evolved from animal beginnings, that still allowed for a specifically human soul with an origin and nature of the traditional, immaterial, kind. But the Darwinian approach obviously raised the possibility that the kind of rationality possessed by human beings was just another step in the evolution of intelligence among animals, and that there was no need to think that souls existed at all. The acid was threatening to leak out in the upward direction.

A similar kind of possibility also applied to the lower links in the chain. If there is no good reason to think that explanation of a Darwinian kind must stop with the higher animals, might it not also start before the lower animals, and account for the emergence of life from inanimate matter? Even though Darwin did not pursue this idea, the possibility is obviously there; and if this bridge can be crossed, the full danger of the Darwinian inversion becomes clear. If the unplanned interactions of 'bare incogitative matter' really can account for the emergence of life, and simple life for the emergence of complex life and intelligence, then we may literally have risen from the dust, without any assistance from anything higher.

Of course, that would still leave the problem of accounting for the existence of the world itself, and although (as Dennett implies) some enterprising physicists are busy trying to use Darwinian principles to explain the existence of our universe, it is not at all clear – at least yet – how this could work. But whether or not that can be done, the problems in understanding how matter could have arisen from nothing are not obviously more serious than those involved in explaining how God could have arisen from nothing; so if Darwinism could get as far as explaining how human capacities could have resulted from the ordinary characteristics of matter, it might have done all the damage necessary.

This is all obviously extremely serious, because if the inverted order of explanation can get this far, there no longer seems any reason to believe in the existence of skyhooks at all. If God and the angels are no longer needed to explain anything, there may be no reason to believe they exist. And if that stage is reached, human beings appear not in the middle of the Great Chain of Being, a little lower than the angels, but (as far as we know) at the top: the highest point yet reached by mindless cranes toiling upwards out of the mud. This is a very long way indeed from the traditional view of our own situation.

So although Darwin himself did not venture far beyond this middle ground of animal and human evolution, at least in public, and seems to have had doubts about whether skyhooks could be eliminated entirely from the scheme of things, the idea of natural selection at least raised as a serious possibility the idea that the animate and the conscious, together with all the ideas and culture we have traditionally regarded as inspired by higher things, could have developed from the inanimate without the intervention or addition of anything else. It raised, more seriously than ever before, the idea that no supernatural life breathed into matter to make it animate, and that no soul was infused to make it conscious. Consciousness and all that goes with it – culture, art, science, philosophy, moral ideas – are just things that appear when matter gets into these arrangements, and the idea of natural selection shows in principle how these arrangements are possible.

And since it has traditionally been these outside elements – intelligent, immaterial, and unreachable by science – that have been thought to distinguish us from the lesser creation, the threat of their being taken up into a Darwinian synthesis opens the way for the scientific explanation of all that we regard as most distinctive about ourselves. It may mean that what we tend to think of as our most essential characteristics are ultimately to be explained as devices that exist only because they have been successful in achieving our evolutionary survival. It is hardly surprising, therefore, that Darwinism has seemed to threaten everything traditionally regarded as most fundamental about our nature.

The question of the extent to which these threats are all that they seem is the subject of this book.

The potential of the Darwinian revolution can be best understood as a continuation of the first scientific revolution. The first revolution, of Copernicus and Newton, broke down the traditional distinction between the earth and the heavens, and showed the universe to be the same throughout. But it did not alter the prevailing view that it was impossible to explain the complexity of life and movement and thought in terms of the workings of inanimate matter. This was what Darwin's view began to upset, because he altered the direction of explanation, producing non-teleological explanation in a context where teleology had always seemed necessary.

Since traditional views of the world have held mind, or spirit, to be distinct from matter, and to account for all the most important aspects of our nature, the Darwinian revolution seems to present a radical threat to our understanding of ourselves and our potential.

2 The sceptics

The previous chapter was more about Darwinism than philosophy; this one is more about philosophy than Darwinism. It uses controversy about the truth of Darwin's theory to introduce wider questions about epistemology and philosophy of science, and to disentangle different kinds of scepticism.

Scientists now claim that the essentials of the Darwinian theory have been established beyond any doubt, and this chapter addresses the question of whether they are entitled to any such claim. It does not deal (except in outline) with the *scientific* arguments for certainty, but addresses the wider question of whether we are ever justified in claiming certainty for anything. This raises two levels of question. The first, which comes into philosophy of science, is about the claim that whatever scientists discover may always be overthrown by later evidence. The second is about radical philosophical scepticism, and introduces briefly the subjects of metaphysics and epistemology.

Philosophical scepticism is often treated as a subject of purely academic interest, but it becomes of practical relevance when it is inadvertently entangled with questions about the strength of scientific evidence. The last section of this chapter distinguishes specific doubts about Darwinian theory from all-encompassing doubts of different kinds, and in doing so draws distinctions between levels of argument that will be crucial in later chapters. It also makes use of these issues to introduce the problems of practical decision-making against a background of ignorance and uncertainty, which will reappear in the discussion of politics in Chapter 9.

But is it true?

It is all very well to say that Darwinian ideas present threats to deeply rooted ideas about ourselves, but whether any or all of these threats are fulfilled depends in the first instance on whether the theory is true. If it is not, we have no need to worry about its potentially alarming implications. And, as is well known, many people still resist the Darwinian account of our origins altogether.

The most energetic and conspicuous of these are the spiritual heirs of the Victorian fundamentalists: the so-called creationists, who still flourish in America, and whose starting point is a conviction of the literal truth of the Genesis account of creation. Nearly all systematic resistance to Darwinism as a whole comes from religion (which is not, of course, to say that all religions resist all aspects of Darwinism). Still, it is also worth mentioning doubts of a more diffuse kind. According to the Darwinian biologist John Maynard Smith:

> Something very odd has happened during the past five years or so. The public has been persuaded that Darwinism, as an explanation of evolution, has been exploded.

> I find repeatedly, when discussing my work with non-biologists, that they are under the impression that Darwin has been refuted ... *The Times* ... marked the centenary of Darwin's death with an article (by a non-biologist) attacking his views, and a cartoon of Darwin slipping on a banana skin ... *The Guardian* ... every now and then ... carries an editorial attacking 'mechanistic biology'. Television joined in the anti-Darwinian crusade, with an *Horizon* programme 'Did Darwin get it wrong?' [which] left the impression that the producer had wandered round the US thrusting a microphone in front of anyone who would say anything that sounded anti-Darwinian.
>
> (Maynard Smith (1988), p. 23)

This book is primarily about the implications of Darwinian theory, rather than about its truth, so there are severe limits to how much space can be given to the justifiability of doubts such as these. Questions about the nature and strength of the evidence raise large issues in philosophy of science as well as in science itself, and if we went far into those we should never get to the problem of implications. On the other hand, there is no point in embarking on questions about the implications of Darwinism if the reader is likely to be thinking all the time that the most important issue of all has simply been ignored.

It is clear from the story so far that the question of whether Darwinism is true cannot be a simple one, because of all the questions about how far Dennett's acid can seep beyond its original container. The most important current debates are not between pro- and anti-Darwinians, but among people who have crossed the Darwinian threshold but disagree about how far beyond it Darwinian explanation can take them. But questions about how far Darwinian explanation can stretch arise only if it can get off the ground at all, on Darwin's central ground of organic evolution; and the question of whether this can be done is what most people still have in mind when they hear disputes about the truth of Darwinism. So that is the first question to address.

Scientific confidence

When the question of the truth of Darwinism is clearly intended as being about the fundamental theory of organic evolution by natural selection, the answer is almost uncontroversial among scientists. Virtually all scientists agree that the evidence for organic evolution by natural selection is now so overwhelming that its essential truth is beyond question. Acceptance of the theory went into something of a decline towards the end of the nineteenth century and at the beginning of the twentieth; but since then, and in particular since the discovery of DNA and the explosive development of genetics in the second half of the twentieth century, confirmations have piled on from all directions.

The main evidence depends on scientific detail, but as this is not a book about science – and as there are innumerable books on Darwinism that are – I shall not go into these details. All that is needed here is an account of the *kinds* of reason scientists have for claiming that the central core of Darwinism must be regarded as beyond serious scientific doubt; and to this question Dennett again gives a succinct answer:

> The fundamental core of contemporary Darwinism, the theory of DNA-based reproduction and evolution, is now beyond dispute among scientists. It demonstrates its power every day, contributing crucially to the explanation of planet-sized facts of geology and meteorology, through middle-sized facts of ecology and agronomy, down to the latest microscopic facts of genetic engineering. It unifies all of biology and the history of our planet into a single grand story. Like Gulliver tied down in Lilliput, it is unbudgeable, not because of some one or two huge chains of argument that might – hope against hope – have weak links in them, but because it is securely tied by hundreds of thousands of threads of evidence anchoring it to virtually every other area of human knowledge.
>
> (Dennett (1995), p. 20)

In other words, the reason why the theory of evolution by natural selection is regarded by scientists as certainly true is that it is not an idea on its own. What puts it beyond question is its detailed interlocking with innumerable other areas of science.

You can see the point here, once again, by means of a comparison with what happened during the transition from Aristotle to Newton. When the Aristotelian/Ptolemaic account of the universe was generally accepted everyone knew the theory faced serious problems, but they nevertheless had good reason to accept it, and there was no serious rival. When Copernicus's ideas appeared on the scene they seemed to solve some of these problems, but they also faced many new difficulties, not suffered by the existing view. Both theories fitted some of the facts but seemed incompatible with others, so it was not clear which should be rejected and which, if either, accepted. But then came Galileo and, eventually, Newton. Newton's theory was compatible with a refined version of Copernicus, but not with the Ptolemaic system or with astrology. This was not enough on its own to show that Copernicus was (more or less) right and Ptolemy wrong; but it was only the beginning. After Newton all kinds of new questions could be asked and new predictions made, and the success of the theory began to stretch into areas that the earlier one had not begun to reach. When Ptolemaic astronomers found planets following inappropriate paths, for instance, they had to invent convolutions of epicycles, and even then could not achieve accuracy. When post-Newtonian astronomers found that Neptune turned out to be following not quite the path that Newtonian mechanics predicted, astronomers proposed that a hitherto unknown planet might be pulling it out of orbit, and when they looked in the appropriate place they found Uranus. When Uranus's orbit itself turned out to be slightly different from what was expected, they looked again and found Pluto. Ptolemaic astronomy had been able to achieve nothing like this. Newton's theory superseded Aristotle not because of any simple, direct proof that Aristotle's was wrong, but because

Newton's theory was so successful. Different parts of science were coming together, and reinforcing each other.

Darwinian science is not just going, but has gone, the same way. One standard creationist criticism of Darwinism, for instance, used to be that the evidence was circular, because the rock strata were used to date the fossils, and the fossils to date the strata. The theory of evolution is no longer just about strata and fossils. Neo-Darwinism, the modern version of the theory that incorporates the astonishing discoveries of genetics, is too closely integrated with everything else we know about, and the things we do every day, to leave any room for reasonable doubt. We know how heredity works, we know about mutations, and we know so much about the details of which bits of genetic material do what that we can move genes from one creature to another. It makes as much sense to doubt the Darwinian explanation of life while complaining about genetically modified tomatoes and the prospect of human clones as it would to work on the intricacies of rocket design while thinking that the heavenly bodies might, after all, be circling a stationary earth on crystalline spheres propelled by angels.

That, as it stands, is of course just assertion; and critics of this kind of view – mainly religious fundamentalists – still insist that the details of the scientific evidence are not enough to establish the truth of evolution, and, at least in America, campaign for Darwinian evolution to be referred to in schools as 'only a theory', and for children to be taught 'the arguments against evolution' and 'intelligent design theory' as well. If you suspect there may be anything in these objections, there is no difficulty in finding literature that expounds them, and responses by scientists.

But in the meantime, there are also challenges to scientific claims of certainty that have nothing to do with the details of scientific evidence, but are instead based on more general claims that scientists are never entitled to claim certainty for their theories because, no matter what the evidence, they may always be wrong. And this kind of general scepticism about science is so widespread, and so frequently confused with doubts about particular theories like Darwin's, that it needs at least some discussion.

The rest of this chapter deals with questions around this issue. The next section is about the idea, familiar among scientists themselves, that any theory, however well supported, may be overthrown by later discoveries. This discussion can be regarded as a brief introduction to issues that arise in philosophy of science.

Following that comes a section about the more fundamental philosophical problem of radical scepticism: the question of whether we can ever know anything for certain. This serves partly as an introduction to problems of epistemology (theory of knowledge), but I also use it to raise the wider problem of making practical decisions against a background of ignorance, which will be an important issue in Chapter 9.

Finally, under the general heading 'Shifting goalposts', there are two sections about the confusions that can arise if different kinds of challenge to the claims of scientists are not clearly distinguished from each other. The topic is introduced through the work of a nineteenth-century naturalist who was also a Christian fundamentalist, and whose argument against his sceptical contemporaries depended on just such a mistake. The discussion is then extended to a wider consideration of the danger of unnoticed shifts of level in mid-argument, which is directly relevant to several later parts of the book.

The perpetual threat of overthrow

Scientists themselves, and not merely their critics, are often heard to claim that you can never be certain of the truth of any theory, because no matter how long some belief has been going, or how successful it has been, there is always the possibility that it may be overthrown by some new discovery. People who make this claim cite the way in which, throughout the history of science, theories have always been ousted by others, and they refer approvingly to the ideas of the philosopher Karl Popper (1902–94), who argued that you could never prove scientific theories true, but only falsify them. If this is true, it must apparently be wrong to claim that scientists have now proved the essentials of Darwinism beyond serious doubt.

The question of whether scientists should be trying to confirm theories or falsify them is interesting in itself, and, if only because of the number of scientists who claim to be Popperians, important. But Popper's arguments go into kinds of technicality that are beyond our scope. There is a large area of philosophy of science that deals with questions about the rational basis of evidence, but here it will be necessary to take a short cut, and address more directly the question of how plausible this idea is.

Once again, the earlier scientific revolution will help to put current problems into perspective. At first sight the history of ideas about the universe may seem to provide all the proof necessary that nothing can ever be established with certainty. For, it will be said, people felt certain about Ptolemy and Aristotle, whose views were overthrown by those of Copernicus and Newton. Then they claimed to be certain about those, but Newton was overthrown by Einstein. Therefore anything, no matter how well established, no matter how rationally believed, may be overthrown by later discoveries. Scientists are therefore never justified in claiming certainty.

Is this true? What needs to be established is the truth of the statement:

> All claims made by scientists, no matter how well supported, may be overthrown by future evidence.

This statement takes the form of a universal generalization, and a universal generalization can be proved wrong by a single counterexample: the claim that all As are Bs is false if you can find an A that is not a B. (This is the basis of Popper's claim about falsifiability.) If, therefore, you can find a scientific claim you think could not possibly be overthrown by future discoveries, you will conclude that the statement is false. Does it seem to you that there are any such claims? If it seems that there are not, consider a related question. Are scientists entitled to claim that any previous ideas about the universe are definitely *wrong*? Is there any chance at all, for instance, that the earth may, after all, be at the centre of a finite, spherical universe, and that the planets may be made of a quite different kind of substance, carried by intelligences pushing crystalline spheres?

When the question is put that way round, few people would claim to have any doubts at all. We know that the Ptolemaic system cannot be true, because we know too much that is incompatible with it. If it were true, we could not be sending up space probes that depend on the finest calculations of gravity and momentum, and doing such sophisticated things as using the gravity of one planet to change the trajectory of rockets to direct them to the next. If the heavenly bodies were made of a quintessence rather than the kind of thing we find on earth, we could not have people walking on the moon and bringing back lumps of perfectly recognizable substances. It is out of the question that there is an unchanging sphere of fixed stars, because we now have sophisticated ways of measuring the heavens, and we know that there are millions of other galaxies in which change is happening all the time.

Perhaps the question of whether previous views of the world are certainly false seems quite different from that of whether anything we now believe is certainly true; but in fact these are two aspects of the same question. To whatever degree you think it certain that we cannot go back to Ptolemy, to that same degree you think all the claims about evidence against Ptolemy are themselves certain. It is only because we have no doubt at all that rockets are going up, that scientists are making detailed calculations to control them, that pictures and (soon) rock samples from planets will be coming back, and that scientists just could not be getting all this right unless they knew in extraordinarily detailed ways about many of the objects in space, that we can be certain the conflicting theories are false.[2] If we think some earlier theories are certainly false, we must believe that the evidence that proves them false is certainly true. If we think theories can be overturned, we must think there is something certain enough to do the overturning.

But, it may be said, what about Einstein? Surely he overthrew Newton? And until Einstein came along, surely people were completely confident about the truth of Newtonian mechanics?

To assess this claim, consider again the kinds of thing most people regard as so certain that they completely rule out the possibility of our returning to Ptolemy and Aristotle. For instance, given all the familiar facts about space exploration, we must think that among the things we are certain about are such matters as the arrangements of planets and other heavenly bodies in space, their gravitational attraction, their orbits round each other, and so on. We obviously do not think of beliefs about *those* ideas as having been overthrown by Einstein, since we still hold them; but nearly all such ideas were part of Newton's scheme. Einstein made no difference at all to the idea that the earth was one of a series of planets circling the sun, and made of the same kind of matter, or that the universe contained other galaxies. And many of the Newtonian ideas that his theories did affect (gravity, infinite space) were only slightly affected. Newton's theory of gravity was very nearly right as an account of how matter behaves.

The point is that a theory such as Newton's is not an all-or-nothing matter, to be accepted or rejected as a whole, with each of the details either wholly right or completely wrong. Large theories can be largely right, even if not entirely so; particular beliefs can be very close to the truth, even if not precisely true. Einstein changed some parts of the Newtonian view of things completely, significantly modified others, and added some completely new elements, but large tracts of the Newtonian description of things remain beyond any possibility of revision. And this was also true of Aristotle's overthrow by Newton. A great many elements of the Aristotelian system were never in any doubt, and were unaffected by the Newtonian revolution. Newton did not shift the Aristotelian idea that the earth was round, for instance, or that the heavenly bodies had certain kinds of movement in relation to it, or that stones fell to the earth and fire rose.

There is nothing puzzling about this; it is perfectly familiar from many contexts. To say that there are always some scientific claims we can be certain of, even though we may not be certain of all aspects of them and may not have the theoretical details right, is no more remarkable than your being absolutely sure that some friends of yours have at least three children, while at the same time not knowing whether they have more than three, being wrong about the age and sex of one of them, and mistakenly thinking they have a dog. And this, in essence, is why scientists claim to be certain about genetics and Darwinism in general. The fact that there is a great deal we do not know or are unsure about, and (undoubtedly) that there are many things we think we know but are wrong about, does not alter the fact that there are innumerable things about which there cannot possibly be any reasonable doubt. Nobody can now reasonably doubt the existence of chromosomes and genes, for instance, or the basic mechanisms of reproduction and heredity.

This is why Dennett concludes the paragraph quoted in the last section by saying:

> New discoveries may conceivably lead to dramatic, even 'revolutionary' *shifts* in the Darwinian theory, but the hope that it will be 'refuted' by some shattering breakthrough is about as reasonable as the hope that we will return to a geocentric vision and discard Copernicus.
>
> (Ibid., p. 20)

The shifts he considers possible are like the Einsteinian change: a more powerful theoretical approach that explains more, and reveals hitherto unknown entities and influences. But there is no more chance of our giving up neo-Darwinism – the version of Darwinism that depends on modern genetic theory – than there is of our giving up the idea that we are on a planet orbiting the sun.

Radical sceptics and rational bets

Reaching this conclusion, however, depends on a willingness to accept that there is anything at all about which we are entitled to claim certainty, and many people have disputed even this. May we not be mistaken even in our most fundamental and confident beliefs about what the world is really like?

There is a long tradition of such radical philosophical scepticism. The most famous case is that of Descartes (1591–1650), who considered the possibility that the world might not really contain all the objects he had always assumed it did, and that all his experiences might really be dreams, or even directly caused by an evil genius bent on deceiving him. Descartes himself was not, in fact, a sceptic. His evil genius was a methodological device, rather than a seriously entertained possibility. What Descartes wanted to do was to find out whether anything could be known for certain, and his evil genius was part of a thought experiment. If such a being existed, and devoted all its energies to deceiving him, would there be anything about which it could not possibly deceive him? Descartes did think that he could establish a foundation of certain knowledge on which to build: the evil genius could not be deceiving him into thinking he existed when he did not, because he would have to exist even to be deceived. This is the context in which he produced his famous 'Cogito ergo sum' – 'I think, therefore I am' – a proposition he regarded as 'so firm and sure that the most extravagant suppositions of the sceptics [were] incapable of shaking it'. But few philosophers accept that he succeeded in building a structure of certain knowledge on this foundation, and the problem of radical scepticism has persisted.

In its most general form the problem is that the evidence we have for what the world is like and how it works comes through experience. But in that case, why do we feel entitled to make claims about anything more than that experience itself? Why do we think there are real objects, existing independently of ourselves, when all we have is our sensations? How, for instance, can we tell that life is not all a dream? It is no good doing experiments, or trying to wake ourselves up, because if life actually is a dream, all those experiments, and our waking up, will all themselves be part of the dream. It is no good trying to prove that the cat currently trying to nudge your hand away from the page really exists, and is not an illusion created by Descartes's evil genius, because whatever experiments you do to test it for genuine catness, the results of those experiments could all be more illusions with the same cause. Or maybe you are nothing but a brain in a vat, being manipulated by some brilliant but probably unhinged scientist, who is systematically preventing you from ever finding out your true situation by inducing new and convincing illusions every time you have doubts. Maybe your sister is nothing but a robot, with no sensations or experiences. It is no good trying to disprove this claim by asking subtle questions, or sticking pins into her, because whatever her responses are, they consist only of more behaviour. You cannot get directly at her sensations or experiences, and therefore you can never be sure that anything lies behind that behaviour.

This is what is important about radical scepticism. When people are sceptical in the ordinary way about some claim, rather than in the radical way, they are saying that you have not enough evidence for what you are claiming. People who were sceptical about Copernicus's ideas when they were first put forward, before Galileo and Newton, would have said that he had not enough evidence, or that the evidence went against him. But what the radical sceptic does is claim that all *possible* evidence is useless. No matter how much you had, you would still not have proved your point. Whatever evidence you produce, the radical sceptic will say it is irrelevant to your claim. However much evidence there is for the universe of Copernicus and Newton, all that evidence presupposes that there is underlying our sensations an orderly world that our investigations can discover, and if there is not, the evidence is worthless. And the same applies to Darwinism. Scientists may claim absolute certainty about genes and chromosomes, but that certainty itself depends on a belief that the world really is as it seems to be, and that our experience as a whole is not just a gigantic illusion.

Arguments like these are just the kind of thing that drives people who are not of philosophical inclinations away from the subject in droves, muttering about angels on the heads of pins, and making their way off to history, or computer programming, or some other sensible subject. And, of course, philosophers themselves do not go through the world in a perpetual state of anxiety in case Descartes's evil genius is hiding behind the next tree.

Still, the question of whether the radical sceptic can be proved wrong is philosophically interesting, and philosophers have responded to the challenge in a variety of ways. They obviously cannot use empirical evidence; that would be begging the question – presupposing the point at issue – since the whole problem is whether empirical evidence can tell us anything. However, they have produced many other kinds of argument. Descartes, for instance, thought he could demonstrate that there was an orderly world underlying our sensations, first by proving the existence of God and then arguing that he could rely on his senses because God could not be a deceiver. Others, such as Berkeley, have concluded that there is no problem because material objects are themselves actually collections of experiences, rather than the causes of them. Others still, such as the Logical Positivists in the twentieth century, have denied that there is a genuine problem, claiming that propositions that could not be verified empirically were meaningless, and therefore that all metaphysical questions – questions about the reality underlying our experience, which cannot themselves be answered by experience – were pseudo-questions.

However, that vast philosophical quagmire extends far beyond the scope of this modest enquiry. If any headway is to be made here in defending scientific claims of certainty against the onslaughts of radical scepticism, it will once again be necessary to take a short cut. This will also have the additional advantage of covering some ground that will be needed for the arguments of Chapter 9.

Consider again where we are. The argument so far has been in two stages. First came the claim – asserted, but not justified in detail here – that the *scientific* evidence supports the essentials of Darwinian theory. Second came a counter claim, that new evidence may appear at any time to overturn what seems certain, which was replied to by the argument that if we think mistaken beliefs can be decisively overturned, we must think there is something certain enough to do the overturning. But now we come to a deeper level of scepticism still. The critic now says that this conclusion – that there are some things we can be certain of – itself depends on the assumption that the world behind our sensations is as we think it is: independent of our experience and orderly in its behaviour. But if we are wrong about that – if, to take Descartes's fantasy, we are in the power of an evil genius, or a mad scientist controlling our thoughts – then all our conclusions about certainty go by the board. The evil genius could change the course of things and fool us at any moment. So we cannot prove, after all, that any theory is either false or true.

Now we cannot – at least without going deep into metaphysics, and probably not even then – deal with that question directly here. But perhaps we do not need to. If we think of these arguments about Darwinism (or any other part of science) in context, where the question is whether scientists are justified in claiming certainty for what they say, one of our main concerns is about how we should *act*. We are asking whether we should *treat* Darwinian scientists as having the knowledge they claim – act on the basis of their theories – or whether we should treat them with scepticism. For instance, we want to know whether we should allow their theories to be taught as fact in schools, or whether we should say, as creationists do, that it is 'just a theory', and demand that no special authority is claimed for it. We also need to know whether we should give out government research grants on the assumption that scientists are entitled to claim this kind of certainty, or whether we should be more tentative and scatter the money more widely, among them and their critics. Even if we have an intellectual interest in the metaphysical question of whether the world really is as we think it is, what really matters in practical and scientific contexts is whether we are justified in *treating* particular ideas as certain. We can, then, usefully reconsider the matter of scepticism from that point of view. Does the radical sceptic give us any reason to *act* as though Darwinian theory is not certain?

For the sake of the argument, start by conceding the sceptic's basic claim: that we cannot be *certain* that the world is as we think it is, and that the evil genius may in fact have us in his clutches. The question now becomes a different one: not about what we know, but about how it is rational to behave given that we do *not* know. This question is one of practical decision-making against a background of uncertainty.

This problem is another that is famous in the history of philosophy, in the argument known as Pascal's Wager. Pascal (1623–62) was trying to decide the rational way to run his life in the face of uncertainty about the existence of God and a life after death. Deciding what to do in the absence of adequate evidence is particularly pressing in the case of traditional religion and ideas of immortality, since eternity is a bad thing to make mistakes about. This was the basis of Pascal's Wager. Pascal thought that although it was impossible to know for certain whether God existed or not, it should still be possible to work out, rationally, the best basis on which to live his life. And (to give a decidedly free account of the matter) what he did was produce a *risk analysis* of the situation, along these lines.

He started, in effect, with a matrix setting out the various possibilities. Along one of the axes he put two possibilities for the truth about the world: God exists, God does not exist. Along the other he put two possibilities for ways he might spend his time: in a life of secular pleasure, or in a life of religious observance. He then filled in the cells of the matrix with the *payoffs*: the outcome for each of the possible combinations of circumstances, which came out more or less like this:

	Life of religious duty	Enjoyable life
God exists	short-term austerity eternal bliss	short-term pleasure eternal damnation
God doesn't exist	short-term austerity nothing else	short-term pleasure nothing else

And considering this range of possibilities, Pascal decided the best risk to take was that of a life of religious duty. It was true he might be wasting the only life he would ever have in austerity, but that was nothing like as bad as risking eternal damnation if he took the other option. The winning stakes were infinitely better, too: this might get him eternal bliss.

The problem with Pascal's argument is in the details of its setting out. He considered two possibilities – whether God existed or did not exist – but the way he thought about this amounted to the question of whether the Catholic Church was right or whether it was not. But the alternatives are not as simple as that. Suppose, for instance, that the views of some extreme Protestants are right. In that case, your life of Catholic virtue might destine you to eternal damnation just as effectively as a life of secular pleasure. This kind of argument can work only to the extent that it takes account of all significantly different possibilities. Still, the problems of detail in Pascal's case do not undermine the principle of this kind of reasoning, so might it help with the problem of how to act rationally in science?

Consider again what the problem is. The challenge to claims of scientific certainty that we are now considering is not that there is too little evidence, or that new evidence may appear unexpectedly, but that *all* evidence will be useless if the world underlying our experience is in some way illusory. So the question here is not about whether we ought to believe in the claims of Darwinism in particular, but about whether there is any point in undertaking scientific enquiry *at all* – because if it is rational to act as if all evidence is useless, there is no point in science. What we need to decide is whether it is rational to engage in science at all, *given* that we do not know whether the world underlying our experience is orderly or whether it is not. What, then, should the decision matrix look like?

The two rows, giving possible states of affairs, can be described for brevity as 'orderly world' and 'disorderly world', and the two possible courses of action, in the columns, as 'do science' and 'don't do science'. And for filling in the payoffs, the relevant points seem to be that doing science involves a lot of work, but that it has enormous potential rewards in allowing us to predict and control the world. That suggests a matrix along these lines:

	Do science	**Don't do science**
Orderly World	Have the trouble of doing science (−2) Find out about the world, and be able to predict and control events (+50) (Total +48)	Save the trouble of doing science (+2) Fail to find out about the world and to predict and control events (−50) (Total −48)
Disorderly world	Have the trouble of doing science (−2) No advantage: nothing to be found out, so no opportunity to predict and control (0) (Total −2)	Save the trouble of doing science (+2) No disadvantage; nothing to be found out, so no opportunity to predict and control (0) (Total +2)

The figures given for the payoffs are of course purely notional, but they are quite useful for illustrating the point. They are based on the assumption that it is plausible to regard the effort of doing science as some disadvantage, say −2, and the advantage of not doing it as +2. But the advantage of being able to predict and control the world is enormous, say +50. Failing to find out how to do this when you could have done, I am counting as −50, since you waste the opportunity to predict and control the world. Perhaps it should count as 0, since your situation is the same under that circumstance as if there were no under-lying order; I am not sure, but it makes no difference to the overall conclusion. On these assumptions, the most you can get by not doing science is +2, whereas although doing science may land you with −2, there is also the chance that it will give you +48. So the question is whether you think it worth while to gamble the chance of a small loss against the possibility of a huge gain, or go for the certainty of a small gain.

Given that analysis, there seems no doubt which course of action is the rational bet. Doing science gives you the chance of success if success is to be had; not doing it saves you trouble, but means that there is no chance of success even if it could have been had. Most people would presumably rather try for the high stakes even though there was a chance of failure, unless of course there was nothing they dreaded more than work.

It goes without saying that that argument is highly simplified and schematic, but it makes a useful point. There are sometimes ways of making rational decisions against a background of uncertainty, on the principle of making rational bets. If, as in Pascal's case, one course of action has the possible outcomes of a small loss and a huge gain, and another has the possible outcomes of a huge loss and a small gain, and we do not know how likely each of them is, there seems no doubt about which to go for. And if this is the right response, it provides an answer to the challenge of the radical sceptic who claims that we cannot know that an orderly world underlies our experience. We may not be able to claim knowledge that the world has an underlying order, but we can still claim that it is *methodologically rational* to act as though it has. It is a better bet.

This is like another point made by Locke, in a rather similar context:

> If we will disbelieve everything, because we cannot certainly know all things, we shall do much what as wisely as he who would not use his legs, but sit still and perish, because he had no wings to fly.
>
> (Locke (1976 edn), p. 3)

If there is any coherence in the structure of things (which experience so far suggests, since we have a huge amount of practical scientific success) then our only chance of finding out what that is lies in investigation. We may be wrong, and wasting our time; Descartes's evil genius may just be lulling us into a false sense of security. But we *certainly* will not get anywhere if we decide to presuppose underlying disorder, and 'sit still and perish'. One way gives the possibility of success; the other the certainty of failure.

Now return to the original question of science and certainty: the claim of scientists to be certain of the truth of the core Darwinian theory, and the question of whether they are entitled to claim such certainty in the face of radical scepticism. How should Darwinian scientists respond to the radical sceptic who insists that they are wrong to claim certainty for any of their conclusions?

What they can do is rephrase their claims of certainty in terms of methodological rationality. Given that science can proceed only on the presupposition of underlying order (whether that presupposition is right or wrong), any conclusions reached must be understood in that light. If there is an underlying order, then the Darwinian account of evolution is certainly true. If there is not, then it is not; *but then neither is any other scientific theory*. So the scientific claim of certainty can be understood as being that it would be methodologically absurd, given the amount of evidence we have, to treat the fundamentals of Darwinism as anything other than certainly true. That is the practical answer to anyone who persists with radical doubt, even though it does not solve the metaphysical problem.

Another way of putting the matter is this. Someone who argues that there is not enough evidence to accept a scientific theory, or that a theory is wrong, is making the assumption that the world is orderly and its workings are discoverable, just as is someone who argues that a theory is certainly true. Any claim about the evidence for or against a particular theory presupposes that the available evidence is relevant to the question. Radical scepticism is a challenge to the idea that evidence is relevant *at all*, and therefore undermines claims that evidence is inadequate to just the same extent as it undermines claims that it is adequate. When a scientist claims that a theory is certain, the relevant contrast is not with the kind of uncertainty caused by the possibility that Descartes's evil genius might be deceiving us, but with theories that are *not* adequately supported, or are proved wrong, by the evidence. The implication is that whereas the evidence might have been inadequate, in fact it is adequate. A critic can respond to this claim by showing that it is inadequate in comparison with what would count as adequate, but not by saying that no evidence could be adequate.

People who say that we cannot be certain of the truth of Darwinism on the grounds that nobody can be certain of anything have given up science. They can, if they like, pursue their metaphysics in philosophical monasteries (or philosophy departments), but, as their own reasoning would lead them to agree, they are of no relevance to scientists.

Exercise 2.1

1 Which of the following challenges take radically sceptical forms, as opposed to expressing ordinary grounds for doubt (i.e. about how good the evidence is)?

   (i) You can't be sure she has got over it; she was always very good at hiding her feelings.
   (ii) The behaviour of animals provides no evidence that they are suffering; they could just be sophisticated machines made to respond to stimuli in that way.
   (iii) Your controlled experiments don't give the slightest reason for doubting that telepathy exists. Of course something like that doesn't work when there are sceptics around; it will probably never work for you.
   (iv) The world could have been created ten seconds ago, complete with all historical records and apparent memories.

2 For each of the following, suggest two challenges that might be made by someone trying to deny the claim, one of which expresses ordinary

grounds for doubt and one of which appeals to radical scepticism. (It does not matter how fanciful the suggestions are, as long as they make the point.)

(i)   That car is perfectly safe.
(ii) Cutting down plants isn't cruel.
(iii) I shall definitely be here tomorrow.

3   What is meant by its being methodologically rational to accept that something (such as the underlying order of the physical world) is true?
4   Suppose someone claimed that animals might only be automata with no feelings, and therefore that we had no need to try to prevent animal suffering. It would be irrelevant to claim that they showed all the symptoms of pain, since the relevance of those symptoms is what is being challenged. How, following the kind of argument recommended here, might you reply?

(Answers on p. 274)

Shifting goalposts

Philosophical scepticism is usually treated by non-philosophers as a game, with no relevance to real life; and, as I have just argued, it is certainly rational to *treat* it that way. Nevertheless, this does not mean that it can be entirely ignored, because arguments that make illicit use of it do sometimes encroach upon real life. They have a habit of turning up when people who are losing arguments cannot make any headway by appeals to evidence. Tactics of this kind do not usually look as though they depend on radical scepticism – you are not likely to be taken in by Descartes's evil genius if he appears with horns and a tail – but this is why it is important to be clear about what they are like, and how they differ from the legitimate scientific doubt that comes from lack of adequate evidence. And since one particularly charming and poignant illustration of the illicit use of radical scepticism comes from the early history of the subject we are discussing, that will be an ideal illustration of the general point.

The Omphalos *case*

The case is one of a Christian fundamentalist trying to defend his position against the increasing pressure of threats from geological investigations and burgeoning ideas of evolution. It is something of an anachronism from the point of view of objections to present-day claims of scientific certainty about Darwinism, since the argument was published two years before even Darwin's *Origin*, let alone before the recent work on genetics that is the basis for scientists' current confidence. But even at the time there was a good deal of evidence for evolution of some kind – Darwin's grandfather was an evolutionist – and work in geology was increasingly leading to claims that the earth was far older than the official, Genesis, account implied. The forebears of today's creationists were anxious to stop this dangerous trend of challenging received truth, and the best-known of their attempts was by Philip Henry Gosse (1810–88), in a remarkable book called *Omphalos*.

Gosse was, according to Stephen Jay Gould:

> the David Attenborough of his day, Britain's finest popular narrator of nature's fascination. He wrote a dozen books on plants and animals, lectured widely to popular audiences, and published several technical papers on marine invertebrates. He was also, in an age given to strong religious feeling as a mode for expressing human passions denied vent elsewhere, an extreme and committed fundamentalist of the Plymouth Brethren sect.
>
> (Gould (1985), p. 100)

His problem was therefore to reconcile the findings of natural history and geology with his fundamentalist religious beliefs. He could not cast doubt on the empirical evidence, since he himself knew more about it than most people did, but he devised a quite different strategy for defending his beliefs in the face of what scientists were increasingly regarding as overwhelming geological evidence that the Genesis account could not be true.

Here is part of Stephen Jay Gould's account of the matter.

> The ample fig leaf served our artistic forefathers well as a botanical shield against indecent exposure for Adam and Eve, our naked parents in the primeval bliss and innocence of Eden. Yet, in many ancient paintings, foliage hides more than Adam's genitalia; a wandering vine covers his navel as well. If modesty enjoined the genital shroud, a very different motive – mystery – placed a plant over his belly. In a theological debate more portentous than the old argument about angels on pinpoints, many earnest people of faith had wondered whether Adam had a navel.
>
> He was, after all, not born of a woman and required no remnant of his nonexistent umbilical cord. Yet, in creating a prototype, would not God make his first man like all the rest to follow? Would God, in other words, not create with the appearance of pre-existence? In the absence of definite guidance to resolve this vexatious issue, and not wishing to incur anyone's wrath, many painters literally hedged and covered Adam's belly.
>
> A few centuries later, as the nascent science of geology gathered evidence for the earth's enormous antiquity, some advocates of biblical literalism revived this old argument for our entire planet. The strata and their entombed fossils surely seem to represent a sequential record of countless years, but wouldn't God create his earth with the appearance of pre-existence? Why should we not believe that he created strata and fossils to give modern life a harmonious order by granting it a sensible (if illusory) past? As God provided Adam with a navel to stress continuity with future men, so too did he endow a pristine world with the appearance of an ordered history. Thus, the earth might be but a few thousand years old, as Genesis

literally affirmed, and still record an apparent tale of untold aeons.

This argument, so often cited as a premier example of reason at its most perfectly and preciously ridiculous, was most seriously and comprehensively set forth by the British naturalist Philip Henry Gosse in 1857. Gosse paid proper homage to historical context in choosing a title for his volume. He named it *Omphalos* (Greek for navel), in Adam's honour, and added as a subtitle: *An Attempt to Untie the Geological Knot. . . .*

Gosse began his argument with a central, but dubious, premise: All natural processes, he declared, move endlessly round in a circle: egg to chicken to egg, oak to acorn to oak.

> This, then, is the order of all organic nature. When once we are in any portion of the course, we find ourselves running in a circular groove, as endless as the course of a blind horse in a mill … This is not the law of some particular species, but of all: it pervades all classes of animals, all classes of plants, from the queenly palm down to the protococus, from the monad up to man: the life of every organic being is whirling in a ceaseless circle, to which one knows not how to assign any commencement … The cow is as inevitable a sequence of the embryo, as the embryo is of the cow.

When God creates, and Gosse entertained not the slightest doubt that all species arose by divine fiat with no subsequent evolution, he must break (or 'erupt,' as Gosse wrote) somewhere into this ideal circle. Wherever God enters the circle (or 'places his wafer of creation', as Gosse stated in metaphor), his initial product must bear traces of previous stages in the circle, even if these stages had no existence in real time. If God chooses to create humans as adults, their hair and nails (not to mention their navels) testify to previous growth that never occurred. Even if he decides to create us as a simple fertilized ovum, this initial form implies a phantom mother's womb and two non-existent parents to pass along the fruit of inheritance.

> Creation can be nothing else than a series of irruptions into circles … Supposing the irruption to have been made at what part of the circle we please, and varying this condition indefinitely at will, we cannot avoid the conclusion that each organism was from the first marked with the records of a previous being. But since creation and previous history are inconsistent with each other; as the very idea of the creation of an organism excludes the idea of pre-existence of that organism, or of any part of it; it follows, that such records are false, so far as they testify to time.

Gosse then invented a terminology to contrast the two parts of a circle before and after an act of creation. He labelled as 'prochronic', or occurring outside of time, those appearances of pre-existence actually fashioned by God at the moment of creation but seeming to mark earlier stages in the circle of life. Subsequent events occurring after creation, and unfolding in conventional time, he called 'diachronic'. Adam's navel was prochronic, the 930 years of his earthly life diachronic.

Gosse devoted more than 300 pages, some 90 per cent of his text, to a simple list of examples for the following small part of his complete argument – if species arise by sudden creation at any point in their life cycle, their initial form must present illusory (prochronic) appearances of pre-existence. Let me choose just one among his numerous illustrations, both to characterize his style of argument and to present his gloriously purple prose. If God created vertebrates as adults, Gosse claimed, their teeth imply a prochronic past in patterns of wear and replacement.

Gosse leads us on an imaginary tour of life just an hour after its creation in the wilderness. He pauses at the seashore and scans the distant waves:

> I see yonder a ... terrific tyrant of the sea ... It is the grisly shark. How stealthily he glides along ... Let us go and look into his mouth ... Is not this an awful array of knives and lancets? Is not this a case of surgical instruments enough to make you shudder? What would be the amputation of your leg to this row of triangular scalpels?

Yet the teeth grow in spirals, one behind the next, each waiting to take its turn as those in current use wear down and drop out:

> It follows, therefore, that the teeth which we now see erect and threatening, are the successors of former ones that have passed away, and that they were once dormant like those we see behind them ... Hence we are compelled by the phenomena to infer a long past existence to this animal, which yet has been called into being within an hour.

Should we try to argue that teeth in current use are the first members of their spiral, implying no predecessors after all, Gosse replies that their state of wear indicates a prochronic past. Should we propose that these initial teeth might be unmarred in a newly created shark, Gosse moves on to another example.

> Away to a broader river. Here wallows and riots the huge hippopotamus. What can we make of his dentition?

All modern adult hippos possess strongly worn and bevelled canines and incisors, a clear sign of active use throughout a long life. May we not, however, as for our shark, argue that a newly created hippo might have sharp and pristine front teeth? Gosse argues correctly that no hippo could work properly with teeth in such a state. A created adult hippo must contain worn teeth as witnesses of a prochronic past:

> The polished surfaces of the teeth, worn away by mutual action, afford striking evidence of the lapse of time. Some one may possibly object ... 'What right have you to assume that these teeth were worn away at the moment of its creation, admitting the animal to have been created adult. May they not have been entire?' I reply, Impossible: the Hippopotamus's teeth would have been perfectly useless to him, except in the ground-down condition: nay, the

unworn canines would have effectually prevented his jaws from closing, necessitating the keeping of the mouth wide open until the attrition was performed; long before which, of course, he would have starved ... The degree of attrition is merely a question of time ... How distinct an evidence of past action, and yet, in the case of the created individual, how illusory!

(Ibid., pp. 99ff.)

And Gosse goes on to claim that these circular processes apply to the earth and geology; so that at whatever point God chose to insert the 'wafer of creation', the earth would inevitably show traces of this circling, illusory, past. The geological record therefore provided no evidence that the earth was any older than the Bible implied, or that species had not been created in their present forms.

I have followed Gould in giving these delightful details (which, he says, could go on for ever, and nearly do in the original) – even though they are hardly essential for the philosophical point – partly as a further illustration of how mistaken it is to present the history of science (and religion) in such as way as to make our predecessors look simply silly and superstitious. Gosse's argument is often caricatured as though he said that God had created the earth with the illusion of a past, as a test of faith (which I suppose would have made God into something rather like Descartes's evil genius), but that is not Gosse's point. His point is that given the kinds of creature God decided to create, it was inevitable that at whatever stage in their development God created them, they would show traces of a nonexistent past. There is nothing perverse or faith-testing about this; it was just that if the sort of thing you were creating was something whose nature it was to develop and change in cycles, you would have to create it at some point during this cyclical process, and it would therefore inevitably display traces of the rest of the cycle. Chickens would contain incipient eggs, eggs would contain incipient chickens. These extracts illustrate the detailed work of an outstanding naturalist, who knew all about the teeth of hippos and sharks, and was trying to find a way of reconciling what he saw with his theological convictions.

He really thought he had succeeded in trouncing the sceptics, and was devastated to find that nobody was in the least impressed. He could not see why his argument was not regarded as settling the matter. And, indeed, a lot of the people who are not impressed can't really see why it doesn't work; they are just sure that it doesn't. (You may find it interesting to try to pin down exactly what is wrong with it before reading on.)

There are in fact various problems when you get down to details, in spite of Gosse's impressive understanding of animal development, dental and otherwise. As Gould points out later in his article, the arguments about animals work very well within Gosse's terms, but he has to resort to hand-waving and biblical rhetoric when trying to make out that geological processes have the same kind of cyclical character as animal development; and, as already explained, these were important for Gosse's thesis because the cycles were what made it necessary that whenever creation happened, what appeared would bear the traces of an illusory past. But this point need not concern us, because what gives this case its appearance of spuriousness has nothing to do with the details. It concerns the *kind* of challenge Gosse was making to his opponents.

There are all kinds of ways of challenging opposing scientists' claims. You might, for instance, challenge the reports of their discoveries, and allege that they were misrepresenting the evidence, or suppressing important information that might support an alternative conclusion. You might claim that in spite of your opponents' positive evidence, there was even more evidence that counted against their theory. You might accept their account of the evidence, but claim that it supported your theory better than theirs. Or you might claim that even though the case seemed at that moment to be going their way, there was reason to think that new evidence would come and overthrow this current set of beliefs. All such moves are familiar parts of scientific argument.

However, if you think about Gosse's argument it is clear that he is doing none of these things. He does not dispute his opponents' claims about evidence; he does not bring in new evidence of his own that he claims they have overlooked; he does not claim that the six-days/constant-species theory provides a better explanation of the observed data; he is not suggesting that more sophisticated techniques of dating will eventually show that the rocks really are no more than six thousand years old. He is doing a quite different kind of thing, which shows in a claim Gosse puts forward as an *advantage* of his theory:

> The acceptance of the principles presented in this volume … would not, in the least degree, affect the study of scientific geology. The character and order of the strata … the successive floras and faunas; and all the other phenomena, would be facts still. They would still be, as now, legitimate subjects of examination and inquiry. We might still speak of the inconceivably long duration of the processes in question, provided we understand ideal instead of actual time – that the duration was projected in the mind of God, and not really existent.
>
> (Quoted in ibid., p. 109)

The point is that Gosse's argument is not about how good the evidence on each side is. His claim is that the empirical evidence is *irrelevant* to questions about the date of creation, because no matter what the evidence is, it cannot show that creation happened at a time before the Bible said it did. He is holding on to his claim about the truth of Genesis not by claiming that the geologists have got their science wrong, but that they are misunderstanding the reality underlying the phenomena, which is out of the reach of scientific investigation. He is, in other words, making a *metaphysical* claim, about the reality that lies beyond possible experience.

It is because Gosse is saying that the scientific evidence is irrelevant, rather than that it is inadequate or goes against his opponents' thesis, that his idea comes into the category of radical scepticism. Gosse does not look like a sceptic, because he has such firm beliefs of his own, but his manoeuvre is exactly the same as that of philosophical sceptics who claim that experience cannot give any evidence about the nature of reality. Gosse has responded to the evidence of geologists in the way followers of Descartes might have done if they had appeared in the middle of the nineteenth century, and said the fossils might be illusions produced by the evil genius. But Gosse is not presenting his claim as if it were part of metaphysics; he is offering it as part of the scientific debate.

Consider the context in which *Omphalos* appeared. There was an established belief, derived from the Bible, that the earth had been created in six days, about six thousand years earlier, with species in their modern form. But then along came geologists, whose investigations of fossils and geological processes started to cast doubt on the biblical account. It began to look as though the earth was much older than had been thought, and that life forms had gradually evolved, rather than all being created at the beginning. This was unwelcome to people of fundamentalist beliefs, so they tried to explain the evidence differently, in ways compatible with the Bible. But the geological evidence kept piling up, and made observation less and less compatible with the biblical account.

You can think of the debate between geologists and traditionalist fundamentalists – creationists, as they would now be called – as going along these lines:

Creationist: The Bible gives us evidence (with its genealogies) that the earth is about six thousand years old, and the Bible is the word of God.

Geologist: But we have found fossils of extinct creatures, and seen that simpler ones are in the older strata.

Creationist: The fossils don't contradict the biblical account; they are the remains of species that were destroyed in Noah's flood ... (etc.).

Geologist: That may seem plausible at first glance, but when you start looking closely and fitting all the bits of evidence together, you find that the evidence makes that impossible ... (etc.).

And the geologist seems to be getting the better of it. But then *Omphalos* is published, and suddenly the creationist has a new idea about how to fight back:

Creationist: But what you are talking about is only what Gosse calls prochronic time: you are describing the lengths of the cycles of time which God conceived as natural to the earth. But that doesn't show when creation *really* happened, because whenever God had inserted the wafer of creation, the earth would have shown evidence of the same prochronic past. Creation could therefore have happened at any time, and in fact did happen about six thousand years ago. Your evidence about rocks and fossils is therefore irrelevant.

This discussion starts off as a disagreement about how to interpret the empirical evidence. The creationist refers to genealogies and the Bible and the geologist produces evidence to suggest the Bible is wrong; the creationist tries to counter that explanation with an alternative explanation and the geologist replies with more evidence.

The creationist could have tried to reply with yet more evidence of the same kind, on the same level. This is what the present-day Scientific Creationists of the United States try to do, as they collect evidence intended to show that scientific evidence for evolution just is not good enough. (This is why they call themselves 'scientific creationists'. Their claim is that they can make their case out by ordinary scientific arguments, without dependence on the Bible.) But that is not what happens in the dialogue above. Here the creationist's third move slips to another level, in which he stops trying to meet the geologist's evidence with alternative explanations of that evidence, and instead claims that all the evidence produced by the geologist is irrelevant to the question at issue. His claim now is that the rocks can show nothing at all about when creation really happened. Gosse's disciple is holding on to his claim about creation, by claiming not that the geologists have got their science wrong, but that they are misunderstanding the reality underlying the phenomena, which is out of the reach of scientific investigation. But it does not look as though that is what he is doing. In the dialogue above, he presents his argument as though he is carrying on with the same subject. The final move is presented as part of the original debate.

What this means is that when Gosse produced his thesis he quietly (and almost certainly innocently) changed the subject. The issue started as a real scientific debate between two sides – the traditional fundamentalist and the new geologist – about whose view was best supported by the accumulating geological evidence. The two sides had competing theories, which could not both be right: the earth could not fit Ussher's calculations and be the age geologists were beginning to think it was. Gosse, in defending the biblical account against the geologists, seemed to be coming in on the biblical side of the same argument. But in fact his theory was not a competitor on the same ground – as he himself implied, in pointing out that his argument made no difference to anything that was going on in science. He had moved from science (questions about the world we experience) to metaphysics (questions about underlying reality, to which the details of our experience are necessarily irrelevant).

So the creationist in the imaginary exchange above is implying that this post-Gosse argument is a continuation of the original debate about how to interpret the available evidence, when it is really a claim about a quite different matter. And, furthermore, in switching to the new level, which makes *all* evidence irrelevant to his claim, he is undermining his own original case as well as his opponent's. If he moves to a position of saying that all the geological evidence is irrelevant to the real truth, his own explanation of fossils as the remains of the Flood becomes just as necessarily irrelevant.

The first thing the geologist needs to do, then, is insist on separating the two questions, and not allow the creationist to imply that he is still discussing the weight of the scientific evidence, when he has really changed to a new subject to which scientific evidence is irrelevant.

After that, he might try challenging the creationist directly to produce evidence for his own positive contention that the Bible is to be relied on, because, after all, if what it says is contradicted by all available evidence, that rather suggests it should not be taken very seriously. But that leads off in directions that cannot be pursued here.

Slips of level and sleights of hand

All these ideas about prochronic time and wafers of creation and possible evil geniuses may seem too far-fetched to be relevant to many real-life contexts, but in fact *the pair of mistakes* just described is extremely common. It often happens during arguments that some move shifts the debate to a quite different issue, while presenting itself as part of the original one. Such moves are often also of a kind such that, if they work at all, they make the whole of the original debate irrelevant, while appearing to support one side against the other. And since they confuse all kinds of issues in the Darwinian debates – as will appear in later chapters – it is important to recognize them.

Consider this imaginary conversation – born of the earlier mention of shifting goalposts – which is only slightly far-fetched in detail, and perfectly recognizable in kind. A and B are disputing a referee's decision to send a player off for a foul. A thinks he didn't deserve to be sent off, B thinks he did:

A: It was an accident, not a foul. He only slipped, which wasn't his fault. So he didn't deserve to be sent off.
B: It wasn't clear at the time, but we now have the video evidence. It was quite deliberate; it was his fault. He was entirely responsible for what happened.
A: No he wasn't. Perhaps he lost his temper, but that's just the way his brain chemistry works, and he couldn't help that. It's not fair to penalize him for his chemistry. He shouldn't have been sent off.

A's first contribution is on the familiar subject of whether the player was treated fairly, and that is the point to which B responds. But when B defeats A's original point, A does not respond on the same level (perhaps by arguing that the video was a forgery), but changes the level in a way which, if accepted, undermines the whole basis of the original discussion.

The debate starts as a disagreement about whether, within the rules of football, a particular incident justified a particular penalty. The case was in some doubt, because it was difficult to see what had happened, but then that issue was settled by the video evidence. Instead of accepting it, however, A shifts from the original question – about what should have happened *given the rules of football* – to the quite different question of whether people should be penalized for something that can be explained in terms of the effects of their brain chemistry. And that is quite different, because if you accept A's second point, you are no longer discussing what the rules of football demand, but in effect saying those rules are themselves misguided. If that incident can be explained in terms of brain chemistry, so, potentially, can everything every player does, and no player should ever be penalized for anything. Perhaps football should be a game without penalties and rewards; perhaps (which probably amounts to the same thing) it should not exist at all. But whatever the answer to that, A's rejoinder is not part of the original discussion. Even if A wants to argue that the rules of football are themselves unfair and the game in its present form unjustified, it would be cheating of a preposterous kind to offer that as a reason for saying that *this* referee, working in *this* situation, had made an unfair decision. But that is how it is presented.

There are innumerable ways in which the course of a debate may shift, surreptitiously or accidentally, to claims which are irrelevant to the discussion, and which may undermine the whole of the original debate. Here is another illustration:

A: The newspaper account was biased.
B: No it wasn't; I know how much care they took to get an objective account.
A: There's no such thing as an objective account; all accounts are given from a particular point of view. So of course it was biased.

The original dispute here is about whether or not the newspaper account met certain implied standards. A says it did not, and clearly implies this is a matter for blame; B says the standards were met. A goes on arguing, apparently on the same subject; but what he does is surreptitiously (and perhaps even innocently) change the standard for being unbiased into something that cannot be met *even in principle*, since by this criterion everything must be biased. But whether or not A would want to defend that idea, he cannot use it as the basis for a complaint that this particular account is biased, which is where he started. If A's second claim is true, the first one cannot be – at least, not in the sense which is clearly implied by the context.

Once you start looking for this kind of move, you see it everywhere. When people find themselves driven into an argumentative corner, and are desperately trying to think of anything that will seem to support their case, they often grasp at something that looks extremely potent, without noticing that – if indeed it is as potent as they think – it works just as much against their own case as against their opponents'. It is as though in reaching for the strongest solvent they can find they have taken down one of Dennett's universal acids. They uncork it in the hope of dealing with their opponent's point, but it is too strong; it dissolves theirs too. A universal acid cannot be used selectively. But on the other hand, if their opponents do not notice that that is what they have done, they may get away with it and seem to win their political point.

There are more illustrations of this in the exercise at the end of the section, and, as I have said, there will be several others in the course of the book. There is, however, one particular version worth special mention now, because it is extremely common, and directly relevant to the earlier discussion of radical scepticism. This is the familiar *relativist* claim that scientific theories are all social constructions. Which theory prevails at any time, according to this view, is just a matter of who has the power and what is in fashion; there is no objective truth to be found.

The issue of relativism is, like claims about evil geniuses and reality as projected in the mind of God, something that can be discussed in its own right. But, quite apart from any problems about relativism as such (of which there are many – as will appear later when it is discussed in the context of ethics in

Chapter 8), the practical danger comes when it is used, as it often is, in attempts to undermine *particular* scientific claims. Imagine another possible conversation, again not at all implausible:

A: Astrology should be taught in schools. Children won't be able to understand their characters and control their futures unless they have this kind of understanding.

B: But the Newtonian revolution has completely discredited astrology. It was a plausible theory at the time when it was developed, because then it really did seem that the heavens had a special kind of influence on the earth. But now we know there is no difference between the heavens and the earth, and most of the phenomena that astrology was originally invoked to explain have been explained in other ways.

A: It hasn't been discredited; there's no such thing as objective discrediting. What is taught as fact is just a matter of who is in control. Scientific 'truth' is just a political device: a way of keeping your party in power. Astrologers have as much right to be heard as anyone else.

A is running into serious problems with that second claim in itself, since he is presenting as an objective truth the claim that there is no such thing as objective truth. But quite apart from any problems inherent in the claim, what A cannot do is use the argument to defend his own claim against B's attack. If the second claim is true, it undermines A's own first claim as well as B's. Whatever else may be said about relativism of this kind, it cannot be used selectively, to discredit *particular* scientific claims. As Richard Dawkins robustly says (1995, p. 36), 'Show me a cultural relativist at thirty thousand feet, and I'll show you a hypocrite' – though any such case might show more confusion than hypocrisy. And the same applies to part-time relativists who want trained surgeons rather than witch doctors to operate on them, and would be most unlikely to think that if they were in India they could safely jump out of an upper window because a guru had assured them they could fly. Nobody can be a full-time relativist.

Exercise 2.2

Look back again at the dialogues above about football and biased reporting, which change tack between the second and third exchanges. Construct similar conversations to follow the opening moves given below. Remember that B's reply will meet the point made in A's opening move; A's reply will be presented as a response to B, but will really involve a change of standards, and would undermine A's own first claim just as much as B's:

1 A *(defence):* My client cannot be blamed for the rape. He was encouraged by the woman who is accusing him, and found it difficult to stop.
   B *(prosecution):* ...
   A: ...

2 *A:*   That wasn't altruism; she has only been looking after you because she thought you were rich and might leave money to her in your will.
   B: …
   A: …

(Answers on p.274)

————————————

This chapter has used a discussion of continuing doubt about the truth of Darwinism to introduce various problems in epistemology and philosophy of science. There are still people who resist Darwinian theory in its entirety, in spite of its essential links with so many other aspects of accepted scientific knowledge. Although much of this resistance is motivated by fundamentalist religious views, appeals to religious authority no longer appear much in public debate: instead opponents claim that there are reasonable scientific grounds for doubt.

These claims need individual analysis, but one common line of argument depends on the general idea that scientific knowledge can never be certain. Here it is essential to distinguish between different kinds of doubt: ordinary scientific doubt based on inadequacy of evidence, the wider claim that any theory – no matter how well supported – may be overthrown by later theories, and the radical scepticism which treats all evidence as irrelevant. These levels have all been briefly discussed, but the main conclusion is the importance of distinguishing between them, so that doubts about the possibility of knowledge in general – which would apply equally to all theories – are not applied selectively to suggest doubt about Darwinism in particular.

This kind of shift between levels in mid-argument has been illustrated in the context of scientific theories by the argument of Gosse's *Omphalos*, and then in various non-scientific contexts. The mistake involved will be relevant to the discussion of many issues connected with the implications of Darwinism.

3   Internecine strife

This chapter returns from general philosophical matters to questions specifically about Darwinism. Even though the central core of Darwinism can be taken as established beyond doubt, that is in itself relatively unthreatening to traditional conceptions of the kind of thing we ourselves are. The real danger comes with the possibility that Darwinian explanation might spread further, beyond the range of organic evolution.

The fundamental problem here is to find a way of presenting a complex and confused debate in a way that does not distort the issues. This chapter divides controversies about the application of Darwinism to human nature into two main kinds. The first is about whether Darwinism can give a complete account of our origins, and justify a materialist account of what we are. The other is about the extent to which a Darwinian under-standing of our evolution can provide insight into the details of our character, as is claimed by researchers in the field of evolutionary psychology (sociobiology).

These controversies within Darwinism seem to have further-reaching implications for our view of ourselves than the controversy about whether the theory is true at all, and are the ones about which public debate is most passionate. The chapter outlines these debates, and in particular explains what evolutionary psychologists take their subject to be about.

However, it also argues that there is no possibility of resolving these debates here, and that for the purposes of this enquiry the question of which view is right will have to be left open.

A spectrum of Darwinism

The previous chapter claimed that the core Darwinian theory of organic evolu-tion by natural selection must now be regarded as settled beyond any reasonable doubt. That, however, does not mean that serious Darwinian controversies are at an end. There is still the question of whether Darwinian explanation can be confined to this core, or whether it really is the universal acid Dennett suspects it is; and from the point of view of understanding the implications of Darwinism, the disagreements between Darwinists themselves – the people who have crossed the Darwinian threshold, but disagree about how far to go beyond it – look far more momentous than those between Darwinists and their funda-mentalist opponents.

It is of course well known – as part of the great Darwin legend – that Darwin's ideas were regarded with horror by many of his contemporaries. The biblical account of creation was widely accepted at the time as literally true; and, quite apart from anxieties about challenges to the revealed word of God, it was also shocking for refined Victorians, with their sense of natural superiority even to the lesser (human) breeds without the law, to be told that they were related to apes. But when the dust began to settle and people got used to the idea, it became possible to think that not too much had changed after all. Darwin's original thesis was indeed incompatible with biblical fundamentalism, but that was anyway already under attack from several directions; and, furthermore, the idea of evolution by natural selection was not in itself incompatible with a Mind First view of the world as a whole. Many eighteenth- and nineteenth-century naturalists and geologists were clerics, and several were among Darwin's first supporters. It was possible to accept that the human body had evolved from lower animals while still maintaining that God was needed to explain the existence of the world as a whole and the emergence of life from inanimate matter, and that souls were distinct from bodies and separately created by God. Tradition had always accepted that the human body was material, and also, through most of the history of Christianity, that it was generally loathsome and corrupt. Since bodies had always been vile, perhaps it did not matter how they had come to be that way.

Through ideas of this kind many religions, and many people of unfocused religious leanings, have found themselves able to accept the basic idea of organic evolution without too much intellectual and emotional disruption. The Catholic Church, for instance, has taken on this kind of limited Darwinism without any real change of theology. As long as Darwinism can be kept within its original bounds, the implications seem not too alarming after all. The serious trouble seems to set in only if, as Dennett thinks, the Darwinian acid can seep beyond this central area; and the question of how far it can penetrate is the ground on which the aptly named Darwin wars (Brown (1999)) are now being fought. Since the question of the implications of Darwinism for our understanding of ourselves is strongly connected with this dispute, the battle lines need to be explained. The details are as complex as the biology, so the explanation will inevitably involve considerable simplification; what is needed is not so much a detailed account of current opinion as an effective framework within which to classify the wide range of views there is. This is what I shall try to present in this chapter.

The broad question of how much of our nature and situation can be explained in Darwinian terms encompasses two narrower ones. The first of these is Dennett's question about Darwinism as a universal acid, and it concerns the relevance of Darwinism to questions about what we and other things ultimately consist of, and how everything came to be as it is. The second is about the extent to which a Darwinian understanding of our origins can extend our understanding of human nature as it is now.

The first question starts with the idea of Darwinism as essentially a *type of explanation*, involving the ideas of reproduction, variation, transmission of characteristics, and differential survival. Evolution by natural selection occurs as soon as there are reproducers whose offspring take up more space than is available, so that some survive to reproduce themselves while others do not. Its most striking characteristic is that it reverses the traditional direction of explanation, by explaining higher levels of the Chain of Being entirely in terms of the workings of lower levels. It shows how complexity can emerge from simplicity by purely physical processes, without there being any intentions, or designs, or aspirations, at all. In Dennett's terms, explanations of a Darwinian type involve only cranes; and since we have traditionally thought of ourselves and the world in terms of skyhooks, explanations of a Darwinian type are likely to make radical changes to whatever parts of the intellectual landscape they can reach. The more they can encompass, the more disruptive they are likely to be.

This is an issue that stretches far beyond biology. As mentioned earlier (p. 23), some physicists are trying to extend such explanations in the downward direction, to the fundamentals of existence, and experimenting with the idea that Darwinian principles might be involved in the origin of the universe.[3] They are asking, for instance, whether black holes might be generators of universes, of which only the viable survive. And in the upward direction, in enquiries about ourselves and our societies, some people are asking whether Darwinian principles might be applied to the understanding not only of ourselves as organisms, but to quite different aspects of our social and intellectual world. The first suggestion of this kind came from Richard Dawkins in the final chapter of *The Selfish Gene* (1976), where he floated the idea that genes in the organic world might be mirrored by what he called *memes* in the world of ideas, and that the spread of ideas might be understood in terms of replication, variation and differential survival. If so, this could account for a great deal of the way we and our societies worked. This is highly controversial, but many people are seriously interested in the idea; and more recently it has been suggested that other aspects of social organization, such as social roles, should be understood in the same Darwinian way.

The second controversy is also about the scope of Darwinian explanation, but in a different way. This one is not about the ultimate scientific explanation of how anything came into existence or about how much can be explained in cranes-only terms, but about how far the *details* of human nature – our deepest emotions and capabilities – can be revealed by attempts to understand our Darwinian origins.

This point can also be explained by reference to the Great Chain of Being. Corresponding to all its traditional levels there are areas of academic enquiry: physics, chemistry and geology dealing with the inanimate levels, plant biology dealing with animate but insentient organisms, zoology dealing with animals, and so on up to the level of theology, dealing with God and angels. Your attitude to each of these enquiries will obviously depend on what you think about the extent to which the crane/skyhook inversion can spread along the chain. If, for instance, you think you can get rid of skyhooks altogether, theology will go; if you think human beings are entirely material in origin, you will not conduct your enquiries into human psychology by thinking about implanted souls. But even if you agree with someone else about the ultimate nature and origins of any kind of being (living or non-living), you may disagree about how useful the investigation of those origins is for the understanding of present-day phenomena. If you are studying rocks, or animals, or people, to what extent does it help your understanding of them *as they are now* to know about their origins? This is a quite different question from that of what those origins are, and controversial in its own right. There is, for instance, an important current debate within medicine, between people who think that all relevant knowledge comes from a direct study of people and pathogens as they are now, and Darwinians who think that an evolutionary approach is essential for the under-standing of health and disease.[4] There is a similar debate about human psychology and society.

These two questions, about origins and constitution on the one hand and the details of human nature on the other, are in many ways distinct. But since only people who give a strongly Darwinian answer to the first are likely even to raise the second, it is useful to think of the range of views about human beings and Darwinian explanation as occurring on a single scale of deepening Darwinism, ranging from anti-Darwinists at the conservative end, to ultra-Darwinists at the radical end. This is what is shown in the diagram below, with its gradually deep-ening shading from left to right.

THE SCOPE OF DARWINIAN EXPLANATION

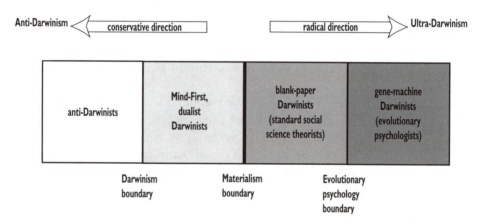

'Ultra-Darwinist', I should mention in passing, was coined as a term of abuse for Darwinian enthusiasts, by the occupants of less deep positions, and carries for them the same kind of negative spin as 'skyhooks' in Dennett's terminology. Several such abusive terms are used as missiles in the Darwin wars; but since many of them are usefully graphic, I shall not hesitate to use them. Perhaps if I use abusive terms from all sides, that can count as giving adequate balance. But I shall, anyway, be using all of them as purely descriptive, with no negative connotations intended.[5]

Since both sets of questions are about *how much* can be explained in Darwinian terms, the potential answers are matters of degree; a continuum does not, as such, offer any clear lines of demarcation. But rather in the way that freezing happens quite suddenly while temperatures fall continuously, there are points at which gradually deepening Darwinism seems to produce an abrupt flip to a significantly changed view of the world. These points are the boundaries over which the Darwin wars are being fought, and they are represented by the vertical lines on the diagram.

The first of these lines, labelled as the Darwinism boundary, marks the division between out-and-out anti-Darwinians and people who accept the core Darwinian theory of organic evolution. The anti-Darwinian position will not be discussed here, mainly because from the point of view of controversies about human nature there is not much difference between it and that of their immediate neighbours, just over the threshold. As I have already suggested, you lose fundamentalist interpretations of scripture at the Darwinian threshold, but not traditional conceptions of human nature. So for our purposes anti-Darwinians can count as being in the same category as the next group along.

This next group, who have crossed the Darwinian border to the shallowest part of Darwinism, are the occupants of the position the Church tended to adopt once it got its breath back. People in this position accept the Darwinian account of organic evolution, including the evolution of the human body, but nevertheless insist that skyhooks cannot be removed from the system entirely. There are endless variations of detail in views that take this form, but most of them tend, in practice, to share two elements that are particularly important for our understanding of our own nature and situation. One, the more fundamental, is that the Mind First view still holds: that God or something like God is needed for setting things going in the first place and for sustaining them in their present state. The other, which usually accompanies it even though the two are technically distinct, is that human beings have souls that cannot be accounted for in material terms. Non-materialist views of these kinds are typically – though not necessarily – dualist, in the traditional sense of regarding mind or spirit and matter as distinct kinds of substance,[6] so I shall sometimes refer to them in this way. All three terms – non-materialist, dualist, and Mind First – will be used to refer to this position on the band, since even though they have different meanings, they belong to the same cluster of ideas.

Next comes the materialism threshold – the most significant division on the band – which marks the abandoning of the Mind First idea. As explained in Chapter 1, materialism is a monist view, according to which the only kind of substance is matter, and everything else is derived from that. If matter vanished, minds and ideas would vanish too. The materialist Darwinian view is that life emerged from matter, and consciousness from life, by entirely Darwinian means. Skyhooks disappear altogether, and the laws of physics and natural selection give a complete explanation of our origins and fundamental nature. In practice, the division between Mind First views and material monist views coincides closely – though not perfectly – with the division between religious and secular beliefs about human life.

Finally there is the boundary that marks the battle, within materialist Darwinism, between the supporters and opponents of what used to be called sociobiology, but is now more generally known as evolutionary psychology. The combatants here agree (as the diagram implies) that our origins are entirely material and Darwinian, but they disagree about the extent to which an understanding of those origins can help to explain our nature. Neither side doubts that what we are is the result of interactions between genes and environments, or that environments have a great deal of influence. The difference between them is that evolutionary psychologists think that an understanding of the evolutionary process that made us what we are is essential for understanding the nature of our deepest emotions and abilities, and why different environments have the effects they do. Their opponents, who hold what evolutionary psychologists (probably with disparaging intent) call the *standard social science model* of explanation, believe, in contrast, that we have now evolved to a state of being so much creatures of our culture that our evolutionary origins can tell us little or nothing about what we now are. For reasons that will shortly become clear, it will be useful to describe evolutionary psychologists as taking a *gene-machine view* of human nature, while their opponents hold a *blank-paper view*.

It is important to stress that this spectrum of Darwinism indicates only general beliefs about *the extent* to which we can be understood in Darwinian terms: it does not indicate particular theories. The boxes contain people who have, as it were, immersed themselves in Darwinism to a particular depth, but who may hold quite different views from other people at that depth. This is easy to see in the case of religious views: there is no difficulty in understanding that anti-Darwinists or Mind First Darwinists can disagree radically among themselves about the right religious views to hold. The same is also true on the other side of the materialism divide. Standard social scientists agree about the general approach to the study of human nature, but may well hold quite different theories about how cultural influences shape character. Evolutionary psychologists agree in their assumption that the study of human nature must be rooted in an understanding of evolution, but that does not mean they must agree in their conclusions. The difference between the two positions as wholes is about methodology, rather than about detailed theories. None of these positions should be regarded as a body of doctrine, only as a belief about *how relevant* Darwinism is to our understanding of ourselves.

The diagram will be referred to a good deal in the course of the text, to make it easier to keep track of the analysis. I shall refer to it for short as 'the scope diagram'.

The battle lines

Mind First and Matter First

The division between non-materialism and materialism is the most important on the diagram: far more significant, for our understanding of ourselves and our place in things, than the Darwinian threshold itself. As has already been suggested, not much more is disrupted by the core Darwinian theory than biblical fundamentalism. And the materialism debate is more fundamental than the evolutionary psychology debate, because that is unlikely even to arise until the boundary into materialism has been crossed; if you think of souls as the essential carriers of personality, you presumably think that genes have little or nothing to do with what we are. The real changes start to come when the boundary is crossed to materialism, and therefore to an essentially secular view of the world.

The question of whether a materialist view of human nature is correct involves at least two separate kinds of sub-question. The first is about origins: whether the world as we know it could possibly have originated without conscious intention, and in particular whether life could have arisen by purely physical means from inanimate matter. The other is about the relationship of mind and body, and whether it is possible that mind could just be an attribute of material things, arising out of them, rather than something distinct.

Traditionally, the answers to both these questions have been negative. To many people, Locke's idea that the root of everything must be a cogitative being seems so intuitively obvious as hardly to need defence, and it seems equally obvious that you cannot explain the rationality and consciousness of human beings entirely in terms of the workings of matter.

It is not difficult to understand why these intuitions are so strong. Just as it seemed obvious to ordinary people living ordinary lives on the surface of the earth that the heavenly bodies moved in circles round them, it probably seemed equally obvious that matter on its own could only transmit, and not initiate, motion and change. The material things we are familiar with do not get up and spontaneously move themselves around; they have to be moved by other things. The only things that seem able to generate spontaneous motion are beings with consciousness, like us. When ordinary material things move or change we look for an explanation, and if there is no obvious external physical explanation – something else pushing or pulling – we assume intelligence. The crystalline spheres of the Aristotelian universe were presumed to need intelligences to keep them in motion; when unexplained things happened on earth they were attributed to the workings of gods and spirits and devils, or of fellow humans with access to mystical arts. Against such a background, it is equally natural to think of consciousness as lying at the foundation of everything – sometimes as creator, sometimes as first mover of already existing matter. (Gods were usually thought of, not as producing matter, but as bringing order out of chaos. That is indeed what happens in Genesis: matter already existed, but 'the earth was without form, and void' (Genesis 1.2).)

Furthermore, there seems to be no material difference at all between a living body and a newly dead body, so it is natural to attribute the difference to an invisible extra ingredient: the carrier of the consciousness, abilities and intentions that make the difference between a person and a corpse. Ingrained ideas of a distinction between powerful, active minds and inert, passive matter, are not at all difficult to understand.

However, one of the clearest morals of the earlier scientific revolution is that intuitions arising from common experience and common sense cannot be relied on as representations of reality. The whole history of science has been the story of its gradual encroachment on territories that had previously seemed to lie beyond the reach of natural explanation, and this is just why the Darwinian approach, which suggested a mechanism by which the apparently impossible began to seem possible, was such a revolution. It is increasingly being claimed that explanations of a Darwinian kind can reach downwards, to account for the emergence of life from matter, and upwards, to explain the human mind.

Here, for instance, is Richard Dawkins explaining in outline how Darwinian explanation might account for the development of life from inanimate matter by ordinary physical processes, and how natural selection has the capacity to do at least some of the work originally regarded as possible only through the activity of conscious beings. All that is needed for present purposes is a sense of how this kind of explanation works; it is not necessary to absorb much detail. But the passage is worth quoting at some length partly because it introduces the fundamental concept of a replicator, which will appear again later, and partly because it provides a first glimpse of the genetic revolution that has both extended and vindicated Darwin's theory.

> Before the coming of life on earth, some rudimentary evolution of molecules could have occurred by ordinary processes of physics and chemistry. There is no need to think of design or purpose or directedness. If a group of atoms in the presence of energy falls into a stable pattern it will tend to stay that way. The earliest form of natural selection was simply a selection of stable forms and a rejection of unstable ones. There is no mystery about this. It had to happen by definition.
>
> From this, of course, it does not follow that you can explain the existence of entities as complex as man by exactly the same principles on their own. It is no good taking the right number of atoms and shaking them together with some external energy till they happen to fall into the right pattern, and out drops Adam! You may make a molecule consisting of a few dozen atoms like that, but a man consists of over a thousand million million million million atoms. To try to make a man, you would have to work at your biochemical cocktail-shaker for a period so long that the entire age of the universe would seem like an eye-blink, and even then you would not succeed. This is where Darwin's theory, in its most general form, comes to the rescue. Darwin's theory takes over from where the story of the slow building up of molecules leaves off.
>
> The account of the origin of life which I shall give is necessarily speculative; by definition, nobody was around to see what happened. There are a number of rival theories, but they all have certain features in common. The simplified account I shall give is probably not too far from the truth.
>
> We do not know what chemical raw materials were abundant on earth before the coming of life, but among the plausible possibilities are water, carbon dioxide, methane, and ammonia: all simple compounds known to be present on at least some of the other planets in our solar system. Chemists have tried to imitate the chemical conditions of the young earth. They have put these simple substances in a flask and supplied a source of energy such as ultraviolet light or electric sparks –

artificial simulation of primordial lightning. After a few weeks of this, something interesting is usually found inside the flask: a weak brown soup containing a large number of molecules more complex than the ones originally put in. In particular, amino acids have been found – the building blocks of proteins, one of the two great classes of biological molecules. Before these experiments were done, naturally-occurring amino acids would have been thought of as diagnostic of the presence of life. If they had been detected on, say Mars, life on that planet would have seemed a near certainty. Now, however, their existence need imply only the presence of a few simple gases in the atmosphere and some volcanoes, sunlight, or thundery weather. More recently, laboratory simulations of the chemical conditions of earth before the coming of life have yielded organic substances called purines and pyrimidines. These are building blocks of the genetic molecule, DNA itself.

Processes analogous to these must have given rise to the 'primeval soup' which biologists and chemists believe constituted the seas some three to four thousand million years ago. The organic substances became locally concentrated, perhaps in drying scum round the shores, or in tiny suspended droplets. Under the further influence of energy such as ultraviolet light from the sun, they combined into larger molecules. Nowadays large organic molecules would not last long enough to be noticed: they would be quickly absorbed and broken down by bacteria or other living creatures. But bacteria and the rest of us are latecomers, and in those days large organic molecules could drift unmolested through the thickening broth.

At some point a particularly remarkable molecule was formed by accident. We will call it the Replicator. It may not necessarily have been the biggest or the most complex molecule around, but it had the extraordinary property of being able to create copies of itself. This may seem a very unlikely sort of accident to happen. So it was. It was exceedingly improbable. In the lifetime of a man, things which are that improbable can be treated for practical purposes as impossible. That is why you will never win a big prize on the football pools. But in our human estimates of what is probable and what is not, we are not used to dealing in hundreds of millions of years. If you filled in pools coupons every week for a hundred million years you would very likely win several jackpots.

Actually a molecule which makes copies of itself is not as difficult to imagine as it seems at first, and it only had to arise once. Think of the replicator as a mould or template. Imagine it as a large molecule consisting of a complex chain of various sorts of building block molecules. The small building blocks were abundantly available in the soup surrounding the replicator. Now suppose that each building block has an affinity for its own kind. Then whenever a building block from out in the soup lands up next to a part of the replicator for which it has an affinity, it will tend to stick there. The building blocks which attach themselves in this way will automatically be arranged in a sequence which mimics that of the replicator itself. It is easy then to think of them joining up to form a stable chain just as in the formation of the original replicator. This process could continue as a progressive stacking up, layer upon layer. This is how crystals are formed. On the other hand, the two chains might split apart, in which case we have two replicators, each of which can go on to make further copies.

A more complex possibility is that each building block has affinity not for its own kind, but reciprocally for one particular other kind. Then the replicator would act as a template not for an identical copy, but for a kind of 'negative', which would in its turn re-make an exact copy of the original positive. For our purposes it does not matter whether the original replication process was positive–negative or positive–positive, though it is worth remarking that the modern equivalents of the first replicator, the DNA molecules, use positive–negative replication. ...

So we seem to arrive at a large population of identical replicas. But now we must mention an important property of any copying process: it is not perfect. Mistakes will happen. ... We tend to regard erratic copying as a bad thing [but] ... erratic copying in biological replicators can in a real sense give rise to improvement, and it was essential for the progressive evolution of life that some errors were made. We do not know how accurately the original replicator molecules made their copies. Their modern descendants, the DNA molecules, are astonishingly faithful compared with the most high-fidelity human copying process, but even they occasionally make mistakes, and it is ultimately these mistakes which make evolution possible. Probably the original replicators were far more erratic, but in any case we may be sure that mistakes were made, and these mistakes were cumulative.

As mis-copyings were made and propagated, the primeval soup became filled by a population not of identical replicas, but of several varieties of replicating molecules, all 'descended' from the same ancestor. ...

The next important link in the argument, one which Darwin himself laid stress on (although he was talking about animals and plants, not molecules) is competition. The primeval soup was not capable of supporting an infinite number of replicator molecules. For one thing, the earth's size is finite, but other limiting factors must also have been important. In our picture of the replicator acting as a template or mould, we supposed it to be bathed in a soup rich in the small building-block molecules necessary to make copies. But when the replicators became numerous, building blocks must have been used up at such a rate that they became a scarce and precious resource. Different varieties or strains of replicator must have competed for them. ... There was a struggle for existence among replicator varieties. They did not know they were struggling, or worry about it; the struggle was conducted without any hard feelings, indeed without feelings of any kind. But they were struggling, in the sense that any miscopying which resulted in a new higher level of stability, or a new way of reducing the stability of rivals, was automatically preserved and multiplied. The process of improvement was cumulative. Ways of increasing stability and of decreasing rivals' stability became more elaborate and more efficient. Some of them may even have 'discovered' how to break up molecules of rival varieties chemically, and to use the building blocks so released for making their own copies. These proto-carnivores simultaneously obtained food and removed competing rivals. Other replicators perhaps discovered how to protect themselves, either chemically, or by building a physical wall of protein around themselves. This may have been how the first living cells appeared. Replicators began not merely to exist, but to construct for themselves containers, vehicles for their continued existence. The replicators which survived were the ones which built survival machines for themselves to live in. The first survival machines probably consisted of nothing more than a protective coat. But making a living got steadily harder as new rivals arose with better and more effective survival machines. Survival machines got bigger and more elaborate, and the process was cumulative and progressive.

(Dawkins (1976), pp. 14ff.)

So Darwinian ideas of natural selection have made considerable progress in the downward extension of cranes-only, non-teleological explanation; and, indeed, there has been a good deal more progress since Dawkins wrote that. Many scientists believe that it is quite possible in principle, even if the details remain elusive, for replication and natural selection to have got underway without the slightest need for anything more than the ordinary behaviour of atoms and molecules. This leads them to conclude that matter could, after all, be the root of everything, and that the Mind First view can be abandoned, as no longer necessary for explanation.

And in the meantime, at the other end of the scale, Darwinian scientists have been trying to explain the development of consciousness and intelligence in much the same terms. Here is Dawkins again, a little later in the same chapter, pushing towards his notorious, ultra-Darwinist, gene-machine conclusion:

Was there to be any end to the gradual improvement in the techniques and artifices used by the replicators to ensure their own continuance in the world? There would be plenty of time for improvement. What weird engines of self-preservation would the millennia bring forth? Four thousand million years on, what was to be the fate of the ancient replicators? They did not die out, for they are past masters of the survival arts. But do not look for them floating loose in the sea; they gave up that cavalier freedom long ago. Now they swarm in huge colonies, safe inside gigantic lumbering robots, sealed off from the outside world, communicating with it by tortuous indirect routes, manipulating it by remote control. They are in you and in me; they created us, body and mind; and their preservation is the ultimate rationale for our existence. They have come a long way, those replicators. Now they go by the name of genes, and we are their survival machines.

(Ibid., p. 21)

Darwinists think that intelligence and sensitivities in animals are closely connected with their abilities to survive the evolutionary competition; and if there is no difficulty in seeing how evolutionary processes can account for increasing intelligence in animals, there seems no reason in principle to doubt that the human mind results from them as well. A great deal of work is now being done on the question of how the human mind can have taken its qualitatively different turn from animal intelligence, with speculation on such matters as the coevolution of mind and language.

Furthermore, however difficult it may be to understand the connection between mind and brain, this view of things seems to be supported on all sides by advances in other areas of scientific investigation. More and more is being discovered about the connection between activity in the brain and states of mind, and about the effects of various chemicals – drugs and hormones – on those states of mind. To many people it now seems that ideas of gods and souls were early explanatory hypotheses that were quite reasonable in their time – as astrology was in its time – but are now unnecessary.

This is why it seems to many Darwinists that their theory really is a universal acid, and that it dissolves the distinction between material and spiritual substance in the way that Newton dissolved the distinction between the heavens and the earth. If they are right, Darwinian thinking shows traditional dualist conceptions of the nature of the world and ourselves to be radically mistaken, and puts matter and the laws of physics at the root of everything.

All these claims, of course, meet with resistance; that is why there is controversy along the materialist divide. Opposition is particularly strong in the United States, where there is a strong, religiously based movement arguing for what is called Intelligent Design Theory. Opponents of materialism produce various arguments in favour of the Mind First view, claiming either that the world as it is could not have come about through chance, or that there are theoretical objections to the idea that life could emerge from inanimate matter, or both. There are also objections to the idea that mind can be explained as an emergent property of matter, and that the differences between them are too great to be overcome in this way.

I shall return to these controversies later.

Exercise 3.1

1 What does Dawkins mean by a replicator?
2 Dawkins agrees that the spontaneous appearance of a replicating molecule, out of the chance interactions of molecules in the primeval soup, was extremely unlikely – far more unlikely (as he might have said if he had been writing now) than the chances of your winning the lottery several weeks in succession. How, then, does Dawkins justify his belief that it happened?
3 How, according to Dawkins, can there be a variety of replicators, given the extreme improbability of the appearance of even one?

(Answers on p. 275)

Blank paper and gene machines

The next controversy is between people who have passed over the threshold of materialist Darwinism, but disagree about the extent to which an understanding of our Darwinian origins can cast light on the details of our psychology.

At the conservative end of the materialist range there is the view that although our origins are entirely Darwinian, we have now evolved to a stage where we have pretty well broken free of them, and are essentially creatures of our culture. According to this view, a Darwinian view of our evolutionary background cannot contribute much to the understanding of human nature as it now is, because most of it must be explained in terms of our social environment. But more radical Darwinists think that much of our evolutionary past remains deep in our nature; and the qualitative flip on this continuum comes with the dispute (one of the fiercest in current Darwinism) between advocates and opponents of evolutionary psychology.

Here is one account of the nature of the disagreement. It comes from Robert Wright, who is on the radical, pro-evolutionary psychology side of the debate:

> The new Darwinian social scientists are fighting a doctrine that has dominated their fields for much of this century: the idea that biology doesn't much matter – that the uniquely malleable human mind, together with the unique force of culture, has severed our behaviour from its evolutionary roots; that there is no inherent human nature, driving human events, but that, rather, our essential nature is to be driven. As Emile Durkheim, the father of modern sociology, wrote at the turn of the century: human nature is 'merely the indeterminate material that the social factor moulds and transforms'. History shows, said Durkheim, that even such deeply felt emotions as sexual jealousy, a father's love of his child, or the child's love of the father, are 'far from being inherent in human nature'. The mind, in this view, is basically passive – it is a basin into which, as a person matures, the local culture is gradually poured; if the mind sets any limits at all on the content of culture, they are exceedingly broad. … Even psychologists – who might be expected to argue on behalf of the human mind – have often depicted it as little more than a blank slate. Behaviourism, which dominated psychology for a good part of this century, consists largely of the idea that people tend habitually to do what they are rewarded for doing and not do what they are punished for doing; thus is the formless mind given form. …
>
> This view of human nature – as something that barely exists and doesn't much matter – is known among modern Darwinian social scientists as 'the standard social science model'. Many of them learned it as undergraduates, and some of them spent years under its sway before beginning to question it. After a certain amount of questioning, they began to rebel.
>
> The various revolutionaries stubbornly refuse to call themselves by a single, simple name, the sort of thing that would fit easily onto a fluttering banner. They once had such a name – 'sociobiology', Wilson's apt and useful term. But Wilson's book drew so much fire, provoked so many charges of malign political intent, so much caricature of sociobiology's substance, that the word became tainted. Most practitioners of the field he defined now prefer to avoid his label. Though bound by allegiance to a compact and coherent set of doctrines, they go by different names: behavioural ecologists, Darwinian anthropologists, evolutionary psychologists, evolutionary psychiatrists. People sometimes ask: Whatever happened to sociobiology? The answer is that it went underground, where it has been eating away at the foundations of academic orthodoxy.

(Wright (1994), pp. 5ff.)

As I said earlier, I shall use 'sociobiology' and 'evolutionary psychology' inter-changeably. This is partly because 'sociobiology' is still probably the more familiar term, but largely because the adjective 'sociobiological' is a lot less cumbersome than 'evolutionarily psychological'.

The basis of evolutionary psychology was well understood by Darwin himself. Any characteristic that gives an organism a reproductive edge over its rivals will tend to spread through a population, and once evolution reaches the stage of producing creatures capable of making choices, the kinds of choice they make will have an enormous effect on how reproductively successful they are. The range of choices available to them will depend partly on their environment and partly on their own physical skills and intelligence, but the choices they actually make will depend, at root, on their emotions. Emotions are what make creatures prefer some things to others, so as soon as emotions evolve they will be part of what determines which lineages survive. If you are a member of a sexual species but not interested in sex, or a female mammal averse to suckling, you will probably leave fewer offspring than others who like both activities. And if any offspring you do succeed in producing and rearing resemble you in these respects, there will still not be much hope for your lineage in the long run. Different emotions have different reproductive potential, just as different phys-ical and intellectual characteristics have.

This meant that the emotions and inclinations of animals could be studied by evolutionary scientists in just the same way as were their physical characteris-tics. Questions could be asked about the survival value of particular psychological tendencies, just as about colouring or beak shape. Tendencies that appeared to have negative reproductive value for individuals (such as the altruism of the social insects – to be discussed later) could be recognized as prob-lems that the theory still had to cope with, along with questions about puzzling physical characteristics, such as how the peacock could possibly have evolved his massive encumbrance of a tail. Such studies of animal emotions, dispositions and habits, therefore, were in principle a straightforward part of evolutionary enquiries into why creatures were as they were.

As with all aspects of evolution, however, a completely new direction for this kind of enquiry was opened up when genes came into the evolutionary picture, and the principles of heredity became understood. The idea of genes as the fundamental reproducers, and organisms as vehicles whose characteristics deter-mined whether those genes would survive or not, transformed the enquiry, and seemed to many biologists to offer quite new solutions to recalcitrant traditional problems.

The breakthrough to this way of thinking was made with William Hamilton's triumphant explanation, in terms of the survival of genes, of the baffling altruism of the sterile social insects (Hamilton, 1964), which will be discussed further in Chapter 4. But the real controversy about explanations of phenotypic behaviour (behaviour of whole organisms) in terms of the success of genes began when the idea was popularized in E. O. Wilson's *Sociobiology* (1975). Nobody had been particularly bothered by sociobiological explanations of ants and bees, but in the last chapter of *Sociobiology* Wilson, like Darwin, extended his ideas to speculations about human psychology and behaviour; and it was there that the real resistance began. Most people working in the field of the social sciences had for some time taken it for granted that most of our character should be explained in terms of the influence of culture.

Wilson's early suggestions about human sociobiology were open to various kinds of reasonable criticism – which were made vociferously, along with criticisms of a totally unreasonable kind – but the work has continued, and so has the debate.

So what exactly is the difference between the two sides? Care is necessary here, because nobody can control the nonsense that may be put out in the name of some idea, and when people are at war you cannot always believe what they say about each other. In particular, it often seems to be thought that evolutionary psychologists think everything about us is determined by our genes; and this is simply not the case. Here is Wright again, explaining further:

> In a way, it's not surprising that the rediscovery of human nature has taken so long. Being everywhere we look, it tends to elude us. We take for granted such bedrock elements of life as gratitude, shame, remorse, pride, honour, retribution, empathy, love, and so on – just as we take for granted the air we breathe, the tendency of dropped objects to fall, and other standard features of living on this planet. But things didn't have to be this way. We could live on a planet where social life featured none of the above. We could live on a planet where some ethnic groups felt some of the above and others felt others. But we don't. The more closely Darwinian anthropologists look at the world's peoples, the more they are struck by the dense and intricate web of human nature by which all are bound. And the more they see how the web was woven.
>
> Even when the new Darwinians do focus on differences – whether among groups of people or among people within groups – they are not generally inclined to explain them in terms of genetic differences. Darwinian anthropologists see the world's undeniably diverse cultures as products of a single human nature responding to widely varying circumstances; evolutionary theory reveals previously invisible links between the circumstances and the cultures (explaining, for example, why some cultures have dowry and others don't). And evolutionary psychologists, contrary to common expectation, subscribe to a cardinal doctrine of twentieth-century psychology and psychiatry: the potency of early social environment in shaping the adult mind. Indeed, a few are preoccupied with this subject, determined to uncover basic laws of psychological development and convinced that they can do so only with Darwinian tools. If we want to know, say, how levels of ambition or of insecurity get adjusted by early experience, we must first ask why natural selection made them adjustable. This isn't to say that human behaviour is infinitely malleable. In tracing the channels of environmental influence, most evolutionary psychologists see some firm banks. The utopian spirit of B. F. Skinner's behaviourism, the sense that a human being can become any sort of animal at all with proper conditioning, is not faring well these days. Still, neither is

the idea that the grimmest parts of the human experience are wholly immutable, grounded in 'instincts' and 'innate drives'; nor the idea that psychological differences among people boil down mainly to genetic differences. They boil down to the genes, of course (where else could rules for mental development ultimately reside?), but not necessarily to differences in genes. A guiding assumption of many evolutionary psychologists, for reasons we'll come to, is that the most radical differences among people are the ones most likely to be traceable to environment.

In a sense, evolutionary psychologists are trying to discern a second level of human nature, a deeper unity within the species. First the anthropologist notes recurring themes in culture after culture: a thirst for social approval, a capacity for guilt. You might call these, and many other such universals, 'the knobs of human nature'. Then the psychologist notes that the exact tunings of the knobs seem to differ from person to person. One person's 'thirst for approval' knob is set in the comfort zone, down around (relatively) 'self-assured', and another person's is up in the excruciating, 'massively insecure' zone; one person's guilt knob is set low and another person's is painfully high. So the psychologist asks: How do these knobs get set? Genetic differences among individuals surely play a role, but perhaps a larger role is played by genetic commonalities: by a generic, species-wide developmental programme that absorbs information from the social environment and adjusts the maturing mind accordingly. Oddly, future progress in grasping the importance of environment will probably come from thinking about genes.

Thus, human nature comes in two forms, both of which have a natural tendency to get ignored. First, there's the kind that's so pervasively apparent as to be taken for granted (guilt, for example). Second, there's the kind whose very function is to generate differences among people as they grow up, and thus naturally conceals itself (a developmental program that calibrates guilt). Human nature consists of knobs and of mechanisms for tuning the knobs, and both are invisible in their own way.

(Wright (1994), pp. 8–9)

Evolutionary psychologists expect environment to have a strong influence on the way people develop, because they take it for granted that something as adaptable as the human species will of course be genetically predisposed to respond differently to different circumstances. The disagreement between them and standard social science theorists is not about *whether* environment influences what we are, but only about the extent to which an understanding of our evolutionary origins can help to show *how, and to what extent*, this happens.

So what exactly is going on in this disputed new area? The subject matter is as wide as human nature itself, and most of the detailed hypotheses put forward are regarded as still highly speculative, even by people who are in no doubt about the underpinnings of the general area of research. We obviously cannot go far into the details; but some sense is needed of what is going on.

This is best given by a particular case; and since the matter of sex is one of the subjects most actively investigated by sociobiologists – as well as one of the most irresistibly fascinating and politically alarming – let us take that as a case study.

The evolutionary psychology of sex

It is worth commenting here that one of the reasons for hostility to sociobiological thinking is that ideas about genetic determinants of character have been used as the basis for some nasty social policies – in particular, ones that have distinguished between fit and unfit people. Partly for that reason (and partly because it is, indeed, true) present-day evolutionary psychologists stress that their concern is not the range of genetic variation between people, but with the characteristics of *the human species*. You can learn human anatomy as a subject, knowing that the information in an anatomy textbook will apply to all human beings, even though you know that individuals vary in their genetic inheritance and that the environment will influence the direction of development, and also that there will be some non-standard oddities. And in the same way, evolutionary psychologists think that a common human nature underlies all the differences between people's characters and temperaments. It is this that they are investigating.

It is useful to remember the study of physiology for comparison, because we have no difficulty, in that context, in understanding that a common physiology can underlie individual variation and the differentiating effects of environments. And it offers a useful comparison in another way as well, because in the case of physiology we also know that there is one great exception to the claim that there is a single underlying description of human anatomy; and that is sex. Sex differentiation is itself a characteristic of the species as a whole. In spite of a few unclear cases, the difference between biological maleness and femaleness is distinct – not, as with race, a matter of a continuum. Anatomy books have to recognize this distinctness, and discuss two kinds of human body. In the same way, many evolutionary psychologists go so far as to talk of two kinds of human nature, male and female.

Given how much of the traditional subjection of women was based on ideas of great differences between the sexes, it is not difficult to see why this idea has produced so much hostility. No one doubts that men and women are by nature physically different in various conspicuous ways; that is what makes them men and women. But as everyone also knows, tradition and folklore have always taken it for granted that the differences go a lot further than simple difference of reproductive apparatus and secondary sexual characteristics. Sex differences have traditionally been taken to pervade every aspect of character, and the separation of the function of the sexes for nearly all purposes was taken to follow from their natural differences as a matter of course. When the first stirrings of feminism were felt, therefore, and ideas about the traditional position of women came under attack, the obvious line of conservative defence depended on the claim that since the sexes were quite different by nature, it was obviously appropriate that they should occupy different social positions.

Here, for instance, is Ruskin:

Each has what the other has not, each completes the other; they are in nothing alike, and the happiness and perfection of each depends on each asking and receiving what the other only can give.

(Ruskin (1974 edn), in 'Of Queen's Gardens')

And here is his contemporary James Fitzjames Stephen, whose ideas will be discussed further in Chapter 9:

> There are some propositions which it is difficult to prove, because they are so plain, and this is one of them. The physical differences between the two sexes affect every part of the human body, from the hair of the head to the soles of the feet, from the size and density of the bones to the texture of the brain and the character of the nervous system. Ingenious people may argue about anything ... but all the talk in the world will never shake the proposition that men are stronger than women in every shape. They have greater muscular and nervous force, greater intellectual force, greater vigour of character.
>
> (Stephen (1991 edn), pp. 193–4)

And these differences, Stephen went on to claim, in line with most other people of his time, made it entirely proper that women and men should be treated differently and have different functions. It justified the sexes' traditional separate spheres:

> This general truth, which has been observed under all sorts of circumstances and in every age and country, has also in every age and country led to a division of labour between men and women, the general outline of which is as familiar and as universal as the general outline of the differences between them.
>
> (Ibid., p. 194)

However, Stephen's arguments were specifically addressed to those of John Stuart Mill, whose book *The Subjection of Women* had been published four years earlier, in 1869; and Mill had, in fact, pointed out clearly the problem with confident assertions of this sort:

> Standing on the ground of common sense and the constitution of the human mind, I deny that any one knows, or can know, the nature of the two sexes, as long as they have only been seen in their present relation to one another.
> ...[it is] a subject on which it is impossible in the present state of society to obtain complete and correct knowledge – whilst almost everybody dogmatizes upon it.
>
> (Mill (1991 edn), pp. 493–4)

Since women were educated and treated in systematically different ways from men – which everybody knew, because that was the situation the people who appealed to claims about the sexes' natural differences were trying to defend – you could not infer a difference of nature at all, let alone anything about the nature of that difference, from the way men and women currently appeared.

And this claim of Mill's is generally true. You cannot infer the genetic origin of any characteristic from its universality (even if it is universal), for the simple reason that there may be a cultural explanation for that universality.

Now since women's traditional position had always been justified by claims about a deep difference of nature between the sexes, it is not surprising that when the idea of environmentally produced differences was thrown into the argument, feminists picked it up and ran with it. The standard social science model of explanation, which attributed most aspects of character to environmental influences, became an article of faith for the political left in general and feminism in particular. But the trouble with this idea was that, from the point of view of evidence, it suffered from just the same problem as the other side. Mill's way of putting the matter was exactly right: we were not in a position to know about the extent of natural differences between the sexes. The existence of systematic environmental differences did undermine the conservative claim to know that the sexes were naturally different, but it was not enough to establish the feminist claim that most of the differences were environmentally caused. It was *possible* that many of them were, but that was all. As Mill had said, it was impossible to establish the matter one way or the other as long as the sexes were in different environments; and environments are not at all easy to control.

This matter of innate sex differences is a particular version of a general problem about human nature. It is extremely difficult to disentangle by direct observation the influences of genes and environments on what we are. Even if it were regarded as morally acceptable to do controlled experiments on people, social environments are far too subtle and complex to be controlled with any degree of confidence. Progress is bound to be difficult and slow.

This is the situation into which evolutionary psychology has come. It offers a different *direction* from which to approach the problem of disentangling the genetic and environmental influences on human nature. The basic idea with which evolutionary psychologists approach questions about sex is that since the different physical constitutions of the sexes would provide different conditions for reproductive success, you would expect males and females to have different natures. If we can work out which kinds of emotional disposition and mental ability *would have been evolutionarily successful* for each sex during our evolutionary history, that may give us some clues as to which of the sexual differences we observe are genetic in origin. That is the line on which the evolutionary psychology of sex has been working; and the results are nothing if not interesting.

Here is Dawkins again, setting the evolutionary scene (and, incidentally, in the opening sentence, hinting at another heresy perpetrated by evolutionary psychology):

> If there is conflict of interest between parents and children, who share 50 per cent of each other's genes, how much more severe must be the conflict between mates, who are not related to each other? All that they have in common is a 50 per cent genetic shareholding in the same children. Since father and mother are both

interested in the welfare of different halves of the same children, there may be some advantage for both of them in cooperating with each other in rearing those children. If one parent can get away with investing less than his or her fair share of costly resources in each child, however, he will be better off, since he will have more to spend on other children by other sexual partners, and so propagate more of his genes. Each partner can therefore be thought of as trying to exploit the other, trying to force the other one to invest more. Ideally, what an individual would 'like' (I don't mean physically enjoy, although he might) would be to copulate with as many members of the opposite sex as possible, leaving the partner in each case to bring up the children. As we shall see, this state of affairs is achieved by the males of a number of species, but in other species the males are obliged to share an equal part of the burden of bringing up children. This view of sexual partnership, as a relationship of mutual mistrust and mutual exploitation, has been stressed especially by Trivers [one of the main researchers and theorists in this area]. It is a comparatively new one to ethnologists. We had usually thought of sexual behaviour, copulation, and the courtship which precedes it, as essentially a cooperative venture undertaken for mutual benefit or even for the good of the species!

(Dawkins (1976), p. 151)

In other words, if you consider men and women from the point of view of success in getting their genes into subsequent generations, the simple fact of their physical, reproductive differences suggests different, and to some extent competing, evolutionary strategies. The mental characteristics that make females effective reproducers are likely to be very different from those that make males effective; and if so, genes that are successful in transmitting copies of themselves into future generations are likely to be ones that have different effects in the male and female bodies they construct. A consideration of what these characteristics might be suggests what we might expect to find as deeply rooted differences between the sexes.

Here, to illustrate the kinds of idea that are around, is another, much longer extract from *The Moral Animal*. Wright is not himself a researcher, but he is drawing on the work of a variety of people in the area to present an overview of the way things are going. The details can be read fairly quickly; what is important is to understand in general the kinds of claim he is and is not making – especially if you are inclined to be horrified by them.

Playing God

The first step toward understanding the basic imbalance of the sexes is to assume hypothetically the role natural selection plays in designing a species. Take the human species, for example. Suppose you're in charge of installing, in the minds of human (or prehuman) beings, rules of behaviour that will guide them through life, the object of the game being to maximize each person's genetic legacy. To oversimplify a bit: you're supposed to make each person behave in such a way that he or she is likely to have lots of offspring – offspring, moreover, who themselves have lots of offspring.

Obviously, this isn't the way natural selection actually works. It doesn't consciously design organisms. It doesn't consciously do anything. It blindly preserves hereditary traits that happen to enhance survival and reproduction. Still, natural selection works as if it were consciously designing organisms, so pretending you're in charge of organism design is a legitimate way to figure out which tendencies evolution is likely to have ingrained in people and other animals. In fact, this is what evolutionary biologists spend a good deal of time doing: looking at a trait – mental or otherwise – and figuring out what, if any, engineering challenge it is a solution to.

When playing the Administrator of Evolution, and trying to maximize genetic legacy, you quickly discover that this goal implies different tendencies for men and women. Men can reproduce hundreds of times a year, assuming they can persuade enough women to cooperate, and assuming there aren't any laws against polygamy – which there assuredly weren't in the environment where much of our evolution took place. Women, on the other hand, can't reproduce more often than once a year. The asymmetry lies partly in the high price of eggs; in all species they're bigger and rarer than minuscule, mass-produced sperm. (That, in fact, is biology's official definition of a female: the one with the larger sex cells.) But the asymmetry is exaggerated by the details of mammalian reproduction; the egg's lengthy conversion into an organism happens inside the female, and she can't handle many projects at once.

So, while there are various reasons why it could make Darwinian sense for a woman to mate with more than one man (maybe the first man was infertile, for example) there comes a time when having more sex just isn't worth the trouble. Better to get some rest or grab a bite to eat. For a man, unless he's really on the brink of collapse or starvation, that time never comes. Each new partner offers a very real chance to get more genes into the next generation – a much more valuable prospect, in the Darwinian calculus, than a nap or a meal. As the evolutionary psychologists Martin Daly and Margo Wilson have succinctly put it: for males 'there is always the possibility of doing better'.

There's a sense in which a female can do better, too, but it has to do with quality, not quantity. Giving birth to a child involves a huge commitment of time, not to mention energy, and nature has put a low ceiling on how many such enterprises she can undertake. So each child, from her (genetic) point of view, is an extremely precious gene machine. Its ability to survive and then, in turn, produce its own young gene machines is of mammoth importance. It makes Darwinian sense, then, for a woman to be selective about the man who is going to help her build each gene machine. She should size up an aspiring partner before letting him in on the investment, asking herself what he'll bring to the project. This question then entails a number of sub-questions that, in the human species especially, are more numerous and subtle than you might guess.

Before we go into these questions, a couple of points must be made. One is that the woman needn't literally ask them, or even be aware of them. Much of the relevant history of our species took place before our ancestors were smart enough to ask much of anything. And even in the more recent past, after the arrival of language and self-awareness, there has been no reason for every evolved behavioural tendency to fall under conscious control. In fact, sometimes it is emphatically not in our genetic interest to be aware of exactly what we are doing or why. (Hence Freud, who was definitely onto something, though some evolutionary psychologists would say he didn't know exactly what.) In the case of sexual attraction, at any rate, everyday experience suggests that natural selection has wielded its influence largely via the emotional spigots that turn on and off such feelings as tentative attraction, fierce passion, and swoon-inducing infatuation. A woman doesn't typically size up a man and think: 'He seems like a worthy contributor to my genetic legacy'. She just sizes him up and feels attracted to him – or doesn't. All the 'thinking' has been done – unconsciously, metaphorically – by natural selection. Genes leading to attractions that wound up being good for her ancestors' genetic legacies have flourished, and those leading to less productive attractions have not.

Understanding the often unconscious nature of genetic control is the first step toward understanding that – in many realms, not just sex – we're all puppets, and our best hope for even partial liberation is to try to decipher the logic of the puppeteer. The full scope of the logic will take some time to explain, but I don't think I'm spoiling the end of the movie by noting here that the puppeteer seems to have exactly zero regard for the happiness of the puppets.

The second point to grasp before pondering how natural selection has 'decided' to shape the sexual preferences of women (and of men) is that it isn't foresightful. Evolution is guided by the environment in which it takes place, and environments change. Natural selection had no way of anticipating, for example, that someday people would use contraception, and that their passions would thus lead them into time-consuming and energy-sapping sex that was sure to be fruitless; or that X-rated videotapes would come along and lead indiscriminately lustful men to spend leisure time watching them rather than pursuing real, live women who might get their genes to the next generation. This isn't to say that there's anything wrong with 'unproductive' sexual recreation. Just because natural selection created us doesn't mean we have to slavishly follow its peculiar agenda. (If anything, we might be tempted to spite it for all the ridiculous baggage it's saddled us with.) The point is just that it isn't correct to say that people's minds are designed to maximize their fitness, their genetic legacy. What the theory of natural selection says, rather, is that people's minds were designed to maximize fitness in the environment in which those minds evolved. This environment is known as the EEA – the environment of evolutionary adaptation. Or, more memorably: the 'ancestral environment.'. . .

To figure out what women are inclined to seek in a man, and vice versa, we'll need to think more carefully about our ancestral social environment(s). And, as we'll see, thinking about the ancestral environment also helps explain why females in our species are less sexually reserved than females in many other species. But for purposes of making the single, largest point of this chapter – that, whatever the typical level of reserve for females in our species, it is higher than the level for males – the particular environment doesn't much matter. For this point depends only on the premise that an individual female can, over a lifetime, have many fewer offspring than an individual male. . . .

Men and women

One of the more upbeat ideas to have emerged from an evolutionary view of sex is that human beings are a 'pair-bonding' species. In its most extreme form, the claim is that men and women are designed for a lifetime of deep, monogamous love. This claim has not emerged from close scrutiny in pristine condition.

The pair-bond hypothesis was popularized by Desmond Morris in his 1967 book *The Naked Ape*. This book, along with a few other 1960s books (Robert Ardrey's *The Territorial Imperative*, for example), represent a would-be watershed in the history of evolutionary thought. That they found large readerships signalled a new openness to Darwinism, an encouraging dissipation of the fallout from its past political misuses. But there was no way, in the end, that these books could start a Darwinian renaissance within academia. The problem was simple: they didn't make sense.

One example surfaced early in Morris's pair-bonding argument. He was trying to explain why human females are generally faithful to their mates. This is indeed a good question (if you believe they are, that is). For high fidelity would place women in a distinct minority within the animal kingdom. Though female animals are generally less licentious than males, the females of many species are far from prudes, and this is particularly true of our nearest ape relatives. Female chimpanzees and bonobos are, at times, veritable sex machines. In explaining how women came to be so virtuous, Morris referred to the sexual division of labour in an early hunter-gatherer economy. 'To begin with', he wrote, 'the males had to be sure that their females were going to be faithful to them when they left them alone to go hunting. So the females had to develop a pairing tendency.'

Stop right there. It was in the reproductive interests of the males for the females to develop a tendency toward fidelity? So natural selection obliged the males by making the necessary changes in the females? Morris never got around to explaining how, exactly, natural selection would perform this generous feat.

Maybe it's unfair to single Morris out for blame. He was a victim of his times. The trouble was an atmosphere of loose, hyper-teleological thinking. One gets the impression, reading Morris's book, and Ardrey's books, of a natural selection that peers into the future, decides what needs to be done to make things generally better for the species, and takes the necessary steps. But natural selection doesn't work that way. It doesn't peer ahead, and it doesn't try to make things generally better. Every single, tiny, blindly taken step either happens to make sense in immediate terms of genetic self-interest or it doesn't. And if it doesn't, you won't be reading about it a million years later. This was an essential message of George Williams's 1966 book, a message that had barely begun to take hold when Morris's book appeared.

One key to good evolutionary analysis, Williams stressed, is to focus on the fate of the gene in question. If a woman's 'fidelity gene' (or her 'infidelity gene') shapes her behaviour in a way that helps get copies of itself into future generations in large numbers, then that gene will by definition flourish. Whether the gene, in the process, gets mixed in with her husband's genes or with the mailman's genes is by itself irrelevant. As far as natural selection is concerned, one vehicle is as good as the next. (Of course, when we talk about 'a gene' for anything – fidelity, infidelity, altruism, cruelty – we are usefully oversimplifying; complex traits result from the interaction of numerous genes, each of which, typically, was selected for its incremental addition to fitness.)

A new wave of evolutionists has used this stricter view of natural selection to think with greater care about the question that rightly interested Morris: Are human males and females born to form enduring bonds with one another? The answer is hardly an unqualified yes for either sex. Still, it is closer to a yes for both sexes than it is in the case of, say, chimpanzees. In every human culture on the anthropological record, marriage – whether monogamous or polygamous, permanent or temporary – is the norm, and the family is the atom of social organization. Fathers everywhere feel love for their children, and that's a lot more than you can say for chimp fathers and bonobo fathers, who don't seem to have much of a clue as to which youngsters are theirs. This love leads fathers to help feed and defend their children, and teach them useful things.

At some point, in other words, extensive male parental investment entered our evolutionary lineage. We are, as they say in the zoology literature, high in MPI. We're not so high that male parental investment typically rivals female parental investment, but we're a lot higher than the average primate. We indeed have something important in common with the gibbons.

High MPI has in some ways made the everyday goals of male and female humans dovetail, and, as any two parents know, it can give them a periodic source of common and profound joy. But high MPI has also created whole new ways for male and female aims to diverge, during both courtship and marriage. In Robert Trivers's 1972 paper on parental investment, he remarked, 'One can, in effect, treat the sexes as if they were different species, the opposite sex being a resource relevant to producing maximum surviving offspring'. Trivers was making a specific analytical point, not a sweeping rhetorical one. But to a distressing extent – and an extent that was unclear before his paper – this metaphor does capture the overall situation; even with high MPI, and in some ways because of it, a basic underlying dynamic between men and women is mutual exploitation. They seem, at times, designed to make each other miserable. . . .

What do women want?

For a species low in male parental investment, the basic dynamic of courtship, as we've seen, is pretty simple: the male really wants sex; the female isn't so sure. She may want time to (unconsciously) assess the quality of his genes, whether by inspecting him or by letting him battle with other males for her favour. She may also pause to weigh the chances that he carries disease. And she may try to extract a precopulation gift, taking advantage of the high demand for her eggs. This 'nuptial offering' – which technically constitutes a tiny male parental investment, since it nourishes her and her eggs – is seen in a variety of species, ranging from primates to black-tipped hanging flies. (The female hanging fly insists on having a dead insect to eat during sex. If she finishes it before the male is finished, she may head off in search of another meal, leaving him high and dry. If she isn't so quick, the male may repossess the leftovers for subsequent dates.) These various female concerns can usually be addressed fairly quickly; there's no reason for courtship to drag on for weeks.

But now throw high MPI into the equation – male investment not just at the time of sex, but extending up to and well beyond birth. Suddenly the female is concerned not only with the male's genetic investment, or with a free meal, but with what he'll bring to the offspring after it materializes. In 1989 the evolutionary psychologist David Buss published a pioneering study of mate preferences in thirty-seven cultures around the world. He found that in every culture, females placed more emphasis than males on a potential mate's financial prospects.

That doesn't mean women have a specific, evolved preference for wealthy men. Most hunter–gatherer societies have very little in the way of accumulated resources and private property. Whether this accurately reflects the ancestral environment is controversial; hunter–gatherers have, over the last few millennia, been shoved off rich land into marginal habitats and thus may not, in this respect, be representative of our ancestors. But if indeed all men in the ancestral environment were about equally affluent (that is, not very), women may be innately attuned not so much to a man's wealth as to his social status; among hunter–gatherers, status often translates into power – influence over the divvying up of resources, such as meat after a big kill. In modern societies, in any event, wealth, status, and power often go hand in hand, and seem to make an attractive package in the eyes of the average woman.

Ambition and industry also seem to strike many women as auspicious, and Buss found that this pattern, too, is broadly international. Of course, ambition and industriousness are things a female might look for even in a low-MPI species, as indices of genetic quality. Not so, however, for her assessment of the male's willingness to invest. A female in a high-MPI species may seek signs of generosity, trustworthiness, and, especially, an enduring commitment to her in particular. It is a truism that flowers and other tokens of affection are more prized by women than by men.

Why should women be so suspicious of men? After all, aren't males in a high-MPI species designed to settle down, buy a house, and mow the lawn every weekend? Here arises the first problem with terms like love and pair bonding. Males in high-MPI species are, paradoxically, capable of greater treachery than males in low-MPI species. For the 'optimal male course', as Trivers noted, is a 'mixed strategy'. Even if long-term investment is their main aim, seduction and abandonment can make genetic sense, provided it doesn't take too much, in time and other resources, from the offspring in which the male does invest. The bastard youngsters may thrive even without paternal investment; they may, for that matter, attract investment from some poor sap who is under the impression that they're his. So males in a high-MPI species should, in theory, be ever alert for opportunistic sex.

Of course, so should males in a low-MPI species. But this doesn't amount to exploitation, since the female has no chance of getting much more from another male. In a high-MPI species, she does, and a failure to get it from any male can be quite costly.

The result of these conflicting aims – the female aversion to exploitation, the male affinity for exploiting – is an evolutionary arms race. Natural selection may favour males that are good at deceiving females about their future devotion and favour females that are good at spotting deception; and the better one side gets, the better the other side gets. It's a vicious spiral of treachery and wariness – even if, in a sufficiently subtle species, it may assume the form of soft kisses, murmured endearments, and ingenuous demurrals.

At least it's a vicious spiral in theory. Moving beyond all this theoretical speculation and into the realm of concrete evidence – actually glimpsing the seamy underside of kisses and endearments – is tricky. Evolutionary psychologists have made only meagre progress. True, one study found that males, markedly more than females, report depicting themselves as more kind, sincere, and trustworthy than they actually are. But that sort of false advertising may be only half the story, and the other half is much harder to get at. As Trivers didn't note in his 1972 paper, but did note four years later, one effective way to deceive someone is to believe what you're saying. In this context, that means being blinded by love – to feel deep affection for a woman who, after a few months of sex, may grow markedly less adorable. This, indeed, is the great moral escape hatch for men who persist in a pattern of elaborate seduction and crisp, if anguished, abandonment. 'I loved her at the time', they can movingly recall, if pressed on the matter.

This isn't to say that a man's affections are chronically delusional, that every swoon is tactical self-deception. Sometimes men do make good on their vows of eternal devotion. Besides, in one sense, an out-and-out lie is impossible. There's no way of knowing in mid-swoon, either at the conscious or unconscious level, what the future holds. Maybe some more genetically auspicious mate will show up three years from now; then again, maybe the man will suffer some grave misfortune that renders him unmarketable, turning his spouse into his only reproductive hope. But, in the face of uncertainty as to how much commitment lies ahead, natural selection would likely err on the side of exaggeration, so long as it makes sex more likely and doesn't bring counterbalancing costs.

There probably would have been some such costs in the intimate social environment of our evolution. Leaving town, or at least village, wasn't a simple matter back then, so blatantly false promises might quickly catch up with a man – in the form of lowered credibility or even shortened life span; the anthropological archives contain stories about men who take vengeance on behalf of a betrayed sister or daughter.

Also, the supply of potentially betrayable women wasn't nearly what it is in the modern world. As Donald Symons has noted, in the average hunter–gatherer society, every man who can snare a wife does, and virtually every woman is married by the time she's fertile. There probably was no thriving singles scene in the ancestral environment, except one involving adolescent girls during the fruitless phase between first menstruation and fertility. Symons believes that the life-style of the modern philandering bachelor – seducing and abandoning available women year after year after year, without making any of them targets for ongoing investment – is not a distinct, evolved sexual strategy. It is just what happens when you take the male mind, with its preference for varied sex partners, and put it in a big city replete with contraceptive technology.

Still, even if the ancestral environment wasn't full of single women sitting alone after one-night stands muttering 'Men are scum', there were reasons to guard against males who exaggerate commitment. Divorce can happen in hunter–gatherer societies; men do up and leave after fathering a child or two, and may even move to another village. And polygamy is often an option. A man may vow that his bride will stay at the centre of his life, and then, once married, spend half his time trying to woo another wife – or, worse still, succeed, and divert resources away from his first wife's children. Given such prospects, a woman's genes would be well served by her early and careful scrutiny of a man's likely devotion. In any event, the gauging of a man's commitment does seem to be part of human female psychology; and male psychology does seem inclined to sometimes encourage a false reading.

That male commitment is in limited supply – that each man has only so much time and energy to invest in offspring – is one reason females in our species defy stereotypes prevalent elsewhere in the animal kingdom. Females in low-MPI species – that is, in most sexual species – have no great rivalry with one another. Even if dozens of them have their hearts set on a single, genetically optimal male, he can, and gladly will, fulfil their dreams; copulation doesn't take long. But in a high-MPI species such as ours, where a female's ideal is to monopolize her dream mate – steer his social and material resources toward her offspring – competition with other females is inevitable. In other words: high male parental investment makes sexual selection work in two directions at once. Not only have males evolved to compete for scarce female eggs; females have evolved to compete for scarce male investment.

Sexual selection, to be sure, seems to have been more intense among men than among women. And it has favoured different sorts of traits in the two. After all, the things women do to gain investment from men are different from the things men do to gain sexual access to women. (Women aren't – to take the most obvious example – designed for physical combat with each other, as men are.) The point is simply that, whatever each sex must do to get what it wants from the other, both sexes should be inclined to do it with zest. Females in a high-MPI species will hardly be passive and guileless. And they will sometimes be the natural enemies of one another.

What do men want?

It would be misleading to say that males in a high-male-parental-investment species are selective about mates, but in theory they are at least selectively selective. They will, on the one hand, have sex with just about anything that moves, given an easy chance, like males in a low-MPI species. On the other hand, when it comes to finding a female for a long-term joint venture, discretion makes sense; males can undertake only so many ventures over a lifetime, so the genes that the partner brings to the project – genes for robustness, brains, whatever – are worth scrutinizing.

The distinction was nicely drawn by a study in which both men and women were asked about the minimal level of intelligence they would accept in a person they were 'dating'. The average response, for both male and female, was: average intelligence. They were also asked how smart a person would have to be before they would consent to sexual relations. The women said: 'Oh, in that case, markedly above average.' The men said: 'Oh, in that case, markedly below average.'

Otherwise, the responses of male and female moved in lockstep. A partner they were 'steadily dating' would have to be much smarter than average, and a marriageable partner would have to be smarter still. This finding, published in 1990, confirmed a prediction Trivers had made in his 1972 paper on parental investment. In a high-MPI species, he wrote, 'a male would be selected to differentiate between a female he will only impregnate and a female with whom he will also raise young. Toward the former he should be more eager for sex and less discriminating in choice of sex partner than the female toward him, but toward the latter he should be about as discriminating as she toward him.' As Trivers knew, the nature of the discrimination, if not its intensity, should still differ between male and female. Though both seek general genetic quality, tastes may in other ways diverge. Just as women have special reason to focus on a man's ability to provide resources, men have special reason to focus on the ability to produce babies. That means, among other things, caring greatly about the age of a potential mate, since fertility declines until menopause, when it falls off abruptly. The last thing evolutionary psychologists would expect to find is that a plainly postmenopausal woman is sexually attractive to the average man. They don't find it. (According to Bronislaw Malinowski, Trobriand Islanders considered sex with an old woman 'indecorous, ludicrous, and unaesthetic'.) Even before menopause, age matters, especially in a long-term mate; the younger a woman, the more children she can bear. In every one of Buss's thirty-seven cultures, males preferred younger mates (and females preferred older mates).

The importance of youth in a female mate may help explain the extreme male concern with physical attractiveness in a spouse (a concern that Buss also documented in all thirty-seven cultures). The generic 'beautiful woman' – yes, she has actually been assembled, in a study that collated the seemingly diverse tastes of different men – has large eyes and a small nose. Since her eyes will look smaller and her nose larger as she ages, these components of 'beauty' are also marks of youth, and thus of fertility. Women can afford to be more open-minded about looks; an oldish man, unlike an oldish woman, is probably fertile.

Another reason for the relative flexibility of females on the question of facial attractiveness may be that a woman has other things to (consciously or unconsciously) worry about. Such as: Will he provide for the kids? When people see a beautiful woman with an ugly man, they typically assume he has lots of money or status. Researchers have actually gone to the trouble of showing that people make this inference, and that the inference is often correct.

When it comes to assessing character – to figuring out if you can trust a mate – a male's discernment may again differ from a female's, because the kind of treachery that threatens his genes is different from the kind that threatens hers. Whereas the woman's natural fear is the withdrawal of his investment, his natural fear is that the investment is misplaced. Not long for this world are the genes of a man who spends his time rearing children who aren't his. Trivers noted in 1972 that, in a species with high male parental investment and internal fertilization, 'adaptations should evolve to help guarantee that the female's offspring are also his own'.

All of this may sound highly theoretical – and of course it is. But this theory, unlike the theory about male love sometimes being finely crafted self-delusion, is readily tested. Years after Trivers suggested that anticuckoldry technology might be built into men, Martin Daly and Margo Wilson found some. They realized that if indeed a man's great Darwinian peril is cuckoldry, and a woman's is desertion, then male and female jealousy should differ. Male jealousy should focus on sexual infidelity, and males should be quite unforgiving of it; a female, though she'll hardly applaud a partner's extracurricular activities, since they consume time and divert resources, should be more concerned with emotional infidelity – the sort of magnetic commitment to another woman that could eventually lead to a much larger diversion of resources.

These predictions have been confirmed – by eons of folk wisdom and, over the past few decades, by considerable data. What drives men craziest is the thought of their mate in bed with another man; they don't dwell as much as women do on any attendant emotional attachment, or the possible loss of the mate's time and attention. Wives, for their part, do find the sheerly sexual infidelity of husbands traumatic, and do respond harshly to it, but the long-run effect is often a self-improvement campaign: lose weight, wear makeup, 'win him back'. Husbands tend to respond to infidelity with rage; and even after it subsides, they often have trouble contemplating a continued relationship with the infidel.

Looking back, Daly and Wilson saw that this basic pattern had been recorded (though not stressed) by psychologists before the theory of parental investment came along to explain it. But evolutionary psychologists have now confirmed the pattern in new and excruciating detail. David Buss placed electrodes on men and women and had them envision their mates doing various disturbing things. When men imagined sexual infidelity, their heart rates took leaps of a magnitude typically induced by three successive cups of coffee. They sweated. Their brows wrinkled. When they imagined instead a budding emotional attachment, they calmed down, though not quite to their normal level. For women, things were reversed: envisioning emotional infidelity – redirected love, not supplementary sex – brought the deeper physiological distress.

The logic behind male jealousy isn't what it used to be. These days some adulterous women use contraception and thus don't, in fact, dupe their husbands into spending two decades shepherding another man's genes. But the weakening of the logic doesn't seem to have weakened the jealousy. For the average husband, the fact that his wife inserted a diaphragm before copulating with her tennis instructor will not be a major source of consolation.

The classic example of an adaptation that has outlived its logic is the sweet tooth. Our fondness for sweetness was designed for an environment in which fruit existed but candy didn't. Now that a sweet tooth can bring obesity, people try to control their cravings, and sometimes they succeed. But their methods are usually roundabout, and few people find them easy; the basic sense that sweetness feels good is almost unalterable (except by, say, repeatedly pairing a sweet taste with a painful shock). Similarly, the basic impulse toward jealousy is very hard to erase. Still, people can muster some control over the impulse, and, moreover, can muster much control over some forms of its expression, such as violence, given a sufficiently powerful reason. Prison, for example.

(Wright (1994), pp. 35–9, 55–8, 59–67)

There is much more along these lines. In the next chapter, for instance, Wright argues that, evolutionarily speaking, polygyny is better for women (more of them get high quality men) but worse for men (some do not get any women) and dreadful for society (because the sex drive is strong and frustrated men are dangerous). Our present arrangement of serial monogamy is the worst of all worlds because it leaves lots of unattached, and therefore dangerous, men and lots of abandoned older women, as the high-status men monopolize the fertile years of the females.

You will have to read the rest of Wright's book, and several others, to get the full flavour of what is going on, in the study both of sex and of many other areas of human nature. This extract offers only an indication. Still, this is more than enough to show why it is all widely regarded as alarming, and hot political stuff. The controversy in this area is probably even more impassioned than that on the materialist divide – at least in Britain. As Philip Kitcher says in a passage that will be discussed in Chapter 9:

Friends of sociobiology see the 'new synthesis' as an exciting piece of science, resting soundly on evidence and promising a wealth of new insights, including some that are relevant to human needs. To critical eyes, however, the same body of doctrine seems a mass of unfounded speculation, mischievous in covering socially harmful suggestions with the trappings and authority of science.

(Kitcher (1985), p. 8)

This brief account of what is going on in the evolutionary psychology of sex is probably enough to show just what he means.

Exercise 3.2

It is easy to misunderstand the kinds of claim Wright is making, and important not to. These exercises are designed to pre-empt common misunderstandings.

1 Wright is careful to explain that his discussion of the intentions of genes is shorthand, and that it is necessary to remember that questions about evolution are backward-looking (about what has made some characteristic survive) rather than forward-looking (about what will make it survive). As always, it is a useful exercise to translate this shorthand, to make clear the real contrast between Darwinian thinking and the teleological approach that it replaced. Try translating this teleological claim from the previous passage:

> Each new partner offers [a male] a very real chance to get more genes into the next generation – a much more valuable prospect, in the Darwinian calculus, than a nap or a meal.

2 In each of the following three sets of statements, which represents most closely Wright's claims in the preceding passage? Explain briefly why the others are not accurate representations. (Remember that this is only about what the claims are, not about whether you think they are true.)

    (i)   (a) Evolution has given the members of our species a desire to have as many offspring as possible.

            (b) Evolution has given the members of our species a desire to get as many genes as possible into the next generation.

            (c) Evolution has given members of our species desires that would have tended, in the early stages of human evolution, to have the effect of getting genes into future generations.

            (d) Evolution has given members of our species desires that will tend to have the effect of getting genes into future generations.

    (ii)   (a) All men want a wide variety of sexual partners.

            (b) All true men want a wide variety of sexual partners.

            (c) Men who want a variety of sexual partners have more offspring than monogamous men.

            (d) A desire for a variety of sexual partners has been a genetically successful male strategy in our species.

            (e) It is unnatural for a man not to have a wide variety of sexual partners.

            (f) We should not blame men who want a wide variety of sexual partners.

    (iii)   (a) Men systematically cheat women by promising to be faithful when they have no intention of it.

    (b) Evolution may have produced in men a genuine intention to be faithful to each new woman, because that makes them more efficient attracters of women, even though in fact they will soon be interested in others.

    (c) Men who are unfaithful to women will get more genes into the next generation.

3   According to current theories of evolutionary psychology as presented by Wright in this extract (either explicitly or implicitly):

    (i)   Why are there so many urban bachelors who roam around looking for brief relationships?

    (ii)   Under what circumstances are women likely to be emotionally inclined to commit adultery?

    (iii)   Under what circumstances are men likely to be emotionally inclined to commit adultery?

    (iv)   Why do the sexes seem 'designed to make each other miserable'?

    (v)   Why do men give women presents during courtship, rather than the other way round?

    (vi)   Would a woman be likely to lose sexual interest in an attractive man if she discovered he was infertile?

(Answers on p. 275)

Persisting controversy

Now look again at the scope diagram on p. 54, and consider where we are.

    The overall project of the book is to consider the implications of Darwinism for our understanding of what we are and how we fit into the wider scheme of things. There have been fears ever since Darwin's time that if the Darwinian theory of evolution is right, we shall have to recognize that many of our most deeply rooted beliefs about ourselves and hopes for our destiny are unfounded. Not surprisingly, therefore, there has always been a good deal of anxious debate about whether Darwinian claims are true.

    But the question looks rather different in the light of the way the Darwinian debate is now going, and the kinds of disagreement that persist within the Darwinian view itself. This way of looking at the matter suggests that it is not the fundamental claims of Darwinian evolution that carry the real threat to traditional ideas about ourselves, because the most conservative forms of Darwinism are compatible with most traditional, dualist, ideas about human nature. The real trouble seems to start with the thoroughgoing materialism according to which Darwinism offers a complete, skyhookless, account of our origins and nature; and it seems to intensify with the idea that those origins are still so deeply reflected in our nature that Darwinian thinking can offer detailed insights into our emotions and abilities. These questions of *how much* of our

nature and situation can be explained in Darwinian terms seem far more significant for our understanding of human nature than the simple fact of Darwinian
evolution itself.

Apparently, therefore, anyone concerned with the question of the extent to
which Darwinism forces us to change our understanding of the kind of thing we
are needs to decide between these different degrees of Darwinism. But here
there are formidable obstacles.

The first of these is actually getting to the questions themselves, which – given
the massive amount of public debate in these areas – presents considerably more
difficulties than might be imagined. And although I am about to give what might be
considered disproportionate emphasis to this problem, in comparison with the
extremely brief remarks that will be made about the difficulty of actually
answering the questions, the pervasiveness of Darwinian literature and debate
makes it important to say something about the nature of public controversy.

If you do much in the way of reading about or listening to the disputes that
go on between the various Darwinian factions, you will already be well aware
that this is a war zone; and when people find themselves in the middle of wars
their usual impulse seems to be to make a quick identification of goodies and
baddies so that they can see which side to join. After that, it is easy to start
interpreting everything claimed by the enemy in such a way as to justify all the
hostility, and for the real issues to vanish in the smoke. In practice, as a result,
much of what is presented as arguments about the issues turns out, on closer
inspection, to be about the *people* who are supposed to be associated with the
different depths of Darwinism.

This matter of the extent to which the debate is about people rather than issues is
a subject of study in its own right, and not something that can be covered in any
detail here. (It will be considered further in Chapter 9.) Nevertheless, the problem
is so pervasive that it is worth a brief illustration. The following passage is taken
pretty well at random from Steven Rose's *Lifelines* (1997), which is itself taken
pretty well at random from the polemics in this area.

> My principal target is the dogmatic gene's eye view of the world that ultra-
> Darwinism offers. There is more, much more, to life, and to evolutionary change,
> than is dreamt of in the ultra-Darwinists' philosophy. As will become apparent as
> the argument unfolds, their position is tenable only on the assumption ... of a
> direct and relatively unmodifiable line between gene and adult phenotype. There is
> no room within the model for the processes of development or for the internal
> physiological processes which constitute the organism ...
>
> (Rose (1997), p. 215)

This makes it clear that Rose is going to be arguing against the 'assumption ...
of a direct ... line between gene and adult phenotype'. This looks like, and
indeed is, a statement of an intention to discuss an issue. But it is not only that.
It is a claim about what a particular *group of people* (headed, as the rest of the
book makes clear, by Dawkins) believes: a claim that they believe there is such a

direct line between gene and phenotype (the observable characteristics of an organism, as opposed to the unobservable genes), and that it leaves no room for the processes Rose describes. The claim that these people have these beliefs is a claim about the *people*, not about the issue itself. There are also strongly implied claims about their characters. 'Dogmatic' is not a word that describes a view; it can apply only to the people who hold that view. He also refers to this supposed view as an *assumption*, which in turn implies that they have not put forward arguments for these (putative) beliefs. This paragraph promises a discussion of the issue later in the book, but it is itself entirely about the *people* who are being opposed.

I do not want to go into the details of this claim of Rose's, or any other particular case, but it is perhaps worth commenting in general that if you follow up in detail any of the claims about what opponents are supposed to have said in this debate, you may be quite startled by the extent of misquoting, quoting out of context, looking for the worst interpretation of what is said, and flagrant misrepresentation that goes on. You cannot, in this debate (nor, indeed, in most others) take it for granted that people actually do say what they are alleged by their opponents to say. You can consider in its own right Rose's arguments against the position he says he is going to dispute; but the question of whether the people to whom he attributes it actually hold it – as well as whether they have the implied moral and scientific character defects – is a quite separate one. (You might like to consider Rose's remarks in the light of what Wright says in the extract on pp. 65–6). Do evolutionary psychologists seem to you to be making an assumption about 'a direct … line between gene and adult phenotype'? Do they seem to think the genes determine everything about how an organism develops?)

Furthermore, even if particular authors do actually say what they are alleged to say, and are open to the criticisms made of them, that must still not be mistaken for an objection to all ideas in that general neighbourhood. Even if particular authors present bad arguments for some view, there may still be others who offer good arguments to the same conclusion. Even if they hold versions of a view that are easily demolished, that demolition may leave intact more carefully stated views of a similar kind. So even if there are people around who hold the views Rose attributes to ultra-Darwinism, and even if his criticisms of those views are right, that will not in itself necessarily mean that all ideas at the ultra-Darwinist end of the spectrum have been disposed of.

So the first obstacle to reaching a conclusion about which degree of Darwinism is true is penetrating the hand-to-hand fighting between factions and getting to the issues themselves. The next difficulty is that even when the real issues are identified, the problems are genuinely difficult. Many of them turn on scientific details which are disputed between experts, and about which most non-experts are simply not in a position to reach judgements. And although there are plenty of philosophical questions in the area, as well as the scientific ones – for instance, about the relationship of mind and body, and the status of evidence for the existence of God – these are difficult too, and there is perhaps even less agreement about these than about many of the empirical claims.

This is not meant to suggest that all the controversial questions are genuinely wide open, and that there is nothing to choose between the arguments put forward by the different sides: the mere existence of controversy is never enough to show that a case really is finely balanced. But what is certainly true is that such matters cannot possibly be settled here. For the purposes of this book, it will be necessary to leave the controversy between these different degrees of Darwinism unresolved.

Exercise 3.3

1   Read the following two passages from Mary Midgley's book *Evolution as a Religion*. For each passage list separately (and briefly) what she claims or implies about *people* and what she claims or implies about *issues*. It doesn't matter whether you understand properly what her claims are; this exercise is just about sorting out the two elements.

(i)   The effect on [the] public of these quasi-scientific superstitions, once any physical scientists take them up, can therefore be rather serious, and their strength is remarkable. The case most publicized so far – the resurgence of Social Darwinist[7] egoism in sociobiological literature – is indeed an alarming one. Officially, sociobiological writers understand the objections to this view perfectly. They rehearse familiar refutations of it with references to the naturalistic fallacy[8] and the like; they treat Social Darwinism as obsolete. But because the intensely competitive attitude from which it originally sprang is still their own, because competition is what they live and breathe, because they are totally culture bound and do not know that human life can proceed in any other way, they continue to project this picture on to the cosmos and to treat it as part of science.

(Midgley (1986), p. 24)

(ii)   Glover's discussion[9] is interesting because his tone and official intention are so different from the naïve, evangelistic Utopianism we have just been seeing. But at root I think he is just as machine-struck, just as carried away on a wave of undiagnosed faith in technology as such. On the surface he is highly moderate and reasonable ... He notes the difficulty of deciding who is to be in charge, warns us of the twin dangers of totalitarian, state-organized transformation and of anarchic, unbalanced changes produced by free enterprise in the 'genetic supermarket' so amazingly proposed by Robert Nozick. He does not, however, seem to notice the idiocy of this proposal. Nozick, while rejecting a genetically engineered Utopia on the grounds mentioned earlier, advises such a market 'meeting the individual specifications (within certain moral limits) of prospective parents'.

(Ibid., p. 48)

2   Suppose you are trying to decide whether you should believe some

controversial claim, such as the claims made by Wright about the differences between male and female natures, and that someone who opposes the theory makes the assertions that follow.

Consider each assertion individually. If the person who makes it can persuade you that it is *true*, how, if at all, should it affect your attitude to the theory in question? (Should it convince you that the theory is false, or that there is no reason to believe it true, or that there is less reason than you thought to believe it true, or that it makes no difference either way, or what?)

(i)   The people who make these claims are all incompetent scientists: they don't understand the difference between a wild speculation and something carefully supported by evidence.

(ii) The proponents of the theory are mainly men who hope it's all true, because they think that will justify their philandering.

(iii) If these claims are true, it will mean that feminism is misguided from top to bottom, and women will have to resign themselves to their traditional role.

(Answers on p.276)

The most important Darwinian controversies now are not between Darwinians and anti-Darwinians, but between people who have crossed the Darwinian threshold but disagree about how far to go beyond it. The purpose of this chapter has been to identify and explain the main areas of dispute within Darwinism, which are about materialism – the question of whether Darwinian explanation can extend far enough to overthrow the traditional Mind First view of the world – and evolutionary psychology – the question of whether an understanding of our evolutionary origins can cast significant light on the details of human nature.

There is a good deal that might be said about these controversies; the fact that controversy persists does not mean that the evidence on all sides is equally good. But it is difficult to establish, through the smoke of the Darwin wars, even what the detailed problems are, and as even specialists disagree about the answers there is no chance of settling them here. For the purposes of this enquiry, the question of which of these views is right will have to be left open.

4 Implications and conditionals

This short chapter is another that is more about philosophical technicalities than about Darwinism in particular, but is essential for the analysis that follows.

If there is no point at this stage in trying to establish, as a basis for the enquiry into implications, which of the Darwinian factions is closest to the truth, the best procedure is to investigate the implications of each of them. This will show how much *turns on* the question of which version is true.

This involves investigating a series of conditional statements, about what follows *if* each version is true, without investigating whether it is true or not. The chapter concludes by setting out a method for the systematic investigation of conditionals, which will be used throughout the book.

Where to go from here

Now it may seem that if we have to leave unresolved the question of which degree of Darwinism is right, that sabotages the whole project of this book. Its concern is the implications of Darwinism for our understanding of ourselves; but if the earlier arguments have been right, merely crossing the threshold to the first level of Darwinism does not make much difference to traditional views about the human situation. The real threats to tradition seem to come with the later transitions, first to materialism, and then to the gene-machine idea and evolutionary psychology. Surely, then, we cannot find out about the implications of Darwinism for ourselves until we have decided which degree of Darwinism is right?

The first part of the answer to this challenge is simple. We *can* ask about the implications of Darwinism for the things that matter to us, even without resolving the matter of truth, because we can do it for *each* of these views individually. Instead of asking simply what Darwinism implies for our understanding of human freedom, for example, we can ask a series of conditional questions. *If* materialism is true, what follows for human freedom and responsibility? *If* evolutionary psychologists are right, is serious political change impossible? And so on. There is no more difficulty in asking about the implications of different Darwinian positions without knowing whether they are true than there is about wondering what the implications of alternative courses of action are – going to live in the country or staying in London – before making a decision. It is something we have to do all the time.

But still, it may be objected, if our purpose is to understand our own situation, then surely it is not enough to know what the implications are *if* one or other version of Darwinism is true. If we want to know whether we have free will, for instance, there is no point in knowing that (perhaps) *if* materialist Darwinism is true we are not free, but *if* dualism is true we are, or whatever. To know what to think about ourselves we shall still need to find out which of the two is true; and until then it may seem that there is no point in thinking about implications. It may seem a waste of time to consider three sets of implications when only one is going to turn out to be relevant, and that we should find out what the truth is before we start worrying about implications.

In fact, however, it is not necessarily best to start with questions of truth, and leave questions about implications until those have been settled. Sometimes it is better to start with the implications.

Suppose, for instance, you think you are the long-lost only child of a recently deceased billionaire. You (and half a dozen others with the same idea) may leap to the conclusion that you should spare no effort to establish your claim, and you may – at considerable trouble and expense – start digging out documents and hiring lawyers and advertising in newspapers. But if you do rush ahead in that way, it is because you are presupposing the truth of the conditional statement *if I am the only child, then I get the money*; and you may be wrong. The deceased may have left all his money to the cats' home, or to you irrespective of whether you are his child or not, or specifically not to you under any circumstances. In any such case, the direction of the bequest will not *turn on* the truth of your claim about paternity, and you will be wasting all the time and money spent on trying to establish it. It may be better for you to start by trying to find out whether the presupposed conditional ('If I am the only child, then I get the money') is true. Then, if you find that it is, you can go on to the arduous matter of trying to establish your claim. If it is not, you can save yourself the trouble.

Whether it is better to start by investigating how much turns on the facts of your paternity, or by trying to establish those facts themselves, will depend on the situation. There is no general principle about whether it is better to start with the question of truth or the question of implications: you will need to judge such matters as how easy each kind of investigation looks, and what are the probabilities of success. If it is difficult to find out whether the conditional is true, it may be better just to go ahead with your attempted proof of paternity and risk wasting the effort; if proving paternity looks more difficult than finding out what turns on it, it will be better to start with the conditional.

This is strongly relevant to the situation here. If the debate between the different degrees of Darwinism is complicated, and agreement not yet in sight, that in itself suggests the worthwhileness of making investigations in other directions. We may find, if we go into the matter of implications, that fewer issues turn on the question of which version is true than at first appeared. Until we look, we shall not know.

The difficulty of settling the questions of fact in this area is significant in another way as well. I have said that the debates on these issues are pretty passionate; but how many of the people who take these sides are in a position to understand the ins and outs of the evidence for their positions? What is the basis of their conviction that they are right about their claims? Obviously some of the main protagonists are experts in their fields; but experts in some areas may not be experts in others, and passion about these matters extends far beyond expertise in anything at all.

How many people who eagerly defend the ideas of God and souls against materialism, for instance, have much understanding of cosmology or subatomic physics or molecular biology, or of the philosophical problems about bodies and minds, and reach the conclusions they do because of them? During the time this book was being written an immense stir was caused in America by a book that claimed to prove the Mind First view – so-called Intelligent Design Theory – at the level of molecular biology (Michael J. Behe's *Darwin's Black Box: The Biochemical Challenge to Evolution*). But how many of the people who enthusiastically accepted this purported proof had the faintest idea of how to assess the arguments? How many even read the detailed rebuttals of Behe's arguments that immediately appeared,[10] or wondered whether his being a molecular biologist, rather than an evolutionary specialist, gave any reason to doubt his expertise? The controversy here turns on the scientific detail, but far more people have taken sides than know anything about the details. And much the same is true of the debate on the evolutionary psychology boundary.

If people engage in passionate defence of some position without knowing much about the evidence, and in particular without caring much about it, it is obvious that the evidence is not what underlies the passion. No doubt what does underlie it is complex; much of the side-taking is probably to do with personal loyalties and accidents of intellectual geography. But it seems pretty clear that much of the anxiety stems from concerns about unwelcome *implications* of other positions, and that this lies at the root of the determination, mentioned by Dennett, to contain Darwinism within some partial revolution. Opponents of the more radical positions are anxious to show that the onward march of Darwinism can be stopped before it encroaches on the territory that matters most to them. This may also be why there is so much misunderstanding and misrepresentation around. Opponents are seen as people who hold alien views about ourselves and our situation, and the allegations about what they say may result from presumptions about what people like that could be expected to say.

Indeed, much of this concern about implications is explicit. People will sometimes give the supposed implications of their rivals' position as the reason for advocating their own. American creationists, for instance, can often be heard defending the teaching of creationism in schools on the ground that evolution is a morally dangerous theory; after the Columbine High School massacre in 1999 a US senator proclaimed that this was what happened if you taught children that they were descended from monkeys. Opponents of sociobiology also used to claim (not so often now) that the theories couldn't be true because the political implications were so appalling, and can still often be heard to say that the theories are sexist, or racist, or elitist, and seeming to recommend their rejection on those grounds.

It goes without saying that dislike of implications is irrelevant to questions of truth – though it might provide a reason for trying to mislead people – but what is significant in the present context is the fact that the implications of the different positions are so often taken for granted. Questions about implications are, in general, far too little discussed in their own right. You will find, if you start reading in this area, that when the debate between the various factions does not consist of exchanging insults with opponents, it is usually about which of the rival positions is *true*. The controversy is hardly ever about implications. People argue about whether we need to give up ideas of souls and a creator, or whether there is any justification for the claims of evolutionary psychology, but on the whole they do not discuss separately the question of what follows *if* these things are true. This is partly because it tends to be regarded as obvious; but it may also be because conditionals are thought of as too abstract to be worth serious consideration. Just as politicians often try to deflect the probings of journalists by implying that it is illegitimate to ask hypothetical questions, many people who pride themselves on having their feet on the ground and dealing with the practicalities of the real world are inclined to think it is silly of philosophers to spend a lot of time arguing about conditionals. Why ask what follows *if* something is true, when you don't know whether it is or not?

But journalists ought to reply to this evasive manoeuvre, much more often than they do, that the answers to hypothetical questions are often highly relevant to what is going on. You need to know how someone *would* behave under certain circumstances to know what sort of job that person is likely to do; and in the same way, to whatever extent the disputes about Darwinism are motivated by anxieties about implications, people involved in those disputes need to be sure the different views really do have the implications they are supposed to have.

It is often crucial to understand what does and what does not turn on the truth of the rival Darwinian theories; and for this reason the rest of the book will be concerned neither with the question of which degree of Darwinism most accurately represents the truth, nor with whether individuals actually make the claims their opponents accuse them of making, but only with questions about what follows *if* a particular view is true. I hope that by the end of the book it will be clear why it is worth going about things in this way.

Exercise 4.1

1   The following claims all make presuppositions which can be expressed in the form of conditionals. What are they? (This may be more difficult than it looks. The way to tackle it is to think of the statements as arguments with a missing premise and then see what premise you need to insert to make the argument valid.)

   (i)   We're going to be able to live on Mars one day; they've found water there.
   (ii)   They've discovered water on Mars, so we may be able to live there one day.
   (iii) There's no chance of her enjoying reading; they had no books in the house when she was a child.

(iv) You'll never become a concert pianist; you practise less than four hours a day.

(v) Materialism hasn't been proved, so we may have free will.

(vi) We are not entirely selfish, so Dawkins's selfish-gene theory obviously isn't true.

2   In the following situations, assume you do not know the answer to either question in the pair. Which should you try to answer first: (a) (the conditional) or (b)? If the answer is not clear, on what basis would you make your decision?

(i) You want to transplant some of the rhododendrons in your current garden to the garden you will shortly be moving to.

(a) Is it true that if the soil is alkaline, you can't grow rhododendrons?
(b) Is the soil alkaline?

(ii) You don't want to end up in Hell, if it exists.

(a) If the Bible is the word of God, will unbelievers go to Hell?
(b) Is the Bible the word of God?

(iii) You have been for years an active campaigner for various feminist causes; now someone says that sociobiology has proved that male dominance and the subordination of women is too deeply ingrained in human nature to be eradicated, and that women were happier before feminism.

(a) Is it true that if male dominance is a natural and ineradicable consequence of evolution, feminism is misguided?
(b) Is male dominance a natural and ineradicable consequence of evolution?

(Answers on p. 277)

The assessment of conditionals

From now on, then, my concern will not be with the truth of indicative statements such as 'The world arose entirely from the workings of inanimate matter,' or 'Men are genetically inclined to philander,' but with conditional statements such as '*If* the world arose entirely from inanimate matter, then we can have no free will,' or '*If* men are genetically inclined to philander, then we can't blame them if they do.' This means that the first problem to be addressed is how to set about investigating a conditional statement.

There is no mechanical way of churning out correct answers to questions about the truth of conditionals in general, any more than about statements of any other kind. It is easy to think of any number of conditionals whose truth there would be no real chance at all of settling, such as 'If there are dinosaurs on planets in a galaxy retreating from ours faster than the speed of light, they have not developed feathers.' How difficult it is depends entirely on the conditional. On the other hand, it is possible to get the investigation into some kind of order, to clarify the issues and provide a check against certain kinds of mistake.

The approach I shall outline is not one people intuitively take when they are in the thick of argument – and I have seen no trace of it in the debates about Darwinism – but there is nothing obscure about it; there is not likely to be any problem about understanding it, or seeing why it works in the way it does. If it sounds obscure or complicated when described in abstract, it will fall into place as it is applied to particular cases in the following chapters.

Consider again the conditional statement:

If I am the only child, then I get the money.

In this case, we are supposing, you want to find out whether the conditional is true because you want to know what turns on your being the child. You do not want to go to all the effort of establishing your own claim, and disproving the pretensions of your rivals, if the facts of your paternity are irrelevant to the outcome.

A conditional statement is a statement like any other, and therefore has truth value: it can be true or false. (Or, of course, nearly true, approximately true, true a hundred years ago but not now, and so on; but those complications are not relevant here.) It may be true that if you are the only child you get the money, or it may not. And as with any other statement, to decide whether or not it is true, you need to consider the appropriate evidence.

In the case of ordinary indicative statements, such as 'I am his only child,' or 'I shall get the money,' there is not much difficulty in understanding what counts as evidence – even though there may be difficulties in collecting it, or deciding whether you have enough. But what kind of evidence is relevant to establishing the truth of conditionals such as '*If* I am the child, *then* I get the money'?

The first point to make is obvious but easily overlooked. Finding out the truth of the conditional is not a matter of finding out whether the antecedent is true (whether you are the only child), or whether the consequent is true (whether you get the money). Even if you proved conclusively that either of those was true or false, you would still have no evidence at all for the truth of the conditional. Whether it is true or false that you are the child, or whether it is true or false that you will get the money, has on its own no bearing on the claim that *if* you are the child you get the money. In fact, even if you proved both antecedent and consequent true, or both false, or the consequent true and the antecedent false, that would still have no bearing on the truth of the conditional. In all these cases, the conditional could be either true or false – as experiment will quickly show.[11]

This is because a conditional is a statement which is not about the truth of any individual proposition, but about a particular kind of connection between two. It asserts that when the antecedent is true, the consequent is true as well.

To put it more technically, a conditional is true when the truth of the antecedent is a sufficient condition of the truth of the consequent. When a conditional is true, knowing the truth of the antecedent entitles you to infer the truth of the consequent.

The first rule about assessing conditionals, then, is that it is irrelevant to find out whether their antecedents and/or consequents are true. To find out whether a conditional is true, you need to find out whether this kind of connection does exist between the two elements, irrespective of the truth of either. To find out the truth of the conditional 'If I am the only child, I get the money,' you need to look into the laws of inheritance and the circumstances of this particular case. And then, if you wanted to demonstrate to someone else that the conditional was true, you would give the relevant information as your reason: 'It's true that if I'm the only child I get the money, because the law says that children always get the money irrespective of the provisions of any will,' or whatever. Anyone who doubts your claim about the truth of the conditional can then challenge the reason you give.

The fact that a conditional claims that the truth of the antecedent is a sufficient condition of the truth of the consequent suggests a useful way to formalize this kind of investigation. A conditional can be regarded as the outline of an argument, with the antecedent as the premise and the consequent as the conclusion, thus:

I am the only child.
_____
Therefore I get the money.

And since a conditional is true when the truth of the consequent can be *inferred from* the truth of the antecedent, the question can be recast as that of whether *a sound inference* can be made from premise to conclusion – or, to put it differently, whether if the premise is assumed to be true, the argument as a whole is sound. If it is true that 'I get the money' can be inferred from 'I am the only child' (irrespective of whether it is true that you are the only child), the conditional 'If I am the only child I get the money' is true.

Now in some cases of conditionals, you can make the inference from premise to conclusion directly. For instance, the conditional 'If I am the only child, I have no nephews or nieces' translates into argument form as:

I am the only child.
_____
Therefore I have no nephews or nieces.

Which is obviously a sound inference, since being an only child is incompatible with having siblings who have children. That means the conditional is true.

In other cases, it would be immediately obvious that this could not be done. The conditional 'If I am the only child, my nephew may try to murder me' translates into argument form as:

I am the only child.
_____

Therefore my nephew may try to murder me.

Which is obviously an unsound inference, since being an only child is inconsistent with having a nephew at all. That means the conditional is false.

However, conditionals like these are special cases. They are *necessarily* true or false, because there is a logical relationship (entailment in the first case, contradiction in the second) between the antecedent and consequent, and therefore between premise and conclusion of the corresponding argument. But most conditionals are not like that. Their truth or falsity is *contingent*, which means that whether or not they are true depends not on the meanings of the words, but on what the world is like.

That is the case with the conditional under consideration here. The statement:

I am the only child.

on its own neither entails nor contradicts the statement,

I get the money.

This means that you cannot directly infer the truth or falsity of the second from the truth of the first, and the conditional is not *necessarily* true or false. On the other hand, you may, by adding more premises, be able to construct a sound argument (a valid argument with true premises) to link the antecedent and the consequent. If you can, you will have shown that the conditional is *contingently* true, and therefore that the antecedent is, contingently, a sufficient condition of the truth of the consequent.

To find out whether you can do that in this case, start by expressing the conditional as an outline argument:

I am the only child.
_____

Therefore I get the money.

This argument is obviously unsound as it stands, since it is not even valid. It is not a fallacy – positively invalid – but it is incomplete. To think of it as valid, you must regard it as an *enthymeme*: an argument with at least one suppressed premise. So what you need to do is try to make the argument valid by filling the logical gap between being the only child and getting the money with a statement of a possible reason for accepting the truth of the conclusion.

Producing a *valid* argument in this way is usually not difficult. For instance:

I am the only child (of the deceased).
Children are always entitled to whatever is left by their parents.

Therefore I get the money (what the deceased left).

is a valid argument.

(I shall, by the way, throughout this book, signal newly-added elements of arguments by putting them in italics.)

This means that if the added premise is true, so that the inference from first premise to conclusion is sound (or, to put it the other way, the argument as a whole is sound if the first premise is assumed true), the truth of the first premise (the antecedent) is a sufficient condition of the truth of the conclusion (the consequent), and the conditional is true. The truth of the first premise is not sufficient on its own, of course; if it were, the conditional would be necessarily true. But given the truth of the added second premise, the conditional is contingently true.

The next step, therefore, is to decide whether the candidate added premise is actually true. You may decide that it is false (as this one, indeed, is); and in that case the inference, although valid, is not sound. Even if the first premise is true, the conclusion may not be.

Under such circumstances the conditional has not yet been shown to be true; but of course that does not mean it has been shown to be false. All it means is that the conditional has not been proved true *by this argument*. You could try again with other ways of making the argument valid, and seeing whether they fared any better. For instance, you might try completing the argument like this:

I am the only child.
Children are entitled to whatever is left by their parents unless a will
   positively states otherwise.
There is no will in this case.

Therefore I get the money.

And perhaps the added premises here can be shown to be true. If so, the inference is sound: the truth of the conclusion can be inferred from the truth of the first premise, and the conditional is true. If not, you can go on looking for other ways to complete the argument; and if you are doing a serious job of trying to find out whether the conditional is true you will try any plausible ways you can think of. (There is of course no point in trying implausible premises. There are usually indefinitely many ways of completing an incomplete argument to make it valid, but there is nothing to be gained by showing that a string of manifestly implausible ones does not work.) If you keep on failing, you are increasingly likely to conclude that the conditional is probably false, or at least that there is no good reason to believe it true.

There is nothing very momentous, and nothing at all mysterious, about this procedure. But it is nevertheless highly effective, because what it does is expose what is hidden by the conditional statement itself: the question of whether there is an adequate justification for the assertion that if the antecedent is true, so is the consequent. The conditional simply asserts the existence of the connection; the attempt to construct an argument helps you to assess whether the connection actually exists. It exposes invalid justifications, and shows the kind of evidence that would be needed to establish the soundness of valid ones. And, as I hope will become evident, this simple method will bring to light all kinds of confusions and dubious assumptions about the implications of the different degrees of Darwinism.

So, to summarize, a conditional is an assertion that the truth of the antecedent is a sufficient condition for the truth of the consequent. One way to find out whether this is true is to see whether it is possible to construct a sound argument to link the antecedent, as premise, with the consequent, as conclusion.

There is of course far more than this to be said about investigating the truth of conditionals in general; this should not be taken for a complete account. However, this will be enough to clarify the range of conditionals relevant to working out the implications of Darwinism.

Now, to conclude, return to the specific issue of Darwinism, and the use to be made of all this.

Consider again the scope diagram (p. 54). The problem is going to be to assess the implications of each of the three degrees of Darwinism for our understanding of ourselves, so that we can see how much *turns on* which one of them is true. The aim will be to establish what follows for our understanding of ourselves *if* each of them is true.

Following the account just given of how to assess conditionals, this will involve taking statements drawn from the different positions on the band of deepening Darwinism as the antecedents of the conditionals, and statements of their supposed implications – usually the ones that people are worried about – as the consequents. So we shall be investigating conditionals such as:

> If evolutionary psychologists are right about the nature of the sexes, feminism is misguided from the foundations.
> If we are ultimately material, we can have no free will.
> If we are still constrained by our evolutionary past, we are incapable of genuine altruism.
> If there is no God, there are no objective moral standards.

Each conditional to be investigated will be set out in argument form, so that it is clear what is needed to decide, in each case, whether accepting the antecedent provides a justification for believing the consequent. So, to take the first example from the list above, we shall be starting from outline arguments such as:

> The sexes are by nature as evolutionary psychologists claim they are.
> ───────
> Therefore feminism is misguided from the foundations.

The problem will then be to see whether it is possible to construct a sound argument to link the two elements, and in doing so show the conditional to be true.

The accumulation of these investigations will, I hope, cast light on the general fear that the deeper into Darwinism we are forced to go, the more we shall have to resign ourselves to losing what we have traditionally valued about ourselves.

You will see how this works – and discover some complexities not yet discussed – in the discussions of particular cases. This method is not an algorithm that generates the correct results in a mechanical way, but at the very least it will keep the structures of the arguments clear, and prevent the issues from being confused with each other. This in turn will make it obvious where any problems do lie. This is not enough to guarantee all-round success, but it can very effectively block certain ways of going wrong.

There are of course indefinitely many conditionals whose truth might be investigated. You can enquire into the truth of any conditional you like, and although the ones that are discussed in the following chapters do represent some important concerns, they are only a sample of the possibilities. I am not for a moment meaning to imply, by discussing these, that they are the only ones worth discussing. But that is another reason for approaching the issues by making the methodology explicit. It means that if you want to investigate issues that are not raised here, what is done here will nevertheless provide a guide to further investigations.

I think that anyone new to philosophy will also find some of the results surprising enough to show how crucial it is that problems of these kinds should be brought into the open and made a familiar part of the debate, and how essential it is to recognize the philosophical aspects of some very familiar questions.

Exercise 4.2

1   The first step towards producing a sound argument is to produce a valid one. For each of the following arguments:

      (a)   Say whether it is valid as it stands.

      (b)   If it is not, say what is wrong with it. Is it actually fallacious, or just incomplete? (In other words, could it be made valid by the addition of further premises?)

      (c)   If it is only incomplete, say where the logical gap comes (which elements need to be bridged by additional premises).

      (d)   Suggest one way of completing it to make it valid (but not necessarily sound).

      (e)   Check that what you have suggested really does make it valid.

   (i)   The earth is a cardboard box and all cardboard boxes are round, so the earth is round.

   (ii)   That must be an earwig; it's two inches long and all earwigs are about two inches long.

   (iii) She can't have any cousins; neither of her parents has brothers or sisters.

(iv)   That balloon is floating upwards; it must contain helium.
(v)   All my friends are unfaithful to their spouses, which shows that all my friends are men.
(vi)   All men are unfaithful to their spouses, and none of my friends is a man, so none of my friends is unfaithful to her spouse.
(vii) Yoghourt is dangerous because it contains micro-organisms, and micro-organisms are the cause of all human diseases.
(viii) All deliberate taking of human life is murder, so abortion is murder.
(ix)   She didn't have children of her own, so she'll probably be an excellent grandmother.
(x)   Homosexuality doesn't do anyone any harm, so there's no justification for trying to prevent it.

2   Complete the following incomplete arguments to make them valid. Do each in at least two different ways, making one argument plausible (arguably sound) and the other manifestly implausible.

(i)   Animals are sentient beings.
      _____
      Therefore we should not eat them.

(ii) Boxing is a dangerous sport.
      _____
      Therefore boxing should be banned.

(iii) That mountain is magnificent.
      _____
      Therefore we should not build a railway up it.

3   Show how you might use the techniques just described to set about investigating the truth of the conditional:

      If women's inclination to put their families ahead of their careers is genetic, there is no hope of changing it.

(Answers on pp. 277-8)

————————

Since it is at this stage not possible to resolve conclusively the controversies within Darwinism, the investigation of implications must be done for each of the rival positions. It may seem that this will not advance our understanding of human nature, since an enquiry of this kind can only establish that *if* one of the Darwinian views is true, something follows for our understanding of ourselves. But that is on the assumption that the implications of the different views really are as different as they are thought to be. An enquiry into the implications of the different degrees of Darwinism is needed to find out how much actually turns on the question of which is true, and it may appear that this is less than the nature and ferocity of the Darwin wars would suggest.

The way to proceed is through the investigation of a series of conditionals – *If* this Darwinian view is true, *then* what follows for our understanding of our own nature and situation? – without any consideration of whether each antecedent is itself true. A systematic way of approaching this problem is to think of the antecedent and consequent as first premise and conclusion of an outline argument, and then see whether it is possible to construct a sound inference – valid and with true premises – from premise to conclusion. This will keep the structure of the analysis clear, and make it clear how to apply it to other questions that cannot be covered here.

5   Biology as destiny

This chapter is the first of two about the idea that Darwinism presents a threat to our idea of ourselves as free and capable of responsibility, and that the deeper you go into Darwinism, the greater the threat. The accusation of denying freedom is made both by dualists against materialists and by standard social science theorists against evolutionary psychologists.

This chapter concentrates on a problem within materialist Darwinism: the question of whether the truth of the more radical, gene-machine view would deprive us of the power to control or change our destiny, in a way that the blank-paper view would not. It works through a series of such problems, setting them out in the way described at the end of the previous chapter, and reaches the substantive conclusion that there are no differences of implication of the kinds considered.

The arguments are taken quite slowly, because the purpose of this chapter is as much to show how the method works as to deal with the issues themselves. It also begins to introduce and demonstrate, as they arise, a range of philosophical terms, distinctions and techniques.

Introduction

The first problem to be considered is that of whether the truth of Darwinism would show us to be mistaken in our idea that we are free agents, responsible for our actions.

This is anyway one of the central concerns about the implications of Darwinism, but it is particularly suitable as a starting point for this enquiry, with its question about the different implications of the different depths of Darwinism. Blank-paperers often claim that gene-machinists cannot allow for human freedom – a capacity for genuine responsibility – and holders of the Mind First view typically think the same about materialists. This in itself demonstrates that the matter of implications cannot be as straightforward as it may seem, because these claims, simply understood, cannot both be right. If the capacity for responsibility is lost at the materialism threshold, it cannot be lost again to evolutionary psychology.

The discussion of this topic will be spread over this chapter and the next. The next deals specifically with the ideas of responsibility and blame, and with questions about the effects of crossing both the materialist and the evolutionary psychology thresholds. This chapter deals with the more limited question of the extent to which we have the power to change our destiny, and deals only with the controversy on the evolutionary psychology boundary.

Robots and puppets

It is not really surprising that standard social scientists frequently accuse evolutionary psychologists of ruling out human freedom. Dawkins's remarks about
gigantic lumbering robots, constructed by genes for their own purposes, and
Wright's about puppets whose puppeteer has not the least concern for their
happiness, do rather lend themselves to that kind of interpretation. And you can
also see why the accusation is often expressed in terms of evolutionary psychologists' believing in biological, or genetic, determinism: the idea that we are
forced to do what our genes dictate.

Still, even a pinch of charity would show that this was not the right interpretation to give Dawkins's and Wright's remarks. The robots and puppets are
clearly metaphors. Dawkins does not for a moment think we are mindless and
insensate, as robots (at least currently) are, and Wright does not believe either
that evolution has purposes, or that we lack them. It is important to be clear
about what the difference between the standard social scientists and evolutionary psychologists really is. Both are materialist, in accepting that all the
complexity we know has arisen from the workings of matter according to the
ordinary laws of physics, and that if matter disappeared, so would all
substance.[12] But evolutionary psychologists think that our characters contain
deeply ingrained, genetically induced, residues of our evolutionary past, which
are resistant to removal by upbringing (the gene-machine view), while standard
social scientists think that we have evolved to the stage of being able to take off,
mentally and emotionally, in any direction we like, and that culture is the main
determinant of our nature (the blank-paper view). So is it true that evolutionary
psychologists think that human nature is more constrained by our genes than
their opponents do? If so, does it imply that they can be accused of denying
human freedom, in a way that standard social scientists cannot?

To introduce this problem, start by reading another extract from Dawkins.
This is from *The Extended Phenotype* (1982), a book intended mainly for
professional biologists. The beginning of the book, from which the passage
comes, is largely given over to replies to critics of Dawkins's earlier book, *The
Selfish Gene* (1976) – and since we are not concerned with details of Dawkins
exegesis, I have left out the bits where he is correcting impressions about what
he personally said. I have concentrated on including passages directly concerned
with the implications of the view that we are gene machines.

As I suggested earlier, discussions of the *implications* of the different views
are actually quite rare; most of what you find on the subject consists of arguments about which position is true, and tends to take the matter of implications
for granted. This is quite a short passage, but it raises most of the important
issues connected with freedom, responsibility and the gene-machine view. In it
Dawkins mentions three people who make claims, or seem to hold beliefs, about
what is implied about our capacity for choice and responsibility by views
like those of Dawkins himself and E. O. Wilson (the author of *Sociobiology*).
These beliefs catch quite effectively a range of familiarly held ideas about the

implications of thinking of ourselves as vehicles for the propagation of genes. Dawkins argues that these ideas are wrong.

The passage will, by the way, provide further illustration of the animosity that often exists between the proponents of the various degrees of Darwinism. What you see is characteristic of the battle on this particular front, and, indeed, has characterized Darwinian battles since the very beginning. Most of the venom, perhaps not surprisingly, seems to be directed against the more radical positions by the relative conservatives whose views seem under threat; some hints of that appeared in the previous chapter. But the second paragraph of this extract – which deals with technicalities not directly relevant to the matter of implications – has been included because it shows that brickbats can fly in both directions. (Because this extract will be referred to in some detail, the paragraphs are numbered.)

[1]   A reviewer of Wilson's (1978) *On Human Nature*, wrote: 'although he does not go as far as Richard Dawkins (*The Selfish Gene*) in proposing sex-linked genes for "philandering", for Wilson human males have a genetic tendency towards polygyny, females towards constancy (don't blame your mates for sleeping around, ladies, it's not their fault they are genetically programmed). Genetic determinism constantly creeps in at the back door' (Rose 1978). The reviewer's clear implication is that the authors he is criticizing believe in the existence of genes that force human males to be irremediable philanderers who cannot therefore be blamed for marital infidelity. The reader is left with the impression that those authors are protagonists in the 'nature or nurture' debate, and, moreover, dyed-in-the-wool hereditarians with male chauvinist leanings.

[2]   In fact my original passage about 'philanderer males' was not about humans. It was a simple mathematical model of some unspecified animal (not that it matters, I had a bird in mind). It was not explicitly (see below) a model of genes, and if it had been about genes they would have been sex-limited, not sex-linked! It was a model of 'strategies' in the sense of Maynard Smith (1974). The 'philanderer' strategy was postulated, not as the way males behave, but as one of two hypothetical alternatives, the other being the 'faithful' strategy. The purpose of this very simple model was to illustrate the kinds of conditions under which philandering might be favoured by natural selection, and the kinds of conditions under which faithfulness might be favoured. There was no presumption that philandering was more likely in males than faithfulness. Indeed, the particular run of the simulation that I published culminated in a mixed male population in which faithfulness slightly predominated (Dawkins 1976, p. 165, although see Schuster and Sigmund 1981). There is not just one misunderstanding in Rose's remarks, but multiple compounded misunderstanding. There is a wanton eagerness to misunderstand. It bears the stamp of snow-covered Russian jackboots, of little black microchips marching to usurp the male role and steal our tractor-drivers' jobs. It is a manifestation of a powerful myth, in this case the great gene myth.

[3]   The gene myth is epitomized in Rose's parenthetic little joke about ladies not blaming their mates for sleeping around. It is the myth of 'genetic determinism'. Evidently, for Rose, genetic determinism is determinism in the full philosophical sense of irreversible inevitability. He assumes that the existence of a gene 'for' X implies that X cannot be escaped. In the words of another critic of 'genetic determinism' (Gould 1978, p. 238), 'If we are programmed to be what we are, then these traits are ineluctable. We may, at best, channel them, but we cannot change them either by will, education, or culture.'

[4]   The validity of the determinist point of view and, separately, its bearing on an individual's moral responsibility for his actions, has been debated by philosophers and theologians for centuries past, and no doubt will be for centuries to come. I suspect that both Rose and Gould are determinists in that they believe in a physical, materialistic basis for all our actions. So am I. We would also probably all three agree that human nervous systems are so complex that in practice we can forget about determinism and behave as if we had free will. Neurones may be amplifiers of fundamentally indeterminate physical events. The only point I wish to make is that, whatever view one takes on the question of determinism, the insertion of the word 'genetic' is not going to make any difference. If you are a full-blooded determinist you will believe that all your actions are predetermined by physical causes in the past, and you may or may not also believe that you therefore cannot be held responsible for your sexual infidelities. But, be that as it may, what difference can it possibly make whether some of those physical causes are genetic? Why are genetic determinants thought to be any more ineluctable, or blame-absolving, than 'environmental' ones?

[5]   The belief that genes are somehow super-deterministic, in comparison with environmental causes, is a myth of extraordinary tenacity, and it can give rise to real emotional distress. I was only dimly aware of this until it was movingly brought home to me in a question session at a meeting of the American Association for the Advancement of Science in 1978. A young woman asked the lecturer, a prominent 'sociobiologist', whether there was any evidence for genetic sex differences in human psychology. I hardly heard the lecturer's answer, so astonished was I by the emotion with which the question was put. The woman seemed to set great store by the answer and was almost in tears. After a moment of genuine and innocent bafflement the explanation hit me. Something or somebody, certainly not the eminent sociobiologist himself, had misled her into thinking that genetic determination is for keeps; she seriously believed that a 'yes' answer to her question would, if correct, condemn her as a female individual to a life of feminine pursuits, chained to the nursery and the kitchen sink. But if, unlike most of us, she is a determinist in the strong Calvinistic sense, she should be equally upset whether the causal factors concerned are genetic or 'environmental'.

[6]   People seem to have little difficulty in accepting the modifiability of 'environmental' effects on human development. If a child has had bad teaching in

mathematics, it is accepted that the resulting deficiency can be remedied by extra good teaching the following year. But any suggestion that the child's mathematical deficiency might have a genetic origin is likely to be greeted with something approaching despair: if it is in the genes 'it is written', it is 'determined' and nothing can be done about it; you might as well give up attempting to teach the child mathematics. [These] environmental causes are in principle no different from each other. Some influences of both types may be hard to reverse; others may be easy to reverse. Some may be usually hard to reverse but easy if the right agent is applied. The important point is that there is no general reason for expecting genetic influences to be any more irreversible than environmental ones.

[7]   What did genes do to deserve their sinister, juggernaut-like reputation? Why do we not make a similar bogey out of, say, nursery education or confirmation classes? Why are genes thought to be so much more fixed and inescapable in their effects than television, nuns, or books? Don't blame your mates for sleeping around, ladies, it's not their fault they have been inflamed by pornographic litera-ture! The alleged Jesuit boast, 'Give me the child for his first seven years, and I'll give you the man', may have some truth in it. Educational, or other cultural influ-ences may, in some circumstances, be just as unmodifiable and irreversible as genes and 'stars' are popularly thought to be.

(Dawkins (1982), pp. 9–13)

What views are expressed here about the implications of the gene-machine view?

The first comes from Steven Rose, in a review of Wilson's *On Human Nature*. He thinks that if there are genes that predispose you to philander, then you cannot reasonably be blamed for philandering. (He says this with manifest sarcasm; he seems to be taking this supposed implication of sociobiology as a reason for thinking sociobiology absurd.) The second comes from (Stephen Jay) Gould – whom you have already encountered as the author of the Gosse article in Chapter 2 – who says that if a predisposition is genetic, it is ineluctable. The third is attributed to the young woman at the sociobiology lecture, who, if Dawkins is right in his diagnosis of her distress, thinks that if there are genetic differences in the psychology of the sexes, of the kind that evolutionary psychologists claim, she will be condemned to a life of traditional feminine pursuits, 'chained to the nursery and the kitchen sink'. Her genes will force her to pursue this kind of life whether she likes it or not.

Here, then, are three claimed implications of the gene-machine thesis: the ideas that if we are genetically predisposed in certain directions, then (a) it is inevitable that we shall end up doing the things the genes predispose us to, (b) it is impossible to change any of it and (c) we can't be blamed for it. These are typical ideas about what is implied by the thesis that genes underlie deep aspects of our character, so we can usefully take them as the basis of the discussion. It does not matter whether Dawkins was right about his interpretation of the woman's distress – or even, for that matter, whether these brief quotations from

Rose and Gould are accurate representations of their views – since all these ideas about the implications of evolutionary psychology are in the air of public debate, and are important to discuss irrespective of whether they are correctly attributed to particular individuals. As always, our concern will be with the problems themselves, and not with attacking or defending particular people.

The task now is to try to establish whether ideas like those of Dawkins do have these implications. Is it true that if the gene-machine thesis is right, then the woman's fate is sealed, and the man cannot be blamed for obeying the promptings of his genes to seek out sexual variety, and, furthermore, that it is hopeless to try to change any of it?

There are two broad issues to consider. The young woman and Gould are concerned with the idea that the gene-machine view makes certain things *inevitable*: the idea that (to use a familiar expression) biology is destiny. That is the subject of the rest of this chapter. Rose is concerned with the related but different matter of *responsibility*, which is dealt with in Chapter 6.

Setting out the argument

Consider first the concerns of the young woman described by Dawkins. Her distress reflects a general feminist anxiety about evolutionary psychology: the idea that if sociobiological ideas about sex differences (such as the ones described by Wright (see pp. 70ff.)) are true, women are forced by their biology into something alarmingly like their traditional role. Even when the cage door is open, the genes will determine that the bird does not fly away. Since she thinks the claims of evolutionary psychologists have these unwelcome implications, she desperately hopes they are not true.

The task here is not to try to decide whether those claims are true or not, but to work out whether she is right to think they have these implications. Is it true that if the differences of sexual character are deep in the genes – rather than mainly produced by the cultural environment – and if sociobiologists are right about the nature of that character, then women are forced into lives of traditional domesticity whether they like it or not?

Feminist worries of this kind extend far beyond the domestic matters of nurseries and kitchen sinks mentioned by Dawkins. As the Wright extract in the previous chapter clearly implied, there are enough ideas being tossed around in evolutionary psychology circles to send armies of feminists to early graves. And since that extract was about relationships between the sexes rather than about predispositions to maternity and domesticity, which is also the topic of Rose's remarks about philandering men, it may be useful to start by giving Dawkins's young woman a different kind of worry, and think of her as having been reading Wright. As a result of this, she finds herself contemplating with horror a conditional along these lines:

> If current theories of evolutionary psychology are right, and evolution has given women sexually possessive emotions that dispose them

to want sole possession of a high-status man, I shall spend my life first in seeking out and competing for as high-status a man as I can get, and afterwards in desperately trying to hold on to him, jealously watching for signs of interest in other women. And then, when he philanders and shows signs of going off with younger women, as he probably will, I shall go along the time-honoured female path of 'losing weight, wearing makeup, trying to win him back', instead of throwing the louse out as he deserves, which is what he would do to me ...

This is hardly a feminist's vision of delight; so, since she is appalled by the (rather long) consequent of her conditional, she desperately hopes the antecedent is not true.

The question to be investigated here on her behalf, however, is not whether the *antecedent* is true, but whether the conditional is true: whether *if* evolutionary psychologists are on the right track, then she is doomed in the way she thinks she is.

It will help to start by simplifying that long conditional, to make it manageable. The simplified version is intended only as a marker for the long version, not an accurate summary of it, but this will not matter. Since we are concerned with general questions about the implications of our having genetically ingrained characteristics of *any* kind, rather than these kinds in particular, the details will make no difference to the line of argument. Something like this will do:

> If evolution has given women sexually possessive emotions, then (whether I like it or not) I shall spend my life acting in a sexually possessive way.

Like all conditionals, this is an assertion. It states that the truth of the antecedent (women's having sexually possessive emotions) is a sufficient condition of the truth of the consequent (this woman's life being spent in trying to catch and keep a man). To find out whether the assertion is true, we need to find out whether the truth of the antecedent gives a sufficient reason for believing the truth of the consequent. And if this question is approached by way of the method outlined at the end of the last chapter, the first step is to set out the antecedent and consequent as the premise and conclusion of an argument, thus:

> Evolution has given women sexually possessive emotions.
> ————
> Therefore I shall spend my life acting in a sexually possessive way.

The question now is whether this outline can be expanded into a sound argument. If it can, there is good reason to make an inference from premise to conclusion, and the conditional is true.

The first step is to identify any logical gaps, and then to fill them in the most plausible way possible. Here there are at least two. (And at this point, as in many similar places throughout the book, you may be interested to try to identify them before reading on.)

The first of these is so conspicuous that it may, paradoxically, be invisible; we so automatically supply the missing premise that we hardly notice its absence. There is a clear logical gap between 'women' in the first premise, and 'I' in the conclusion. You cannot get from a claim about what women do to a claim about what any particular person does unless that person is a woman. This probably seems too obvious to be worth saying, but it is often in the spelling out of details that it becomes possible to see where the problems arise, so for now, at least, it will be useful to make such infillings explicit.

That gives us:

Evolution has given women sexually possessive emotions.
I am a woman.

———————

Therefore I shall spend my life acting in a sexually possessive way.

That fills the most obvious logical gap, but there is still another. The first premise is only about *emotions*; the conclusion, in contrast, is about *actions*.

This begins to show the point of working in this detailed way. Setting the argument out makes it clear that to make this argument valid you need another premise, connecting the possession of these emotions with actually acting in this way.

The most obvious way to do this is along these lines:

Evolution has given women sexually possessive emotions.
I am a woman.
Whatever people's emotions dispose them to, they are bound to do.

———————

Therefore I shall spend my life acting in a sexually possessive way.

This is not by any means the only way in which the argument could be completed, but it is a plausible start. It seems to meet one necessary condition for the truth of the conditional, in producing a structurally valid argument linking its antecedent and its consequent. It now needs to be checked in more detail.

In a case like this, where more than one premise has been added, it is often helpful to divide the argument into two, with the conclusion of the first becoming the first premise of the second, thus:

Evolution has given women sexually possessive emotions.
I am a woman.

———————

Therefore I have sexually possessive emotions.

I have sexually possessive emotions.
Whatever people's emotions dispose them to, they are bound to do.

―――――

Therefore I shall spend my life acting in a sexually possessive way.

These two arguments can now be considered separately.

Exercise 5.1[13]

Statements are not in themselves either premises or conclusions; those terms refer only to the position of a statement in an argument.

1   For each of the following statements construct a pair of valid (not neces-sarily sound) arguments, which make the statement the conclusion of the first argument and a premise of the next. (In each case there are indefinitely many ways of doing this.)

(i)   Animals do not have a right to life.
(ii)   Boxing should be forbidden by law.

2   Turn each of the following arguments into two arguments, of which the conclusion of the first is a premise of the second:

(i)   The castaway devastated the island before he died.
       There were no sentient beings on the island.
       The only thing that matters is harm to sentient beings.

       ―――――

       Therefore what the castaway did did not matter.

(ii)   We arose entirely as a result of the laws of physics and natural selection.
       The laws of physics and natural selection can produce only automata.
       Automata are of no moral importance.

       ―――――

       Therefore we are of no moral importance.

(Answers on pp. 278–9)

Assessing the argument

First step: 'women' to 'woman'

The first of the two arguments is:

Evolution has given women sexually possessive emotions.
I am a woman.
_____

Therefore I have sexually possessive emotions.

This argument seems structurally valid; and in this case there also seem to be no problems about the truth of the premises. We are not asking about the truth of the first, because our concern is to find out the *implications* of such sociobiological claims rather than to decide their truth, and in the imaginary case we are considering – the one derived from Dawkins's story – the second premise is obviously true. So must we conclude that the inference from first premise to conclusion is sound? So it may seem, but there is still a problem about this argument, which I shall approach by way of a more general discussion.

You can often tell that an argument is not valid – that its conclusion does not follow from its premises – just by looking at its structure. You can see this in the case of the familiar formal fallacies known as *denying the antecedent* (if all swans are white, and this is not a swan, then this is not white) and *affirming the consequent* (if all swans are white, and this is white, then this is a swan). The argument above, however, does not commit any such fallacy. It looks structurally valid, so it has fulfilled that necessary condition for validity.

However, structural validity, although necessary for overall validity, is still not sufficient. There are other ways in which arguments can be invalid; and one extremely common fallacy, which has nothing to do with structure, is the *fallacy of equivocation*. This is what occurs when the meaning of a word or phrase changes during the course of the argument, and makes an apparently valid argument invalid.

The following example is so flagrant that nobody could possibly make a mistake about it, but it illustrates the point:

Mary is the one who wears the trousers in that house.
I saw all the inhabitants of that house yesterday, and the only one
    wearing trousers was a man.
_____

Therefore Mary is a man.

If you just go by the words, this argument looks valid. But 'wearing the trousers' is metaphorical in one premise and literal in the other. In spite of the similarity of the words, therefore, the expression means completely different things in the two premises, and the argument is invalid.

Or consider this argument:

If you are caught over the limit, you are disqualified from driving.
He was caught over the limit yesterday.
_____

Therefore he's bound to be disqualified.

'Over the limit' is ambiguous: it might mean over the alcohol limit or over the speed limit. If 'over the limit' means the same in both premises the argument is valid; if its meaning changes, it is not. So there is no single answer to the question of whether this argument is a fallacy of equivocation; it depends what is meant in the circumstances.

This begins to show why logic is much more complicated in real life than in logic textbooks. Logic books can teach the formal fallacies, and when you come across a formal fallacy you know there is something wrong. For instance, if you come across an argument like this:

If you are caught over the limit, you are disqualified from driving.
He was disqualified from driving.

_____

So he must have been caught over the limit.

you can tell that it is invalid (it is a case of affirming the consequent) quite irrespective of which way the ambiguous terms are interpreted. But when you find an argument that does not manifest any formal, structural fallacies of this kind, it may still be invalid because of equivocation, or it may be valid on some interpretations and invalid on others. And there may often be room for dispute about whether a meaning has or has not changed during the course of the argument.

With this in mind, consider again the original argument:

Evolution has given women sexually possessive emotions.
I am a woman.

_____

Therefore I have sexually possessive emotions.

Does there seem to be any scope here for equivocation?

The problem in this argument is that the first premise, 'Evolution has given women sexually possessive emotions,' is not only ambiguous, but multiply ambiguous. You can use it to mean all kinds of different things, as you can easily tell by considering familiar traditional claims such as 'Men are cleverer than women.' Even if you disregard problems about the exact meaning of 'clever' (and, of course, all questions of truth), a statement like that can mean all sorts of things: 'All men are cleverer than all women,' 'No woman is as clever as the cleverest man,' 'Most men are cleverer than any woman,' 'The average man is cleverer than the average woman' and many more. Someone intending any of these might, without violence to the language, express it as 'Men are cleverer than women.' This means that if such a claim is used as a premise in an argument, you cannot tell whether the argument is valid until you have clarified the meanings of all relevant parts. The argument might be valid on some interpretations of the premises and conclusion, and invalid on others.

So, for instance, suppose you have an argument that goes like this:

Women are not as clever as men.
Only the very cleverest people should be university professors.
_____

Therefore no women should be university professors.

Whether it is valid or not depends on the interpretation of the first premise. If it is interpreted as meaning 'No woman is as clever as any man,' the argument is valid. But if it is taken as a claim about the average woman and the average man, the conclusion does not follow. Even if men were cleverer than women on average, it would still be possible for some non-average women to be brilliant. Indeed, it would even be possible for men to be cleverer than women on average while *all* the very cleverest people were women – as long as the rest of the women were stupid enough to make the average for women lower than that for men.

You will find, if you look, that most of the traditional arguments designed to keep women in their place have involved fallacies of equivocation of this kind – quite apart from problems about the truth of the premises. Equivocation with general claims about groups is a favourite tool of the argument-fudger, because you can make the claims sound plausible by implying that you intend them in one of the weak interpretations (about the average characteristics of a group, for instance), but then shift surreptitiously to strong interpretations for the purpose of drawing the conclusions you want.

Now consider, in the light of all this, the specific argument at issue here:

Evolution has given women sexually possessive emotions.
I am a woman.
_____

Therefore I have sexually possessive emotions.

Whether that argument is valid depends on how you interpret the first premise. We could ask about the implications of any of the possible interpretations, as an abstract intellectual exercise, but since our concern here is with the kinds of claim sociobiologists are making, it is most useful to consider what they seem most likely to mean, and to take Wright as guide. How does it seem that he would interpret this kind of claim – or any other – about the nature of women?

He does not say anything precise about this matter, but it is nevertheless clear what he does *not* mean. He clearly is not suggesting that all women (or all men) must have the characteristics sociobiologists think is typical of their sex, let alone that they have it to any particular degree. If he took the claim to be universal it would be obviously false: it would not, for instance, allow for the existence of lesbians. The idea is much weaker than that. It is just that since you would expect different kinds of emotional makeup to have reproductive success in males and females, you would expect strong ingrained tendencies to differ-ence between the groups as wholes. But that still allows for a great deal of difference between individuals and overlap between groups. So the claims of evolutionary psychology must be understood as being about *tendencies* in the sexes, or about the *average* woman and the average man, or something of the kind. The details do not matter here; all that matters is that evolutionary psychology does not make claims about all women, or about any particular degree of possessiveness.

Now consider again the original argument. Its premise was that women were emotionally possessive, and if we are considering the implications of sociobiological claims, we need to interpret that appropriately. So, in line with what has just been said, the argument appears as something like:

> Evolution has given most women/the average woman sexually posses-
> sive emotions.
> I am a woman.
> _____
> Therefore I have sexually possessive emotions.

Is this argument valid? Obviously not – as you can see by thinking of any characteristic in which you personally differ from the average member of your group. If the average woman is six feet tall, and you are a woman, it obviously does not follow that you are six feet tall.

For the argument to work, the first premise would need to be interpreted as a claim that *all* women had these possessive emotions. The inference from first premise to conclusion would then be sound; but since the first premise would no longer be a statement of what sociobiology was claiming, it would be irrelevant to the matter of working out the implications of a sociobiological view of things.

So the claim that any *particular* woman will have a tendency of this kind, let alone a strong one, is *not* a consequence of sociobiological theories about women. Dawkins's woman should conclude, on the basis of these theories, only that she is *likely* to have *some* inbuilt degree of these evolutionarily advantageous female characteristics, but not that she is bound to have them to a strong degree, or, necessarily, anything of them all.

It may, perhaps, seem that this kind of detailed, logic-chopping analysis misses the real point. Our imaginary woman would probably be nearly as worried by the likelihood of her having these female characteristics as about its certainty – just as she might worry that she was in a high-risk group for breast cancer. She might also be altruistically anxious about the majority of women, even if she herself could be sure of being in the clear. So pointing out that sociobiology implies nothing about all women may seem just a quibble.

And of course from the point of view of her worries, it probably is just a quibble. If we were discussing the issue with such a woman, and implied that as a result of this argument she would be silly to go on worrying, we would be falling into the fallacy of *ignoratio elenchi*, which is a close relation of the fallacy of equivocation: that of arguing against a claim which is not the one your opponent is making, and which you are purporting to rebut. But this is another point at which it is important to remember that the purpose of this analysis is not to discuss particular people and their worries and beliefs, but to investigate issues – if only because the issues need to be sorted out in general terms before particular worries can be properly addressed.

So this has not been intended as an argument that the woman we have imagined was being silly, or worrying about nothing. Rather, the purpose has been to investigate the implications of sociobiological ideas by analysing an argument, and what has been achieved so far is one small step in the direction of clarification. Many mistakes are made in argument as a result of insufficient care with meanings, and philosophical progress depends on paying attention to small details, just as scientific progress does. (If people had just taken an approximate view of the movement of the heavens, instead of attending to tiny details that did not fit, the Copernican revolution would never have happened.) Even if the clarification looks like a quibble here, there are many contexts in which this kind of slip has serious consequences, and it is important to be aware of the danger.

Exercise 5.2

1 What is a fallacy of equivocation?
2 In the following arguments, what interpretation of the first premise is needed to make the argument valid? Is this the most plausible interpretation?

(i)   Men are stronger than women.
      I am a man, you are a woman.
      _____

      Therefore I can lift heavier weights than you can.

(ii) Men are stronger than women.
      We know there will be six men pulling one way in tomorrow's tug-of-war, and six women pulling the other, but nothing else about the situation.
      _____

      Therefore it is rational to expect the men to win.

(iii) Scientists say that smoking causes cancer.
      But my grandfather smoked 60 a day and lived to be 98.
      _____

      Therefore the scientists are wrong.

(iv) New Yorkers are richer than Londoners.
      Andy is a New Yorker, Bruce is a Londoner.
      _____

      Therefore Andy is richer than Bruce.

3 Go through the preceding arguments again, taking the most plausible

interpretation of the first premise. If this makes the argument invalid, rewrite the conclusion to make the argument valid. (This will usually mean making the conclusion less specific.)

4   Write any conditional statement, and use it as the first premise of (a) a valid argument, (b) an argument that commits the fallacy of denying the antecedent, (c) one that commits the fallacy of affirming the consequent.

(Answers on pp. 279–80)

Second step: dispositions to actions

Now, with those matters clarified, move on to the second half of the original argument. This was:

I have sexually possessive emotions.
Whatever people's emotions dispose them to, they are bound to do.

Therefore I shall spend my life acting in a sexually possessive way.

Since the first premise of this argument is derived from the conclusion of the first argument, it should be modified in some way – perhaps by the addition of 'probably' – and the conclusion adjusted accordingly. But that will not affect the matter of assessing the soundness of the inference from premise to conclusion, so it can be left as it stands.

So is this inference sound? The second premise, which was added earlier, seems to have made it valid, but is the premise true? Do people who have a strong inclination or emotion always or necessarily act in a way determined by it?

This is, of course, an empirical question; but it is not a difficult one that can be answered only by new research. It is obviously *not* true that all emotions determine corresponding actions. Emotions are what incline you to act in particular ways; but on the whole, in advanced animals, they do not force you to. It would be impossible for them to do this all the time anyway, since people and higher animals have conflicting emotions. If a creature is rather low down the intelligence scale, its emotions (if they can be called emotions at that level) will actually determine what it does; the proto-emotions of worker bees mean that they *certainly will* look after the queen and the grubs and collect nectar. But this applies less and less directly as you go up the intelligence scale, and creatures develop complex and competing emotions. Behaviour will depend on such things as what other emotions an animal has, its ability to calculate what will best suit its overall concerns, and its capacity to control immediate impulses for the sake of longer-term advantages. Dogs are certainly capable of restraining their impulses in the interests of calculation even without training; so are chimpanzees. In humans the case is stronger still, and there is usually no necessary connection at all between a particular emotion and its manifestation in behaviour.

Occasionally, of course, an emotion is so overpowering that a person is no longer capable of control, but that is a situation we count as mental disorder or illness, or, when temporary, a state of diminished responsibility. If evolutionary psychologists claimed that genetically ingrained emotions were typically of this kind – a kind that constituted mental illness – that would, of course, be enough to prove that evolutionary psychology was nonsense. But, as the Wright extract makes clear, evolutionary psychology makes no such claim. The claims of evolutionary psychology are about the *origins* of human dispositions, not about how strong they are.

What this means is that if the young woman's fears about sociobiology are based on the assumption that emotional dispositions force you to act in particular ways, and deprive you of any power to do otherwise, those fears are unjustified. Whatever its origin, any single emotion, even a strong one, is only one component of a complex character. Even if the woman experiences the possessive emotions that make her want to catch and keep a man, she is likely to have others too – indeed, her having other emotions is proved by the very fact that she is alarmed by the possibility that sociobiological ideas about women might be true – and she may decide that no matter how emotionally distracting she finds her possessiveness, she absolutely will not allow it to wreck her career in opera or banking, and simply refuse to act in particular ways. Or, a different kind of possibility, she might feel desperately possessive, but realize that if she acted directly on the basis of these feelings she would make things even worse for herself, and so make determined efforts to restrain her impulses.

This means that the added second premise of the argument is false, and that this second inference does not go through either. Even if Dawkins's woman has a strong dose of the emotions attributed by evolutionary psychology to women, that does not in itself determine what she will *do*. It will be an important element in the situation, but nothing like the whole.

Third step: unchangeability

Even if she accepts all this, however, the woman may still feel unconsoled. The characteristically female emotions said by sociobiologists to be innate may not force her into unwelcome courses of action, but she will still be in danger of being tormented by them. Even if she pursues her career with gritted teeth and a bright smile, and manages never to subject men to expressions of jealousy and doubt, she may feel all the time like Hans Christian Andersen's mermaid, who chose to become human even though the price was that every step she took would be like treading on daggers. And if the daggers are genetic, there will be nothing she can do to get rid of them.

This leads to the next idea about the implications of the gene-machine thesis: the one expressed by Gould in the Dawkins extract above (paragraph 3, p. 103):

> If we are programmed to be what we are, then these traits are ineluctable. We may, at best, channel them, but we cannot change them either by will, education, or culture.

The woman may be afraid that if she has these feelings, and they are genetic, there will be nothing anyone can do about it. She may defy them, but (unless she is very lucky in her circumstances) she is bound to suffer from them. How justified is this form of anxiety? Once again, the problem is to assess the truth of a conditional, which is something like this:

> If (sociobiology is right, and) women's emotional attitudes towards men are genetic in origin, then (however successfully they refuse to allow their actions to be manipulated by their emotions) women who have these emotions have no way of avoiding them (and their unwelcome effects).

This is why she is anxious for sociobiological ideas about women not to be right. This conditional translates into outline argument form along these lines:

> Women's emotional attitudes to men are genetic in origin.
> _____
> Therefore women who have these emotions have no way of avoiding them.

And, once again, the problem is to decide whether a plausible argument can be found to link premise and conclusion. The missing connection here is obviously between 'genetic' and 'ineluctable', and Gould himself makes it clear how he would complete the argument:

> Women's emotional attitudes to men are genetic in origin.
> *Genetic traits are ineluctable.*
> _____
> Therefore women who have these emotions have no way of avoiding them.

That makes the argument structurally valid, and there seems to be no other obvious candidate for the second premise. The question now is whether it is true. Are genetic traits ineluctable?

The belief that they are is essentially the 'gene for' idea. If you have the gene for brown eyes you get brown eyes; and in the same way, the idea seems to be, if you have the gene for female possessiveness about men, possessive you will feel. So the first thing to stress is, once again, that this is nothing like what evolutionary psychology claims. Even if evolutionary psychologists are right in the idea that women in general have such traits, they do not doubt either that women vary in their natural possession of them, or that their environmental background will have an effect on how strongly the genetic predispositions make themselves felt.

Still, whatever may be said about variation and possibilities for environmental tuning, this is not an adequate reply. It cannot be denied that any trait open to investigation by evolutionary psychology must be quite deeply ingrained. The idea underlying evolutionary psychology is not that everything is determined by genes, but that you may be able to find which characteristics are most deeply ingrained in any kind of creature by considering what would have been conducive to reproductive success in its evolutionary past. The traits that can be found by this method, therefore, must be ones that are likely to manifest themselves in one way or another under most circumstances the creature in question is likely to encounter. Even that allows for the possibility that unfamiliar forms of culture and environment, or special kinds of education, could bring about changes; but still, with that qualification, it can be accepted that Gould is at least close to the truth in saying that if sociobiologists are right in saying that certain characteristics are of an evolutionarily useful type, we shall not be able to change them 'either by will, education, or culture'. In Wright's terms, such influences may affect the tuning, but will not get rid of the knobs.

But does accepting Gould's contention amount to accepting that these characteristics are ineluctable, and that the added second premise is true?

Gould makes it sound as though 'ineluctable' means the same as 'unchangeable either by will, education, or culture'; but these are not the same. The claim that traits are unchangeable by will, education or culture is that they cannot be changed *by these particular means*; but to say that particular means of change are ineffective is not to say that *all* means of change must be so. Quite apart from the possibilities raised by our increasing understanding of genetic manipulation, for instance, we know that there are pharmacological ways of altering states of mind and emotion, and our understanding of these, too, is increasing all the time. Might there appear a kind of gyno-Prozac, perhaps, to make women unconcerned about men? There may also be kinds of mental exercise that would do the job. Some people claim there are.

The point here is essentially the one Dawkins makes in paragraph 6 above (p.103–4): that causes which are normally hard to reverse may be easily reversed if the right agent is applied. Infections that were once lethal could be cured easily once penicillin had been discovered; and in the same way we may discover ways to undo characteristics that are – for evolutionary reasons – strongly resistant to change under familiar conditions. There is no reason to think that the changing of a genetically induced trait is intrinsically impossible, even though it is likely to be resistant to change under familiar circumstances.

Of course that still leaves open the question of whether it would be *right* to change our nature in such ways, but that question will be left until Chapter 9. For the moment the issue is only whether the gene-machine thesis would imply that change was *impossible*, and the answer is that it would not.

Tu quoque

Nevertheless, in spite of all these academic quibbles, you may still feel that our imaginary woman is entitled to feel dejected at the thought that current theories of evolutionary psychology might have any foundation. These theories may not entail that all women have the genetic dispositions supposed, or have them strongly, but that is not much consolation to the women who do have them and wish they had not. They may not entail that women who have these dispositions must have their behaviour determined by them, but that still leaves them in permanent danger of being tussled by their emotions, ravaged by conflicting pressures, and dangerously susceptible to harm by men whose evolutionary psychology disposes them to philander – and of whom the worst are probably, for good evolutionary reasons, the very ones women are likely to find most attractive. And although it may be possible in the long run to change these characteristics by genetic engineering or chemical intervention, that is of little comfort to women who already exist and have no access to such pharmacological remedies for ingrained femininity.

Should Dawkins's young woman then still desperately hope that current theories of evolutionary psychology are unfounded, and that these traits are not deep in women's nature? It may seem so, but this raises another important aspect of this investigation into the implications of Darwinism in its various degrees. It is also one that is very commonly overlooked.

Consider again where we are on the band of deepening Darwinism. We have been considering the implications of the most radical position on the scale, and the argument so far has concluded that although the claims of evolutionary psychology do not have quite the alarming implications someone like Dawkins's woman may think they have, the modified versions that survive the analysis are likely to be quite bad enough to distress many women. This is what is implied in the diagram opposite, where the alleged implications of evolutionary psychology are crossed out and replaced with the modified versions.

But now consider another aspect of the matter. If the woman we are imagining is to be justified in her hope that the deeper level of Darwinism – the gene-machine view – is not true, she needs to show not only that *it has* the unwelcome implications she is afraid of, but also that the position she is hoping to defend *has not*. She needs to show that the unwelcome consequences *turn on* which of the two Darwinian positions is true – because if they do not, it does not matter which is true.

What, then, is the ground she is hoping to defend? Since our woman is constructed as a thought experiment, we can put her on any ground we like. But let us for now attribute to her the position from which most allegations about the implications of sociobiology are made: the blank-paper/standard social science view, which comes next to the gene-machine view on the scale of deepening Darwinism.

To see whether she is right to hope that this view is right, she needs to find out whether the blank-paper view does *not* have the unwelcome implications of the more radical position. This is what is implied, in the diagram below, by the question marks in the blank-paper column. The questions are about how the implications of the standard social science view *compare* with the unwelcome implications of the evolutionary psychology view.

blank-paper Darwinists (standard social science theorists)	gene-machine Darwinists (evolutionary psychologists)
Men and women *do not* have, on average, different (and possibly unwelcome) emotions. ?	~~Men's and women's different lives and choices are determined entirely by their genes.~~ Men and women have, on average, different (and possibly unwelcome) emotions. ✓
Familiar differences between men and women are easily changed or prevented. ?	~~Familiar differences between men and women are impossible in principle to change or prevent.~~ Familiar differences between men and women may eventually be changeable or preventable, by unfamiliar means, but not yet. ✓

What she needs to do, therefore, is assess the truth of a series of conditionals which have a statement of the blank-paper view as their antecedent:

If the characters of the sexes are mainly determined by cultural conditioning ...

and have the *negation* of the unwelcome implications of the evolutionary psychology view as consequents.[14] So she needs as consequents something like:

... women are *not* likely to have sexually possessive emotions.
... women are *not* likely to suffer from the ravages of sexually possessive emotions.
... sexually possessive emotions in women can (easily) be changed.

Then each of these conditionals can be analysed in the way now familiar.
The first conditional is:

If the characters of the sexes are mainly determined by cultural conditioning, women are not likely to have the emotions that make them sexually possessive.

This becomes in outline argument form:

The characters of the sexes are mainly determined by cultural conditioning.

Therefore women are not likely to have sexually possessive emotions.

This argument needs a premise to link the likelihood of having the characteristic with the claim about its origins, presumably along these lines:

> The characters of the sexes are mainly determined by cultural conditioning.
> *Women are not in a cultural environment that causes sexually possessive emotions.*
> _____
> Therefore women are not likely to have sexually possessive emotions.

That looks structurally valid, but is the added premise true?

The question of what causes emotional possessiveness is of course part of the dispute between standard social scientists and evolutionary psychologists. But one thing does seem clear. People who accept the standard social science model, and think that most differences of character between the sexes result from different environmental pressures on essentially similar material, do not think that women in general have escaped traditionally female ways of thinking and feeling. They must, therefore, think the traditional environment is still hard at work. So I think that the inserted premise would be rejected as implausible by most standard social science advocates themselves.

If this is right, women are about as likely to have traditional female characteristics as a result of their culture, if the standard social science model is right, as they are as a result of their genes, if the evolutionary psychology thesis is right. From the point of view of her own prospects, Dawkins's young woman seems to to be just as badly off in the shallower waters of standard social science Darwinism as in the deeper waters of evolutionary psychology.

This conclusion means that the second of the conditionals she needs to consider is easily settled. This one is:

> If the characters of the sexes are mainly determined by cultural conditioning, women are not likely to suffer from the ravages of sexually possessive emotions.

But this hardly needs separate discussion. If women are just as likely to have the sexually possessive emotions under the standard social science view as under the evolutionary psychology view, they are just as likely to suffer from them. The implications of the two views still seem the same.

That leaves the third conditional, about the possibility of improvement:

> If the characters of the sexes are mainly determined by cultural conditioning, sexually possessive emotions in women can (easily) be changed.

This gives the outline argument:

The characters of the sexes are mainly determined by cultural conditioning.
_____

Therefore sexually possessive emotions in women can (easily) be changed.

To fill the gap in this argument, we need a claim connecting type of origin with ease of change. Something like:

The characters of the sexes are mainly determined by cultural conditioning.
Culturally caused emotions and abilities can (easily) be changed.
_____

Therefore sexually possessive emotions in women can (easily) be changed.

That seems structurally valid, but is the added premise true?

Here care is needed to distinguish two quite different ways in which environments can affect actions and emotions. One way is immediate. How we act and feel at any time must obviously be strongly influenced by the situation we are in and the range of options open to us as well as by our own character, and if we move between different situations our behaviour and feelings may change radically even while our underlying character remains the same. On *any* understanding of the roots of human nature, therefore, people's behaviour and emotions may be radically changed by changing environments, as may even the abilities they display. Everyone sings better in a good choir; a woman with a faithful husband may never feel any jealousy, and as a result presume jealousy is not in her nature. To that extent, no one doubts that the way we behave, feel and appear are strongly influenced by environment.

That, however, is not the question at issue here, since this is not a point of disagreement between blank-page and gene-machine theorists. Their disagreement is about the *formative* effects of environment: about the nature of influences that give you the kind of underlying character you have. So the question here is specifically about whether environmental influences on underlying character are easy to undo.

This again goes back to the point Dawkins makes in paragraph 6 (pp. 103–4). There is no reason at all to think, in general, that differences between people that result from differences of environment are easier to change than differences resulting from genes. It has already been suggested that characteristics deeply rooted in genes might be changed quite easily if we knew how to do it, and the converse is also true: some environmentally caused characteristics are quite impossible to undo. Nobody can unbake a baked potato. And difficult and unsettled as the social sciences are, it does seem well established that certain kinds of environmental deprivation in children are never undone in the adults. There seems no reason at all to think that if a characteristic is caused by the environment – in the specific sense that an individual with a particular set of genes would have turned out differently in a different environment – it can be easily undone. If women's environment, rather than their genes, makes them grow up with characters disposed to emotional possessiveness about men, that may make the possessiveness easy to undo, but it may not. And, as with genetic causes, it will certainly depend on knowledge of how to do it.

This means that if our imaginary woman is anxious about traditionally female characteristics in her temperament, and wants to make sure they do not get in her way, there is no point in her hoping, in general, that standard social scientists rather than evolutionary psychologists are right about the origins of female nature. Either way, what she needs to know is whether these unwelcome characteristics can be undone, and if so how. The question of whether the main causes are environmental or genetic is irrelevant.

Finally, for the sake of completeness, consider just one further possibility. Let us suppose the woman has realized that the question about blank paper and gene machines is not one whose answer affects her own prospects of escape from traditional femininity, but, on the baked-potato principle, is still concerned about the implications of the evolutionary psychology view for her daughters and granddaughters. Are the prospects better for *them* if standard social scientists are right? Will that give them better prospects of not getting baked in the first place?

Once again, what is needed is a comparative investigation to see whether the implications of sociobiology are worse than those of the standard social science model. This means considering two conditionals in parallel:

If female possessiveness is genetically induced, it is difficult to prevent.

and

If female possessiveness is socially induced, it is not difficult to prevent.

The most plausible way to spell out the relevant arguments seems to be:

Female possessiveness is genetically induced.
Whatever is genetically produced is difficult to prevent.

Therefore female possessiveness is difficult to prevent.

and

Female possessiveness is socially induced.
Whatever is socially induced is not difficult to prevent.

Therefore female possessiveness is not difficult to prevent.

Do the two added premises seem plausible?

The first one has already been discussed. If a characteristic is of a kind to be studied by evolutionary psychologists, it will show itself in most normal circumstances, but that does not preclude the possibility of finding non-normal methods of preventing its appearance. Maybe we shall find genetic and pharmacological ways of making changes, if we want to. At the present rate of genetic progress, it is hard to set limits on what we might be able to do for our great-granddaughters. Everything depends on the particulars.

What, then, about the added premise in the second argument: the claim that if characteristics are mainly socially induced they are easy to prevent? The converse problem arises. Even if the general thesis that the environment is the most powerful formative cause is true, how easy it is to prevent any particular outcome depends entirely on the details. First you need to know enough about how the influence in question works, and second, you need to be in a position to control it. So far there is no agreement even about the first of these, even among people who presuppose the standard social science model. Experiments in changing human nature by large-scale political reorganization do not yet seem to have shown much sign of achieving their purpose; and if you claim that that is because it has never been done properly, that shows, if nothing else, how difficult it is to do it properly.

Once again, then, even if what is at issue is the fate of future generations, there seems no general reason to hope that blank-paperers, rather than gene-machinists, are right about the origins of human nature.

All this connects with the point made in the long paragraph just before the scope diagram, on p. 54. The disagreement between evolutionary psychologists and standard social science theorists is about the *general approach* that should be taken to the study of human psychology and society, and whether an understanding of evolutionary origins is or is not an essential part of such an enquiry. Within each of these general views there can be any number of different theories about detail. The point that emerges from these analyses is that the anxieties felt by our imaginary woman, which she sees as turning on which approach to human psychology is right, turn only on the *details* of what the truth is, and not on whether, in general, the main differences between women and men can be attributed to differences that come from different pressures in natural selection, or just different pressures from the environment. No more inevitability is implied by the gene-machine view as such than by the blank-paper view as such.

Notice, once again, that all this has only been about the *possibility* of change, and not about its desirability or legitimacy. A quite different reason for hoping that the blank-paper view was right would depend on the idea that it might often be desirable to change society, but that we should not be trying to change genetically induced characteristics. That will be discussed in Chapter 9.

Exercise 5.3

1   This section draws a distinction between (a) the formative effects of environment on character and development, and (b) environment as affecting the way someone acts or appears. In each of the following, say which of the two is at issue:

   (i)   'What is now called the nature of woman is an eminently artificial thing, the result of forced stimulation in some directions, and unnatural repression in others' (J. S. Mill).
   (ii) You'd steal too if you were starving.
   (iii) My wartime upbringing has made me habitually frugal.
   (iv) Ever since the attack she has started at the slightest noise.
   (v)   Animals brought up in captivity don't know how to hunt.
   (vi) Some cats don't bother to hunt because they are so well fed.

2   According to the arguments of this section, which of the following claims *turn on* the question of whether the blank-paper/standard social science or gene-machine/evolutionary psychology view of human nature is right (i.e. which of them would be true under one circumstance and not, or not necessarily, under the other)? (Note that this question is not about the *truth* of any of them.)

   (i)   Most women are likely to feel strong sexual possessiveness if their men show signs of interest in other women.
   (ii) It is almost inevitable that any adult woman will have a possessive disposition.
   (iii) Women are bound to act in a jealous and possessive way in certain circumstances.
   (iv) It is easy to change women's disposition.

(Answers on p. 280)

———————

This chapter has begun the analysis of the implications of differing degrees of Darwinism slowly, because part of the purpose has been to show the method of analysing conditionals in action, and to deal with relevant techniques of analysis as they appear. It has discussed, in particular, the difference between structural fallacies and informal fallacies such as the fallacy of equivocation, and illustrated this with the different possible meanings of general claims about groups.

   The investigation has mainly been into claims about the implications of the gene-machine view of human nature. It is often implied that if this is right, the genes must determine the whole course of our lives: that, for instance, it is useless for women to struggle against their female role, or to hope that women in the future may be different.

This is one reason why people who do not like the present female role hope that evolutionary psychology is not true.

If the arguments have been right, there are two main kinds of reason for claiming that this is an unfounded hope. First, the implications of evolutionary psychology are nothing like as strong as this view implies. Evolutionary psychology makes claims only about tendencies, not about characteristics' universal distribution or irresistible strength. It also allows for the possibility of radical change by extraordinary means, such as genetic and pharmacological manipulation.

But, equally important, to the extent that the gene-machine view does have unwelcome implications, it seems that the blank-paper view has them as well. When considering the implications of any of the degrees of Darwinism, it is essential to *compare* them with the implications of rival views. Unwelcome implications of one view may turn out to belong to others as well.

6 Blameless puppets

This chapter continues the discussion of genes as determining our fate by moving on to our idea of ourselves as possessing free will and the capacity for responsibility. The discussion starts with questions about the evolutionary psychology boundary, as in the previous chapter, but then extends to the debate between materialists and their opponents. It concludes, again, that when the details are looked at with enough care, there is no difference of implication between the different positions.

The chapter also provides an introduction to the philosophical problem of free will, and continues the process of introducing, as they arise, various other technicalities such as necessary and contingent non-existence, the scope of negation (contraries and contradictories), and intrinsic and instrumental values. It also makes use of the analysis to revisit shifts of level in mid-argument, and to expose familiar confusions in arguments about responsibility and punishment.

Philandering gene machines

The Dawkins passage at the beginning of the last chapter (pp. 102ff.) contained three alleged implications of the gene-machine thesis. Two of them have now been discussed: the young woman's fear about her pre-ordained future, and Gould's claim that genetic characteristics are ineluctable. In both cases I have argued that the implications of the gene-machine thesis are nothing like as strong as is often implied, and that the rival blank-paper view is, in itself, no better.

We come now to the third claim about the implications of the gene-machine thesis – that of Rose, whose remark is about responsibility and blame. He implies that if evolution has bred into us dispositions to act in certain ways, then we cannot be blamed for acting in those ways. If sociobiological ideas about men are right, it follows that women should not blame their philandering mates.

The Rose remark starts to raise fundamental questions about responsibility. What he says hovers between two quite different ideas; and these need to be distinguished, because while one of them refers back to the ground that has just been covered, the other points forward to the large philosophical problem of free will, which needs separate consideration. This section will form a bridge between the two; the rest of this chapter will be about free will and responsibility.

Rose, as quoted by Dawkins (paragraph 1), says:

> although he does not go as far as Richard Dawkins in proposing sex-linked genes for 'philandering', for Wilson human males have a genetic tendency towards polygyny, females towards constancy (don't blame your mates for sleeping

around, ladies, it's not their fault they are genetically programmed). Genetic determinism constantly creeps in at the back door.

Rose is, in other words, asserting (by rhetorical implication) the truth of a conditional. He is claiming that if, as evolutionary psychologists claim, males have evolutionarily ingrained emotions that incline them towards polygyny (or, more generally, to wanting sex with a lot of women), then we are forced to the conclusion that they cannot be blamed for philandering.

This means that the conditional to be investigated is something like:

> If men are genetically inclined to polygyny, they should not be blamed for philandering (acting polygynously).

This gives the outline argument:

> Men are genetically inclined to polygyny.
> _____
> Therefore they should not be blamed for philandering.

The question now is whether it can be completed to provide a sound inference from premise to conclusion.

Since in the last chapter the way to complete the arguments seemed obvious, it is worth stressing that there may be contexts in which it is not at all obvious how to complete an outline argument. There are indefinitely many ways in which this argument could be completed to make it valid, and there may be several that could, or might, make it sound. The most obvious way seems to be:

> Men are genetically inclined to polygyny.
> *People should not be blamed for doing what they are genetically inclined to do.*
> _____
> Therefore we should not blame men for philandering.

This does, of course, raise the potential for equivocation with different interpretations of the first premise: even if the average man should not be blamed for philandering, on this argument, it does not follow that any particular man can get off the hook in this way. However, since the question of how many men can be excused for philandering cannot possibly be settled until it has been established that a genetic inclination would provide such an excuse, we can disregard that complication here, and assume that we are dealing with an interpretation of the first premise and conclusion that makes the argument valid.

What, then, about the truth of the added premise? I said at the beginning of this section that we were approaching philosophically deep waters, and it may be clear that they are already well above the ankle. Making the added premise explicit does, as usual, help to clarify the issue, by showing starkly the kind of presupposition that underlies the assertion of the conditional. On the other hand, it shows at the same time that judging the truth of this conditional is not going to be straightforward, because the matter of blame – with all the associated problems of responsibility and desert – raises thickets of philosophical controversy. Is it true that people cannot be blamed for doing what they have a genetic tendency to do? And if so why? This is complicated, and will have to be taken a step at a time.

One way to approach the matter is this. Since the problem is to decide whether a genetic predisposition to philandering means that you should not be blamed for philandering, a plausible way to start is by considering in a general way the conditions under which we normally agree that people should not be blamed for something they have done. Then, having identified those, we can try to decide whether a genetic predisposition to polygyny would put a philandering man into any of these blameless categories.

Start, then, by thinking in ordinary, unphilosophical terms about questions of blame. Imagine, for instance, you are an ingenious defence lawyer, always ready to find ways of trying to persuade the court that although your clients may actually have *done* the things they are accused of – like stealing, or killing – they are not actually *to blame*, or much to blame, for doing them. What kinds of excuse might you have in your repertoire? Under what circumstances, if you could establish the truth of the claim you were making on behalf of your client, would most judges and juries agree that blame disappeared or was much mitigated? There seem to be three main familiar kinds of claim you might make.

One is that the apparently wrong action, although it really occurred, was not really wrong. For instance, an apparent murder may really be a case of justified killing in self-defence, or a burglary may be for the purpose of retrieving stolen papers from a blackmailer.

Another is that external circumstances severely restricted the available options. For instance, a woman who murders her husband because she is terrified and can think of no other way to escape domestic violence is regarded as less blameworthy than another who murders her husband just to get his money, or to make it easier to marry her lover, even though in both cases the action was wrong in itself. The idea here is that the difference between the first woman and the blameless majority of people who would not dream of murder is not of moral character, but of available options. In their position she would have been as virtuous as they are; in hers, they might have made the choice she did.

The final possible claim is that there was mental incapacity of a relevant kind: diminished responsibility, criminal insanity, or severe intellectual incompetence. In this kind of context we regard blame and punishment as inappropriate, although we may say that anyone persistently incapable of acting in a socially responsible way must be controlled or confined for the protection of everyone else.

Does any of these apply to the case under consideration here? If men have genetically induced inclinations to polygyny, does that provide them with an exemption from blame for philandering on any of these grounds?

Many people do seem to think that the first kind of argument applies here:

that if philandering is in this sense natural, there is nothing wrong with it. However, although this is in itself a crucial issue in the debate about evolutionary psychology it is not relevant to Rose's point, which is obviously about *responsibility* for philandering rather than about its rights and wrongs. There are two elements involved in judgements about blame: one of whether an action is wrong, the other of whether the agent is responsible for it. Since Rose says 'it's not their fault', he is considering responsibility, which is our concern in this chapter. Questions of whether genetic dispositions affect questions about what is right and wrong will be discussed in Chapter 9, but they are not relevant to the problem here.

The second kind of argument, in contrast, is about responsibility. However, the lessening or removal of responsibility in this kind of case has to do with the existence of *environmental* freedoms and constraints, rather than with the nature of the individual. Claims about the effects of genes are about the nature of the person, not the environment. So this is not relevant to Rose's point either.

What, then, about the third possibility? If a tendency is in the genes, does that mean that people who have such a tendency come into the third category, and must be regarded as the slaves of irresistible impulses, incapable of self-control and rational action?

Rose's remark, with its use of 'programmed' and 'genetic determinism', seems to imply that this is what he thinks is implied by the gene-machine/evolutionary psychology view. But the point that needs to be made here is the one made earlier, on p. 115. Evolutionary psychology claims that various aspects of our character are deep in our genes, but it does not suggest for a moment that any particular emotion is overwhelming to the extent of preventing self-control or rational judgement. Its claims are about the *origins and depth* of particular tendencies, not about pathological force. Once again, the dispute between evolutionary psychology and the standard social science model is not about whether individuals have emotions of a particular kind, or how strong they are; that is something that can be found out only by studying individuals as they are. The disagreement is about the *origins* of the emotions. The standard social science model explains male polygynous tendencies as rooted in particular social backgrounds, and implies that in a different kind of situation they would not exist; evolutionary psychology regards these tendencies as hard-wired into the male psyche, and likely to manifest themselves in some way no matter what the cultural environment. (That is connected with the point made in reply to Gould, above. If evolutionary psychology can explain a characteristic, it must be the kind of thing that manifests itself to some extent in most backgrounds.)

So evolutionary psychology does not claim that genes generate overwhelming, irresistible desires; only that there is a strong genetic element in the overall *explanation* of human emotions, and, in consequence, of human behaviour. It predicts that most men will have inclinations to philander; but whether they give in to these inclinations will depend on all sorts of other things: how strong their feelings are, what the prevailing social conventions are, whether they are already attached, what their feelings are for their partner, whether they are committed to honesty in relationships, whether they think God or the next-door neighbour is watching, and whether they think the newspapers will find out.

This means that the third of the grounds on which we normally say that blame should be withdrawn or lessened does not apply here either. The truth of sociobiological theories about male philandering would not provide the basis of a general plea of incapacity or diminished responsibility. On either the evolutionary psychology view or the standard social science model, individuals have mixtures of emotions and desires and impulses, and you find out what those are, and how strong they are, by considering the individuals. Either kind of cause might, in principle, produce either strong or weak, controllable or uncontrollable, emotions. To know whether people are incapable of responsibility for their actions – and therefore not suitable for treatment as part of the normal community – it is not necessary to know anything at all about the origins, in genes or culture, of the characteristics in question.

So far, then, there seems no reason at all to accept Rose's implied allegation that a sociobiological explanation of emotions and inclinations would provide men with an exemption from blame for philandering, or anyone from anything.

That, however, is by no means the end of the argument.

Exercise 6.1

1   Claims about individual freedom are sometimes about (a) the capacity of individuals to make choices, and sometimes about (b) the external freedom that determines the scope they have to exercise that capacity. Which is each of the following about?

  (i)   We are no freer in a democracy than under totalitarianism; in both cases all the choices we make are determined by our nature and our environment.
  (ii) She has never had much freedom; her husband prevented her from doing what she wanted to do.
  (iii) Women are still not truly free; society is still full of subtle obstacles that make it difficult for them to do what they want to do.
  (iv) Women are still not truly free; their choices are conditioned by their feminine upbringing.

2   A lawyer defending a woman who had killed her husband might make any of the following claims in mitigation on her behalf. For each of them, say whether the attempt would be to show that (a) the action was not wrong (it was the right choice to make under the circumstances) (b) there were mitigating external circumstances (she made the wrong choice, but she had so few choices open to her that she was less to blame than most other people would have been if they had done the same thing), or (c) she was not responsible for her actions at the time.

(i)   She was suffering from pre-menstrual syndrome.

(ii)   She was badly treated by him, and was being pressed to kill him by a group of extreme radical feminists who provided her only support.

(iii) She was afraid that if she ran away he would pursue her and kill her.

(iv) He was in terrible pain and asked her to kill him.

(v)   She thought he was an incarnation of the Devil.

(vi) She killed him in self-defence.

(vii) She suddenly snapped after years of provocation.

(Answers on p. 280)

Real responsibility

Now consider once again where we are. The problem has been to assess the truth of a conditional, implied by Rose's remark about the implications of the gene-machine view:

> If men are genetically inclined to polygyny, they cannot be blamed for philandering.

That was spelt out in argument form as:

> Men are genetically inclined to polygyny.
> *People should not be blamed for doing what they are genetically inclined to do.*
> _____
> Therefore we should not blame men for philandering.

I have just been discussing the added premise, and so far found no reason to accept it. The genetic origin of a characteristic does not provide exemption from blame of any of the familiar kinds considered. In particular, it provides no reason to regard its possessors as insane, or the slaves of uncontrollable desires. The truth of evolutionary psychology would not imply that men were genetically *determined* to philander, and therefore exempt from blame on that account.

However, as already stressed, there may be many different ways of constructing arguments to link the antecedent and consequent of conditionals, and a failure to make one kind of argument work does not show the conditional to be false. Other arguments may do the job this one has failed to do. Even if the familiar grounds for exemption from blame so far considered do not apply in this particular case, perhaps others would. And even in Rose's remark – an ironic throwaway, obviously not intended as a worked-out argument – there is the suggestion of a quite different idea, which needs careful disentangling from the one that has just been discussed.

The previous section picked up the theme of programming and biological determinism: the idea that if men did have an inborn disposition to polygyny, they would have no choice but to philander. That is not true: a genetic disposition to polygyny in men in general would not amount to a permanent state of sex-crazed insanity in any of them, let alone most. But Rose also says that it is not men's *fault* if they are programmed this way, which raises a quite different matter. And because the purpose of this enquiry is to test the *best* argument that can be found to link premise and conclusion, it is important to investigate that possibility.

Consider, then, an argument along these lines. Even though evolutionary psychology does not claim that any particular genetic tendency is on its own an emotional steamroller crushing all before it, it does nevertheless claim that when a man does philander, his genetic background is a significant part of the explanation. It implies that *but for* that genetically ingrained inclination, he would not have philandered. But he is not responsible for his genes, nor, therefore, for what those genes cause. If the theories of evolutionary psychology are right, then, they have the implication that no matter how sane and responsible a man may seem, he is not really responsible – really to blame – for his philandering.

In other words, Rose's (obviously true) claim that you cannot be held responsible for your genes seems to suggest an alternative argument linking the antecedent and consequent, which goes more or less like this:

> Men are genetically inclined to polygyny.
> *But for this genetic inclination they would not philander.*
> *People cannot help having the genes they have.*
> *People should not be blamed for what they cannot help.*
> _____
> Therefore men should not be blamed for philandering (acting polygynously).

So this is another way of interpreting Rose's remark. The idea now is that evolutionary psychology implies not a genetic inclination to polygyny that forces them to philander (which is what is implied by the claim of genetic determinism), but that men would not philander unless they had a genetic inclination to philander, and they cannot help having this genetic inclination.

This is a line of argument that many people do seem to accept, or at least find plausible, and not just in the context of male philandering. It seems to be increasingly widely accepted that if a causal connection can be found between your genetic constitution and your behaviour, you cannot justifiably be blamed – or indeed praised – for that behaviour. It is even being used in law courts, as well as less formally. I shall say more about that later.

Now, if we followed the procedure established so far, the next step would be to assess this argument for soundness. However, I said earlier that Rose was on the edge of philosophically deep waters; and an attempt at this stage to make a proper assessment of the argument would blow the discussion miles off the Darwinian track, and leave it in danger of sinking in the philosophical complexities of free will. This problem will be discussed before the end of the chapter, but for now I shall miss out this stage, accept provisionally that the argument is sound, and move straight on to the matter of comparison with the implications of the rival blank-paper view of human nature.

If these arguments are indeed right, as many people seem to think, the gene-machine position – which lies at the radical end of the Darwinian spectrum – implies that men are not to blame for philandering. But if Rose or someone in his position is to present this implication as a hazard of deepening Darwinism, and a reason either for hoping that evolutionary psychology is not true or for regarding the whole idea as absurd, he needs to show that his own position – some version of the next one along in the conservative direction, the blank-paper view – does *not* have this implication. He needs, in other words, to show the truth of some such conditional as:

> If men's inclination to polygyny is (not genetic, but mainly) the result of cultural conditioning, men can be blamed for philandering.

(Technically speaking, that should be 'it is not the case that men cannot be blamed for philandering', but this will not affect the argument.)

This gives the outline argument:

> Men's inclination to polygyny is the result of cultural conditioning.
> ————
> Therefore men can be blamed for philandering.

But how can this argument most plausibly be completed? If, in the previous argument, the conclusion that we are not responsible for our actions is supported by the claim that we are not responsible for our genes, it looks as though what is needed here must be something like this:

> Men's inclination to polygyny is the result of cultural conditioning.
> *We can help our cultural conditioning.*
> *We can be blamed for anything we can help.*
> ————
> Therefore men can be blamed for philandering.

But, of course, the first of the added premises is patently false. We can to some extent determine our current environment (get out of bad company, stop inflaming ourselves with pornographic literature, take philosophy courses), but not the environment that made us what we are. If the evolutionary psychologist's view entails that we cannot be regarded as responsible for anything because everything we do is ultimately caused by genes for which we were not responsible, then exactly the same applies to the standard social scientist's own position.

This is what Dawkins is saying in his 'inflamed by pornography' remark. If you are a materialist, as he presumes Rose is, you may not agree with evolutionary psychologists about the relative weights of genetic and environmental influences on the finished human product, but you still believe that everything about us is ultimately a product of genes and environment in some combination, and we are clearly no more responsible for the formative environment part than we are for the genes.

And there is the overall problem. If blank-paperers want to accuse gene-machinists of denying us responsibility for our actions, they need to show that the gene-machine position removes responsibility for actions *in a way that their own position does not*. But this does not seem possible. Whether we are entirely determined by genes, or entirely by environment, or (as all materialists believe) by some combination, the forces that made us what we are were in full swing before we existed to have any power over them. As Dawkins says, it seems to be *determinism*, rather than *genetic* determinism, that causes the trouble here. The worry is that if everything about us and our environment is ultimately determined by things that happened before we existed, no matter what those are, it is impossible for us to be genuinely responsible for anything.

The challenge from dualism

This last point leads directly to the next set of enquiries. Consider yet again the overall picture of where we are.

I have suggested that there is a general tendency for people on the conservative side of any Darwinian controversy to accuse people on the more radical side of holding views that demand our giving up some of our most fundamental ideas about the kind of thing we are. The subject now at issue is freedom of the will and responsibility (where freedom of the will counts, as it usually does, as the capacity for responsibility); and I have been considering the controversy between the two materialist positions at the radical end of the degrees-of-Darwinism band. Adherents of the blank-paper/standard social science view of human nature often allege that the truth of the gene-machine/evolutionary psychology view would remove human freedom, and leave us incapable of responsibility for our actions.

What I have argued so far is that this is mistaken. If what is at issue is what might be called the capacity for *ordinary* responsibility – the capacity to control our impulses, think through what to do, and judge between competing desires – the answer is that most of us have it and some of us have not; but the difference is between individuals *as they are now*, and has nothing to do with whether genes or environment made us what we are. The gene-machine view does not imply that men are sex-crazed maniacs who cannot control their actions; only that their tendency to have more interest than women in a large number of sexual partners is rooted in a genetic difference between the sexes rather than a difference in their upbringing. If, on the other hand, the question is whether we have a capacity that makes us genuinely responsible for our actions in the sense of being *ultimately* responsible for being what and where we are – the answer on either view is that we are not. Whatever the proportions of genetic and environmental input, we are still – on both views – the product of natural forces that were working before we existed, and for which we obviously cannot be responsible. So whichever kind of capacity for responsibility is under consideration, the two materialist views have the same implications.

And this, of course, is exactly what is typically thought by the inhabitants of the next position along in the conservative direction, on the other side of the materialism boundary. They see the threat to our ideas of freedom of the will as lying not in the difference between blank paper and gene machines, but in materialism itself. This is because, as Dawkins points out, his standard social science opponents, as much as he, are determinists. Both forms of materialist Darwinism hold that everything about us came about, without skyhooks, through the ordinary workings of the laws of physics. Matter is usually presumed to work deterministically, and determinism to rule out free will.

This is the next subject to investigate. As usual we need to consider two conditional claims: that if we are entirely material, we cannot have free will, and that if we are not entirely material, we can.

The problem of determinism

Consider first the idea that the truth of materialism would rule out freedom of the will.

There are various ways in which this might be expressed as a conditional. I shall discuss the slightly awkward form:

> If our origins are entirely material, free will is impossible [for us].

This is mainly because it will make things easier later on, when non-materialism and indeterminism are discussed. I think the details will make no difference to the discussion, but anyone who suspects it does can experiment with variations.

This version gives the outline argument:

> Our origins are entirely material.
> ———
> Therefore free will is impossible.

How might that be completed, on the basis of what has been said so far? There are many different ways of going about it, depending on how much detail and argument you want to include, but the simplest way seems to be something like this:

> Our origins are entirely material.
> *Matter is deterministic.*
> *Determinism is incompatible with free will.*
> ———
> Therefore free will is impossible.

This argument seems valid, so we can move on to the assessment of the added premises.

The first of the added premises claims that material things are deterministic. A deterministic system is one in which everything that happens is entirely caused by what went before: one in which the entire course of events is an inexorable series of causes and effects. If the world is wholly material, must it be like that?

It is often taken for granted that it must be; but it should be said for the sake of completeness that this is a subject of considerable philosophical and scientific controversy. Many people now, particularly those who have any knowledge of quantum physics, say that science has demonstrated the existence of undetermined events.[15] I shall not be going into that – it will not be necessary for our purposes – but it is important to be aware that the connection of materialism and determinism is not uncontroversial. Many people try to use claims about indeterminism in the material world as a basis on which to argue that even though fully material in origin, we can be free.

The second added premise, that determinism is incompatible with free will, is also a matter of dispute. Many philosophers, known as compatibilists, think that free will and determinism are compatible – and even that determinism is necessary for free will. For now I shall not go into this either (though I shall return to it later), but instead consider the *reasons* why so many people regard it as obvious that determinism would rule out free will, and therefore see the deeper levels of Darwinism as a threat to it.

The problem of reconciling free will and determinism was explained earlier (p. 134). Free will is thought of as the capacity to be genuinely responsible for actions and genuinely deserving of praise or blame for the choices that are made; a deterministic state of affairs is one in which everything that happens is determined by what happened before. Consider, then, the situation of one of those polygynously inclined men when he finds himself in a situation of opportunity. If he believes he has free will he probably thinks the future is open until he makes his choice. He also probably regards himself as responsible for the choice he makes and therefore for what happens as a result, and also (if he is morally conscientious and agrees that this instance of philandering would be wrong) that he will deserve blame and perhaps punishment if he makes the wrong choice. But if the world is deterministic, how can any of this be possible? His deliberations and his eventual choice are not what determine the future course of events, but themselves just part of a course of events that has been inevitable since the beginning of the universe. If so, he cannot help what happens, and therefore cannot be responsible for it. In turn, therefore, he cannot deserve blame, let alone punishment. All these elements of our usual idea of what is involved in making choices seem to be illusions if determinism is true.

The problem of indeterminism

For now, then, accept, at least provisionally, that non-materialists – as well as many materialists like Dawkins – are right in thinking that materialism does preclude free will, and turn to the other aspect of the problem. Before we can conclude that this is a case where progression from conservative to radical versions of Darwinism does imply the loss of something we value, we must, as usual, consider whether if we can stay on the non-materialist side of the divide, free will is possible. We need to set up an argument to test the conditional:

If our origins are not entirely material, free will is possible.

This gives the outline argument:

Our origins are not entirely material.
_____
Therefore free will is possible.

And someone who accepted the previous argument as sound would presumably complete it like this:

Our origins are not entirely material.
Non-material things are not deterministic.
Indeterminism can allow for free will.

_____
Therefore free will is possible.

Note that 'not deterministic' in this argument is just the negation of 'determin- istic' in the first argument. A deterministic state of things is one where everything that happens is caused, so one that is not deterministic (or is *indeter- ministic*, which means the same), is one in which *it is not the case that everything is caused*. This means it is one where at least some things are not caused by what went before, *not* one where *nothing* is caused by what went before. It is always necessary to take care with the scope of negation: the matter of how much is covered by the 'not'. 'Not (everything is determined),' or 'It is not the case that everything is determined' is quite different from 'Everything is not-determined.' This point will be discussed more fully later.

With this explained, the argument looks structurally valid, and it also looks in line with traditional views of our own nature. Traditionally we have always thought of ourselves as partly material and partly immaterial, with a body subject to all the usual laws of physical nature but also with an immaterial mind that is free from such constraints. And it is to this other part of our nature – the immaterial, skyhook part – that freedom of the will has traditionally been attributed. So, once again, we can see why dualism (non-materialism) is widely thought to allow for freedom of the will.

What, then, should we think about the added premises? Consider first the claim that non-material things are not deterministic. Given the foregoing defini- tion of indeterminism (not-determinism), this is the claim that a non-material world would contain at least some uncaused happenings. Is it true?

Some people immediately respond to this by saying that nothing can possibly happen without a cause. (In fact they tend to express this by asking rhetorically *how* anything can happen without a cause – thereby begging the question, because that 'how' presupposes that an appropriate answer must be causal.) That is yet another huge topic beyond the scope of what we are doing here; and, like the question about materialism and determinism, one that fortunately does not need to be addressed for our purposes. Notice, however, that if you do think that uncaused events are impossible, you think determinism must be true – in the non-material world, if it exists, as well as in the material world – and, by the previous argument, that free will cannot exist.

The other question to ask about the first added premise is whether there is any reason to think that non-material things, in particular, must be indeterministic. It often seems to be taken for granted that non-materialism goes with non-determinism, just as materialism goes with determinism, but it seems to me no more obviously necessary in this direction than the other. People who believe in non-material substances presume that there are causal connections between them, and between the non-material and the material. Minds are supposed to be able to influence matter; and, in most conceptions of these things, they are also supposed to be able to influence other minds (by prayer, telepathy and so on). Why should it be presumed that they have aspects that do not act in a strictly causal, deterministic way? You could say that it is because minds have free will and free will needs indeterminism, but that begs all the questions.

However, I shall go on leaving questions about the connection of materialism with determinism, and non-materialism with indeterminism, aside, and concentrate on the relationship of determinism and free will. The previous argument connected determinism with the impossibility of free will. Now consider the second added premise of this argument, and decide whether, if the world is not deterministic, freedom of the will is possible.

If indeterminism is to allow us free will while determinism does not, it must offer the things we intuitively regard as essential aspects of free will, and of which determinism seems to deprive us. Can it do this? Consider again the potential philanderer, this time deciding to resist temptation. In a deterministic world his decision is the result of a series of causes and effects going back to the beginning of time, and therefore set in motion before he existed. His decision is part of that sequence rather than an interruption of it, and therefore, it seems, he did not really choose to resist; his resistance was just something that happened to him. He was not really responsible for his decision, and did not deserve praise – just as he would not have deserved blame if he had gone ahead. What happens to all this if we imagine the world as indeterministic, with uncaused events appearing in the sequence? There is certainly one improvement. If the world is not deterministic, the course of events is not laid down from the beginning of time. It is genuinely unpredictable, even in principle. In a genuinely indeterministic world all our actions, and all the events following our actions, might have gone differently. The future is genuinely open, and the philandering may go ahead or it may not.

That, however, is only the start of the answer. What about the other elements that seem essential to free will? Do such matters as choice, responsibility and desert fare better in a state of indeterminism?

This calls for a series of thought experiments, in which uncaused events – literally uncaused, not just with unknown causes – occur at various points in the sequence. We can put them wherever we like, and see if anywhere we put them gives the non-philanderer the capacity for the genuine responsibility that we would regard as constituting freedom of the will. (It is, of course, irrelevant to ask how we could know that these uncaused events had occurred. We probably could not; but this is a thought experiment, whose purpose is only to clarify the problem.)

It is clear, in the first place, that most uncaused events we might imagine would do nothing whatever to help to make the hero of this episode ultimately responsible for his forbearance. We could throw in a few uncreated comets and uncaused earthquakes and the spontaneous generation of tadpoles, but such irrelevancies would obviously do nothing to make him responsible for what he did in an otherwise deterministic world. Any relevant failure of determinism must be connected with him in some way. But how?

We could try starting before his birth. Perhaps there could be an uncaused happening at his conception, breaking the connection with his parents' genes. But he obviously could not have been responsible for that; and it is hard to see how it could make any difference to his responsibility later on.

What happens, then, if we put the uncaused event much nearer the time of his choice? Perhaps his brain was chugging along in a deterministic way, and then, suddenly, the idea of not philandering flashed, completely uncaused, over everything else. But again, if it just appeared, uncaused, and everything else followed deterministically after that, how could that make him responsible for what happened? He did not produce the uncaused flash; if he had done, it would not have been uncaused. And, indeed, if the idea of refraining was genuinely uncaused, and came from nowhere, it seems much *less* his choice, and his responsibility, than if it had been the product of his character and his brain. (This may begin to suggest why many philosophers argue that determinism is essential for free will and responsibility.)

Perhaps, then, we should try making the uncaused event the action itself: his turning away from the object of temptation, immediately after having made the decision not to go ahead. But that seems no better. To start with, it seems very odd that the turning away should happen after the decision to turn away, if the second did not actually cause the first. Why, having decided to turn away, should he not have just started on his seduction or broken into song or committed suicide? And second, if the turning away really was unconnected with the decision, that seems positively to preclude his being responsible for it.

What happens if you follow a familiar suggestion in this context, and try thinking of some event in the sequence as *partially* caused? Perhaps his act of resistance was partly caused by the way his brain was working, but there was a genuinely uncaused element as well; perhaps his brain would not have produced that effect all on its own. But that does not help either: it just combines the problems of determinism and indeterminism. He is not responsible for the caused part, because that was set in motion before he existed; and he is not responsible for the uncaused part, because it came from nowhere.

You can try any other way you like; but what these cases begin to show is that the difficulty is not one of finding the right place for an uncaused event to come into the sequence. We are up against a deeper problem than that. The point is that what responsibility requires precisely *is* the man's having caused the event in question; and the trouble with trying to bring non-determinism into all this is that uncaused events are, by definition, things for which *nobody and nothing* can be responsible.

This seems to mean that from the point of view of responsibility, we are if anything even worse off with indeterminism than determinism. At least with determinism the non-philanderer and his intentions did cause the event, even though he was not the ultimate cause of himself or his intentions. If you start throwing uncaused events into the sequence, you have things for which there can be no responsibility.

The situation then seems to be this. If the world is deterministic there is no free will and responsibility, because if everything that happens was determined from the beginning of time, we cannot freely choose, or be really responsible for, any of it. But the only difference between a deterministic state of things and an indeterministic one is that some of the determined (caused) events are replaced by undetermined (uncaused) ones, for which no one and nothing can be responsible. That can hardly make us responsible for them. And if we cannot be responsible, it means that an indeterministic state of things is incompatible with free will as well. Either way, free will cannot exist.

This is why there was no need to go into the question of whether materialism really did go with determinism and non-materialism with indeterminism. Even if traditional ideas about human nature as partly spiritual, or claims of physicists about uncaused events among subatomic particles, can be justified, they do not help in the least to justify our ideas of freedom of the will.

And if all this is right, the situation is yet again that there is no difference between the implications of the two degrees of Darwinism. If non-materialists are right in saying that the materialist position precludes free will because we cannot be ultimately responsible for our choices, they are faced with the problem that their own does too. So the conclusion is once again that an issue that seems to turn on the question of which version of Darwinism is true, in fact does not. We do not need to find out which version is right to know whether or not we have free will. In either case, we have not.

Exercise 6.2

1   Which of the following have been argued for in this section?

(i)   Determinism is true.

(ii)   Determinism is not true.

(iii)   Materialism implies determinism.

(iv)   Immaterialism implies indeterminism.

(v)   If the world is deterministic we are not free.

(vi)   Freedom of the will is incompatible with both determinism and indeterminism.

(vii) Minds work non-deterministically.

(viii) We are not free because we are determined.

(ix)   If the world is indeterministic we are free.

(x)   Determinism and indeterminism are irrelevant to the question of free will.

(xi)   Non-materialist Darwinism is the only variety that makes freedom of the will possible.

(xii) Evolutionary psychology precludes freedom of the will because it is deterministic.

2   It is often thought that materialist Darwinism precludes free will because materialism is deterministic. This discussion has left open the question of whether materialism is deterministic, as well as whether non-materialism is indeterministic. Why, if these arguments are right, does this not matter?

3   If these arguments have been right, how should you respond to the familiar question 'Are we free or are we determined?'

(Answers on pp. 280–81)

The root of the free will problem: kinds of non-existence

Since the project of this book is to find out how many of our ideas about ourselves turn on questions about how far Darwinian explanation can extend, there is in a sense no more to be said here on the subject of free will and capacity for responsibility. If these arguments are right the conclusion is, rather surprisingly, that the issue is unaffected by the matter of how much of our nature and situation can be explained in Darwinian terms. This is because if you consider the capacity for *ordinary* responsibility, all of the views allow for it, but if you take the capacity for *ultimate* responsibility – which is what is usually meant by having free will – none of them does.

On the other hand, it would be very unsatisfactory to end the discussion here; it seems to leave the puzzle in mid-air. And anyway, to understand the extent to which ideas about human nature are affected by the development of science – Darwinian or otherwise – it is necessary to see why some of the problems about understanding the kind of thing we are seem to be unaffected by the outcome of scientific controversies such as these. So, even though there is no space to go far into the philosophical question of free will in its own right, a little more does need to be said.

The problem we have been dealing with is that of whether free will exists or not, and therefore whether or not we are genuinely responsible for our actions. Questions about whether various things exist are, in themselves, perfectly familiar, as when we ask whether there are (exist) mice under the floorboards, or monsters in Loch Ness, or unicorns in the garden, or intelligent life on other planets, or ways of achieving cold fusion, or things that can move faster than the speed of light, or intelligences pushing Aristotelian crystalline spheres. For answering most such questions the advance of science (or empirical investigation at a less exalted level) is highly relevant, because investigation is needed to tell us what the world is like, and these questions about what exists are about what kinds of thing the world contains. The world may be such that they do exist, or it may be such that they do not. To find out we must, as it were, compare our description of the thing whose existence we are interested in with the world, and see whether the world contains anything that matches the description. You know what you mean by mice under your floorboards; to see whether the world contains anything that corresponds to that specification you can pull up the floorboards and look.

It is natural, therefore, to assume that establishing whether free will exists or not will also be a matter of finding out about what the world is like: that if the facts turn out one way, free will exists, and that if they turn out another way, it does not. Against this background, it seemed likely that questions about whether we had free will might well turn on the question of which degree of Darwinism was true, because the question of how far Darwinian explanation can stretch is itself a question about what the world is like. But this is not what seems to have happened. Free will – the capacity for genuine responsibility – seems not to exist whichever of the degrees of Darwinism is true.

That in itself is not surprising; it is quite possible for incompatible views about the world to have some implications in common. For instance, consider these statements:

> The world is as Aristotle described it.
> The world is as Newton described it.

Those are incompatible, but they both have the implication that the world does not have an edge over which incautious sailors might fall.

Now since Newton's description of the world is incompatible with Aristotle's, those two statements are *mutually exclusive*. If one of them is true, the other cannot be. But they are not, as philosophers say, *jointly exhaustive*: they do not exhaust all the possibilities. There are (indefinitely many) other statements that are incompatible with both of them, for instance:

> The world is a disc supported by four elephants.

And some of these (indefinitely many) possible, mutually exclusive views of the world do have the implication that there is an edge you might fall over, while others do not. Whether the world has an edge turns on which of the incompatible (mutually exclusive) views of the world is true.

When statements are mutually exclusive, but not jointly exhaustive, they are called *contraries*.

But now consider another pair of mutually exclusive statements.

> The world is a disc supported by four elephants.
> The world is not a disc supported by four elephants.[16]

This pair is quite different from the other one, because these propositions are also jointly exhaustive. Between them, they exhaust the possibilities. (I believe Bertrand Russell once said that when you met a man there were exactly two possibilities: either he was Ebenezer Weelkes Smith, or he was not.) The second embraces all the other possible descriptions of the world, such as those of Aristotle and Newton.

When two statements are both mutually exclusive and jointly exhaustive, they are called *contradictories*. And what is important about contradictories is that although they are like contraries in that they cannot be true together, they are unlike contraries in that they cannot be false together either. Between them they exhaust all the possibilities, which means that if one of them is false, the other must be true.

This is, by the way, one reason why it is so important to be careful about the scope of words like 'not' (see above, p. 137). If the scope of negation is a whole proposition (if, for instance, you put 'it is not the case that' in front of it) you produce a pair of contradictories. If the 'not' goes elsewhere, you may produce only contraries. This is the essence of what goes wrong in Pascal's Wager (see p. 34). His argument works on the assumption that his possible states of affairs are contradictories – that they are jointly exhaustive as well as mutually exclusive – but this is not so. They would be if 'God exists' and 'God does not exist' were interpreted as meaning 'There exists some god or other' and 'There exists no god', but that interpretation is incompatible with the way he completes his matrix. The way he estimates the payoffs shows that his alternatives are 'God as conceived by Catholicism exists,' and 'There is no god at all.' These are only contraries, and his argument fails because he treats them as contradictories.

The relevance of all this to the subject in hand is that we have been discussing the implications, for freedom of the will, of two incompatible propositions:

> The world is deterministic.
> The world is indeterministic.

When those terms were introduced (pp. 137ff.), I emphasized that 'indeterminism' referred, not to a state where *everything* was uncaused, but to a state where *at least some things* were uncaused. It is probably now clear why it was important to emphasize this. If you take the propositions:

Everything that happens has a cause.
Nothing that happens has a cause.

they are mutually exclusive. But they are only contraries: they are not jointly exhaustive. It is easy to think of another proposition that is incompatible with both, such as:

Every sixth thing that happens has no cause.

But if, on the other hand, you take the propositions:

Everything that happens has a cause.
At least some things that happen do not have a cause.

They are mutually exclusive *and* jointly exhaustive. They are contradictories, which means that one of them must be true. If either is false, the other is true. Between them they exhaust all the possibilities.

This means that one of the propositions:

The world is deterministic.
The world is indeterministic (i.e. it is not the case that the world is deterministic).

must be true, because there is no further possibility. We may not know which is true, but we know as a matter of logic that one or other of them must be. That is why it is so significant that free will seems to be incompatible with both determinism and indeterminism. If that is true, the non-existence of freedom of the will is not just a *contingent* truth: something whose truth turns on the question of which possible description of the world is true. It is a *necessary* truth; something that is true, as philosophers say, in all possible worlds.

What this means is that there seem to be two quite different kinds of non-existence. Some things do not exist, but might have existed if the world had been different. Other things seem so thoroughly nonexistent that they could not possibly have existed whatever the world had been like.

Why is this? Why do some things just happen not to exist, while others could not have existed under any circumstances?

Consider again what is involved in trying to decide whether anything exists. Typically what we want to know is whether there is anything that *corresponds to a particular description*. If we want to know whether there is (exists) a unicorn in the garden, we start with an idea of what a unicorn is and where our garden is, and see whether there is anything corresponding to the description of one inside the other.

But now consider how a description works. If we are to understand anything at all by the word 'unicorn', we must understand when it is appropriate to use it and when it is not. If 'unicorn' is defined as 'white horse with a single horn', that means by implication that it is *not* a great many other things, such as pink with blue spots, equipped with a beak and webbed feet, and ideally suited for spreading with plates for a dinner party.

And notice, incidentally, that this is just as true if you are like Humpty Dumpty in *Alice Through the Looking Glass*, and insist that words mean whatever you want them to mean. It is also true, for that matter, even if you are an ultra-perverse Humpty Dumpty and change those meanings every half-hour. You may decide to define 'unicorn' to mean what the rest of us call a dining table; but then if a white horse with a single horn comes along it is not, in your eccentric sense of the word, a unicorn.

What all this means (to go back to the familiar definition of 'unicorn') is that if you say there is at the bottom of the garden a unicorn with pink spots, webbed feet and two horns, you are making it impossible for your claim to be true, because anything that met one part of your specifications would necessarily fail to meet the other. Something whose description contains conflicting elements in this way is nonexistent in all possible worlds.

This way of putting it shows why it is mistaken to say that we cannot be certain that such things cannot exist, and that it is only our finite imaginations that prevent our recognizing the possibility. You can see this by considering that even an omnipotent god could not create these things. An omnipotent god is (*inter alia*) one who can meet any challenge you offer; but if you come up with a self-contradictory challenge, such as a demand for a two-horned unicorn, you have in effect failed to produce a challenge at all, since anything that met one part of it would, in doing so, automatically fail to meet another. The inability to produce two-horned unicorns is no reflection on omnipotence. All it demonstrates is confusion in the challenger.

The fact that free will as we have specified it seems to be nonexistent in all possible worlds suggests that we may be working with a self-contradictory conception of free will: a set of ideas such that correspondence to some of them would involve non-correspondence to others.

If that is so, it is likely not to be obvious; we are not likely to go around with ideas of freedom that are obviously incoherent. But most of our ideas turn out to be riddled with inconsistencies when they are looked at closely enough – which is one of the reasons why progress in philosophy, as in science, depends so much on taking care with the details. And if there is such an incoherence in our concept of free will, we should be able to work out what it is by seeing why determinism and indeterminism both seem to make it impossible.

Consider again, then, the case of the non-philanderer, stoutly resisting temptation. He certainly seemed to choose to resist; he thought about the implications of his action and made his decision accordingly; it was not as though he failed to philander because he had a heart attack or was interrupted by his secretary. Why, then, did it seem that in a completely deterministic system this apparent choice would not have been a real choice, for which he was genuinely responsible? The problem seemed to be that the state of mind that caused the action was itself, like everything else, brought about by the previous state of the world, and therefore fixed in advance, before he even existed. Since no other course of events was possible, he did not make a real choice and was not ultimately responsible for anything that happened. Determinism seems to preclude free will because determinism precludes ultimate responsibility.

Why, on the other hand, did this state of affairs seem not to be improved by indeterminism? It was because even though what he did was not laid down from the beginning of time, uncaused events are, by definition, not something that he, or anyone, could possibly be responsible for. So even if you think of any of the events leading up to the decision as uncaused, the man still cannot be responsible for them. He chose in the *ordinary* sense to resist (his decision was the cause of what happened, and he was not in a state of diminished responsibility), but *ultimately* he did not choose to be in the state of mind he was in when he made the choice, or to be the kind of person who was in that state of mind. And if that makes him not free, it follows that in order to be free, he would have to be responsible for those states of mind.

There are, of course, ways in which you can be responsible for your own state of mind. If you drink too much you are responsible for being in a frightful temper the next day, or (it is said) if you go in for yoga or deep breathing you can put yourself into a calm state of mind. You can alter your state of mind by taking drugs, or going for a course of psychotherapy, or, perhaps, changing your job. But the question still arises of where the states of mind came from that made you choose to take the drugs or change your job; and even if you claim that those states of mind resulted from previous choices, it is obvious that this process can go back only so far. What is quite certain is that you cannot have chosen to be in the state of mind that resulted in the first choice you ever made. You cannot be the *ultimate* cause of the state of mind you are in, because to do that you would have had to be responsible for your own existence and nature, and to do that you would have had to exist before you existed, which is self-contradictory. It is something that not even an omnipotent god could bring about. We know what we normally mean by wanting to make choices – to have things happen as a result of our intentions and desires – but we get into (infinitely) deep water if we complain that we are not free unless we also choose to be in the state of mind from which each choice arises.

It seems, then, that the vague concept of freedom of the will which allows for ultimate responsibility is one to which no state of affairs could possibly correspond. The individual ideas that form our composite ideal of free will do not fit together; and for that reason we not only do not, but cannot, have free will *in this sense*. If we want to find out whether free will exists as a matter of contingent fact, we need to start with a coherent account of what we would *count* as free will, and only after that try to find out whether the world is such as to allow for it. Given our existing cluster of ideas, it is, as it were, not the fault of the world that it does not contain freedom of the kind we want. It is our fault for demanding something self-contradictory, so that whatever the world was like we should still be dissatisfied. Neither Darwinism, nor materialism, nor determinism has anything to do with the matter.

If so, no form of Darwinism holds any threat for our traditional conception of ourselves as fundamentally free, or ultimately responsible for what we do and deserving of praise and blame. But this is not because these things can withstand Darwinism; it is because we were mistaken in thinking that pre-Darwinian views would allow for them. No possible world could allow for them.

Exercise 6.3

1 What is the distinction between contraries and contradictories?
2 Give the contradictory and one contrary of the following:

   (i)   Blue tulips do not exist.
   (ii) Some of the houses in this street are four storeys high.
   (iii) No cats eat lettuce.

3 Check the contraries you have given by constructing a third statement incompatible with both the original and its contrary (i.e. a statement whose truth would make them both false).
4 What does it mean to say that something's non-existence is contingent?
5 List half a dozen things whose non-existence you take to be contingent, and another half-dozen whose non-existence you take to be necessary.
6 If your fairy godmother offers to grant you three wishes, how should she respond to your request for a spherical golden cube?

(Answers on p. 281)

More shifts of level and sleights of hand

I am not meaning to suggest that this is a full philosophical analysis of the problem of free will. I (and others) think it is on the right track, and that the various elements we intuitively think of as necessary for free will cannot be fitted together into a coherent whole. But there is a good deal more to be said even about this track, and there are anyway many other philosophical opinions on the subject of free will, generating mountains of literature and endless controversy. Some philosophers (the already-mentioned compatibilists) think that when the idea of free will is properly understood it does not contain the incoherent element of what I have called ultimate responsibility, and so understood is compatible with determinism (we are free and determined). Others (called libertarians) think that free will is not compatible with determinism, but that all the elements of ultimate responsibility can be fitted into a coherent whole, and that free will so understood does exist. Yet others have claimed that the idea of free will does not even make sense: Locke, for instance, said 'it is as insignificant to ask whether a man's will be free as to ask whether his sleep be swift or his virtue square' (Locke (1964 edn), p. 199). And there are many other variations on these ideas.

For our purposes, however, there is (fortunately) no need to go further into all this. The problem here is not to settle the general question of free will, but only to consider whether the different degrees of Darwinism have different implications for the question of whether we are capable of genuine responsibility or not. And the very fact that the matter is so much debated by philosophers helps to make the most important point that needs to be made about the whole issue, which is that there is a philosophical problem to sort out before the scientific one even arises. You have to decide what you mean by responsibility – what would *count* as having a capacity for responsibility – before there is any point in asking whether people really have it or not, just as you need to know what unicorns are before trying to find out whether they exist.

The fear that deepening Darwinism is a threat to our capacity for responsibility is based on the mistaken assumption that the idea of responsibility is clear: that we know what we mean by it, and the only question is about whether we have it. (Rose seems, in this passage, to regard the idea as straightforward; and even Dawkins – while recognizing the existence of the philosophical problem – writes as though he knows what free will is. He says we can be regarded as having it even though we have not, and clearly thinks of it as opposed to determinism.) What I have argued here is that when the matter is looked at more closely, it appears that we have two quite distinct ideas about what counts as a capacity for responsibility. First, there is the idea of what can be called the ordinary capacity for responsibility, which we say people have when they are – as most of us are – in control of their actions, not mentally ill, and so on. And, second, there is the idea of ultimate responsibility, which is incoherent, since it seems to require that we should have existed before we existed. It is the confusion of these ideas that lies at the root of most of the problems in this discussion. Once they are distinguished it becomes clear, as I have argued at length, that the prospects for neither seems to be affected by which version of Darwinism is right. All accounts allow for the first kind of capacity for responsibility; none for the second. The impression that different views have different implications is probably the result of unnoticed slips between these conceptions of responsibility.

Equivocation and punishment

This is not just a matter of abstract interest. Confusions about capacity for responsibility can have serious practical implications in all kinds of contexts. Consider the following exchange, which is imaginary but nevertheless familiar:

Counsel for the defence: I agree that my client's crime was in itself deplorable – he could just have divorced his wife, rather than killing her – but he should not be punished because he was not responsible for his actions. He is normally a mild and considerate man, but he had been under extreme stress because his mother was ill, and his wife's behaviour pushed him beyond endurance until he suddenly snapped. This was a case of diminished responsibility.

Counsel for the prosecution: That's not true. We have evidence that the whole thing was carefully planned long in advance, including the plan to provoke his wife into the behaviour that would seem to give the diminished responsibility defence.

Counsel for the defence: But if you look into his background you will see why he did that. He comes from a long line of unpleasant criminals – there are probably criminal genes in the family – and his father brought him up to be cunning and calculating and concerned only for his own interests. In those circumstances, anybody would have done what he did. He wasn't responsible; it was his genes and his upbringing. So it would be quite wrong to punish him.

You will probably recognize from the familiar format what is going on here, even if it is not obvious anyway. What we have here is another case of an argument that surreptitiously changes its level in the middle, and attempts to make selective use of a universal acid. The first two claims are about whether the man was responsible for his actions in the *ordinary* sense; the third shifts to the idea of *ultimate* responsibility. And, furthermore, the defence has changed tack in a way that, if accepted, would actually undermine the whole of the previous argument, because if you accept this third claim you must accept that nobody is ever responsible for anything, and therefore that questions of the extent to which *particular* people are responsible for their actions does not even arise. But if you do not notice this slip, the defence may trick you into accepting that the defendant was not responsible for his actions in the original sense.

You may already have recognized that slips of level of this kind amount to fallacies of equivocation, which depend on treating terms with different meanings as if they were the same. This shows clearly if you think of the defence as reasoning like this:

> My client should be punished only if he was responsible for his action.
> He was not responsible.
>
> _____
>
> Therefore he should not be punished.

On the face of it, this looks like a sound argument. It looks valid, everyone accepts the first premise, and the defence produces a persuasive argument – the one about genes and environment – to show that the second is also true. The appearance of soundness, however, depends on the assumption that responsibility is the same kind of thing in both premises, and it is not. The second premise is about *ultimate* responsibility, whereas the first is about *ordinary* responsibility, and if you make that distinction clear the argument appears like this:

> My client should be punished only if he was (ordinarily) responsible
> for his action.
> He was not (ultimately) responsible.
> _____
> Therefore he should not be punished.

And this is obviously invalid. Or, alternatively, if you adjust the premises to make the argument valid:

> My client should be punished only if he was (ordinarily) responsible
> for his action.
> He was not (ordinarily) responsible.
> _____
> Therefore he should not be punished.

The second premise (according to the story above) is false, so the argument is still unsound. Its original appearance of soundness depends on equivocation between two kinds of responsibility. But this kind of confusion is increasingly taking hold in practice, with serious practical results – as you will soon find if you start to analyse real-life arguments about responsibility.

Still, you may feel, isn't the conclusion that he should not be punished exactly the one we should reach? If all these arguments prove that we are never ultimately responsible for anything, doesn't that mean that we are all equally victims of fate? And if so, doesn't that mean that all blame and punishment must be wrong, and that it is right to undermine any attempt to distinguish degrees of blame and allocate appropriate punishment? So, even if it means fudging the argument to achieve that end, isn't the defence right to do it?

This is an extremely important substantive question. It is too far off the present subject to discuss in any detail, but it is worth adding a coda to show how the philosophical techniques that have been explained and used so far can be applied to the discussion of issues like this one.

In the courtroom case just considered – as in the football case discussed on p. 47 – two distinct questions arise. One is about the appropriate decision to make *within* a particular framework of rules; another, quite different question, is whether that framework is itself right. A third question – a familiar part of practical politics – is about how you should act if you are working within a framework you consider wrong; but that question does not arise until you have decided whether the framework actually is wrong, so the question about the framework is the one to tackle first. How should we set about making a decision of that kind?

Someone who feels that the defence has reached the right conclusion in the previous argument, even though it is not the conclusion justified by the rules as they stand, seems to be saying something like this:

No one is ultimately responsible for what they do, so punishment is never justified.

This is recognizable as an outline argument, with a premise and conclusion, so it can be set out in the usual way:

No one is ultimately responsible for what they do.
_____

Therefore punishment is never justified.

This makes it clear how the claim can be tested: the question is whether it can be completed to yield a sound inference from premise to conclusion. How can it be most plausibly completed, to make it valid? The most obvious way is this:

No one is ultimately responsible for what they do.
Punishment cannot be justified except in cases where people are ultimately responsible for what they do.
_____

Therefore punishment is never justified.

This makes the argument valid; but is the added premise true? It depends on what you regard as the purpose of punishment. If the only possible justification of punishment were retribution – doing something unpleasant to offenders, *simply because* they had offended, and therefore *deserved* it, then it seems to me that the added premise would be true. But that is not the only possible purpose. A quite different justification is the consequentialist (i.e. broadly utilitarian) one that without punishment it would be impossible to deter anti-social behaviour, and that punishment, although *intrinsically* undesirable, is therefore an essential institution for the good of society as a whole. So even if you cannot justify punishment on the grounds that it is intrinsically appropriate that the guilty should suffer, the institution of punishment may be justified on the different grounds that it is *instrumentally* necessary for the maintenance of social order. And if you take this view, you will regard the second premise as false, and the argument as unsound.

Even if you accept this, it is only the beginning of problems about responsibility and punishment: the simplest forms of utilitarian approach to punishment raise all kinds of problems. But what has been said is enough to show again, in another context, the importance of setting out arguments before engaging in them, and of clarifying concepts that may be confused. If you start to analyse real-life arguments about punishment in any detail, you will soon see that *most* of them not only run straight into confusions about freedom and responsibility, but also work with a conception of punishment that is an incoherent conflation of incompatible approaches.

The need to sort out all such issues is increasingly relevant in practice, as we advance in understanding the influence of both heredity and environment in making us what we are, and claims about criminal genes or the influence of television are brought into court as providers of excuses in particular cases. Confusions have real effects on how people are treated, and if how people are treated matters, it matters to do everything possible to get the arguments right. The philosophical disentangling of such issues is morally essential.

Exercise 6.4

This exercise develops an important distinction mentioned briefly in the last section, between claims about intrinsic and instrumental values.

The following sentences explicitly or implicitly make recommendations and give reasons for them. In each case, say whether the argument as it stands treats the recommendation as *intrinsically* or *instrumentally* desirable or undesirable. (Remember the 'as it stands'. In all of these cases you could adapt the justification to make it instrumental, but the question is about what is going on *in this argument*.)

In the instrumental cases, say what the argument treats as intrinsically desirable.

(i)   We must preserve that building; it's a masterpiece.
(ii)   We must preserve that building; we'll get into dreadful trouble with English Heritage if we start tampering with it.
(iii) Don't eat the cakes with pink icing; they are horrible.
(iv)   Don't eat the cakes with pink icing; they are going to use them for conjuring tricks later.
(v)   If you go by bicycle you will save money, get fitter and help to prevent pollution.
(vi)   Go by bicycle and then you will avoid parking problems.
(vii) It's a lovely day for going by bicycle.

(Answers on p. 282)

This chapter has discussed the idea that the truth of the deeper levels of Darwinism would preclude freedom of the will, and with it the capacity for responsibility. This accusation seems to be made both by standard social scientists against evolutionary psychologists, and by dualists against materialists.

The arguments here have claimed that such ideas are mistaken, and seem plausible only because of confusions about what is meant by responsibility. It is necessary to distinguish between the *ordinary* sense of capacity for responsibility that contrasts with various kinds of mental incompetence, and the idea of capacity for *ultimate* responsibility that is supposed to come from freedom of the will. It is argued here that once this distinction is made the problem disappears: all degrees of Darwinism allow for the first, and none for the second because there is no coherent conception of ultimate responsibility. Darwinism presents no threat to freedom because the kind that seems threatened is one that cannot exist in any possible world.

The conclusion is important in illustrating the way problems that are at root philosophical – such as that of free will – may not be recognized as unproblematic, with the result that the truth of claims about free will and responsibility are thought to turn on the empirical question of which level of Darwinism is true. Many questions need philosophical sorting out before the empirical ones can even be asked coherently. Furthermore, these philosophical mistakes can have serious practical consequences, as the brief concluding discussion of punishment shows.

The chapter has also discussed various technical issues that arose in the course of the analysis, in particular the distinction between contraries and contradictories, necessary and contingent impossibilities, and the nature of contradiction. It also returned, in the context of responsibility and punishment, to the earlier discussion of changes of level in mid-argument and the selective use of universal acids, and it connected shifts of this kind with the discussion of equivocation in Chapter 5.

7 Selfish genes and moral animals

This chapter introduces the problem of Darwinism and morality by discussing the familiar claim that if we are entirely products of evolution we must be inherently incapable of anything but self-interested action, and therefore of genuine morality. This is often regarded by dualists as an implication of the materialist forms of Darwinism.

The chapter argues that this is another misconception, and tackles the issue in three stages. The first discussion is essentially scientific, and deals (briefly) with the way in which the problems of altruism encountered by classical Darwinism were solved by the genetic theories of neo-Darwinism. After that there are two sections considering claims that the kinds of altruism allowed for by neo-Darwinism are spurious, and therefore that accusations of radical selfishness must stand. It is argued here that these claims, too, are mistaken, and that the radical forms of Darwinism do allow for genuine altruism.

The chapter extends the use of the analytic techniques used so far by adapting them for the critical assessment of texts. It also recapitulates earlier issues by illustrating other contexts in which there are dangers of equivocation, and where apparently clear ideas turn out to be incoherent. It also analyses the accusation of reductionism, which is one of the main sources of confusion in Darwinian controversy.

Introduction

The threat to freedom is the most fundamental threat to our idea of ourselves as moral beings. Moral behaviour is a matter of making some choices rather than others, and therefore if we lack the capacity to make choices at all, morality seems impossible. I certainly do not think that the previous chapter is going to remove all doubts about our capacity for choice and responsibility; it is more likely to have raised previously unthought-of worries. For now, however, set those concerns aside and accept, at least for the sake of argument, that we can make choices, and go on to the next question, of whether those choices can be moral.

The traditional idea of human nature was that our earthly bodies dragged us down – often literally and morally at the same time – while skyhooks did their best to pull us in the opposite direction, towards God and the good. But what happens if you have reached the conclusion that there are no skyhooks, and that we are ultimately nothing more than animated dust, configured into our present forms by the purposeless forces of natural selection?

If we are entirely the result of evolution by natural selection – the process that is popularly known as survival of the fittest – that surely seems to imply that we are inherently incapable of the altruism that is necessary for any kind of moral action. Moral behaviour, whatever its details, must involve the capacity to subject your own interests to the good of others, or to the requirements of moral principles of other kinds. No account of human nature doubts that there are severe limits to most people's capacity for selflessness, but at least traditional views of human nature allowed us enough of a divine spark to understand how far we fell short of the ideal, and to start the work of moral improvement. But if we have evolved by the kind of cut-throat competition that natural selection seems to involve, does that not mean that we could not exist unless we had, deep in our nature, a ruthless determination to put our own interests first? Evolution would presumably dispose us to put immense care into the survival and reproductive abilities of our own offspring; but would that not be all? If evolution is (as Herbert Spencer said) a war of all against all, surely it should leave us unconcerned with the interests of others – except to the extent that the ability to show some appearance of concern might be necessary to manipulate other equally selfish beings, equally preoccupied with their own interests.

Even if there are no problems about our capacity to choose and act, therefore, it may seem that the skyhookless versions of Darwinism, according to which we are entirely a product of natural forces, undermines our idea of ourselves as moral beings from this other direction. If so, it is again no wonder that the radical forms of Darwinism may be regarded as a threat to what we have regarded as most valuable in our ideas about ourselves. This chapter investigates the truth of such ideas.

Evolution and altruism

By a capacity for altruism or unselfishness (I shall use the words synonymously) I shall mean throughout only the ability to feel genuine concern for the interests of other individuals, and to give those at least some weight against our own. That is intended to leave open the extent and strength of such concern. I am not taking altruism to demand the kind of exalted selflessness that gives no weight to self-interest, or regards it as only of secondary importance. We have a capacity for altruism in the sense intended if we care *at all* about the interests of others. How strong it is, and in particular whether it is strong enough to make us act against our own self-interest, is a separate question. (The fundamental evolutionary questions are once again about emotions rather than actions.)

I am also inclined, by stretching the term a bit, to include in the idea of altruism the ability to put other kinds of good before self-interest, even if that good is not necessarily the interests of other people or other sentient beings. You would be altruistic in this extended way if you wanted to preserve some beautiful landscape even though you would never see it, and perhaps even if you thought it unlikely that anyone else would ever see it either. You would also be altruistic (in an even more extended sense) if you acted against your interests simply on principle of any kind. It does not matter for our purposes about stretching the concept in these ways, because the question here is about whether any of the Darwinian positions rule out all such possibilities, by proving that the only thing we can possibly care about is our own (and our children's) interests. However, nothing in these arguments depends on whether this extension is regarded as legitimate.

The problem of how much genuine altruism there is is a perfectly familiar one. We see people being flagrantly selfish, and we see people being apparently unselfish. But are the unselfish acting considerately only because they have calculated – at some level of consciousness – that by doing so they are likely to fulfil more of their own selfish desires? Other people will do much more for us if they like us, and because they are also selfish they will like us if we seem to care about them; is that why we show concern for them? Or, for that matter, are people who seem altruistic just trying to get on the right side of whatever god they believe in? Religious people sometimes claim that only religion can guarantee genuine self-sacrifice; but this is baffling to the secular, since religions nearly always promise that self-sacrifice now will reap enormous rewards later.

As it stands, the question of the extent to which apparent altruism is genuine is an empirical one, to be investigated in the same way as other questions about the world, by observation and controlled experiment. For instance, we can try to establish what people do when the prospect of reward is removed; and often, when we do this, apparent altruism does turn out to have ulterior motives. But this is by no means always the case. We often find altruistic behaviour for which no ulterior motive appears; and it is when this happens that people's beliefs about the extent to which we are explainable in Darwinian terms starts to influence their beliefs about what is going on. There are two typical kinds of response. Some people think that because such genuine altruism obviously does exist, the idea that human beings originated entirely by material Darwinian processes must be false; we need the divine spark to account for unselfish behaviour. Others work the argument the other way round. Because they accept that we arose entirely by natural processes, without skyhooks, they conclude that what appears to be altruism must really be well-disguised selfishness.

Those two views are, of course, opposed; but they both presuppose that *if* we arose entirely as a result of Darwinian selection, *then* we must be fundamentally selfish, and altruism an illusion. Once again it is conditionals like this that will be investigated here.

In the discussion of freedom in the previous chapter, it was important to distinguish between all three of the Darwinian positions on the scope diagram (see p. 54), because it was clear that the accusation of denying human freedom was levelled both by blank-paperers against gene-machinists, and by dualists against materialists. Here the claims that might be made are less clear. It seems likely that many dualists think that if we are entirely the result of natural selection we must also be entirely selfish, and that the altruism necessary for moral action is possible only if there is an immaterial element that is exempt from evolutionary forces. What is less clear is whether many blank-paper materialists see a difference of implication between their position and that of gene-machinists. Some may, perhaps, think that if the gene-machine thesis were right, selfishness would be inevitable, but that as we are now creatures of culture we can – in the right kind of culture – escape our inborn selfishness.

However, our concern is once again with the issues – the question of what the implications of the various positions actually are – rather than with what different people say about them. I shall start by asking about the implications of the most radical form of Darwinism – the gene-machine view – because if that can escape the implication that we must be entirely selfish, so, with stronger reason, can any less radical view. If, on the other hand, it turns out that the gene-machine view does have that implication, we can then go on to see whether the blank-paper view is different enough to escape the same conclusion.

Exercise 7.1

A conditional premise can support two familiar forms of valid argument: *If p then q, p, therefore q* (modus ponens) and *If p then q, not-q, therefore not-p* (modus tollens).

What conditional premise is presupposed by each of the following pairs of arguments?

(i)   They left before midnight, so they can't have missed the one o'clock train; they missed the one o'clock train, so they can't have left before midnight.
(ii) My cat has been on my sofa all day, so he can't have unravelled the knitting in your kitchen; your cat unravelled the knitting in my kitchen, he can't have been on your sofa all day.
(iii) The earth was created in six days, because the Bible says so; that can't be what the Bible says, because it wasn't created in six days.
(iv) Brown eyes are genetic in origin, so they can't be changed; they've found a way of changing the colour of eyes, so eye colour can't be genetic.
(v)   Men can't be blamed for philandering, because they have a genetic tendency to polygyny; men can be blamed for philandering, so they haven't any such genetic tendency.

(Answers on p. 282)

Unselfish gene machines?

What, then, is the first conditional whose truth is to be investigated? As usual there is no single formulation here – we can investigate whatever conditional we like – but if we are considering the idea that the gene-machine/evolutionary psychology thesis precludes genuine altruism, we seem to need something like this:

> If our fundamental dispositions and emotions (not just our bodies) are products of natural selection, we must be incapable of altruism.

This gives as an outline argument:

> Our fundamental dispositions and emotions are products of natural selection.

—————

Therefore we are incapable of altruism.

How might this most plausibly be completed? It is probably clear by now that there is often a good deal of choice about how to complete an argument. You can do it in the simplest possible way to make it valid, and then discuss any added premises separately, or you can include supporting arguments to defend those premises in the main argument. Which way you go about it makes no difference to the outcome, but it seems to be easiest (I say on the basis of endless experiments) to start with the simplest valid argument you can, and discuss the truth of added premises separately.

In this case, the simplest form of completion seems obvious:

> Our fundamental dispositions and emotions are products of natural selection.
> *Natural selection cannot produce anything capable of altruism.*

—————

> Therefore we are incapable of altruism.

This looks, provisionally, valid. As usual, much may depend on the details of how you interpret the premises and conclusion, but valid interpretations do seem possible. The next step is to begin detailed testing for soundness by considering the added premise – which is, of course, a statement of the central problem here. Is it true that natural selection is incapable of producing anything unselfish?

Now this is, at least in the first instance, a question about science, and there is a limit to how much can be said about the science here. But a sketch is needed; and – to give in advance a sense of where things are going – scientists of gene-machine inclinations do not accept the truth of the second premise. Their very preoccupation with genes gives them a way to escape the problems that altruism posed for classical Darwinism.

In ordinary language, 'altruistic' is a word used only in the context of animals advanced enough to have feelings and make choices. Altruism is something we think of as occurring in emotions that involve genuine concern for the interests of others, and in actions that involve putting the interests of others ahead of your own. Biologists use the word in a different, metaphorical sense, according to which altruism occurs when an organism of any kind – sentient or not – behaves in any way that amounts to giving resources to others rather than keeping them for itself. It is altruism of this extended, metaphorical kind that raises the primary problem for classical Darwinism, because biologically altruistic behaviour amounts to enhancing others' fitness at the expense of your own, and should therefore be evolutionary suicide. Every time chance threw up an altruistic organism it should be quickly outbred by the beneficiaries of its altruism, and the characteristic should die out. But altruism of the familiar, non-metaphorical kind is in most ways a special case of the extended, biological sort, and seems just as doomed by classical Darwinism. As soon as a creature developed that was capable of choice, and had emotions that led it to make some choices rather than others, those emotions must have been part of what determined its reproductive success. Whenever an animal's emotions disposed it to be generous to other animals, therefore, rather than devoting all its efforts to the interests of itself and its offspring, that organism and its altruistic offspring should quickly be eliminated by the selfish, who would flourish at their expense.

But of course the problem for anyone who interpreted classical Darwinism as giving a complete account of the origins of life, rather than trying to hold on to a modified view with room for skyhooks, was that altruism – of both the biological and the familiar kind – apparently did exist. Many animals seemed to act in ways that, according to Darwin's original theory, made no reproductive sense at all. Even if you could explain all the appearances of human altruism as disguises of self-interest (which itself took some doing), this idea became increasingly implausible as you descended the scale of animal intelligence, and quite absurd by the time you got down to the level of the social insects – let alone plants. As already mentioned, the social insects always presented a particularly striking problem, since they all have sterile worker castes whose members do not reproduce at all. In the case of bees, for instance, the queen reproduces for the whole hive, and all the workers – the other females – are not only sterile, but also individually self-sacrificing. They will defend the hive by stinging intruders, even though the sting is lethal for the bee, and devote their entire efforts to the care of the queen and her brood. How could evolution persuade them to act in that way, since they had no offspring to whom to transmit those altruistic characteristics?

This remained a problem for a long time, with some people trying to use the existence of altruism as evidence that there were non-Darwinian forces at work, while others tried to find solutions within a framework of classical Darwinism. The most familiar kind of attempt was one that considered group, rather than individual, selection, and a few biologists still think there is some hope for explanations of altruism that take that form. But most concluded that all such attempts were flawed, and the bafflement continued until, nearly a hundred years after Darwin, classical Darwinism was overtaken by neo-Darwinism. This was the version of Darwinian theory that followed the genetic revolution, and which, in showing how reproduction worked and how characteristics were transmitted from one generation to the next, opened the way to solving problems that had been intractable in classical Darwinism.

The way in which neo-Darwinism differs from classical Darwinism has already been introduced, indirectly, by the extract from Dawkins in Chapter 3 (pp. 58–61). Classical Darwinism saw natural selection as a competition between organisms, whose characteristics had a strong influence on whether they thrived, reproduced and passed on those characteristics to their offspring. Of course organisms do reproduce, and do produce offspring that in many ways resemble themselves; but what the genetic revolution did was show how this came about. The phenotype (the way the organism as a whole turns out) is ultimately determined by its genotype (its genetic constitution), because this will determine from the start how the developing organism interacts with its environment. What happens during reproduction is that parental genes are copied, shuffled, and – in the sexually reproducing species that include nearly all the ones of which we are normally aware – mixed with the genes of a mate; but although the combination of genes in the offspring is new, the individual genes are usually precise copies of parental genes.

This means that the fundamental reproducers are the genes, which simply replicate. The looser resemblances among related organisms result from differing combinations of precisely replicated genes. The fundamental evolutionary competition, therefore, is not between organisms but between genes. The genes that succeed in getting themselves into the next generation are the ones that build bodies (Dawkins's survival machines) that are good at helping those genes to get copies of themselves transmitted into future generations. Combining with other genes to produce reproductively successful organisms is, as it were, the gene's device for getting copies of itself spread around.

The importance of this shift of emphasis from organism to gene is that it considerably affects the kind of question you can ask about why organisms are the way they are. Classical Darwinians tried to understand the selected characteristics of organisms as the ones that would give the organism an advantage over its rivals in the competiton to leave offspring. But when neo-Darwinians ask why the elephant has its trunk, or why ants live in colonies, or why humans have such slowly developing offspring, they no longer ask how it helps any particular *organism* to produce descendants; instead it can be asked how it helps the *genes that construct the organsims* to keep copies of *themselves* going. Typically the answers will be similar whichever way the question is asked: the gene that gets a lot of copies into the next generation will usually be in an organism that itself has a lot of offspring, and competes with other individuals with the result that they have fewer. But this need not be the case. The gene may pursue its ends by less direct means, and it may sometimes do better to build bodies that are not in outright competition with each other, or even which do not have offspring of their own. In other words, the gene may do better if the phenotype shows some degree of altruism to other organisms. And once this is understood, all kinds of previously puzzling anomalies start to fall into place.

This approach is potentially relevant to the investigation of all organisms, including plants (which can show altruism in the biological sense) but it is particularly interesting when it comes to the minds and emotions of animals. To understand animal emotions, and in turn animal behaviour, you need to ask not how the disposition serves the interest of the individual animal, but how it serves the interest of the genes according to whose blueprint that animal is constructed. If a gene is to survive in an organism of a particular kind, in a particular kind of environment, what kinds of characteristic should it (as it were) try to give that organism? In the case of complex organisms like us, what kinds of emotion should it give us? What kinds of inclination would propel us to use our intelligence and other abilities to do its work? Once again, the most obvious

way for a gene to get copies of itself into the next generation is to get its
organism to go and do likewise, and be a ruthless, self-interested reproducer. But
this is not the only possible method. Under certain circumstances, organisms
that developed altruistic attitudes to certain other organisms, counting their
interests as intrinsically important and sometimes even as more important than
their own, might actually do a better job of gene transmission than the purely
selfish kind.

Here is what Dawkins says about the matter in the introduction to *The
Selfish Gene* (1976).

> If we were told that a man had lived a long and prosperous life in the world of
> Chicago gangsters, we would be entitled to make some guesses as to the sort of
> man he was. We might expect that he would have qualities such as toughness, a
> quick trigger finger, and the ability to attract loyal friends. These would not be
> infallible deductions, but you can make some inferences about a man's character if
> you know something about the conditions in which he has survived and prospered.
> The argument of this book is that we, and all other animals, are machines created
> by our genes. Like successful Chicago gangsters, our genes have survived, in some
> cases for millions of years, in a highly competitive world. This entitles us to expect
> certain qualities in our genes. I shall argue that a predominant quality to be
> expected in a successful gene is ruthless selfishness. This gene selfishness will
> usually give rise to selfishness in individual behaviour. However, as we shall see,
> there are special circumstances in which a gene can achieve its own selfish goals
> best by fostering a limited form of altruism at the level of individual animals.
> 'Special' and 'limited' are important words in the last sentence. Much as we might
> wish to believe otherwise, universal love and the welfare of the species as a whole
> are concepts which simply do not make evolutionary sense.
>
> (Dawkins (1976), pp. 2–3)

I am not sure that I think much of Dawkins's gangster analogy if you take it as
an argument, since he does not think the genes are selfish in the sense of having
motives. The selfishness of genes (it is essential to remember) is, like the
altruism of plants, obviously metaphorical, and the use of the term is just a vivid
way of making the logical point that anything which survives and reproduces in
a system of natural selection must be good at bringing about its own survival
and transmission, rather than that of others. It is not obvious that we might be
expected to take on real selfishness just because we were designed by things that
were metaphorically selfish; it does not sound much like keeping bad company.
However, Dawkins does not need the analogy to make his point. If organisms
are the way they are because they have been effective propagators of the genes
whose survival machines they are, you would expect one aspect of that to be
their being good at keeping themselves going and reproducing at the expense of
rival machines with rival genes.

But, on the other hand, you would not expect this as a matter of course. There
might be all kinds of ways in which genes would do better if they got their

survival machines to be nice to each other; and whenever evolution threw up this possibility, you would expect the metaphorically selfish genes to produce machines with some kinds of altruism towards other machines. If you want to think of the gene as a gangster, you could say that it had already discovered, in building bodies (gangs), that it could make a very good niche for itself by cooperating, on an honour-among-thieves principle, with other genes. And, furthermore, it might well discover that it could do better still by getting its gang to cooperate with other gangs, to their mutual advantage. There are limits to this, of course. You could not possibly get a survival machine that put the interests of all other machines before its own. As Dawkins says, this would not make evolutionary sense; those genes would have no chance in natural selection. But that still allows for the evolution of many kinds and degrees of altruism.

There are two main kinds of altruism recognized by evolutionary psychologists: kin-directed altruism and reciprocal altruism.

Kin-directed altruism

If you were a gene, in what ways might you advance your metaphorically selfish purposes by helping to make your survival machines individually capable of altruism? The most obviously useful strategy would be to get those machines disposed to help other machines who also carried copies of you, so that you could as a result of their cooperation do better than you could have done if they had all been competing with each other. Because gene transmission comes about through the reproduction of organisms, the other organisms most likely to carry copies of you are the organisms related to the one you are in. So if you can manage to instil into the survival machines that carry copies of you an inclination to be nice to their relations – more or less in proportion to their relatedness, because that is also the probability of their carrying copies of you – you may get yourself much more effectively transmitted than genes that tried the strategy of making their organisms go for each other's throats.

To test this theory, and see to what extent this possibility is realized in practice, we need to know how a creature that shows altruism to its relatives works genetically. In the case of animals like us, it is straightforward: you share half your genes with your children and your siblings, a quarter with your cousins and grandchildren, and so on. And that does indeed seem to fit the pattern of familial concern pretty well – especially if you make adjustments for age, which considerably influences breeding prospects. But not all animals are like this; and in fact the breakthrough to this whole new, gene-centred way of looking at the problem of altruism was made when William Hamilton (1964) succeeded in explaining the evolutionary success of those puzzling social insects, who seemed more concerned to help their mother to breed more sisters than to produce offspring of their own. It turned out that the Hymenoptera (such as bees and ants) had a complicated genetic structure that meant that the workers were actually *more* closely related, genetically, to their sisters than they would be to their offspring if they had any. The genes will therefore do best by inducing in a bee a proto-emotion that disposes it to help its mother to reproduce and produce more sisters; and in the Hymenoptera they have apparently done a splendid job in achieving just that.

So altruism to kin is easy to explain in evolutionary terms, at least in outline, once the gene rather than the organism is seen as the basic unit of natural selection. The problem of classical Darwinism turns out to be easily soluble in neo-Darwinian terms.

Reciprocal altruism

That, however, does not explain altruism to unrelated others, who share comparatively few of your genes. Once again if altruism, however limited, is a matter of giving consideration to others, that means, however minimally, giving them advantages at the expense of yourself and, if those others are unrelated, your kin. This sounds like an evolutionary dead-end for any genes that dispose you to act that way. Evolution works by the accumulation of tiny advantages; and you would expect genes that disposed their carriers to behave selfishly to anyone other than kin to drive out the genes of the altruists – because the genes for altruism would actually be helping the genes for selfishness to perpetuate themselves.

We know, of course, that cooperation – which involves attending to the interests of others, rather than going all out for your own all the time – can be the basis of a strategy that is beneficial to everyone. There are many situations that take the form of the well-known Prisoner's Dilemma, in which individuals' pursuit of their own interests produces an outcome that is worse for all of them than if they all cooperated. For instance, if everyone files out of a theatre in an orderly way, nearly everyone will be better off than if there were a stampede. But although this shows in general terms how a society of altruists could be better off than a society of selfish individuals, it also implies that evolution by natural selection could not possibly produce such a state of affairs, because the essence of a Prisoner's Dilemma is that it is always in your interest to defect, whatever other people do. Whether the rest of the theatre audience is filing out or stampeding, it is still in your individual interest to push to the front. We can to some extent solve problems of that kind through social institutions, since selfish individuals can all see that it is in their interests to set up cooperative arrangements with built-in sanctions to prevent defection. But evolution has no such foresight and can proceed only by individually advantageous steps. This seems to imply that every time genes conducive to altruism were thrown up by chance, they would be quickly driven out by the selfish.

The breakthrough to the solution (at least in outline) came from Robert Trivers, in 1971. The reasoning involved did not demand the kind of detailed gene-centred thinking needed for the solution of the kin-selection problem, but it came in a different way from the kind of mathematical and game-theoretical thinking that characterized the neo-Darwinian approach to these problems. The idea was that genes can (as it were) experiment with instilling different kinds of emotional response into their vehicles. The chances of evolution are not just going to throw up pure altruists and pure cheats; they will throw up creatures with complex responses; and that raises the question of whether there are kinds of complex response that would result cumulatively in a greater total benefit than could possibly be achieved by a group of pure cheats, but which would not be susceptible to being ousted by cheats.

This is the idea of what is called reciprocal altruism; and the best-known illustration comes in the result of a computer tournament set up by Robert Axelrod (Axelrod, 1984). He asked people to write computer programmes to represent creatures with different ways of responding to the behaviour of other creatures, and then ran the programmes against each other to see which had most success. One of the simplest programmes entered in the competition, called Tit-for-Tat, represented a creature whose rule was simple: be nice to others on first meeting, and after that respond directly to what they do to you: nice to nice, nasty to nasty. And the important point from the point of view of the evolution of altruism was that this was a more powerful strategy than the nastier, straightforwardly selfish ones, because it could get the benefits of cooperation while at the same time keeping cheats out. What this meant was, in effect, that if evolution could throw up a group of Tit-for-Tatters, it would be – within certain environments – highly resistant to invasion by other strategies. Cheats that tried to infiltrate the society would do badly, because everyone else would treat them badly, while treating the cooperators well.

Of course, Tit-for-Tat is very simple, and only a first approximation to an idea that might work; real life and real creatures are much more complicated than that. But it does illustrate the possibility that what biologists call an *evolutionarily stable strategy* might result from the development of complex emotions that included unselfish ones. Altruism, a real concern for the feelings of others, could prompt the initial niceness, as long as other feelings, perhaps of indignation and resentment, would prevent the continuing of these feelings if the other organism responded badly.

Here is Wright on the subject:

> Tit for Tat's strategy – do unto others as they've done unto you – gives it much in common with the average human being. Yet it has no human foresight. It doesn't understand the value of reciprocation. It just reciprocates. In that sense it is perhaps more like Australopithecus, our small-brained forebears.
>
> What feelings would natural selection have instilled in an australopithecine to make it employ the clever strategy of reciprocal altruism in spite of its dimwittedness? The answer goes beyond the simple, indiscriminate 'sympathy' that Darwin stressed. True, this kind of sympathy would come in handy at first, prompting Tit for Tat's initial overture of goodwill. But thereafter sympathy should be dished out selectively, and supplemented by other feelings. Tit for Tat's reliable return of favours might emerge from a sense of gratitude and obligation. The tendency to cut off largesse for mean australopithecines could be realized via anger and dislike. And the tendency to be nice toward erstwhile meanies who have mended their

ways would come from a sense of forgiveness – an eraser of suddenly counterproductive hostility. All of these feelings are found in all cultures.

(Wright (1994), p. 197)

In other words, the genes might achieve the success of Tit-for-Tat by happening to produce in their carriers emotions of gratitude, resentment, forgiveness and so on – all of which would have had the effect of making them behave in a Tit-for-Tat-like manner, even though nobody had calculated any of it.

The details of all this are complicated, and a subject of active research at the interface of mathematics, computing and biology. We can immediately recognize the plausibility of some of this, but it is only a start; even if this is on the right lines, we do not know much about the details, or – very importantly – how much scope there is for differential tuning of these knobs of our natures. But the details are not essential to our purpose here, which is simply to answer the claim that evolution cannot produce unselfishness. This line of argument demonstrates the possibility that (metaphorically) selfish genes could produce individuals with a genuine concern for the well-being of others. Evolution must inevitably produce in individuals some disposition to individual and kin-directed selfishness and self-concern, because totally self-sacrificing individuals who did not care about their own interests at all, or whom they sacrificed them for, would be evolutionary dead ends. But it is possible to develop certain kinds and degrees of altruism, and genuine, immediate sympathy with the feelings of others. Now we understand the mechanism of evolution and the nature of genes, we can see how natural selection could have produced kin-directed altruism (presumably first), and then more generally altruistic attitudes, through the mechanism of reciprocity.

And that is, very roughly, the biology of the matter: the principle of how natural selection can produce altruism. It of course leaves open the question of how much it actually *does* produce, and the substantive moral question of whether we can or should be trying to increase the genetically induced amount. But it is enough to show that the most straightforward biological arguments against the possibility of altruism do not work. Neo-Darwinism has solved, at least in principle, the problems raised by classical Darwinism.

It is, by the way, rather ironic that Dawkins's well-known expression 'the selfish gene' has apparently entrenched in the popular mind the idea that evolution can produce only selfishness, when the shift to a metaphorical selfishness at the level of genes was precisely what allowed for real altruism at the level of organisms. Perhaps 'selfish gene' is popularly misinterpreted as 'gene for selfishness'. Whatever the reason, the expression seems to have misled a great many people.

Exercise 7.2

Chapter 1 explains the essence of Darwinian explanation as non-teleological. Darwinian scientists often think through their problems by asking what use it would be to a gene to build certain kinds of emotion and instinct into animal bodies (as Wright explains at the beginning of the long extract (pp. 70–71)); but the gene has no intentions at all, and it is important to be aware of the full translation of the teleological abbreviations. Translate the following claims from teleological into Darwinian language (as in Exercise 1.3 (p. 18)). Some of these exercises involve going beyond what has been said above, but in ways it should not be difficult to work out.

(i)   'The gene may pursue its ends by less direct means, and it will sometimes do better to build bodies that are not in outright competition with each other, or which do not have offspring of their own' (Dawkins; see quotation above).

(ii)   The interests of the gene and the interests of the organism need not be the same.

(iii)   Genes build themselves survival machines to propagate themselves and defend their interests more effectively.

(iv)   Hedgehogs used to be genetically inclined to curl up in dangerous situations, because that was the best way to protect them from predators, which were their main threat. But for hedgehogs near roads the main threat became the car, and curling up was the worst possible defence in that case. So the genes developed a hedgehog that ran away when danger approached.

(v)   Genes have designed males to be competitive and sexually eager, and to take risks.

(vi)   Genes must instil in female mammals a strong disposition to care for their young.

(vii)   Genes often have to trigger different emotions, according to which sex of animal they find themselves in.

(viii) Genes are selfish.

(Answers on pp. 282–3)

True altruism?

So far this chapter has been mainly about science, but we now come to the philosophical aspects of the problem of evolution and altruism.

We are in the process of assessing another conditional: the idea that if our fundamental dispositions are entirely the result of evolutionary competition, we must be fundamentally selfish. That was expressed, in argument form, thus:

Our fundamental dispositions and emotions are products of natural selection.
Natural selection cannot produce anything unselfish.
_____

Therefore we are fundamentally selfish.

That led, as usual, to assessing the argument for soundness by consideration of the added premise.

The familiar justification for believing that premise is the classical Darwinian view that if organisms have characteristics that dispose them to divert resources from themselves to other organisms, those characteristics will necessarily die out. But, as the last section argued, neo-Darwinism has refuted this idea by demonstrating mechanisms by which organisms disposed to divert resources to other organisms might develop by natural selection.

However, even though the original argument in defence of the added premise does not succeed, this is not the end of the problem of altruism and materialist Darwinism. Now comes an objection of a quite different sort: the idea that the kind of altruism allowed for by neo-Darwinism is not real altruism. Even if we can produce a genetic explanation of altruism, it is said, surely the very fact that this *is* the explanation – that these feelings are just generated by the genes for their own selfish purposes – means that the deflection of resources to others is not really altruism at all.

So we cannot regard the question of whether the gene-machine view precludes the possibility of altruism as settled yet. Unless we can answer the objection that the kind of altruism produced by the genes does not come up to the standards of real altruism, we may still have to conclude that the added premise is true.

Reciprocal selfishness

Here, to raise the first objection, is a passage from David Barash, an early writer on sociobiology, in a passage from his book *Sociobiology: The Whisperings Within* (1979).

> The sturdy Chukchee people of Siberia used to travel great distances with their reindeer herds. As with the proverbial seaman who had a woman in every port, adult Chukchee males could count on finding one at every encampment on their journeys. But such an arrangement could not be left to chance; the harsh Arctic environment would not permit it. The northland places a very great premium on cooperation, and so Chukchee men made reciprocal wife-lending contracts with other men in distant parts of their range. Each man entered into a wife-sharing agreement with several others, each of whom lived in a region normally traversed by him. It was basically 'You scratch my back, I'll scratch yours', only for the Chukchee the guarantee was that someone else would be provided to do the back scratching.
>
> The men making these arrangements did not have to be related at all. And, in fact, they were not really altruistic at all. They profited from their 'generosity' by the guarantee that they would receive equivalent benefits when they were out on the trail. The Chukchee case exemplifies another important aspect of the biology of altruism, second only perhaps to kin selection and the concept of inclusive fitness: reciprocity. The linking of reciprocity and fitness is the brain-child of

Harvard sociobiologist Robert Trivers, who pointed out that under certain conditions, apparent altruism can be adaptive even between individuals who are totally
unrelated. The primary requirement is that the giver will be the getter at some
later time. This being so, genes for such behaviour could be spread by natural
selection, since the ultimate effect of entering into a mutually-beneficial system is
that each participant profits and increases his or her fitness.

So reciprocity – sometimes misnamed 'reciprocal altruism' – is not altruism at
all. It is selfishness, pure and simple, since it takes place in the expectation that the
personal rewards will exceed the costs.

(Barash (1979), p. 155)

To assess any argument, the first thing to do is identify what the author is
arguing *for* – or, in other words, establish the conclusion of the argument.

Barash is discussing the phenomenon neo-Darwinists call reciprocal altruism,
and he thinks it is not altruism at all. He makes this quite clear in the last two
sentences, since he says it is *misnamed*, and that it is *pure selfishness*. This is
reinforced where he says (in the second paragraph) that *apparent* altruism can
be adaptive; whereas Trivers claimed, along the lines I have just described, that
altruism could be adaptive. ('Adaptive' means advantageous from the point of
view of natural selection.)

This means that the conclusion of his argument seems to be:

The (so-called) reciprocal altruism that can be produced by natural
selection is not true altruism.

Now what is the argument by which he defends that conclusion?

There is more than one possible approach to identifying an argument that is
presented, like this one, in text form. The most obvious way is to try to set out
in summary form the argument as it appears in the text, and then assess it in
the usual way: identify unstated presuppositions, check the truth of premises,
and so on. Another way, however, is to work from the other direction, and start
by trying to construct a valid argument to the conclusion, making as much use
as possible of what the author says and making plausible suppositions where
there are obvious gaps. This really amounts to the same thing in the long run,
but it can be helpful when writers do not set their arguments out clearly. It is
also a particularly effective way to work if your concern is to try to make a
judgement about an *issue*, rather than to assess the *author*, since this way of
approaching the matter makes the best possible use of the materials the author
gives, and may suggest ways of improving the argument. Setting about the
matter this way is a variation on the method used so far for assessing conditionals, and it is effective in all textual analysis.

Start, then, with the conclusion:

The reciprocal altruism that can be produced by natural selection is
not true altruism.

The first thing to do, if the aim is to construct the best possible argument to that conclusion on the basis of Barash's text, is to see whether there are any kinds of premise that a valid argument to that conclusion *must* contain. Do there seem to be any?

In this case one, at least, is obvious. Since Barash is going to be concluding that what Trivers has identified does not meet the requirements of true altruism, there must be a premise saying what those requirements are.

Barash does not say explicitly what he means by true altruism, but he does clearly *imply* what he would count. He says that reciprocity is not true altruism because the expected rewards exceed the costs, and the action is therefore in the person's own interests. That implies that true altruism must involve the expected rewards' *not* exceeding the costs. So his premise would be something like this:

> *True altruism involves doing favours without expectation of return.*
>
> _____
>
> Therefore the reciprocal altruism that can be produced by evolution is not true altruism.

Now, again, just by looking at the argument as it stands, you can see another premise that is needed. A link is needed between the standards of true altruism set out in the premise and the shortcomings of the kind of altruism produced by evolution; and it is clear what is needed here, whether Barash actually says anything about it or not. A premise is needed stating that the kind of altruism produced by evolution does *not* do favours without expectation of return.

That gives:

> True altruism involves doing favours without expectation of return.
> *The reciprocal altruism that can be produced by evolution involves doing favours in the expectation that they will be returned.*
>
> _____
>
> Therefore the reciprocal altruism that can be produced by evolution is not true altruism.

This is now structurally valid, and seems to catch the essence of Barash's argument. The next step is to assess it for soundness. Are the premises true?

The first premise does seem true, or at least a close enough approximation to pass in this context. But what about the second? This is more difficult to assess, because the sketch of evolutionary biology and reciprocal altruism in the previous section was so brief. However, it did contain enough information to provide the answer – which is that the claim is not true. The altruism identified by evolutionary psychology is *not* a matter of doing favours in the expectation of returns.

Of course the arrangement Barash describes among the Chukchee is not altruistic in this way, and that may well be true of many, if not most, of our social transactions. We often do things for people because we think they will be able to help us, and will feel an obligation to return our favours – and evolutionary psychology sees us as well adapted to make such arrangements. But that is why it is important to distinguish the genetic claim about the possibility of a capacity for *altruism* from related ideas about our capacity to make mutually beneficial arrangements. We can see that such arrangements are good, and set up conventions and institutions to constrain individually selfish desires: we find it much better to have queueing conventions than to have everyone pushing. Genes cannot make arrangements like that, because they cannot look forward and plan for future benefits. On the other hand, what they may do is produce complex emotions that have similar kinds of *effect* by giving individual creatures emotions that lead them to genuine altruism.

The genetic claim is that there are indeed conditions under which genuinely altruistic emotions have evolved, where concern for others is not a matter of getting a return. The idea is that the genes have, as it were, done (by the trial and error of variation and natural selection) an overall calculation of their interests, and discovered that if they instil into some of their survival machines a genuine concern for the interests of other such machines, and a genuine willingness to sacrifice their own, the overall effect will be better for the metaphorically selfish genes than a race of literally selfish survival machines would be. There would have to be limits to this, of course. Evolution cannot produce a totally and indiscriminately altruistic creature (even the totally self-sacrificing bees are making their sacrifices for particular other bees), and it would need to inculcate some kind of Tit-for-Tat-like emotions to prevent the altruists' being driven to the wall by the selfish. But that is quite compatible with a real willingness to help, say, people whom you will never see again, or who are too weak to give you any return. *Genuine* and *limited* concern are not opposed.

What Barash has done in this passage is, I think, conflate two quite different issues. On the one hand there is the matter of mutually beneficial arrangements made by selfish individuals: the sort of thing we enter into when we agree to queue rather than push, as long as everybody else does. On the other, there are the mutually beneficial arrangements of selfish genes, which have (as it were) discovered that if they do the same kind of thing – produce organisms that in certain circumstances act against their own immediate interests – they can do better for themselves than if they had produced straightforwardly competitive organisms. In the second case the *organisms* are not selfishly doing good in the expectation of reward. The selfishness is only at the genetic level, and then only metaphorical.

So this idea about the non-genuineness of reciprocal altruism simply mistakes the nature of the theory, and can be disregarded for that reason. If there is to be a doubt about the genuineness of evolutionarily produced altruism, it will have to take another form.

Ulterior genetic motives

Consider now a different kind of allegation from Barash, this time about something evolutionary psychologists really do claim. This argument would also apply to the case of reciprocal altruism, but I shall discuss it only in the kin-directed form Barash considers here.

> When a parent rushes into the street to snatch his child from an oncoming car, he is endangering himself and, hence, his genes. On the other hand, he is saving a portion of his 'soul' – one-half to be precise. Perhaps in doing so he seems to be 'altruistic', since he is helping someone else at real risk to himself. Now, given the fundamental selfishness of evolution, true altruism should never occur, since any genes producing altruism should be less fit than genes that produce selfishness. So is the rescuing parent an evolutionary anomaly? Not at all. In fact, he is not really an altruist, since his genes are doing neither more nor less than saving some of themselves. The same can be said of any behaviour by one individual toward another, so long as the two have some genes in common. Caring for our own children or for others with whom we share genes is, then, just a special case of those genes selfishly promoting themselves by watching out for others in whom they also reside.
>
> (Ibid., p. 133)

The conclusion of this argument is, once again, that what appears to be altruism – this time parental altruism – is only apparent, not real. You can tell this from the explicit claim that the parent is not really an altruist, and from the phrase 'seems to be "altruistic" ', where both the 'seems' and the inverted commas imply that this altruism is not the real thing. So the conclusion is something like this:

> Therefore parental altruism is not true altruism.

Once again the form of the conclusion shows the kind of premises that are needed to make the supporting argument valid. As in the previous argument we need a premise saying what true altruism is, and another saying why parental altruism falls short of this standard. What does Barash say or imply about these matters?

As in the previous argument, he says nothing explicit about what altruism is, but gives a clear implication. 'Selfishly promoting themselves' is obviously meant to be what altruism is *not*, since Barash is saying that this is all that the *apparent* altruism is. That seems to give us pretty well the same account of altruism as in the previous argument, so that can go in as a premise:

> *True altruism is acting for the benefit of others at cost to yourself.*
> ———
> Therefore parental altruism is not true altruism.

What is needed now is a claim about the nature of parental altruism which shows it to fall short of the requirements of true altruism. The simplest claim of that form would be 'Parental altruism does not involve acting for the benefit of others at cost to yourself.' Barash, however, does not say anything as simple as that; and if he did it would not be much use, since we would then have to ask why parental altruism fell short of the real thing. The best course here, then, is to put into the argument some of the things Barash definitely does say, and keep on filling the gaps until the argument seems complete and valid.

The basic idea is that caring for children is just a special case of genes' self-ishly promoting themselves. That suggests something like this:

> When you rescue your child at real risk to yourself, your genes are
>   doing neither more nor less than saving some of themselves.
> *True altruism is acting for the benefit of others at cost to yourself.*
> _____
> Therefore parental altruism is not true altruism.

That seems the most plausible way to continue the argument, and certainly in line with what Barash is implying. Is it enough to make the argument valid?

It may perhaps seem so at first glance, but there is still a logical gap, between *yourself* and *your genes*. The first premise claims that the genes are saving themselves; the second premise claims that you are not being altruistic unless you are doing things for others and against your own interests. But unless your interests are the same as your genes' interests, you cannot reach the conclusion. So you need something like this:

> When you rescue your child at real risk to yourself, your genes are
>   doing neither more nor less than saving some of themselves.
> True altruism is acting for the benefit of others at cost to yourself.
> *What is in the interests of your genes is in your interests.*
> _____
> Therefore parental altruism is not true altruism.

Barash does not actually say that your genes' interests are identical with yours, but it is essential for his argument, and his text does strongly imply that he is taking it for granted.

The argument now seems valid, and a fair representation of Barash's claim, so the next question is about the truth of the premises. The second premise can be accepted, since it is the same as in the previous argument we were considering. But what about the other two?

First, is it true that when parents protect their children this is 'neither more nor less than' their genes' saving some of themselves? Is it true that protecting your children must be good for your genes?

As always, the best way to test the truth of a generalization like this is to try to find a counterexample, and in this case it is not at all difficult. If your genetic interest is to get as many copies of your genes as possible into future generations, then it is clear that enormous amounts of parental altruism go into nothing of the kind. For instance, parents may devote their life to a severely handicapped child who is unlikely ever to reproduce, and they may, perhaps, decide not to have other children so that they can care properly for the handicapped one. Or they may encourage a promising girl in the pursuit of her career, even though it seems likely that this will interfere with the production of grandchildren.

This is another important point about evolutionary psychology, and about evolution, in general. The claim that various dispositions evolved because they resulted in the production of successful offspring by our ancestors is not at all the same as saying either that they must always have this effect in individual cases, or even that the overall effect they have now is in the interests of the genes. Evolution is not forward-looking, and evolutionary explanations of characteristics are always in terms of where they came from, not what effects they are having now. (Many of our characteristics are explainable only in terms of our ancestors' having had to adapt to life in the sea. It does not follow that this is what these characteristics achieve now – or even that they achieve anything useful at all.) So evolution, on this account, explains our emotions in terms of their having had *in the past, on average,* a good effect on the passing on of genes while the species was developing its present characteristics. But that does not at all mean that any individual is doing well genetically by acting on them – or even that the species as a whole is, since conditions may have changed.

This means the first premise seems not to be true, and that is enough on its own to make the argument unsound. But consider anyway the second added premise, about your genes' interests being yours. Do your genes' interests seem to be your interests?

The first, pedantic but still important, point to make here is that genes have no interests. The idea that they have, and that they selfishly pursue those interests, is pure metaphor. Selfishness is a forward-looking thing: selfish people are ones whose concern is for themselves, and whose choices are in their own interests. Genes are not forward-looking at all, even metaphorically. The genes that survive are ones that *have been* successful in getting themselves copied into future generations, but they have no plans to carry on that way. A change of circumstances may make them gradually less successful, but they will not do anything about it; they just replicate themselves, and do not adapt at all. All that happens is that other genes do better, and the phenotypes adapt in the sense that the unsuccessful phenotypes, and the genes that produce them, die out.

So we must understand the question as whether your interests are in getting your genes as effectively copied as possible; and it will probably take hardly a moment's thought to recognize that even if you think about the interests of your genes at all, most of your interests have absolutely nothing to do with them. Of course, your interests may well have a considerable effect on gene spread; the deepest characteristics of human nature (according to evolutionary psychology) exist because they have had the effect, on the whole, of being good for the spread of genes. But that does not mean the two are the same; and one of the striking effects of Darwinian thinking is the recognition of how often your genes' as-it-were interests are not yours *at all*. Your genotype reflects what happens to have led to the survival of genes in the past, and if that happens also to be in your interests – conducive to your happiness, flourishing, well-being, dream fulfilment and all the rest – you are *extremely* lucky. As Wright put it, the puppeteer has zero regard for the feelings of the puppets. It was obviously good for our genes to have us bipedal and with babies with enormous heads, for instance; but the resulting effect on childbirth is emphatically not in the interests of the individuals who go through it. And if current evolutionary psychology is anywhere near right about the deep natures of the sexes, that is enough on its own to show that what has been good for the genes can work directly against the interests of the carriers of those genes. The young woman in Dawkins's anecdote in Chapter 3 was appalled by the thought of the disposition her genetic background might have saddled her with; she did not want those emotions, which she saw as getting in the way of her real interests in the way that a disease or injury might.

If this still seems implausible, consider what might be said to be in your genes' interests, and then whether you regard them as being in yours. Suppose some dictator with a eugenics programme decided you were just the kind of person he wanted more of, and forced you to spend your life producing the maximum possible number of offspring, with the technical assistance of suitable partners chosen by the state. Since you cannot personally produce all the offspring you are capable of, most of the process would be arranged artificially (for men by artificial insemination, because that way you can impregnate more women than you could if you had them one at a time; for women by IVF and surrogacy, since you can have far more children that way). That would be wonderful for the genes; but it is unlikely to sound even remotely like what would be in your interests.

Consider also what altruism would have to consist of if your genes' interests really were your own. If acting unselfishly is doing what is against your genetic interests and advances other people's, the unselfish man will refuse to cooperate when his wife wants children, or insist on her having them only by other men; the unselfish mother – who will be a mother only by accident – will neglect her children so that other people's genes have a chance, persuade her daughters to be nuns, and devote her time to anti-contraception and anti-abortion organizations; the unselfish friend will surreptitiously swap her friends' contraceptive pill supplies for placebos and go around pricking holes in their condoms. It opens up a whole new world of altruistic possibilities.

It seems, therefore, that the third premise – which, even though not asserted by Barash, must be regarded as a presupposition if his argument is to be valid – is also completely wrong.

This means that this second attempt to show that evolution cannot produce real altruism also fails. The argument contains two false premises. Our interests and our genes' interests are nothing like identical, and the gene-machine view of human nature has no difficulty in accounting for the fact that we can, and frequently do, act against both. We still have no reason to think that if the radical forms of Darwinism are true, we must be incapable of genuine altruism.

Exercise 7.3

1 It is sometimes claimed that we should not object to intensive farming on grounds of concern for the animals, because what we do is in the animals' interests. These animals have found a highly successful genetic niche in which to propagate their kind: they exist in a kind of symbiotic relationship with us, in which we are really serving their interests as much as they ours.

    Comment on that claim in the light of the foregoing argument.

2 Translate into Darwinian language 'The puppeteer has zero regard for the feelings of the puppets' (where the puppeteer is the metaphorical protector of the interests of our genes, and we are the puppets).

(Answers on p. 283)

Egoism and tautology

Finally, consider one further argument that might seem to justify the claim that natural selection cannot produce anything unselfish, and therefore that if the the gene-machine view is true we must be fundamentally selfish.

Think again of the parent rushing out into the traffic. It has already been argued that such actions may not be in the interest of the parent's genes at all (perhaps she will get killed and not have all the other children she might have had, and her other children will suffer), and that the genes' interests are anyway not necessarily the parent's interests. But, it might be objected, that still does not show that the act is altruistic. If the ideas of evolutionary psychology are on the right track, the genes have actually given us the *desire* to look after our children, and that is why we do it. The genes make us love our children, and often care more for them than for our own safety. The parent would be wretched if the child were killed. This means that, quite apart from any genetic interest, it *really is* in the parent's interests as an individual to save the child, which is why it is worth taking serious risks to do it. So the rescue attempt really is, still, pure selfishness, even at the level of individuals rather than genes.

This is a familiar line of argument, not only in the context of Darwinian altruism, but in everyday life. It is often said, when people are doing something apparently unselfish, that it is not really unselfish because that is how these particular people achieve their own pleasure and satisfaction. Some people happen to get their satisfaction from doing things for other people ('She has a great need to feel she is doing good'), but they are really as selfish as everyone else; they just have a different form of pleasure. Philosophers call this idea – the idea that all our concerns are ultimately for ourselves – 'psychological egoism'.

Does this, then, undermine the claim that the love parents show their children – or, for that matter, the kindness anyone may show to passing strangers – is true altruism? Once again, we can test the idea by putting it into argument form. We need to consider the plausibility of an argument like this:

> In caring for their children, parents are acting according to their own
> desires.
> _____
> Therefore parental care for children is not truly altruistic.

What is needed to complete that argument, and make it valid? Once again, as in the previous two arguments, we obviously need a premise stating what counts as true altruism; but care is needed here. To see exactly what form the statement must take to make the argument valid, we need to be clear about the precise logical gap it needs to fill. Here the conclusion about an absence of altruism needs to be linked to the claim about parents' acting according to their own *desires*:

> In caring for their children, parents are acting according to their own
> desires.
> *To act according to your own desires is not truly altruistic.*
> _____
> Therefore parental care for children is not truly altruistic.

That seems to make the argument valid, so the next question is about the truth of the added premise. On the face of it, this looks much like the ones that were used to complete the earlier arguments, and whose truth was accepted when the soundness of the arguments was being assessed. But in fact it is not. The earlier premises were about altruism and acting in your own *interests*. This one, as was required to make the argument valid, is about acting according to your own *desires*.

This is quite different, because although there is no difficulty in understanding that some of your actions are in your own interests and some against them, there is a sense in which whatever you choose to do is, necessarily, according to your own desires. What you choose to do is what you regard as the best option, and therefore it is what you want – desire – to do in the circumstances, all things considered, even if it has some bad elements you do not desire in themselves. But if we say that whatever you choose to do is acting according to your own desires, and acting according to your own desires is not altruistic, we have *defined altruism out of existence*. Nothing you did could possibly be altruistic according to this account. Even being tortured to death rather than betray your friend would not be altruistic, because, by definition, your choosing to do that would mean that it was according to your own desires, and therefore selfish.

Complaining that there is no altruism when altruism has been defined in this self-defeating way is like complaining there is no free will after it has been defined in a way that demands your making choices before you exist, or that your fairy godmother is a failure because she has still not produced your two-horned unicorn or your spherical cube. In meeting one part of the criterion you are necessarily failing to meet the other. And, of course, if this is the definition of selfishness, everybody and everything is selfish on any possible account of the world: selfishness characterizes all possible choices in all possible worlds, and the idea becomes useless. If the idea of selfishness is to have any purpose at all, there must be a criterion for unselfishness that could in principle be met – however little of it there actually is in practice. Even if you want to claim that everybody is, in fact, selfish, the claim is vacuous unless you could say what they could do to be unselfish.

Notice as well that selfishness defined in this way is one of those universal acids which, like most universal acids, is usually invoked for the purpose of being put to selective use. This account of selfishness makes everything selfish by definition, but in practice it always appears when people want to undermine some *particular* claim about altruism, and cannot find ulterior motives of the usual sort. This is worth watching out for; it happens all the time.

That, however, is a general point. The main conclusion is that once again an argument intended to show that evolutionarily produced altruism is not true altruism has failed. There is still no reason to think that if we originate entirely through natural selection, we must be incapable of the genuine altruism that is a necessary condition of making moral choices.

More shifts of level: reductive explanations

The idea that if altruism has evolutionary origins it is not true altruism raises a general issue about explanation, which connects with a topic already raised more than once in this book.

Consider the following pairs of exchanges, and assume the claims made by both B and C are true.

1   *A:* I'm thirsty; let's get a drink from that lake.
        B: But that's only a mirage.
        C: But that's only a collection of hydrogen and oxygen atoms linked together.

2   *A:* That diamond necklace must be worth a fortune.
        B: But it's only cubic zirconia.
        C: But it's only metamorphosed carbon.

3   *A:* It's a tragedy that all the Old Masters in that gallery were vandalized.
        B: But they were only copies.
        C: But they were only pigments spread on canvas.

In all these cases C's response to A is obviously absurd. What is wrong, however, is not that the replies are false, but that they are *inappropriate*. B's claims are objections to what A has just said: they are assertions that what A is regarding as a real something-or-other is not a real thing of that kind, but false or fake in some way. C's are presented as though they are objections of the same sort –

signalled by the 'but' and the 'only' – but they are not objections at all; they are just a different, compatible, description of the same phenomenon. An explanation of what something is in other terms is not enough to show that it is not a real case of that something.

The absurdity of C's remarks, therefore, comes not in the claims themselves, but in the signals that they are being presented as objections to A. And it is probably already obvious that this is a case of something that has already appeared in other contexts: an equivocation involving a shift of subject to a different level, presented as a continuation of a discussion at the previous level.

Most of the time we have no difficulty in distinguishing between explanations that show some idea to be wrong, and explanations that, although using quite different terms, are compatible with them. But for various reasons – usually their losing the original argument – people do sometimes slip from one level to another, and imply that the explanation or redescription they are giving conflicts with the original claim. This is not something anyone is likely to get away with in simple cases like the ones above, but it is very common in more complex ones.

This is important in all contexts, and I shall give more illustrations in the exercise following this section, but the reason for raising the matter here is its relevance to the arguments about whether apparent altruism is really altruism. The objections raised in the previous two sections to the idea that the altruism produced by evolution can be real altruism are versions of the same phenomenon: a shift of level masquerading as part of the original discussion.

Consider the following:

A: She's very generous; she has agreed to house-sit and look after the dogs while her daughter goes off to the Bahamas, instead of going on holiday herself.

B: It's not generosity at all. It's just a device to make it possible for her lover to stay with her, which she obviously can't manage either at home or by announcing that she's going on holiday alone.

B's claim is an objection to A's, and if B is right, A's claim about generosity is mistaken. B's account *competes* with A's: if B is right, the woman has a hidden motive which undermines the generosity claim. A and B cannot both be right.

But now imagine the conversation going on like this (and now the B can stand for Barash):

A: No, that's not true; her lover will be abroad at the time. And, anyway, her husband will be there as well. It's just straightforwardly inconvenient for her to go dog-sitting. She is disappointed to be giving up her own holiday.

B: But it's just the workings of those selfish genes of hers, which give her a strong inclination to care for her children.

B may well be right about the ultimate, evolutionary explanation of the woman's impulses, but he is not right to introduce the claim with 'but', and say it is 'just' the workings of the genes. In fact he is not right to make the claim at all in this context, because, even though possibly true, it is irrelevant. He is presenting it as though he is giving an objection like the earlier one, and uncovering a hidden motive. But he is not doing that: an explanation is not a motive, and his claim is not in conflict with A's. B's first explanation of what is going on, if true, is in conflict with A's, and undermines the claim of generosity; it is what is sometimes called a *debunking* explanation. But B's second explanation, even if true, is not debunking. It is an explanation on a different level; and to explain the evolutionary origins of generosity is not to show that the generosity is not real, any more than to explain that the water in a bottle is a collection of hydrogen and oxygen atoms is to show that it is not real water – or, to go back to the subject of an earlier chapter, than to show the genetic and social roots of someone's anti-social personality is to show he is not really anti-social.

This is important for the discussion of altruism, but it is relevant to many arguments about evolution. The debate as a whole is rife with this kind of shifting between levels; and one of the commonest signals that this is going on is the way the term 'reductionist' is hurled around as a term of abuse – as anyone who reads much of the literature in this area will know. The direction of hurling is, as usual, from conservative to radical: materialist views are often accused of being reductionist by dualists; evolutionary psychology is said to be reductionist by most of its opponents. This is a complicated matter which needs much more discussion than there is space for here, but a brief indication of the problem will be better than nothing.

Accusations of reductionism are usually just *assertions* made as though it were clear both what they meant and why they were to be understood as criticisms. But since neither of these matters is usually in the least clear, the only productive way to take the issue forward is to get the accuser to clarify exactly what the accusation is supposed to be, or, failing that, to suggest various possibilities and consider them.

This needs to be done in individual cases, but some general points can be made. A reductive explanation is one that explains a set of phenomena by reference to a more fundamental level of explanation and uses quite different terminology. This is what happens, for instance, when heat is explained in terms of the rapid movement of minute particles. It *reduces* the number of separate elements in the situation, by explaining some in terms of others. There is, therefore, a clear sense in which Darwinian explanation – like all scientific explanation – is reductive. Materialist Darwinism claims that the complexity of the organism originated entirely through very simple, mechanical, processes, without any reference to other causal elements traditionally regarded as essential, such as Designers and Life Forces. Evolutionary psychology is reductive in explaining our mental and emotional attributes in terms of the survival strategies of genes. But explaining one thing in terms of another does not give any justification for using 'reductionist' as a term of abuse. If that were generally reasonable you could criticize medicine for being reductionist in virtue of explaining illnesses in terms of bacteria and viruses and genes, or physicists for explaining flashes of lightning in terms of electrical discharges.

Of course there can always be disagreement about whether particular reductive explanations are correct: that is what the disagreements between the different kinds of Darwinist are about. But then they should be accusing each other of simply getting things *wrong*; there would seem no need to add the extra accusation of reductionism. So what exactly is going on?

My guess is that what is happening here is that there is a pervasive conflation of the two kinds of explanation that have been identified in this section. Some explanations simply explain one thing in terms of another, throwing light on its origin or nature without in the least implying that the thing being explained is in any way illusory; others explain things in ways that debunk them, and show them not to be what they seem. My impression is that the accusation of reductionism comes of mistaking the first kind for the second: of thinking that a Darwinian explanation of the existence of, for instance, minds in terms of the laws of physics amounts to a claim that everything we want to say about minds can be said in the language of physics; or that if sexual love can be explained as originating in the survival strategies of genes, that somehow changes its character and proves that love is an illusion. (I suspect Wright of falling into this trap several times, as, for instance, when he writes of the 'seamy underside' of kisses and endearments.) It certainly happens in the context of altruism, when genetic explanations of altruism are said to be trying to explain altruism *away*. This is quite wrong. Explaining is not the same as explaining away. A successful scientific explanation does not prove that the thing it is explaining does not exist. It only shows that rival explanations, *competing on the same ground*, are false.

It is quite difficult to deal with accusations of reductionism in practice, just because they appear as accusations and the natural response to an unjustified accusation is denial. But denial is no good when the problem lies in the way a claim is being presented rather than in its falsity, and the only way to deal with this is to start by demanding clarification – what exactly are you being accused of, and exactly why is it supposed to be bad? – and then be prepared to distinguish between an explanation which competes with some claim, and one which is in different terms, but compatible.

This is what needs to be done in the case of the Barash arguments. He points to the evolutionary explanation of altruism, and implies that it is a debunking explanation: one that proves that altruism is illusory. It does not. Debunking explanations of altruism are ones that allege a selfish motive underlying the apparently altruistic act, and these are quite different from explanations of how altruism comes to exist (i.e. why some motives are altruistic). Explaining how altruism comes to exist no more shows that it is not real altruism than explaining how a cake was made shows it is not a real cake. It is this mistake which leads Barash to conclude that an explanation of why parents are altruistic shows that they are not really altruistic.

In the same way, when Dawkins says we are gene machines, and in doing so claims to be giving a complete explanation of our origins, he is not saying we are *only* gene machines: gene machines *rather than* conscious intelligent beings who are strongly influenced by the material and cultural environment, and capable of abstract reasoning, and subject to strong passions. He is only saying that this is the mechanism by which these things came into existence, and that if we understand their origins we can make a better job of understanding their nature.

It is essential to be on the alert for shifts of level in all the evolutionary debates. They keep happening.

Exercise 7.4

1   In the following list, suppose that each of the claims made is true, and consider its merit as a refutation of the claim that the act in question was altruistic. Say whether each is:

    (a)   genuine (showing that the action was not really altruistic).
    (b)   spurious because making a quite different claim (giving an explanation at a different level, not incompatible with the altruism claim).
    (c)   spurious because depending on a self-defeating definition of selfishness.
    (The spurious ones are the ones where the 'only' is out of place.)

You weren't really being unselfish, you were rescuing the child from the raging torrent at great risk to yourself only because:

(i)   Your fiancée was watching and you wanted to strike an impressive figure.
(ii)   As a child you were given a lot of parental approval whenever you did anything to help other people.
(iii)   You had just seen an inspiring film where the hero rushed around doing good at personal risk.
(iv)   You would get a tremendous feeling of satisfaction from the feeling that you had prevented so much misery.
(v)   Our genetic inheritance gives us a lot of benevolent impulses.
(vi)   There was a television crew on the bank.
(vii)   You knew the child's family was rich, and you thought there would be a big enough reward to justify the risk.
(viii)   It was your own child and you are full of impulses designed by your genes for their own benefit.
(ix)   That was what you wanted to do at the time.

2   Assuming the second part of each of the following assertions is true, does it (or might it) succeed in justifying the first part? (Once again, the question is usually about whether words like 'but', 'only', and 'just' in the second part are appropriate or not.)

(i)   She's not really pleased to see you; she's just a very good actress.
(ii)   You don't really love me, you're just under the temporary influence of a surge of hormones.
(iii)   You say you'll love me for ever, but feelings of love are genetically induced to encourage procreation, and there are good scientific reasons for thinking those feelings won't last.
(iv)   He's not really ill; it's just a hangover.
(v)   You don't really love me; your feelings are just the survival devices of selfish genes.
(vi)   You shouldn't care about having a degree. It's only a bit of paper.
(vii)   They aren't really suffering; putting on a display of agony is part of the ritual.
(viii) That table isn't really solid; it's just a lot of molecules whizzing around in empty space.
(ix)   That table isn't really there; it's just a hologram.
(x)   He's not really ill; it's just that his white corpuscles have gone into overdrive to repel a parasitic micro-organism.

3   In the light of these discussions, comment on the following (real-life) cases:

(i)   A well-known politician was holding a discussion on television with a group of undergraduates. He put forward an argument defending his views, and then asked whether the audience agreed with his conclusion. Most of them didn't. He said, 'It's easy to see what social class you come from.'
(ii)   A student concerned with animal welfare was arguing with a senior medical academic about the sufferings of animals in the process of food production. The doctor said, 'It's all just electrical impulses in the brain.'

(Answers on p. 283)

———————————

This chapter has dealt with the familiar idea that if materialist Darwinism is true, we must be incapable of the capacity for altruism that is a necessary condition of any moral behaviour. The original grounds for holding this belief disappeared when neo-Darwinism superseded classical Darwinism, and the possibility was demonstrated that evolution by natural selection could produce limited altruism. But sceptics responded with a different line of argument, purporting to show that such genetically induced altruism was not real altruism.

Arguments of this kind fall into familiar patterns of mistake. One is a version of the now-familiar confusion of levels in argument, and involves mistaking an *explanation* of some phenomenon for a demonstration that it is in some way *illusory*. This is the basis of the familiar accusation of reductionism that is frequently made by conservatives against radicals in the Darwinian debate, but it depends on a simple conflation of compatible explanations on different levels with incompatible, rival explanations. In this particular case, it depends on overlooking a slip from the metaphorical interests of genes to the real interests of organisms.

Another is a version of the problem already encountered in the context of free will: defining altruism out of existence, and then implying that its non-existence in some context shows something about that case in particular.

8   The end of ethics

Even if materialist Darwinism leaves us capable of the altruism that is a necessary condition of moral behaviour, it may seem to remove the point of moral effort altogether, by removing the whole basis of ethics. This is said by both opponents and supporters of radical Darwinian views. The main lines of argument – in particular the claim that God is essential for both providing and revealing moral standards – are discussed here, and once again the analysis seems to show that there is no difference between the implications of the different degrees of Darwinism.

The chapter also makes a long detour, in the middle, into a discussion of relativism. This discussion has no direct connection with Darwinism, but relativism lurks in the background of many of the claims about Darwinism and ethics, and is worth assessing in its own right. The discussion raises further problems of incoherence and shifts of level, and also introduces the idea of pragmatic self-refutation.

The chapter ends with a sketch of how ethical enquiry can proceed against a background of evolutionary psychology, and connects it with the discussion in Chapter 6 of punishment and responsibility.

———————————

The overall conclusion, if these arguments are right, is that even the most thoroughgoing form of materialist Darwinism allows us a capacity for genuine altruism. The genetic account of altruism does, admittedly, leave it quite limited in extent; but the question has been only about whether the radical forms of Darwinism preclude altruism altogether, and they do not. And anyway, an account of human nature that shows altruism to be limited in extent is hardly revolutionary; no account of human nature has ever claimed otherwise. Religion has never doubted that we are sinful; and advocates of the standard social science view, which attributes more to society than to genes, usually agree that our society makes us pretty selfish. The holders of both these views typically regard us as capable of moral improvement, but there seems no reason why that hope, too, should not apply to the gene-machine view. Once again, then, an issue that might be thought to turn on the question of which version of Darwinism was true seems not to do so after all. All versions allow for altruism; none sees it as all-pervasive.

However, even though the most radical form of Darwinism may, like the others, leave open the possibility of our making moral improvement, it may seem open to a different objection, which would apply to the blank-paper view as well. Can these fully materialist versions of Darwinism allow for there *being such a thing* as genuine moral improvement? Even if we are capable of change, is there any change worth aiming for? Traditional ways of thinking allow us to recognize our moral shortcomings and try to improve, because there are moral standards against which we can compare ourselves and our progress. But if our moral systems and moral intuitions are the result of mindless physical laws and natural selection, can rational consideration endorse our bothering about them at all? If conscience is not a divinely implanted facility for recognizing moral truth, but just a device of the selfish genes for making reciprocal altruism work, why should we take the slightest notice of its promptings, any further than it is in our individual interests to care what other people think?

This chapter is about the question of whether Darwinism undermines ethics at the foundations.

Particular moralities and morality in general

It is common for Darwinism to be accused of undermining moral standards, but it is necessary to be careful about what exactly is meant by this. Usually when people talk of threats to moral standards they mean to the *normative* standards they themselves hold: the particular moral standards they use as the basis for moral judgements of people and policies. But when people abandon or question one set, such as the religious or political principles they were brought up with, that does not necessarily mean that they have given up on morality altogether. Often they are just changing to another set that they regard as better, and that does not imply any doubt about the value of morality as such. Quite the contrary: unless they presumed that there were criteria by which normative standards themselves could be assessed, they would have no basis on which to argue that the ones they were adopting were better than the ones they had rejected. At least on the face of it, debates about which normative standards should be accepted presuppose that there are objective criteria by which they can be assessed. So even if Darwinism undermined particular normative standards, it would not follow that it was a threat to morality as such.

Questions about the effect of Darwinism on particular moral values and ideals are the subject of the next two chapters. In this chapter the issue is the deeper fear that the materialist forms of Darwinism, the kind devoid of skyhooks, undermine morality altogether, leaving only relativism – the kind of do-it-yourself attitude to morality the Archbishop of Canterbury was complaining about towards the end of the 1990s – or total moral scepticism.

Problems about whether there are such things as objective moral values, and if so how we can establish what they are, belong to the philosophical subject of *metaethics*. Normative ethics – the question of what standards we should try to live by – is the familiar part of ethics. But discussions of normative ethics inevitably start to raise second-order questions about what the normative discussion is *about*, and what standards of reasoning and argument it should apply; and these problems about what is going at the normative level are the metaethical ones. Metaethics asks questions such as whether there is such a thing as moral truth, and if so how we can discover it, and if not, what normative disagreements are disagreements about. And sometimes when people reject a particular set of normative standards, this is not because they are recommending instead another set of standards, but because they have reached the conclusion at the metaethical level that there is no such thing as moral truth.

Metaethics is another flourishing area of philosophy in its own right, with a huge literature, and the question of whether there are or could be such things as objective moral standards is a topic of intense philosophical debate quite irrespective of Darwinism. Large numbers of moral philosophers – perhaps the majority at the moment – are sceptical about the possibility. If these sceptics are right, and there are deep, theoretical objections to the idea that there is anything objective to be known about normative ethics – comparable to the deep problems about our familiar ideas about free will and responsibility – then obviously it will follow that which version of Darwinism is true will make no difference to the issue. If objective moral standards are impossible in all possible worlds, then the question of which kind of world we are actually in – the issue that divides the different degrees of Darwinism – will not affect the answer. So the question of whether any particular degree of Darwinism precludes moral objectivity arises only if moral objectivity is possible in principle.

It is hopeless to try to solve such a large question here, though I hope the discussion will clarify several metaethical questions and suggest some ideas about how to regard them. However, we need not set about the question in that way. We can start instead with the situation of someone who presumes that there is such a thing as moral truth – that some things *really are* right and wrong, and some states of affairs morally preferable to others – and consider the specific question of whether acceptance of some particular level of Darwinism would show that this belief should be abandoned. This is obviously a much narrower question than that of whether there are any reasons at all – Darwinian or otherwise – for abandoning a belief in moral truth and the possibility of moral progress.

From this point of view, it seems clear that the first boundary to investigate, on the band of deepening Darwinism, is the one that separates the materialist from the non-materialist varieties. By far the most familiar basis for the idea that materialist Darwinism precludes objective moral standards is the belief that such standards cannot exist without God. That is the obvious place to start the investigation.

Exercise 8.1

1   The following are all explicit or implied complaints. Say whether the critic in each case is complaining about:

(a)   people's failing to act according to a particular set of moral standards;
(b)   their failing to act according to *any* moral standards;
(c)   their recommending or accepting the wrong moral standards;
(d)   their believing there are no such things as objective moral standards.

Each may be about more than one, or the answer may be unclear.

(i)   Nobody cares about moral standards any more; when we were young, if you got married you stayed married. Now people think it's all right to separate by mutual consent.

(ii)   Young people nowadays have no conscience at all.

(iii)   It's wicked to stone adulteresses, even if some religions say you should.

(iv)   You shouldn't eat animals.

(v)   When she lost her religion she decided it didn't matter what she did.

(vi)   He just does whatever he feels like.

(vii)   People aren't honest any more; when people found money in the street, they used to take it to the police station.

(viii)   She thinks it's all right to tell lies if it doesn't hurt anyone, but really lying is always wrong.

(ix)   Moral behaviour is only what your society puts pressure on you to do; if there were no society nothing would be right or wrong.

(x)   You would be wicked to devastate your desert island, even if you were about to die and there were no animals.

(xi)   She always does what is to her own advantage, even though she puts on a good show of consideration for others.

2   Say whether the following questions come within the scope of normative ethics or metaethics.

(i)   If you can prevent massive suffering by punishing an innocent person, is it still wrong?

(ii)   Is it inconsistent to hold that all life is sacred and that it's all right to eat meat?

(iii)   Is moral debate any more than asserting your own intuitive preferences?

(iv)   Would it matter if we blew up a planet with no sentient life on it?

(v)   If powerful people say you should respect the law, does that make it true?

(vi)   If religious tolerance by a government leads to fighting between religious groups, does that make it wrong?

3   On an analogy with this, say whether the following questions are scientific, or about epistemology and philosophy of science. (The distinction is roughly between questions about what is supported by the scientific evidence, and questions about what *counts* as scientific evidence.)[17]

(i)   Is there good evidence that BSE can be transmitted from animals to humans?

(ii)   Is there such a thing as scientific truth, or is it just a matter of what is socially accepted at any time?

(iii)   If everyone in the world thinks something is true, could it still be false?

(iv)   Is it irrational to believe in UFOs?

(v)   What is the evidence that genes are the fundamental replicators?

(Answers on pp. 283–4)

God as necessary for objectivity

Start as usual by clarifying where we are on the scope diagram (see p. 54), and exactly what question we are asking. We are considering a challenge from the conservative direction to the radical direction, this time from non-materialists to materialists. The people making this challenge hold the traditional view that if the materialist view is true, objective moral standards cannot exist. Our question, then, is about the truth of a conditional along these lines:

> If everything, including all life and consciousness, derives entirely from the workings of mindless physical laws and the forces of natural selection (i.e. without God or any other design or intention), there can be no objective moral standards.

This translates into simplified outline argument form as:

> Everything derives from the workings of mindless physical laws.
> ———————
> Therefore there are no objective moral standards.

As always, there is no reason to think that people who accept a conditional will all offer the same reasons for accepting it, and another possibility will be considered later. But if we complete it in the most familiar way – with the idea that presumably underlay the Archbishop's worries – the argument will go like this:

> Everything derives from the workings of mindless physical laws [i.e. without God].
> *Without God there can be no objective moral standards.*
> ———————
> Therefore there are no objective moral standards.

That seems valid; so we come directly to what is obviously the essence of the matter: the question of whether the added premise is true.

The first thing to do is make sure this claim is distinguished from other ideas about God and moral standards. One is that you need God and the threat of Hell to give people enough incentive to take any notice of morality. Perhaps that is true; many atheist philosophers have argued that a popular belief in God is of considerable moral value. However, since that is obviously not what is meant by this claim, it can be disregarded here.

More likely to cause confusion is the idea that you need God to tell you what the objective moral truth is. That will be considered later in the chapter. Here, however, the claim is just that without God it is impossible for there to *be* objective moral standards. Is that true?

Start by focusing the question more clearly. We are considering the question from the point of view of someone who currently takes a Mind First view of things, and also believes in the existence of objective moral truth. So the specific question to ask is whether if the Mind First view were to be abandoned for materialism as a result of Darwinian (or indeed any other) arguments, the belief in objective moral truth would go too. Someone asking this question, therefore, needs to sort out the relationship between God and morality, to see whether the loss of one would entail the loss of the other.

It often seems to be taken for granted by religious believers that this must be true; but in fact controversy about the matter has a long philosophical history, and is the subject of a very old debate within theology. The problem is essentially about whether something is good *because God wills* whatever it is, or whether God wills it *because it is good*. A similar question was raised by Plato in his *Euthyphro*, and it is therefore often called the Euthyphro question. It was continued by the scholastic philosophers in the Middle Ages, and has kept reappearing since. The answer to this question is obviously crucial in this context, because it is only if you take the first of these views – that the good is good *because God wills it* – that the good depends on God.

To work out your own view about the matter, and to get some sense of what is at issue, consider the following series of questions. They are, of course, primarily addressed to religious believers, but if you do not believe in God you might consider how you think you would answer them if you were a believer, or how you think they would be answered by someone you know who is.

Start by considering what your immediate response is to the Euthyphro question. If you say (or were to say) 'God is good', do you (or would you) take it to mean that because of the nature of God, he wills what is good (so that, for instance, we should be grateful that God wills what is good, because a supreme being of different character might have willed what was bad)? That is, in effect, what Plato argued for in *Euthyphro*, and has been the position held by many Catholic philosophers. Or do you think its meaning is the other way round, and that what is good is, by definition, what God happens to will – so that whatever God willed would be good? This second view is often known as the *Divine Command theory* of ethics, or *voluntarism*, and has been held by various philosophers and theologians, including Descartes, Calvin and Luther.

Now consider a second question. If you say 'God is good', do you take yourself to be saying something *about the nature of God*? How does your answer to this question compare with your answer to the first?

If you answered the Euthyphro question with the Divine Command view, saying that the good was good in virtue of being willed by God, you are saying nothing about the nature of God in saying that God is good. You have made the goodness of God a matter of definition, because whatever God did would be good. 'God is good' means something like 'God wills what God wills'. This means you have not made any substantive claim about the nature of God.

If, conversely, the claim that God is good is to be understood as a claim about the nature of God, you must answer the Euthyphro question by saying that God wills what is good because it is good. In other words, you must have an understanding of 'good' that is different from 'what God wills': a conception of good that is independent of God.

The point of this thought experiment is not to show, directly, how the Euthyphro question should be answered, but to clarify the relationship between different ideas. It may not be obvious, until you consider questions as direct as these, that if you accept the Divine Command view you can no longer meaningfully claim that God is good, and recognizing the conflict is the first step towards reaching a coherent overall view. If you did find a conflict, you need to decide – at least provisionally – which idea you are going to abandon for the other. Then test your answer further by going on to the next question.

Suppose somebody produced compelling evidence that God had said there was nothing wrong with torturing innocent people at random for fun, and that it was an ideal way to spend the Sabbath. (Perhaps impressive new research showed that part of the scriptures had been wrongly translated, and this was its real meaning.) How would you respond? What are the implications of your answer to this for your answer to the Euthyphro question?

There seem to be three possible responses here. You could say 'I hadn't realized that was good; I shall go off and do it immediately'; or you could decide that the evidence was obviously worthless, since God was good and therefore could not possibly will such a thing; or you could conclude that God was not, after all, good.

If your response is the first, you are accepting that whatever God wills must be good because God wills it. For consistency, that is the answer you should have given to the Euthyphro question. If, on the other hand, you have given either of the other answers, you should have answered the Euthyphro question by saying that that the good was something independent of God's will, which God happened to will or not to will depending on whether God really was good. The first answer uses a belief in the goodness of God to deny the new evidence, the second uses the new evidence to deny the goodness of God, but both take the good to be something whose nature does not depend on the will of God.

Once again, if your answers were inconsistent, decide which direction you think you should take, and consider one final question, about the traditional Problem of Evil. The question of why there is so much suffering in the world if God is both good and omnipotent has long been recognized as a problem for Christianity, and more widely for believers in the goodness of God. Do you think that this is a question someone who believes in a good, omnipotent God needs to answer (perhaps by arguing that we do not fully understand the divine plan), or that there is no problem?

If you think that an answer is needed – that there is at least a *prima facie* problem here – it shows that you do not accept the Divine Command theory. If whatever God willed must be good, the problem would not arise. We could just say 'War is a good thing after all', or 'Since God thinks it's a good idea to let children die of painful diseases, let's see if we can do some genetic engineering to arrange more of it.' The problem of evil arises only if you reject the Divine Command theory, and have a conception of goodness that is independent of the will of God. Without an independent conception of the good, you could not be puzzled about how to reconcile the state of the world with the goodness of God.

Now, in the light of this extended thought experiment, consider again the added premise of the original argument:

> Everything derives from the workings of mindless physical laws.
> *Without God there can be no objective moral standards.*
>
> ―――――――――
>
> Therefore there are no objective moral standards.

If you have concluded that what God wills is, by definition, good, you will think the premise is true, and therefore that the inference is sound. If, on the other hand, you have concluded that the good is independent of God, you must think the inference unsound because its premise is false.

In principle, your overall conclusion about the Euthyphro question could have gone either way. The purpose of most thought experiments like this is to check ideas for consistency, and you could in principle make them consistent in either direction. So what we need to say here is that whether a religious believer should see Darwinian materialism as a threat to the existence of moral truth depends on what that person's view is about the Euthyphro question.

In fact most people – including most theologians – who believe in a good God turn out, when they consider the matter in enough detail, not to think that what is good is good because God wills it; but rather that God wills it because it is good. If so they regard the standard of good as independent of God, and should regard the materialist view of things as being no less compatible with objective moral standards than the non-materialist view.

It was, in fact, largely his deep and increasing understanding of the appalling extent of suffering in nature that gradually turned Darwin into an agnostic, or perhaps a deist (a believer in some power, but not a personal god). This shows that he thought goodness was not dependent on the will of God. If he had thought that the good was whatever God willed, his discoveries about the workings of nature could have led him to conclude that suffering was good after all.

The small minority who find they accept the Divine Command view will consistently see materialism as a threat to the objectivity of moral standards; but they must also recognize that materialist Darwinians are no more opposed to their beliefs than are fellow-believers who believe in the objectivity of the good.

Yet again, then, we have failed to find a reason for thinking the different degrees of Darwinism have different implications. The argument so far suggests that – for most people – which side of the materialist divide you are on need have no implications for whether or not you think there are such things as objective moral standards.

Exercise 8.2

On the assumption that you have rejected the Divine Command theory, has each of the following been demonstrated by the preceding arguments?

(Be careful. The point of this exercise is to clarify exactly, not approximately, what has been shown in this section. The conflation of similar but not identical claims is what leads to fallacies of equivocation.)

(i)   There are such things as objective moral truths.
(ii)   Whether God exists or not, there are such things as objective moral truths.
(iii)   The existence of objective moral truth does not depend on the existence of God.
(iv)   The question of whether there is such a thing as objective moral truth does not turn on whether Darwinian materialism is true or not.
(v)   No reason has yet been found for thinking that the existence of objective moral truth depends on which version of Darwinism you accept.
(vi)   The non-existence of God would not prove the non-existence of objective moral truth.
(vii)   If Darwinian materialism rules out the existence of objective moral truth, it must be for some other reason than its atheism.
(viii) The non-existence of God is not sufficient for the non-existence of moral truth.
(ix)   The truth of materialism is sufficient for the non-existence of moral truth.
(x)   The truth of materialism is not sufficient for the non-existence of moral truth.

(Answers on p. 284)

Evolution as sufficient for non-objectivity

Of course, the failure of this argument linking materialism to the non-existence of objective moral standards does not mean there is no such link. Other arguments might be tried, and might fare better. The one we have just been considering claims that God is a *necessary* condition of objective moral standards; but there are also signs in the wind of a reciprocal belief from the other direction: that a gene-machine account of our evolutionary origins is a *sufficient* condition of there being *no* objective moral standards.

This belief seems to be held mainly by gene-machinists who are in the thick of game-theoretical analyses of the origins of our moral impulses, though their opponents on the other side of the materialism divide may well agree with them. The general idea seems to be that since we are now in (or close to) a position of being able to explain the evolutionary origins of all our moral impulses, and account for them all in terms of the survival of genes or societies, we now know that there is no more to ethics than this. Ethical standards come from the strategies of genes, not from a perception of some external standard of truth. The only legitimate kind of enquiry into ethics, therefore, is into the question of exactly how we come by the ideas we have, and what their adaptive significance is. There is no separate question of what is *really* right or wrong. Ethics as a substantive subject in its own right is simply replaced by evolutionary and anthropological enquiry into its origins.

Now the trouble with this is that although the idea is undoubtedly around, it is very difficult to see what the arguments are supposed to be, or even, in any detail, what exactly the claims are. This makes them difficult to discuss. However, the advantage of a method-centred approach to these problems is that it is possible to anticipate claims of this kind in outline, so if you do encounter anyone who seems to have some such idea, it is clear how to set about clarifying and assessing it.

First, as usual, the conditional needs to be stated. This may not be easy in any particular case, but it is essential to get that matter clear before any discussion begins. There is no limit to the number of conditionals that might be asserted, but as an illustration suppose someone said, along the lines just mentioned:

> If there is an evolutionary explanation for all our moral intuitions and standards, questions of whether those intuitions and standards are correct does not arise.

That would give as an outline argument:

> There is an evolutionary explanation for all our moral intuitions and standards.
> ————
> Therefore questions of whether those intuitions and standards are correct does not arise.

How might an argument along those lines be completed? There is a logical gap – not to say chasm – between the existence of an explanation and the non-existence of particular kinds of question. Of course it would be the job of whoever was making the claim to show how it could be done, and thereby justify it. (This is an important point to remember, because sometimes people who make assertions imply that they should be presumed true until critics can prove them false.) It might at this stage turn out that no argument was forthcoming, and that the inference was just taken to be self-evident; but if so, this approach would immediately make it clear that this was happening. But perhaps something like this might be tried:

> There is an evolutionary explanation for all our moral intuitions and standards.
> *If a natural explanation can in principle be given for some belief,*

> *there can be no further question about whether it is correct or incor-*
> *rect.*
> _____
>
> Therefore questions of whether those intuitions and standards are
> correct does not arise.

And then the added premise can be assessed as usual. Is this one true?

The most obvious way to test it is to consider counterexamples; and a moment's consideration shows this one to be false. If the materialist view of the world is right there is, in principle, a natural explanation for everything, including all our beliefs, but we do not for a moment think that shows there is no question about whether what we believe is true. All our ideas about science and mathematics come into the category of beliefs that we presume have causal explanations, but that does not remove the question of truth. There is in principle a causal explanation of why one person gets an arithmetical answer right and another gets it wrong, but that does not mean there is no such thing as a right answer. In fact one of the questions we can, and do, ask about evolution is why some of our intuitions are more reliable guides to truth than others. (An interesting illustration of this will come at the end of this chapter.)

When this point is put to people who have vague ideas along these lines, they say that of course that is obvious, but ethics is different. We might, then, try narrowing the added premise to make it apply only to ethics:

> There is an evolutionary explanation for all our moral intuitions and
> standards.
> *If a causal explanation can be given for some moral belief, there can*
> *be no further question about whether it is correct or incorrect.*
> _____
>
> Therefore questions of whether those intuitions and standards are
> themselves correct or incorrect cannot arise.

But if we are to accept this narrower version of the added premise, even though the wider one is not true, we need a justification – and it is not in the least clear what it might be. It is no good simply asserting that ethics is an exception because there are no objective moral truths, because that begs the question; our whole problem, here, is to see whether an evolutionary explanation would provide a reason for the conclusion that there could be no moral truth, so it can't be asserted in one of the premises.

As I say, it is difficult to discuss this further without more concrete examples, so the main conclusion to draw – apart from the fact that there so far seems no reason whatever to accept the conditional – is that if this method of analysis is available, it can be applied to any candidate that does appear. But perhaps it is worth adding a couple of speculations about the source of the idea that evolutionary materialism precludes the possibility of moral truth, and of philosophical – as opposed to scientific – enquiry into ethics.

One possibility is a misunderstanding of the nature of philosophy: the idea that it is somehow a study of things ethereal and essentially connected with skyhooks, so that if the skyhooks go, so does the subject that studies them. If so, this is a simple misconception. Philosophy is not a subject that deals with a particular kind of entity, whose subject matter would vanish if those entities turned out not to exist. It is concerned with non-empirical questions that arise in all subjects of any depth.

Another possibility, which I suspect gives the real answer, would come from mistakes about reductionism of the kind discussed at the end of the last chapter. Maybe it is assumed that if we have shown that our moral ideas are ultimately the survival strategies of genes, we are entitled to conclude that they are *only* the survival strategies of selfish genes. If so, it should now be clear why that is a serious mistake.

So far, then, there still seem to be no good reasons for thinking that materialist Darwinism, even in its most radical gene-machine form, precludes the existence of moral truth.

Relativism: a detour

Until other candidate defences appear of the idea that materialist Darwinism undercuts morality altogether, there is little more to say about that particular topic. However, in spite of that, it still seems worth discussing a matter that is generally taken to be closely connected with it. Non-objectivity is often taken to imply in its turn moral relativism. This is an idea that has no single clear formulation (for reasons that will become clear), but it appears all the time in well-known claims to the effect that values and standards are nothing more than social constructions, and that we should respect everybody's values equally rather than trying to impose our own on other people.

Since relativism of this kind is usually drawn from the idea that there are no objective moral standards and values, it is not directly connected with Darwinian controversies at all. So far there seems no reason to think that materialist Darwinism entails moral non-objectivity; and, conversely, many philosophers who deny the existence of objective moral values do so for reasons unconnected with materialism. That is why I describe this section on relativism as a detour. Nevertheless, the belief that materialism and relativism are connected seems to have strong currency on both sides of the materialist divide. It is widely established as popular wisdom among the secular, as well as causing corresponding anxiety among archbishops about the prevalence of do-it-yourself morality. So the detour seems important on practical grounds, even though it is off the official subject. It is also of general importance in ethics, and a discussion of it should help in the sorting out of metaethical views in general. And, furthermore, it will allow another illustration of the ways in which arguments can be sent awry by unnoticed shifts of level in mid-flight.

Consider, then, the truth of this conditional:

> If there are no objective moral standards, we should respect all moral standards equally, and allow everyone to follow their own.

The consequent here expresses only one possible formulation of relativist ideas; it is not meant to be definitive. As always, if you think there are better formulations you can discuss those afterwards or instead, but this version will raise the issues that are central to all the variations.

This translates into argument form as:

> There are no objective moral standards.
> _____
> Therefore we should respect all moral standards equally, and allow everyone to follow their own.

This argument is obviously not valid as it stands: there is a conspicuous logical gap between the claim of the premise that there are no objective moral standards, and the conclusion about what we should do. So it is natural (given what we have done so far) to try to fill this gap, perhaps along these lines:

> There are no objective moral standards.
> *Without objective standards there can be no basis for moral judgements.*
> _____
> Therefore we should respect all moral standards equally, and allow everyone to follow their own.

In fact, however, this is not the right thing to do in this case. There are deeper waters here.

The problem is that the argument is not just an incomplete one that can be made valid by the addition of more premises, as have been most of the others discussed so far. If you look back to the end of Chapter 4 (pp. 93ff.), where the analysis of conditionals was introduced, you will see that the first two conditionals mentioned were *necessarily* true or false, because the antecedents on their own either entailed or contradicted the consequents. In the first case, no inserted premise was needed because the argument from premise to conclusion was sound without it. In the second, where the antecedent contradicted the consequent, no possible inserted premise could make the argument valid. And the second of these – the case of contradiction between antecedent and consequent – is more or less the situation here.

First, consider the conclusion, which asserts that we should respect all standards equally. On any normal understanding of a statement like that, to make it is to make a moral claim about what we should do. But what do you take yourself to be doing when you make a moral claim? Suppose, for instance, you say that it is totally wrong to torture for fun, and someone else says that there is nothing wrong with it. The two of you seem to be disagreeing, and you presumably think that your opponent is simply *wrong* (mistaken) to say that torture for fun is not wrong (morally wrong). But if you think the claim that torture is not (morally) wrong is itself wrong (mistaken), that seems to mean – on any normal interpretation – that you think there are such things as objective moral standards, and that your opponent is quite simply mistaken about what those standards are.

The same applies here. The conclusion seems to be asserting, quite positively, that people who do not respect other people's standards, and try to impose their own views on others, are doing something that they should not do. And if this is what the conclusion is supposed to mean, the problem with the argument is not just that the premise does not entail the conclusion, but that it actually *contradicts* it. You cannot derive a conclusion intended to express a moral truth from a premise stating that there are no such things as moral truths. The conditional 'If there are no objective moral standards we should respect everyone's views equally ... ' is necessarily false.

Now I did say that on any *normal* understanding of the conclusion you would be making a moral claim; so you might try to escape this problem, and keep the conclusion consistent with the premise, by giving a different (and decidedly non-normal) interpretation of the conclusion. You might, for instance, try claiming, as philosophers have done and still do, that in making a statement about what people should do you are not making an assertion you take to be *true* at all, but are simply expressing your feelings. You might insist that in saying 'You shouldn't torture for fun,' or 'You should respect everyone's views equally,' all you mean is that torture, or failing to respect views equally, makes you react in an emotionally negative way. This is the metaethical view known as *emotivism*, which is one version of the idea that there are no objective moral truths. And if you take that view of the conclusion you do indeed avoid the contradiction, by denying that the conclusion is an assertion at all.

This is pretty implausible as an account of what most people actually mean when they make moral claims, even if some philosophers claim that it is all they are entitled to mean. If you say 'It is wrong to torture for fun,' you are most unlikely to intend nothing more than a report of your own feelings. You mean people *really shouldn't* do this – even when they are alone on a desert island with only animals left. But anyway, even if you did insist that this was all you meant in claiming that something was wrong, it would not help to make the argument valid. The expression of an emotion cannot be the conclusion of an argument at all. Even with this interpretation you cannot infer relativism as a moral claim from a claim about the non-objectivity of moral standards.

However, even though the relativist conclusion cannot be derived from the non-objectivity claim, it might perhaps be defensible on other grounds. So even though it takes the problem still further from directly Darwinian matters, consider the relativist conclusion on its own:

> We should respect all moral standards equally, and allow everyone to follow their own.

The way to find out whether you can really endorse a moral value or principle that seems plausible is to work out its *implications*. You do a series of thought experiments, to find out how you would have to act in various situations if you accepted that principle, and then see whether you can accept those implications, or whether you regard them as *counterexamples* which show the principle to be unacceptable.

As a first step on this path, think of the matter in a fairly superficial and intuitive way. If the claim seems plausible, start by considering whether you really do think you should respect everybody's values, and allow them to act on them. Can you think of actual or possible cases of people with values you would not think you should respect? Can you think of situations where you would certainly try to impose your own views on other people, and try to prevent them from acting on theirs?

Nearly everyone will be able to think of indefinitely many such possibilities. One obvious candidate for intervention might be situations where people believed that women and children should be regarded as the possessions of men, for men to treat in any way they liked; others might be that it was right to kill adherents of other religions or members of other races, or that animals had no moral importance of any kind, or that physically and mentally handicapped people should be killed to avoid burdens on the rest of society. Most people find, when they think about the details, that their ideas about letting other people follow their own standards and values are of severely limited extent. If this is what you have found, it means you do not accept relativism – at least in this form. (I shall say more about this in a moment.)

In fact, however, counterexamples of this kind are rather misleading, because they hide the depth of the real problem about relativism. This real problem shows if you provisionally set aside the question of whether you *approve* of what the relativist principle would demand your doing, and see whether you can get to the earlier stage of even sorting out what its requirements would be.

Suppose, for instance, you are a relativist dictator, trying to make laws to deal with the passionate pro- and anti-abortionists under your jurisdiction. What laws and institutions will your relativist principles tell you to establish? The pro-abortionists must of course be given the freedom to follow their own principles and provide abortions for anyone who wants them. They may assure you that they agree with your approach, and of course have no objections to anti-abortionists' being allowed to follow their own principles as well. But in saying this (as, indeed, many real-life pro-abortionists do), they are misrepresenting the principles of the anti-abortionists. Anti-abortionists are not merely against abortion for themselves. They think abortion is murder, and their principles demand their doing all they can to prevent that murder – even, perhaps (depending on the details of those principles) if that means killing the abortionists. If you allow them to act on their principles, therefore, you will no longer be allowing the pro-abortionists to act on theirs. To do that, you will have to restrain or deter the anti-abortionists, but then you will be preventing them from acting on their principles.

There is no mystery about this. Any set of moral standards must include, as part of those standards, criteria for the appropriate treatment of other people – even if that appropriate treatment consists in completely ignoring what other people do. This means there are necessarily conflicts, when some people think they should do what other people think they should not be allowed to do. And, indeed, the *essence* of what it is for people to have different moral principles is disagreement: if there were no disagreement, there would be no difference. And since there is disagreement, it follows that not everyone *can* be given the freedom to follow their own principles. No matter how great your dictatorial powers, you can no more give everyone this freedom than you can give them two-horned unicorns.

There is also an even more fundamental problem, if that is possible. As a relativist, you are saying that everyone's principles should be equally respected, and everyone should be free to follow their own. Even if you have not yet noticed that you are not going to be able to put that into practice because it is incoherent, there is still the question of what you take yourself to be doing in trying to implement this principle. You are saying that certain things ought and ought not to be done: that people ought to respect others' views, and not try to prevent their acting on the basis of them. But *in doing that, you yourself* are not treating all views as equal, because you are saying your own takes precedence over the others. In making this claim about what should be done, you are doing what you say should not be done. This is what is known as *pragmatic self-refutation*. In the very act of making the claim about what it is right to do, you are presupposing its falsity.

It is no doubt obvious where all this is going. Relativism in its familiar formulations is incoherent. It specifies that no principle should be given precedence over others, but in doing so gives itself precedence; it says that you should not impose your principles on others, but in doing so attempts to impose itself on the holders of other views, and displace theirs. And as well as that, what it specifies you should do is itself incoherent.

This goes back to the point made in the discussion of ultimate responsibility in Chapter 6 (pp. 144ff.): that any word or set of words that has any meaning must exclude certain possibilities. A general principle about not imposing your moral views on other people is something that makes no sense – since if you have moral views at all about how to act, those views will necessarily demand your disagreeing with the moral judgements of people with different moral views, and often your actively opposing them. This is what it *is* to have a moral view. A moral view that ruled nothing out would not be a moral view at all. This is, of course, why it is difficult to find a plausible formulation of relativism. It is difficult to express something that is essentially incoherent in a way that sounds plausible.

Now this does not, of course, imply that all the intuitions that lead people to profess relativism are nonsense. The point of thought experiments in philosophy is essentially the same as of experiments in science, to test hypotheses and refine them in the light of what is discovered; and most people who think they are relativists are likely to retreat at this point, and say that their point is not that we should never impose our views on other people, but that other people should be left to their own preferences as long as these do no harm. That view is certainly potentially coherent and indeed plausible, but it is no longer relativism. That is the kind of view expressed by John Stuart Mill's well-known harm principle – that you may interfere with someone's freedom only in order to protect others from harm – which is the basis not of relativism, but of liberalism. All varieties and degrees of liberalism demand freedom of expression for different moral views, and also tolerance for personal and cultural preferences within definite moral limits; but that is very different from relativism because it is a positive moral principle, and as such positively opposed to others. Liberals do think that anti-liberals should be prevented from acting on their views; they would not be liberals if they did not. And most relativists find, when they settle down to working out a detailed theory of how they think people should act, that they are really some variety of liberal after all. If they think they are not, that is probably because they are not recognizing how wide the range of broadly liberal views can be.

The conclusion from the point of view of the overall enquiry, then, is that the materialist versions of Darwinism do not entail relativism. This is not just because there seems to be no necessary connection between Darwinism and non-objectivity, or between non-objectivity and relativism, but because relativism is incoherent and is therefore not allowed for, let alone entailed, by any view. The problem is like that of free will. No version of Darwinism, or anything else, can allow for your having the kind of ultimate responsibility that demands your making choices before you exist, and in the same way no version can allow for holding a moral view which claims that no moral view has any special status, and which anyway cannot specify what its adherents should and should not do.

Relativism is an essentially unstable and slippery position. Anyone who reaches that stage should really be a total moral sceptic, and deny that there is any real right or wrong, or good or evil, at all. The fact that people do not often do this, and try to go down the relativist path of hanging on to bits and pieces of objective ethics while denying their existence, is interesting in itself.

Relativism and shifts of level

Although that is the main point, it is worth emphasizing the possibility of confusion between liberalism and relativism, partly because it generates the potential for yet another of those shifts of argument level that sometimes cheat the unwary.

Consider this dialogue, for instance:

A: Female circumcision is just a cultural rite of passage, like bar mitzvahs and coming-out parties. We should respect other people's traditions, not try to suppress them and impose our own.
B: But it isn't just a cultural rite of passage. The others you mention are acceptable because they don't harm anyone. But female circumcision – which is a euphemism for genital mutilation – causes terrible pain, often for life, and carries a serious risk of infection and death. It also deprives women of sexual pleasure. It is inflicted on children without their consent. This is all totally wrong.

A: That's just cultural imperialism. You are trying to impose your own Western ideas of what matters, and how men and women should relate to each other, on other cultures. You may think pain and the deprivation of sexual pleasure are bad, but that's just your cultural preference. Other cultures think this is in their children's interests. You shouldn't impose your standards on others.

You can see what is wrong with this exchange (which is, incidentally, only a slight exaggeration of a real one I had some years ago) by considering what principle A is appealing to in each of the statements, and what *kind of disagreement* B has with A. In the first paragraph, A seems to be appealing to the liberal principle that you should, as far as possible, leave people to follow their own cultural preferences. You should not try to get rid of other cultures' practices just because you prefer your own. She (it was, surprisingly, a woman in my original case) implies that this principle makes female circumcision permissible.

B's disagreement, in the second paragraph, is not with the liberal principle; the impression given is that she agrees with it. The disagreement is with A's implied claim that female circumcision is allowed by that principle. The liberal principle draws the line at harm, and also at making one group subservient in this way to the interests of another. B's claim is that female circumcision does not, in fact, come into the category of things allowed by liberalism. So the dispute so far is not about what principle to accept, but about A's application of it to this particular case.

A's reply looks at first glance as though it is still appealing to the original principle of liberalism, and disputing B's claim that it does not apply to this case. This makes it look like a continuation of the same argument. However, it is not. A has in fact *switched principles*, and is now claiming that you should not impose *any* kind of view on other people – not just cultural preferences. That is not liberalism, but an incoherent relativism. Although trying to seem neutral, and above particular ethical views, A is in fact expressing the positive view that it is more important to go along with the cultural tradition than to prevent cruelty and the control of one group by another. But if B does not notice this shift, because she is a bit hazy about the difference between liberalism and relativism, she may be persuaded that her own liberal principles of toleration make it wrong, after all, to oppose female circumcision.

Notice, by the way, that in this analysis I have not committed myself to any positive moral claims at all. I have not claimed that liberalism is good or that female circumcision is bad. I have just been discussing the logic of the exchange, and that goes badly wrong quite irrespective of the merits of the case at issue. So even if you think there is nothing wrong with female circumcision you should have produced more or less the same analysis of this argument.

Since appeals to relativism can be used to oppose any moral claim, it is clear that relativism is a particularly virulent kind of universal acid – which is, as usual, used selectively. People who say you should not impose your views on other people are always talking about *your* views, and resisting the imposition of those views on other people of whom they approve. They are at the same time, of course, trying hard to impose some element of their own incoherent views on you.

It is important to look out for this kind of move; it is a significant disrupter of serious moral enquiry.

Exercise 8.3

1   Which of the following recommendations are in line with liberal principles, and which appeal to a self-defeating relativism?

    (i)   We should allow everyone to express their opinions, and not try to suppress any.

    (ii)   We should not try to impose our tastes on people of other cultures.

    (iii) It is wrong to judge other people by your values.

    (iv) All opinions are equally valuable.

    (v)   Everyone should have a right to have their views heard.

    (vi) Everyone has the right to have their views acted on.

2   For each of the following moral claims, what principle or standard is apparently being appealed to? Suggest two different reasons a critic might give for disagreeing with the claim, one disputing the principle being appealed to, and the other disputing the application of the principle to the matter in hand.

> Example:
>
> We should ban the killing of whales and dolphins, because they are as intelligent as we are.
>
> *Apparent principle:*
>
> Creatures (or species) above a certain level of intelligence should not be killed (or have a right to life).
>
> *Possible disagreements*
>
> *with the principle*:
>
> The right to life shouldn't be based on intelligence, it should be based on possession of a soul;
>
> *with the application:*
>
> They aren't anything like as intelligent as we are.

It does not matter for the purposes of this exercise whether the objections are true or even plausible; the purpose is only to distinguish the two types.

(i)   Abortion is murder, so it's right to try to kill abortionists.
(ii) The police were right to ban the demonstration. Freedom of speech shouldn't extend to the stirring up of racial hatred.
(iii) Animals haven't got rights, so it doesn't matter about killing them.

(Answers on p. 285)

Secular moral enquiry

If these arguments have been right, neither moral objectivity nor relativism has any special connection with any of the degrees of Darwinism. Relativism is incoherent, so it cannot be implied by any of them, and although the question of moral objectivity is much argued about by philosophers, the debate is largely independent of Darwinian views about the kind of thing we are.

However, there is one more question about moral objectivity that must be discussed, and which may seem to turn on the question of whether materialism is true. Even if God is not needed to *set* objective moral standards, it may be argued that God is needed to make clear *what they are*.

A good deal of what underlies the fear that materialism eliminates morality is the idea that it undermines particular sets of moral standards – usually the ones traditionally associated with religion – and leaves us without any way of finding an adequate substitute. Even if there are objective moral truths, and individuals are engaged not so much in do-it-yourself morality as find-it-yourself morality, the results are just as chaotic because people inevitably disagree about what has been found. An omniscient God, on the other hand, knows what the truth is.

Finally, then, consider the question of whether materialist ideas of human nature leave us unable to *discover* the truth about ethics, to whatever extent objective truth exists, while Mind First positions have no such problem. That leaves us still on the borderline between materialism and non-materialism on the scope diagram; and the suggestion now is that it is possible for us to discover moral truth if we stay on the conservative side of that boundary, but not possible if we are forced into materialism. So as usual there is a double question: whether the materialist views cannot solve the problem, and whether the Mind First views can. So there are potentially two conditionals to consider, along these lines:

If God exists, we can reliably discover moral truth.
If God does not exist, we cannot discover moral truth.

I have in general been starting with the implications of the deeper positions, and then looking at the shallower ones only if the deeper ones have turned out to have the alarming implications alleged. But there is no particular reason for doing it that way round. This time it is probably more convenient to start with the shallower versions, and the claim that if God exists we can discover moral truth.

That conditional gives the outline argument:

God exists.
_____

Therefore we can reliably discover moral truth.

The most obvious way to start the infilling seems to be:

God exists.
God (being omniscient) knows the truth about objective moral standards.
_____

Therefore we can reliably discover moral truth.

But this is not yet complete. There is a gap between God's knowing about moral truth and our knowing about it. So we need another premise, about the reliable transmission of moral truth from God to us. Perhaps:

God exists.
God knows the truth about objective moral standards.
God has reliable ways of conveying the truth to us.
_____

Therefore we can reliably discover moral truth.

Now assess the argument for soundness. Are the added premises true?

The second premise may perhaps be open to theological controversy; but for the purposes of this discussion we can assume its truth as a corollary of the first premise. This means that the third premise is the crucial one.

People who claim to have access to the will of God of course believe there are reliable means of transmission: scripture, authorized intermediaries, conscience, and direct revelation of various sorts. But since there are so many different views about what has been conveyed in these ways, all of whose proponents claim that their information has been reliably transmitted by God, the objective view of this matter must be that there is nothing *reliable* here at all. Even if there is an accurate transmission of truth from God to chosen recipients, that does not constitute reliable knowledge from our point of view unless we have reliable knowledge both that this has happened and of who is in possession of the ungarbled version. For reliable knowledge of moral truth we would have to start with reliable knowledge of which account of God to go for, and then find reliable ways to distinguish the true word of God from spurious interpretations, and the promptings of true conscience from the whisperings of the Devil. There is obviously nothing reliable about any of this. Even if the True God is accurately transmitting knowledge of good and evil to the True Believers, that is of no practical help to anyone who has no idea of how to distinguish the true believers from the millions who are deluded but just as confident.

The conclusion, then, seems to be that whatever problems there may be about discovering moral truths (if they exist) in a completely material world, those problems also exist in a world with God. The conditional

> If God exists we can reliably discover moral truth.

seems not to be true.

Still, it might be claimed that even though the existence of God would not guarantee the *reliable* discovery of moral truth, it would at least hold out the possibility of moral knowledge because God is in a position to know what is true. If materialism is true, on the other hand, and our origins are entirely Darwinian and skyhookless, there is no way in which moral truth can be found at all. So now consider the conditional:

> If the origins of life and consciousness are entirely Darwinian and material, it is impossible to discover, or make reliable progress towards, moral truth.

That gives as an outline argument:

> Our origins are entirely Darwinian and material.
> _____
> Therefore it is impossible for us to discover, or make reliable progress towards, moral truth.

How might that most plausibly be completed? The problem for materialist Darwinism seems to be that if our moral sensitivities and concerns exist only because they happen to have been effective survival devices, and our conscience is just something devised by the selfish genes to make us well-functioning reciprocal altruists, there seems not the slightest justification for regarding any of them as pointing towards objective truth. They exist simply because they were good gene transmitters, not because they are good truth discoverers. Such a pedigree suggests they are not to be trusted at all.

That suggests as the next step:

> Our origins are entirely Darwinian and material.
> *Our moral standards and intuitions, and our consciences, evolved merely because they were effective survival devices.*
> *Survival devices are not reliable indicators of truth.*
> _____
> Therefore it is impossible for us to discover, or make reliable progress towards, moral truth.

But this is still incomplete. You would need to claim that these were the *only* characteristics that could be involved in any enquiry into moral truth: that nothing else could be relevant to the search. That suggests another premise along these lines:

Our origins are entirely Darwinian and material.
Our moral standards and intuitions, and our consciences, evolved because they were effective survival devices.
Survival devices are not reliable indicators of truth.
We have no other characteristics that can help in the discovery of moral truth.

Therefore it is impossible for us to discover, or make reliable progress towards, moral truth.

I am not sure that this is the best way of expressing an argument along these lines, but it will be enough for the main points that need to be made here.

Consider now the three added premises. Are they true?

The second premise, the claim that our consciences evolved because they were effective survival devices, would be accepted by virtually all materialist Darwinians, so that can probably be allowed to pass as a corollary of Premise 1.

The third premise is more problematic. The fact that something evolved for one purpose does not for a moment suggest that it cannot be turned to others later. Evolution is not forward-looking, and characteristics that survived for one reason may continue to survive for quite different reasons, and change in the process. Most of evolution involves the adaptation of old structures to new purposes, so it is not out of the question that we might have capacities that allowed the direct perception of moral truth. Still, there is the same problem as with God as a transmitter of moral truth. We would need to have some other way of recognizing which perceptions really did reflect the truth, before we could judge them to be reliable.

The fourth premise, however, seems obviously false. We certainly have other capabilities. In particular, we have reason.

Here we reach wide-open territory: ground on which philosophical and scientific research have only recently embarked. Not much can be said, yet, about the details of how such research will go, or what it can uncover. But we have very good reason to think that we can make real progress towards truth of various kinds, whatever inadequacies evolution may have saddled us with.

Let me conclude this section with an illustration that is now well known among Darwinian psychologists, and which many see as representative of important new ways of investigating human nature. It is interesting in itself, but it also throws light on the matter of transcending our origins in the pursuit of truth, even though it is not itself about ethics. This is Dennett's account.

How logical are we human beings? In some regards very logical, it seems, and in others embarrassingly weak. In 1969, the psychologist Peter Wason devised a simple test that bright people – college students, for instance – do rather badly on. You may try it yourself. Here are four cards, some letter-side-up, and some number-side-up. Each card has a numeral on one side and a letter on the other:

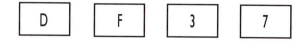

| D | F | 3 | 7 |

Your task is to see whether in this case the following rule has any exceptions: If a card has a 'D' on one side, it has a '3' on the other side. Now, which cards do you need to turn over in order to discover if this is true? Sad to say, fewer than half of students in most such experiments get the right answer. Did you? The correct answer is much more obvious if we shift the content (but not the structure) of the problem very slightly. You are the bouncer in a bar, and your job depends on not letting any underage (under twenty-one) customers drink beer. The cards have information about age on one side, and what the patron is drinking on the other. Which cards do you need to turn over?

| drinking beer | drinking Coke | 25 years old | 16 years old |

The first and the last, obviously, the same as in the first problem. Why is one setting so much easier than the other? Perhaps, you may think, it is the abstractness of the first, the concreteness of the second, or the familiarity of the second, or the fact that the second involves a conventional rule, not a regularity of nature. Literally hundreds of Wason card-sorting tests have been administered to subjects, in hundreds of variations, testing these and other hypotheses. The performance of subjects on the tests varies widely, depending on the details of the particular test and its circumstances, but a survey of the results leaves no doubt at all that there are settings that are hard for almost all groups of subjects, and others that are easy for the same subjects. But a riddle remained … what exactly was it about the hard cases that made them hard – or (a better question) what was it about the easy cases that made them easy? Cosmides and Tooby … came up with an evolutionary hypothesis, and it is hard to imagine this particular idea occurring to anyone who wasn't acutely aware of the possibilities of Darwinian thinking: the easy cases are all cases that are readily interpreted as tasks of patrolling a social contract, or, in other words, cheater detection.

… Framing the hypothesis is not yet proving it, of course, but one of the important virtues of their hypothesis is that it is eminently testable, and has so far stood up very well to a wide variety of attempts to refute it. Suppose it is true; would it show that we can reason only about the things Mother Nature wired us to reason about? Obviously not; it just shows why it is easier (more 'natural') for us to reason about some topics than others. We have devised cultural artefacts (systems of formal logic, statistics, decision theory, and so forth, taught in college courses) that expand our reasoning powers many fold. Even the experts often neglect these specialized techniques, however, and fall back on good old seat-of-the-pants reasoning, sometimes with embarrassing results, as the Wason test shows. Independently of any Darwinian hypotheses, we know that, except when people are particularly self-conscious about using these heavy-duty reasoning techniques, they tend to fall into cognitive illusions. Why are we susceptible to these illusions? The evolutionary psychologist says: For the same reason we are susceptible to optical illusions and other sensory illusions – we're built that way. Mother Nature designed us to solve a certain set of problems posed by the environments in which we evolved, and whenever a cut-rate solution emerged – a bargain that would solve the most pressing problems pretty well, even if it lacked generality – it tended to get installed.

Cosmides and Tooby call these modules 'Darwinian algorithms' … We obviously don't get by with just one such reasoning mechanism. Cosmides and Tooby have been gathering evidence for other special-purpose algorithms, useful in thinking about threats and other social exchanges, and other ubiquitous problem-types: hazards, rigid objects, and contagion. Instead of having a single, central general-purpose reasoning machine, we have a collection of gadgets, all pretty good (or at least pretty good in the environments in which they evolved), and readily exaptable [sic] for new purposes today. Our minds are like Swiss-army knives, Cosmides says. Every now and then, we discover curious gaps in our competence, strange lapses that give us clues about the particular history of R and D that explains the machinery that underlies the glittering facade of culture. This is surely the right way for psychologists to reverse-engineer the human mind, always watching out for QWERTY phenomena.

(Dennett (1995), pp. 488–90)

'QWERTY phenomena', it is probably obvious, refers to the standard typewriter keyboard. Keyboards were originally designed to minimize the chances of adjacent typewriter keys' coming up at the same time and jamming. Nobody would design a keyboard that way now: the layout is extremely inefficient, and typing would be much faster if we rearranged the keys. But this is difficult to do. We can see what would be better, but there is no easy way of getting from here to there; and the consequence is that our modern keyboards are hampered by a fossil of their design history. If we have such difficulty in escaping our own cultural fossils even when we can see clearly what we are trying to get to, a fully Darwinian view of evolution would predict far less good design in nature. In Darwinian nature there is no purpose, and no thinking through ways round obstacles. As Dennett says (somewhat obliquely) in the passage, it is such failures of ideal design that for some time provided the strongest evidence of the fact and the course of evolution, and they are now seen by evolutionary psychologists as offering clues to our evolutionary history.

This is all very interesting, and I shall have more to say about design failures in the next chapter; but the main point to be brought out now is the fact that we can *recognize* such design failures at all. Why do we think of the failures as failures? How do we know that there are some contexts in which our intuitions get the answers right, and others in which they lead us astray? Why do we not just believe all of them? The fact that we do make such judgements shows that we have criteria for right and wrong answers that go beyond our intuitions: the 'systems of formal logic, statistics, decision theory, and so forth' mentioned by

Dennett. It is because we have these *objective* criteria that we can see that our ability to get the calculations right may depend on circumstances. We know that there are all kinds of context in which our intuitive reasoning leads us badly astray; but (whatever the philosophical problems in explaining how) there is no doubt that we do manage to reach objective truth in mathematics, and also in science, or we would not know how badly we were being led astray by what Dennett calls our seat-of-the-pants reasoning in the first place.

Questions about the reliability of intuitive reasoning are being actively investigated in all kinds of areas. There are already, for instance, parts of medicine in which computers are much better at diagnosis than individual doctors exercising their clinical judgement. We are presumably only on the threshold of a major revolution of this kind, which will involve research in innumerable areas. But all that is needed for the purpose of this enquiry is the simple fact that we can in many contexts discover that our intuitions are wrong; and that opens up at least the possibility, if there are such things as objective moral truths, of our transcending our evolutionary starting point in this area too. The unreliability of intuitions cannot be the end of the matter, for the simple reason that we know about that unreliability.

The ways in which we can discover our beliefs to be unreliable have already been illustrated several times in this book. The arguments about the problems of ultimate responsibility, altruism, scientific certainty, shifts of level in mid-argument and many others have all depended, not on comparing our ideas with the standards given by some outside authority, but on discovering conflicts within our own beliefs and intuitions. Finding conflict among intuitions is a clear way of discovering that something is wrong somewhere. If your intuitions tell you that a principle should be followed invariably, but also that some of its implications are quite unacceptable, you know that at least some of your intuitions have to be rejected, even if you do not yet know which.

My own view is that this points the way to the possibility of genuine moral enquiry and discovery. We have to start with our intuitions and our evolutionarily-produced sensitivities and consciences, just as we have to start with what we are born with in all other areas of enquiry. But we are capable of recognizing when these lead to anomalies and contradictions in ethics, just as we are capable of recognizing how unreliable our intuitions often are in science and mathematics, and that alone is enough to allow the possibility of moral progress.

Furthermore, it seems to me that there are also *positive* ways in which, in principle, evolutionary psychology might advance the process of moral reasoning. When we are engaged in moral enquiry we frequently find that our intuitions conflict with each other, and when that happens we cannot keep them all. Traditionally, strong feelings have often been regarded as guides to truth, so when we run into conflicts of intuition we tend to feel we should hold on to the strongest intuition, even if rational consideration would lead to its rejection. But if we can find an evolutionary explanation for our having such a feeling, that may remove the reason for thinking that its intuitive force is a reason for regarding it as a guide to truth.

Here, to conclude, is an illustration of one possibility along these lines. This is speculative, and intended only as an indication of how moral reasoning of this kind might work, but my own suspicion is that this is broadly right.

Consider again the arguments about freedom, responsibility and punishment that appeared at the end of Chapter 6. Many people accept that the arguments about free will and ultimate responsibility really do show that no one can ultimately deserve punishment. People often deserve it in what might be called the *ordinary* sense (which corresponds to the ordinary sense of responsibility), of having done whatever it is they are accused of; but if people cannot be *ultimately* responsible for what they do, it seems impossible for it to be inherently appropriate that they should suffer for it. If so, punishment cannot be justified on the retributivist grounds that it is ultimately deserved, but only on the consequentialist grounds that it is necessary for deterring anti-social behaviour. Punishment may be instrumentally justified, but it is not intrinsically justified.

However, although many people are convinced by this line of argument, they still find themselves with an extremely strong intuition – in particular cases – that it is intrinsically, not just instrumentally, appropriate that the guilty should suffer. There is a conflict in their moral views, but it is not clear which of the incompatible elements to reject for the other. However, if we understand that there are good *evolutionary* reasons for our wanting people to suffer when they have done direct or indirect harm to us, then we can account for our strong feelings about the appropriateness of retribution without presuming that they are a guide to moral truth. We discover the conflict in our intuitions by reasoning; the information from evolutionary psychology may show the direction in which to resolve it. We may be able to recognize our retributivist feelings as a deep and important aspect of our character – and take them seriously to that extent – without endorsing them as a guide to truth, and start rethinking our attitudes to punishment on that basis.

That is just a speculation, and does not even begin to suggest how that rethinking might proceed, but it illustrates the general possibility. There is no reason to think that if materialism is true we must be unable to reason morally. Quite the opposite: it may actually make our moral reasoning better by explaining the origins of puzzling intuitions that reason finds hard to justify.

Once again, then, there seems no reason to think that being forced over the materialist border into deeper Darwinian waters gives us any reason to doubt either that moral truth exists, or that we have a capacity for discovering it if it does. If there are reasons for doubting either of these things, they do not seem in any way connected with any Darwinian understanding of our nature.

––––––––––

The main argument of this chapter is that there seems no good reason to think that a wholly materialist account of the world would support the conclusion that there could be no objective moral truth. The idea that God is essential for the existence of moral standards is one that most religious people themselves reject; and the claims of some evolutionists to have turned ethics into a descriptive science seems to depend on making mistakes about reductivism.

The existence of God is, furthermore, neither necessary nor sufficient for the discovery of moral truth. The reliability of religious claims about moral truth can be no more than that of the foundations of the religion in question; and, conversely, moral enquiry can proceed – in some ways obviously objectively – without any reference to religion. The findings of evolutionary psychology could themselves, in principle, be relevant to this enquiry.

The chapter also goes into a detour on the subject of relativism, even though its connection with Darwinism is rather tenuous, partly because relativist ideas are so prevalent, and partly because it may cast light on some problems of metaethics. This discussion also provides a further illustration of ways in which familiar ideas may be confused or incoherent, and of other contexts in which mistakes can arise from unnoticed shifts of level in argument.

9 Onwards and upwards

This chapter and the next are about the idea that the further you go into Darwinism, the more you risk losing in the way of cherished hopes and ideals. This chapter is about the question as it arises on the evolutionary psychology boundary; the materialist boundary is discussed in the next.

It is widely believed that evolutionary psychology, in seeing our characteristics as deep in our genetic makeup, provides a justification for political and social attitudes of a conservative kind. The chapter analyses this assumption, once again taking sex and traditional attitudes to women as an illustration, and once again concluding that the assumption is mistaken. Although the difference between the gene-machine and blank-paper views may have some implications for the details of aims and methods, broader political and social ideals are not affected.

The first part of the chapter is concerned largely with the recapitulation and development of philosophical techniques introduced earlier in the book: practical decision making against uncertainty, disentangling claims about people from claims about issues, and applying the use of argument structures to the analysis of texts. The broader discussion of evolutionary psychology and political ideals comes in the second half of the chapter ('Ethics and the natural order'), where it is argued that claims about the poltical implications of evolutionary psychology depend on importing into Darwinian materialism presuppositions drawn from traditional, incompatible views of the world.

Introduction

So far in this book the arguments seem to have shown that far less than is often thought turns on the question of which degree of Darwinism is closest to the truth. The differences between them seem to have no significant implications for our understanding of our capacity for freedom and responsibility, or altruism and the possibility of moral progress.

In this chapter, however, we come to questions that go beyond what to *think* about ourselves, to questions that are more directly concerned with what we *do* and how we lead our lives. And here there must be various questions whose answers depend on what the truth about the world is. These different degrees of Darwinism give different accounts of what the world is like; and since getting through life and achieving our aims is a matter of (broadly speaking) manipulating the world, what we believe about the way the world works potentially affects everything we aspire to and everything we do.

This may suggest that there is no longer any point in analysing conditionals. It is pointless to tell people that *if* this view of the world is true they should act one way in their efforts to pursue their aims, but *if* that one is true they should do something else. They want to know what to do, and for this it seems essential to go beyond the conditionals and look at the evidence.

But the trouble is that we cannot just suspend all action until we think we have enough evidence. Sitting around doing nothing has just as much influence on the course of events as the most energetic activity – because the results of the activity do not happen – and therefore itself counts as a kind of action. We have to choose what to do, even if we do nothing; and if we have not got the relevant knowledge, we have to make decisions without it.

This brings us back again into the territory of rational bets. If we do not know what the truth is, we have to work out what is most rational to assume for the purposes of action; and it is here that the matter of the implications of the different Darwinian positions arises.

This is the subject taken up by Philip Kitcher in a passage already mentioned (p. 80), where he is arguing specifically about sociobiology. (He was writing before the term 'evolutionary psychology' was in common use, so I shall tend to keep to 'sociobiology' in this discussion.) He accepts that it is irrational to reject some belief because you do not like its implications; but he does think the implications are relevant to the question of what should be assumed for practical purposes, in the absence of adequate evidence.

Ignorance and rationality

This passage comes from the introduction to *Vaulting Ambition*, Kitcher's 1985 book on sociobiology, whose main theme is the inadequacy of evidence for claims made by sociobiologists. In this introduction he is explaining why it is important to recognize this inadequacy, and arguing that unless we get much better evidence we should, for practical purposes, treat sociobiology as false. His argument for this conclusion connects directly with our continuing analysis of the implications of the different degrees of Darwinism.

It is worth reading this passage not only for Kitcher's substantive claims, but also for further light it sheds on the Darwin wars. It is interesting to work out how much of the persuasive force of the passage comes from real arguments, and how much from innuendo, turns of phrase, and allegations about the people who hold opposing beliefs rather than the beliefs themselves. Perhaps, however, it should also be said – while we are on the subject of distinguishing people from issues – that this passage is included specifically to raise the analysis of the issue, and not necessarily to represent Kitcher. The book is (by the standards of this rapidly moving subject) quite old, and Kitcher has written a good deal since.

[1]   We come to the central theme of this book: The dispute about human sociobiology is a dispute about evidence. Friends of sociobiology see the 'new synthesis' as an exciting piece of science, resting soundly on evidence and promising a wealth of new insights, including some that are relevant to human needs. To critical eyes, however, the same body of doctrine seems a mass of unfounded speculation, mischievous in covering socially harmful suggestions with the trappings and authority of science. From this perspective it might appear that the political considerations could be left behind. After all, if all reasonable people agree that we must

accept hypotheses as the evidence dictates, then the fact that the hypotheses under study can readily be connected with political controversies can be disregarded. The issue reduces to a question about truth, pure and simple.

[2]   Algernon Moncrieff's reminder is apposite – the truth is rarely pure and never simple. Everybody ought to agree that, given sufficient evidence for some hypothesis about humans, we should accept that hypothesis whatever its political implications. But the question of what counts as sufficient evidence is not independent of the political consequences. If the costs of being wrong are sufficiently high, then it is reasonable, and responsible, to ask for more evidence than is demanded in situations where mistakes are relatively innocuous. In the free-for-all of scientific research, ideas are often tossed out, tentatively accepted, and only subsequently subjected to genuinely rigorous tests. Arguably, the practice of bold overgeneralization contributes to the efficient working of science as a community enterprise: hypotheses for which there is 'some evidence' or, perhaps, 'reasonably good evidence' become part of the public fund of ideas, are integrated with other hypotheses, criticized, refined, and sometimes discarded. Yet when the hypotheses in question bear on human concerns, the exchange cannot be quite so cavalier. If a single scientist, or even the whole community of scientists, comes to adopt an incorrect view of the origins of a distant galaxy, an inadequate model of foraging behaviour in ants, or a crazy explanation of the extinction of the dinosaurs, then the mistake will not prove tragic. By contrast, if we are wrong about the bases of human social behaviour, if we abandon the goal of a fair distribution of the benefits and burdens of society because we accept faulty hypotheses about ourselves and our evolutionary history, then the consequences of a scientific mistake may be grave indeed.

[3]   These conclusions do not rest on misty sentimentality or unrealistic standards of evidence but on fundamental ideas about rational decision. A familiar principle of decision making is that agents should act so as to maximize expected utility. The rationality of adopting, using, and recommending a scientific hypothesis thus depends not merely on the probability that the hypothesis is true, given the available evidence, but on the costs and benefits of adopting it (or failing to adopt it) if it is true and on the costs and benefits of adopting it (or failing to adopt it) if it is false. The abstract principle is familiar to us from many concrete cases. Drug manufacturers rightly insist on higher standards of evidence when there are potentially dangerous consequences from marketing a new product.

[4]   The genuine worry behind the political criticism of sociobiology is that, while claims about non-human social behaviour may be carefully and rigorously defended, the sociobiologists appear to descend to wild speculation precisely where they should be most cautious. (Gould expresses admiration for Wilson's non-human sociobiology [Gould (1977), p. 252]; however, even non-human sociobiology has its critics.) Appreciating the worry, we can formulate the central questions about the programme of human sociobiology, the questions that I shall

consider in this book: How good is the evidence for sociobiology? How good is the evidence in the field of human sociobiology? How good is the evidence for certain headline-grabbing claims about human nature made by various practitioners of sociobiology? . . .

[5]   Although the focus of my investigation will be the methodological status of sociobiology, it would be wrong to lose sight of the political implications of the inquiry. In considering the merits of sociobiological claims, we must always be aware that the evidence must not be simply suggestive but must justify us in adopting beliefs that will affect our perception and treatment of other people. Close methodological scrutiny is appropriate precisely because of the consequences for social policies and individual lives if we turn out to be mistaken. As Scott Fitzgerald's narrator reminds us at the end of *The Great Gatsby*, carelessness that results in the destruction or diminution of human life is unforgivable. There is no guarantee that our beliefs about ourselves will be correct, no matter how carefully we weigh the evidence. But the more extensive our inquiry, the more secure we are against error. That, at least, is the hope of human rationality.

(Kitcher (1985), pp. 8–11)

This is clearly an anti-sociobiology piece of writing; and it is interesting to start by pinning down exactly what gives that negative impression. This is only the introduction to the book, and Kitcher's main objections to sociobiology – his claims about the inadequacy of evidence – are still to come. But his opposition is clear almost from the beginning, because although he is apparently just describing two opposed positions – for and against sociobiology – the description leaves no doubt about which side he is on. How exactly is this impression conveyed?

The first symptom is that the people who are in favour of sociobiology are described as its *friends*. 'Friends' is not a neutral word in this context: it implies an inclination that is not scientifically impartial, but a matter of personal preference. 'Body of doctrine' also carries a strong negative spin; you do not refer to scientific claims as doctrine unless you regard their propagators as committed to them irrespective of the evidence (would you speak of Newton's *doctrine* of universal gravitation?). The inverted commas round 'new synthesis' are also significant. They are obviously intended as disparaging (so-called 'scare quotes'), indicating that Kitcher wants to keep his distance from the term. If he had thought there really was a new synthesis he would not have needed inverted commas.

It is important to keep remembering the subtle ways in which language can be used to persuade, especially in debates like this one where passions abound. When you read this paragraph, did you find yourself pulled towards an opposition to sociobiology? If so, note that no *arguments* are given against it. All the negativity is carried in the tone.

Since Kitcher makes his side so clear at the very beginning, we can reasonably take it that the views he attributes to the opponents of sociobiology are his own.

What, then, are his grounds for disapproval? What exactly does he seem to disapprove *of*?

Two claims are immediately clear: one is that sociobiology is *unfounded specula-tion*; another is that it is *socially harmful*. These are of course two quite different matters: one is about the level of evidence, and one about the effects of belief in sociobiology. But it is also significant how much of what he says is not about socio-biology at all, but about *sociobiologists*. This shows even in the term 'unfounded speculation', since that way of putting it implies not only that the evidence is inade-quate, but that the people who advocate it are scientifically careless. There is also an implication of political carelessness or even malevolence, since the implications are 'socially harmful', and are being presented with the 'trappings and authority' of science. 'Trappings' is another word with ominous connotations, implying that the authority claimed is showy and spurious.

The same thing also appears in paragraph 5. The sentence 'The sociobiologists appear to descend to wild speculation precisely where they should be most cautious', in particular, carries strong implications of moral turpitude and intel-lectual dishonesty. The claim is not about *some* sociobiologists, which would imply only a limited range of criticism, but *the* sociobiologists, which seems to imply that they all come into this disreputable category. (Notice the way the word 'the' at the beginning also implies distancing. If you put 'the' in front of expressions like 'animal rights supporters', 'opponents of nuclear power', 'social-ists' and the like, it is a pretty good indicator that you do not count yourself among their number.) 'Descend to wild speculation' implies that these people do not achieve basic scientific standards; 'where they should be most cautious' implies a moral carelessness. 'Headline-grabbing' is also pretty scathing. It seems to imply that practitioners of sociobiology are more concerned about their own fame than the damaging implications of their careless work – though at this point Kitcher does at least say only 'various' practitioners, implying that there may be some non-grabbers among their number.

It is always important to notice how much of the force of a passage comes from innuendo rather than argument, and from allegations about the merits and demerits of people rather than of theories, because so much of the way we are persuaded about issues happens in this kind of way. If sociobiologists are as Kitcher implies they are, that does not bode well for their beliefs. However, it is also important to distinguish this kind of rhetoric from real argument, so, having done this initial disentangling, we are in a position to see what his substantive thesis is. What is it?

This, like the side he is on, is also indicated in the second half of the first para-graph, in the section beginning 'From this perspective'. ('This perspective' must be the perspective of considering the evidence for sociobiology. It looks as though it refers to the immediately preceding sentence, but that would not make sense.) He says it might be thought that the only questions were about 'the truth, pure and simple', and that political considerations were irrelevant. But, as the 'might be thought' signals, he is going to disagree, and say that political implications are important.

The reason he gives for this is directly connected with the problem we are addressing here, of making rational decisions about action against a background of uncertainty. He says that how much evidence is needed before a theory should be accepted is not an abstract matter, but depends on context. If the context is one where the consequences of getting things wrong would be harmful, you need more evidence than you would in a context where mistakes would not be serious.

This point is explained in more detail in the third paragraph, which expresses Kitcher's main point. He is making a general claim about rational methodology, and says that there are two elements we must take into account when deciding whether to assume the truth of some theory as a basis for action. One is the probability that the theory is right; the other is the seriousness of the consequences if it is not. If the consequences of your acting on the basis of X would be disastrous if X were wrong, you demand a higher level of evidence before doing so than you otherwise would.

And then finally, in the fourth and fifth paragraphs, he shows how he takes this general approach to rational decision-making to apply to the particular case of sociobiology. The genuine worry about sociobiology, he says, is that theories are being treated as true in contexts where mistakes are serious. (This is opposed, presumably, to the non-genuine worry that sociobiological beliefs are politically unwelcome, so 'legitimate' or 'justified' would be a better word than 'genuine' here. A worry can be genuine without being justified.) This means that they should not be treated as true without a great deal of evidence; and Kitcher is going to be claiming, in the rest of the book, that the evidence in favour of sociobiological theories is much too weak to justify their use as a basis for action.

Kitcher's Wager

It may already be obvious that what Kitcher is doing here is essentially what Pascal was doing in Chapter 1, when he, too, was trying to decide the rational course of action against a background of ignorance. Although he does not say so, Kitcher is in effect working on the basis of a decision matrix of the same kind.

Pascal was considering two possible states of the world (God exists or does not exist) and two possible courses of action (acting as if God did or did not exist). That gave four possible combinations of circumstance, whose merits and demerits could be compared. And when Pascal considered the possible combinations, he decided that the rational action – since he did not know which possible state of the world actually obtained – was to act on the assumption that God did exist, and lead a sober and upright life. That was the best bet under the circumstances, because it would avoid the worst outcome of eternal damnation, and would also give the chance of the best outcome, of eternal bliss. It carried the risk of wasting a finite life on pointless religious duties when he could have been enjoying himself; but the certain benefits of secular enjoyment were so small – infinitely small, against those eternities – that they did not deserve consideration.

Kitcher is reasoning along similar lines, even though about a very different subject. What he says can also be thought of in the form of a matrix. We do not know what the truth is (whether sociobiology is or is not true), and we have two possible courses of action (act on the basis of its being true or its not being true – the second presumably being a matter of continuing to accept the standard social science model, though that is not said explicitly).

	Sociobiology true	Sociobiology false
Assume sociobiology true		
Assume sociobiology false		

The conclusion he reaches on the basis of this reasoning is clear: as long as there is not enough evidence for sociobiology, the best bet is to work on the assumption that it is false. But how exactly does he get there? Obviously it must depend on how he fills in the payoffs, and as he does not explain his reasoning in terms of a matrix he does not give a direct answer to this question. However, we can make some guesses on the basis of what he does say. Since his conclusion is that it is best to presume sociobiological ideas false until there is strong evidence to the contrary, and since he writes about the harm of making mistakes, we can infer that he thinks the worst of all possible outcomes would be to act on the assumption that these ideas were true if they were in fact false. Presumably he also thinks that if we assume them false while they are in fact true, that will be a mistake, but a less disastrous one. He does not say that, but he does say that we have to take great care when the consequences of making a mistake would be serious, and as he is specifically warning about the dangers of assuming the truth of sociobiology, without any mention of the rival standard social science model, we must presume he thinks the possibility of mistake more serious in this direction than in the other.

My guess is that he would fill in the boxes of the matrix something like I've shown on p. 219 (and I have added totally fictional numbers to make the point).

It is presumably as a result of reasoning along these lines that he concludes that the onus of proof is on sociobiology. The default methodological assumption must be that it is false.

It is a *methodological* assumption, rather than a belief, because the idea is that

	Sociobiology true	Sociobiology false
Assume sociobiology true	Our ideals cannot be achieved, but we make the best of the world as it is (+1)	Our ideals could be achieved, but we act in a way that makes achievement impossible (−10)
Assume sociobiology false	Our ideals cannot be achieved, and we fail to make the best even of the world as it is (−1)	Our ideals can be achieved, and we act in the way most likely to achieve them (+10)

this is the presupposition that should be *acted* on until the evidence for sociobiology is very strong. A useful analogy here is the burden of proof in criminal law: the presumption of innocence until guilt has been established beyond reasonable doubt. Because we generally think it much worse to punish the innocent than to let the guilty go free, the seriousness of a mistake is not equal in both directions, and we demand a high standard of proof for guilt. Even when the balance of evidence may suggest guilt, or even justify a belief that the defendant is guilty, it may still not be strong enough to justify our *acting* on that belief, because the consequences of our being wrong would be so much worse in that direction than in the other. This seems to be just what Kitcher is claiming about belief in the ideas of sociobiology.

So, is he right to conclude that the burden of proof is against sociobiology, and that it should be presumed false until proved true beyond reasonable doubt? The argument depends on his estimate of the payoffs, and his implied claim that it is much worse to assume sociobiology true if it is false than false if it is true. But what justification does he offer for this?

There are in the passage some indications that he thinks harm will follow from mistaken assumptions about the truth of sociobiological theories: there are the previously mentioned 'socially harmful consequences' (paragraph 1), and also 'consequences for social policies and individual lives if we turn out to be mistaken' (paragraph 2), and 'carelessness that results in the destruction or diminution of human life' (paragraph 5). But this does not explain how sociobiological assumptions would result in these kinds of harm, or why mistakes should be worse in this direction than the other. The only point at which he gives any real clue is in the sentence at the end of the second paragraph:

By contrast, if we are wrong about the bases of human social behaviour, if we abandon the goal of a fair distribution of the benefits and burdens of society because we accept faulty hypotheses about ourselves and our evolutionary history, then the consequences of a scientific mistake may be grave indeed.

This is an odd sentence, since the way it is written implies that 'If we abandon the goal of a fair distribution ... ' is just an elaboration of 'If we are wrong about the bases of human social behaviour', when really it is a quite separate point. Still, this does show the nature of Kitcher's concern. He seems to think that if you accept sociobiology, the result must be your abandoning ideals of social justice. That is obviously why he thinks it is better to work on the assumption that it is false. It is better to struggle for justice, even if in fact it cannot be achieved, than to abandon the struggle when justice might have been achievable if only we had tried. It is in effect a secular – and less self-interested – version of Pascal's Wager.

That is pretty obviously the way Kitcher is thinking, and it seems certain that a great deal of hostility to sociobiology is motivated in the same way. Most of the opponents do not explain the methodological point in the way Kitcher does, but it is widely presumed that sociobiology has right-wing political implications of various kinds, and many opponents are determined to believe it false – or at least treat it as false – for that reason.

But are they right about these implications? Kitcher makes the claim, but seems to regard it as too obvious to need any defence. This is what we need to investigate, and it brings us back to our running theme of the implications of rival views about the scope of Darwinian explanation.

Exercise 9.1

For some or all of the following problems about action, make a matrix of the payoffs, and in the light of those see how much evidence you would need in order to decide to act on one assumption rather than the other. You may find it useful to use numbers, however fanciful, for your rankings of the payoffs.

There are no right or wrong answers here. The conclusions can only be approximate at best, and will anyway depend on your own preferences. The purpose of the exercise is to clarify the problem of decision-making against uncertainty.

1   Last week a Boeing 747 crashed. You are going to America next week, on a 747, for your daughter's wedding, but you are worried about the possibility of an accident. (And all other flights are fully booked.)
    Set out a matrix showing possible courses of actions and possible outcomes. Then consider how you would decide in the light of the following evidence:

    (i)   They still don't know what caused the crash.
    (ii) A failure has been found in one of the engines, clearly attributable (they say) to a mistake of an incompetent maintenance engineer, now no longer working for the company.

2   Address the same problem for:

(i)   your boss's daughter's wedding;
(ii)   dinner with the President.

3   You are head of the Committee for the Safety of Medicines, and a drugs company produces what may be a miracle cure for some disorder, but which has not been thoroughly tested for side effects. What do you do if it is for:

(i)   The late stages of AIDS?
(ii)   Morning sickness in pregnancy?

(Answers on pp. 285–6)

Natural premises and political conclusions

Kitcher's fear that the truth of sociobiology would entail our abandoning ideals of social justice is a familiar one; many people of leftward leanings seem to take it for granted that Darwinian ideas about our nature and origins have implications of right-wing and socially alarming kinds.

This association of Darwinism and right-wing ideas has a long history. Long before sociobiology appeared in the landscape, Darwinians were struck by the idea of evolution as working on variations, and eliminating the less good in favour of the better. Since variation was the basis of evolutionary progress, the idea took root that if we wanted to carry on in the onward and upward direction that so inspired the Victorians, we must recognize these natural differences between people, and make sure that the best were the ones that reproduced; and this kind of thinking led to two kinds of social policy which have both acquired terrible reputations.

The first of these was the set of ideas known as Social Darwinism, which (in a simplified caricature) amounted to the claim that you should not prop up the weak, because evolution worked by weeding out substandard designs. If you tried to stop that weeding-out process, by supporting the inferior specimens that nature would have sent to the wall, you would be interfering with the impressive upward course on which evolution had set our species.

The second idea, which followed it, was that of eugenics. Enthusiasts for improvement of the human race became aware that you could not in fact rely on the most impressive people to produce the most offspring, or on the Darwinian losers to curtail their fecundity; and they tried, in a succession of policies – some voluntary, some not – to make sure that the right people multiplied their kind and the wrong ones did not.

It is perhaps not surprising, in the light of all this, that many people's commitment to the idea of environment as the main determinant of character and ability has become a political creed, rather than just a scientific theory. The rejection of the premise about natural differences is seen as essential for avoiding the intolerable political conclusions. This is why someone coming from this direction to evolutionary psychology, which is also concerned with deep genetic traits, may easily see it as the same kind of thing, and carrying the same dangers. The resistance to sociobiology when it first appeared was fuelled mainly by the conviction of its opponents that any claim about genetically ingrained characteristics must be the first premise of an argument for concentration camps, forced sterilization and the abolition of the welfare state.

And in fact Kitcher does this too. The introduction to his book, from which this extract was taken, is called 'A bicycle is not enough', and it is a polemic against the former British system of routine selection of children for different kinds of schooling at the age of ten – and how the consolation prize of a bicycle made no impact on the misery of being rejected at that age. But ideas of this kind mistake the nature of sociobiology, which connects with Darwinian theory in a quite different way. Social Darwinism and eugenics both start from the idea of the random *variations* within species that are the raw materials of selection, and the concern of both movements is essentially forward-looking: to influence the future course of evolution by making sure that some variations rather than others survive. Sociobiology, in contrast, is concerned with the *results*, rather than the materials, of selection, and with understanding the characteristics of species as wholes through consideration of the processes that made them what they are. Its main interest is therefore in what the members of any species have in common, and it is concerned with differences between individuals only to the extent that those are themselves general characteristics of the species and the results of natural selection: differences such as those between the sexes and the castes of social insects, and between individuals of different ages. So even if it were true that the parts of Darwinian theory that are concerned with random variation could provide a justification for unacceptable programmes of eugenics or selective education, that would not apply to the theories of sociobiology. Those theories have no implications whatever for how much random variation in innate abilities there is within a population, or how to identify the possessors of different abilities.

However, there are other ways in which people who defend rightish political views support them with claims about deep human characteristics. Defences of many kinds of tradition – established hierarchies, war, hostility to other races and cultures, and the subjection of women to men – typically appeal to the idea that certain aspects of human nature are too deeply ingrained to be eliminated, and some of these sound ominously like the characteristics for which sociobiologists are claiming evolutionary origins. People of leftward leanings have therefore been inclined to resist the whole enterprise out of hand, as a suborning of science by the political forces of conservatism and authoritarianism.

So the question to be asked now is whether it is true that the claims of sociobiologists have the unwelcome political implications attributed to them. That is what needs to be shown if Kitcher is to justify his claim that sociobiology should be presumed false until there is strong evidence to believe it true.

Sex and the natural order

Since our discussions of sociobiology have so far centred on the matter of sex, that is the appropriate one to discuss here – though it should be said, again, that this is only one context in which it is thought that sociobiological claims have sinister political implications of a conservative kind. The issue is also in many ways atypical, because this is the only context, at the moment, in which evolutionary psychology is concerned with a difference within the species that characterizes a whole life. (Homosexuality is another potential subject here, but although many attempts have been made to explain homosexuality in evolutionary terms there are many problems, and certainly no sign of agreement.) Most of the differences within the species that concern evolutionary psychology – characteristics at different ages, or responses to different circumstances – are not ones that characterize individuals from birth.

Although the sociobiological claims of radical differences between men and women have no sinister implications for policies of eugenics and social Darwinism (even if you think men are superior, you can't, at least at present, breed only from men) the question of innate differences between the sexes is as politically sensitive as any question about innate differences between individuals, because opponents of feminism have always based their conclusions about the appropriate social situations of women and men on claims about the intrinsic natures of the sexes. The feminist movement has on the whole been as strongly committed to the standard social science model as the rest of the political Left. The fear seems to be that if evolutionary psychology were well-founded, the aims of feminism would be misguided from the foundations. The kinds of theory expounded by Wright are widely regarded by feminists as straightforwardly sexist, and just the latest attempts to prop up traditional patriarchy.

(This, by the way, is the basis of the now-familiar use of 'gender' instead of 'sex'. 'Gender' was originally supposed to apply to socially induced characteristics, and its being taken over as a substitute for 'sex' shows the depth of the assumption that sex-linked characteristics are products of social conditioning. Its adoption as a politically correct word shows how political correctness demands the acceptance of the standard social science model. Since I am leaving that matter open, I shall quite deliberately use 'sex' throughout.)

The strength of the political commitment to this idea is once again an obvious reaction to the way in which claims about the different natures of the sexes were traditionally used to justify their relative social positions, and the old idea of the sexes' separate spheres. If traditionalists say that women must be in their subordinate position because of their different nature, the obvious reaction is to deny what is said about that nature. But to do this is in effect to accept what traditionalists said about the *implications* of these claims about male and female nature; and that is just what we need to investigate.

To do this, I want to start by looking in detail at a nineteenth-century argument of this traditionalist kind, which is of particular interest because it depends on ideas that sound rather like some that are put forward by present-day sociobiologists. It is only an illustration, of course, but it will raise most of the important issues.

The argument in question comes from James Fitzjames Stephen, who has already appeared as the author of one of the claims about systematic sex differences quoted in Chapter 3 (p. 68). The passage that follows is part of the chapter from which that quotation came, in which Stephen defends the traditional arrangements for marriage against the kinds of argument that were increasingly coming from campaigners for women's rights, and in particular against John Stuart Mill in *The Subjection of Women* (which was also quoted in Chapter 3 (p. 68)).

At the time when Stephen's book was written (1871), the inequality of rights of men and women in marriage was quite extreme, and few people in Western society – even those of a conservative disposition – now think that women should be legally and conventionally in the power of their husbands. But there are still residues of various sorts, and in many parts of the world the situation is still much worse than it was in Victorian Britain. It is, anyway, instructive to look at the tradition and the traditional arguments, partly because it is as a reaction to these arguments that the feminist commitment to the standard social science model is so strong. And Stephen is particularly interesting, partly because he was offering arguments about social and political arrangements for the general good of society, rather than the theological diatribes perpetrated by many of his conservative contemporaries, but also partly because – as already mentioned – some of the claims he makes about men and women sound very like ideas that are now current among evolutionary psychologists, and were rather unusual in arguments of the time.

At the end of the passage I shall do as I did with the Barash passages in Chapter 7: identify Stephen's line of argument not by trying to summarize the whole, but by starting from the conclusion and then working backwards to construct the most plausible possible argument to that conclusion from the materials in the passage. If you want to try this, note as you go through any points where Stephen seems to be saying what ought to be done and how people ought to act (the conclusion), and also any claims about the nature and natural situation of men and women (particularly women), which seem relevant to the case he is making.

[1]   Now, if society and government ought to recognize the inequality of age as the foundation of an inequality of rights of this importance, it appears to me at least equally clear that they ought to recognize the inequality of sex for the same purpose, if it is a real inequality. Is it one? There are some propositions which it is difficult to prove, because they are so plain, and this is one of them. The physical differences between the two sexes affect every part of the human body, from the hair of the head to the soles of the feet, from the size and density of the bones to the texture of the brain and the character of the nervous system. Ingenious people may argue about anything, and Mr Mill does say a great number of things about women which ... I will not discuss; but all the talk in the world will never shake

the proposition that men are stronger than women in every shape. They have greater muscular and nervous force, greater intellectual force, greater vigour of character. This general truth, which has been observed under all sorts of circumstances and in every age and country, has also in every age and country led to a division of labour between men and women, the general outline of which is as familiar and as universal as the general outline of the differences between them. These are the facts, and the question is whether the law and public opinion ought to recognize this difference? How it ought to recognize it, what difference it ought to make between men and women as such, is quite another question.

[2] The first point to consider is whether [the law] ought to treat [the sexes] as equals, although, as I have shown, they are not equals, because men are the stronger. I will take one or two illustrations. Men, no one denies, may, and in some cases ought to be liable to compulsory military service. No one, I suppose, would hesitate to admit, that if we were engaged in a great war it might become necessary, or that if necessary it would be right, to have a conscription both for the land and for the sea service. Ought men and women to be subject to it indiscriminately? If any one says that they ought, I have no more to say, except that he has got into the region at which argument is useless. But if it is admitted that this ought not to be done, an inequality of treatment founded on a radical inequality between the two sexes is admitted, and if this admission is once made, where are you to draw the line? Turn from the case of liability to military service to that of education, which in Germany is rightly regarded as the other great branch of State activity, and the same question presents itself in another shape. Are boys and girls to be educated indiscriminately, and to be instructed in the same things? Are boys to learn to sew, to keep house, and to cook, and are girls to play at cricket, to row, and be drilled like boys? I cannot argue with a person who says Yes. A person who says No admits an inequality between the sexes on which education must be founded, and which it must therefore perpetuate and perhaps increase.

[3] Follow the matter a step further to the vital point of the whole question – marriage. Marriage is one of the subjects with which it is absolutely necessary both for law and morals to deal with in some way or other. All that I need consider in reference to the present purpose is the question whether the laws and moral rules which relate to it should regard it as a contract between equals, or as a contract between a stronger and a weaker person involving subordination for certain purposes on the part of the weaker to the stronger. I say that a law which proceeded on the former and not on the latter of these views would be founded on a totally false assumption, and would involve cruel injustice in the sense of extreme general inexpediency, especially to women. If the parties to a contract of marriage are treated as equals, it is impossible to avoid the inference that marriage, like other partnerships, may be dissolved at pleasure. The advocates of women's rights are exceedingly shy of stating this plainly. Mr Mill says nothing about it in his book on the Subjection of Women, though in one place he comes very near to saying so, but it is as clear an inference from his principles as anything can

possibly be, nor has he ever disavowed it. If this were the law, it would make women the slaves of their husbands. A woman loses the qualities which make her attractive to men much earlier than men lose those which make them attractive to women. The tie between a woman and young children is generally far closer than the tie between them and their father. A woman who is no longer young, and who is the mother of children, would thus be absolutely in her husband's power, in nine cases out of ten, if he might put an end to the marriage when he pleased. This is one inequality in the position of the parties which must be recognized and provided for beforehand if the contract is to be for their common good.

[4]   A second inequality is this. When a man marries, it is generally because he feels himself established in life. He incurs, no doubt, a good deal of expense, but he does not in any degree impair his means of earning a living. When a woman marries she practically renounces in all but the rarest cases the possibility of undertaking any profession but one, and the possibility of carrying on that one profession in the society of any man but one. Here is a second inequality. It would be easy to mention others of the deepest importance, but these are enough to show that to treat a contract of marriage as a contract between persons who are upon an equality in regard of strength, and power to protect their interest, is to treat it as being what it notoriously is not.

[5]   Again, the contract is one which involves subordination and obedience on the part of the weaker party to the stronger. The proof of this is, to my mind, as clear as that of a proposition in Euclid, and it is this:

(i) Marriage is a contract, one of the principal objects of which is the government of a family.
(ii) This government must be vested either by law or by contract in the hands of one of the two married persons.
(iii) If the arrangement is made by contract, the remedy for breach of it must either be by law or by a dissolution of the partnership at the will of the contracting parties.
(iv) Law could give no remedy in such a case. Therefore the only remedy for breach of the contract would be a dissolution of the marriage.
(v) Therefore, if marriage is to be permanent, the government of the family must be put by law and by morals in the hands of the husband, for no one proposes to give it to the wife.

[6]   Mr Mill is totally unable to meet this argument, and apparently embraces the alternative that marriage ought to be dissoluble at the pleasure of the parties. After much argument as to contracts which appear to me visionary, his words are these: Things never come to an issue of downright power on one side and obedience on the other except where the connection has been altogether a mistake and it would be a blessing to both parties to be relieved from it.

[7]   This appears to me to show a complete misapprehension of the nature of family government and of the sort of cases in which the question of obedience and authority can arise between husband and wife. No one contends that a man ought to have power to order his wife about like a slave and beat her if she disobeys him. Such conduct in the eye of the law would be cruelty and ground for a separation. The question of obedience arises in quite another way. It may, and no doubt often does, arise between the very best and most affectionate married people, and it need no more interfere with their mutual affection than the absolute power of the captain of a ship need interfere with perfect friendship and confidence between himself and his first lieutenant. Take the following set of questions: 'Shall we live on this scale or that? Shall we associate with such and such persons? Shall I, the husband, embark in such an undertaking, and shall we change our place of residence in order that I may do so? Shall we send our son to college? Shall we send our daughters to school or have a governess? For what profession shall we train our sons?' On these and a thousand other such questions the wisest and the most affectionate people might arrive at opposite conclusions. What is to be done in such a case? for something must be done. I say the wife ought to give way. She ought to obey her husband, and carry out the view at which he deliberately arrives, just as, when the captain gives the word to cut away the masts, the lieutenant carries out his orders at once, though he may be a better seaman and may disapprove them. I also say that to regard this as a humiliation, as a wrong, as an evil in itself, is a mark not of spirit and courage, but of a base, unworthy, mutinous disposition – a disposition utterly subversive of all that is most worth having in life. The tacit assumption involved in it is that it is a degradation ever to give up one's own will to the will of another, and to me this appears the root of all evil, the negation of that which renders any combined efforts possible. No case can be specified in which people unite for a common object from making a pair of shoes up to governing an empire in which the power to decide does not rest somewhere; and what is this but command and obedience? Of course the person who for the time being is in command is of all fools the greatest if he deprives himself of the advantage of advice, if he is obstinate in his own opinion, if he does not hear as well as determine; but it is also practically certain that his inclination to hear will be proportioned to the degree of importance which he has been led to attach to the function of determining.

[8]   To sum the matter up, it appears to me that all the laws and moral rules by which the relation between the sexes is regulated should proceed upon the prin-ciple that their object is to provide for the common good of the two great divisions of mankind who are connected together by the closest and most durable of all bonds, and who can no more have really conflicting interests than the different members of the same body, but who are not and never can be equals in any of the different forms of strength.

(Stephen (1991 edn), pp. 193–8)

As often happens in political writing of this sort, this passage contains all sorts of general remarks and sub-arguments, and there is no single way to set out what is going on. However, the overall *conclusion* is clear. It is that law and social convention should (continue to) recognize an inequality of rights in marriage, with the man as superior. It should not change to the equality within marriage recommended by people such as Mill. The reconstructed argument must therefore end:

> Therefore women should be legally and conventionally subordinate to men in marriage.

It is important to notice Stephen's frequent insistence that he is talking about such matters as laws, public morals, and contracts. The passage is not primarily about private morality, or how the sexes should or do treat each other as individuals. This is important, because many arguments both then and now tend to run together claims about what institutions there should be and claims about how individuals should behave.

How does he reach this conclusion? He starts, obviously, with the claim that the sexes are different and unequal, with women at a natural disadvantage to men in most respects. They are (of course) 'weaker in every shape': physically, intellectually, nervously and all the rest. That goes almost without saying; all conservative Victorians took such things for granted. But what makes Stephen more interesting than his similarly-minded contemporaries is that he claims that women have disadvantages of other kinds. They are by nature particularly closely tied to the children, in ways that mean that when they embark on having a family they give up the possibility of supporting themselves. They also lose their sexual attractiveness sooner than men lose theirs. These points are particularly interesting from our point of view, because sociobiologists do make some claims of these kinds. They do think natural selection has resulted in men's keeping their sexual attractiveness longer than women, and in a close natural connection between women and children. Sociobiology also expects greater physical strength in men than in women. It should be emphasized, however, that it has nothing whatever to say about greater nervous or intellectual vigour – unless the risk-taking tendencies of men are to be regarded as manifestations of nervous vigour.

So the framework of Stephen's argument is something like this:

> Women are at many natural disadvantages to men.
> ———————
> Therefore the marriage contract should be one in which the wife is legally and socially subordinate to the husband.

Arguments that take this general form – arguing from claims about the nature of the sexes to political conclusions about their appropriate legal and social treatment – are familiar, and the usual reaction of feminists is an indignant denial of the premises. Sometimes the claims about the differences are dismissed as fantasies; sometimes they are accepted as true, but claimed as socially induced rather than anything to do with nature. The idea of female weakness – apart from brute physical strength – is usually regarded as male wishful thinking; the special bond of women to children and their consequent inability to support themselves are often said to be socially induced, and the same is likely to be said about the idea of women's more rapid decline in attractiveness with age. (This last seems to provoke particular outrage.)

It is perhaps worth noting, in fairness to Stephen, that in his time there were few contraceptives or labour-saving domestic appliances, that housekeeping was for most women a pretty heavy job, and that mothers would have found it extremely difficult to support themselves with outside work – though of course innumerable poor ones had to try. And, of course (since one student of mine indignantly cited Joan Collins as a counterexample to the lessening-attraction-with-age claim), there were rather fewer artificial aids to youth and beauty.

However, we shall not be going into this debate, since our concern will as usual be to investigate the *implications* of these claims. Feminists who feel they must deny the premises if they are to resist the conclusion are presupposing that Stephen and others like him are right in his claims about what those implications are, and that is what is to be investigated here.

As I said, I shall do here as was done with Barash (see pp. 167–75): not follow the course of the text as Stephen sets it out, but, starting with the conclusion, construct the best argument possible from Stephen's ingredients. This is something that can be done with any text, but it is particularly important here, because if you tried to work directly from Stephen's text you would automatically be led to the place where he seems to set out an argument (claiming that it is as clear as any demonstration in Euclid) and that would not be helpful – though it might be an interesting exercise in itself. It will be far more effective to concentrate, as usual, on the logical gap between premise and conclusion, to see first what *kinds of claim* are needed to fill it, and then what is stated or implied in Stephen's text that does the job.

There are innumerable slightly different ways of doing this, but they all come to the same thing in the end. You might find it interesting to see how far you get before reading on.

What follows is, first, a reconstruction of the argument and, second, a section-by-section assessment of its soundness. It is included largely on methodological grounds, as an exemplar of how to conduct this kind of analysis, and an illustration of the way such arguments can go wrong. Anyone who wants to keep to the substantial question of the implications of sociobiology might prefer to skip the details and go directly to the wider view on page 237.

The argument

The outline argument that needs to be filled in is:

Women are at many natural disadvantages to men.
_____

Therefore the marriage contract should be one in which the wife is legally and socially subordinate to the husband.

There is such a huge gap here between premise and conclusion that it is perhaps difficult to see how to set about filling it in in an orderly way. But there is one particularly striking gap which makes an ideal starting point. The premise makes a claim about what *is* the case, and the conclusion says that something *should be* the case.

The inference of an 'ought' (or 'should') statement from an 'is' statement is known to philosophers as the Naturalistic Fallacy. The term was first used by G. E. Moore, in *Principia Ethica* (1903), but the basic problem is well known as one that was identified long before, by Hume:

> In every system of morality, which I have hitherto met with, I have always remarked, that the author proceeds for some time in the ordinary way of reasoning, and establishes the being of a God, or makes observations concerning human affairs; when of a sudden I am surprised to find, that instead of the usual copulations of propositions, is, and is not, I meet with no proposition that is not connected with an ought, or an ought not. This change is imperceptible, but is, however, of the last consequence.[18] For as this ought, or ought not, expresses some new relation of affirmation, 'tis necessary that it shou'd be observ'd and explain'd; and at the same time that a reason should be given, for what seems altogether inconceivable, how this new relation can be deduction from others, which are entirely different from it.
>
> (Hume (1978 edn), p. 469)

Hume is, in other words, claiming that there is a logical gap between statements containing nothing but 'is', and ones containing 'ought'.

So, for instance, if you were considering an outline argument such as:

Horses are gregarious animals.

———

Therefore we should not keep horses alone.

You would need, to complete it, some *general* statement about the kinds of thing we ought and ought not to do, which would apply to this particular case. Here you might do something like this:

Horses are gregarious animals
Gregarious animals are unhappy when they are kept alone.
We should prevent unhappiness whenever we can.

———

Therefore we should not keep horses alone.

The second of those added premises provides a statement of principle, to support the 'should' in the conclusion.

Needless to say, philosophers have disputed this claim about an 'is'/'ought' gap, and I shall consider this matter later. But it certainly *looks* as though there is a gap. We have here a conclusion about what *should* happen, but we have so far no statements of values, or principles about what ought to be the case, in the premises. So in the absence of positive reason to think otherwise, it seems that if Stephen's argument is to make a valid transition from his claim about what men and women are like to conclusions about what marriage ought to be, he needs in the premises a statement of moral values. What does he say, or imply, about the moral standards he thinks we should accept, and which would fulfil this purpose?

Part of his answer, at least, comes in an explicit statement in the last paragraph:

> all the laws and moral rules by which the relation between the sexes is regulated should proceed upon the principle that their object is to provide for the common good of the two great divisions of mankind …

He wants what is *good* for both sexes. So we can start by putting that in, and then deriving from that and the first premise an interim conclusion, thus:

Women are at many natural disadvantages to men.
The laws and customs regulating marriage should be for the good of both sexes.

Therefore these laws and customs should be particularly concerned with the protection of women.

Therefore the marriage contract should be one in which the wife is subordinate to the husband.

The intermediate conclusion does seem to be implied by Stephen, so this seems so far a good representation of his line of argument.

Now what kind of additional premise should we look for? Since Stephen thinks women need protection, and this is going to be part of the argument for his conclusion, he needs to say something about the nature of their vulnerability. In what respects are they vulnerable?

His answer to this is, of course, an amplification of his opening statement about the disadvantageous position of women, so we could have made it part of the first premise. (There is rarely a single way of setting out an argument that is presented as text.) Their vulnerability stems from the fact that in entering marriage a woman becomes dependent on her husband through 'renouncing all professions but one'. She loses her earning capacity because of her strong connection with the children; and, since her attractiveness declines more quickly than that of her husband, she also loses her ability to attract another protector – while he with his continuing attractiveness, it is rather implied, might well be tempted to make off to pastures new. 'A woman who is no longer young, and who is the mother of children, would thus be absolutely in her husband's power, in nine cases out of ten, if he might put an end to the marriage when he pleased.' And this is intended to support the next interim conclusion, that she must be protected from desertion.

So add that to the argument:

> Women are at many natural disadvantages to men.
> The laws and customs regulating marriage should be for the good of both sexes.
>
> ⸻
>
> Therefore these laws and customs should be particularly concerned with the protection of women.
> *Marriage makes women dependent on their husbands.*
>
> ⸻
>
> *Therefore they must be protected from desertion by their husbands.*
>
> ⸻
>
> Therefore the marriage contract should be one in which the wife is subordinate to the husband.

Now what is needed? Stephen presumably needs to say what form this protection should take. He does: he says that marriage must be made permanent, though he seems to regard it as so obvious as to need no argument. So that goes in as the next conclusion, but without any obvious linking premise. (That is a matter to be taken up in the assessment of the argument, which comes later.)

> Women are at many natural disadvantages to men.
> The laws and customs regulating marriage should be for the good of both sexes.
>
> ⸻
>
> Therefore these laws and customs should be particularly concerned with the protection of women.
> Marriage makes women dependent on their husbands.
>
> ⸻
>
> Therefore they must be protected from desertion by their husbands.
>
> ⸻
>
> *Therefore marriage must be permanent.*
>
> ⸻
>
> Therefore the marriage contract should be one in which the wife is subordinate to the husband.

The logical gap now is between the need for permanence in marriage and a marriage contract which makes the wife subordinate. The next premise, therefore, should presumably start to bridge this gap with a claim about the relationship between permanence and inequality. And, indeed, Stephen specifically says that a contract between equals cannot be permanent. This goes in as the next premise, and yields the next intermediate conclusion, that the marriage contract must be unequal.

That gives:

> Women are at many natural disadvantages to men.
> The laws and rules regulating marriage should be for the good of both sexes.
> _____
> Therefore these rules should be particularly concerned with the protection of women.
> Marriage makes women dependent on their husbands.
> _____
> Therefore they must be protected from desertion by their husbands.
> _____
> Therefore marriage should be permanent.
> *A contract between equals cannot be permanent.*
> _____
> *Therefore marriage should not be a contract between equals.*
> _____
> Therefore the marriage contract should be one in which the wife is subordinate to the husband.

That leaves one final gap to be filled, between the claim that inequality is necessary and the conclusion that the inequality should take the form of the subordination of women. Here Stephen says nothing more than that 'no one proposes to give [the government of the family] to the wife' (paragraph 5). Presumably he regards the absurdity of having the wife as the superior as one of those propositions that are difficult to prove because they are so plain. Since women are 'weaker in every shape', anyone who suggested they should be heads of families would, presumably, have entered 'the region at which argument is useless'. Anyway, let us put a marker there for the sake of completeness:

> Women are at many natural disadvantages to men.
> The laws and rules regulating marriage should be for the good of both sexes.
> _____
> Therefore these rules should be particularly concerned with the protection of women.
> Marriage makes women dependent on their husbands.
> _____
> Therefore they must be protected from desertion by their husbands.
> _____
> Therefore marriage should be permanent.
> A contract of equals cannot be permanent.

——————

Therefore marriage should be a contract of unequals.
Women are obviously unsuited to the superior position.

——————

Therefore the marriage contract should be one in which the wife is subordinate to the husband.

That seems to give a pretty good account of the structure of Stephen's main argument – and, I think, a much clearer one than could be obtained by trying to summarize his argument as it stands. (Notice that it makes hardly any use of that Euclidean argument – whose inadequacy would quickly show if an attempt were made to set it out in argument form.) There are various other arguments as well – such as one depending on the claim that any enterprise must have a leader – but this will be enough for our purposes.

The assessment

Now consider the merits of this argument, taking it one sub-argument at a time. The first argument is:

Women are at many natural disadvantages to men.
The laws and rules regulating marriage should be for the good of both sexes.

——————

Therefore these rules should be particularly concerned with the protection of women.

How good is it? It seems valid, at least on plausible interpretations of the premises. The first premise is not being questioned, because we are asking not about the truth of these claims about women, but only about their implications. 'The good of both sexes' in the second premise is rather vague; it gives no indication of what to do in the case of conflicts of interest (about which I shall say more soon). But the second premise seems plausible in itself, and since we then go on to a special concern with protecting women because of their vulnerability, things look all right so far. Most people who accepted the first premise would probably accept the conclusion.

So let us provisionally accept the first sub-argument as sound, and go on to the next:

The rules of marriage should be particularly concerned with the protection of women.
Marriage makes women dependent on their husbands.

——————

Therefore they must be protected from desertion by their husbands.

The first premise is the conclusion of the first argument, so that needs no separate consideration. We have already seen Stephen's justification: it follows from his original diagnosis of the natural disadvantages from which women suffer; it is about women's inability to support themselves once they have 'renounced all professions but one'.

But this begins to raise a problem. Given this justification, the dependence involved is straightforwardly economic. But if that is how the second premise is interpreted, can it support the conclusion? If by 'desertion' were meant simply 'leaving unsupported', it would; but Stephen is clearly intending something stronger than that. He obviously means that the husband must *stay with* the wife, and this is more than can be justified by the premise about the kind of protection women need. If husbands had to leave a great deal of money with deserted wives, for instance, and were legally committed to enormous alimony payments, the wives would not be at too severe a disadvantage from the point of view of maintenance. Women need protection against being left *unsupported*, since that is the form their vulnerability takes, but that is not the same as desertion – if by desertion is meant simply the man's going away.

So I do think Stephen's conclusion here is stronger than can be justified by the most reasonable interpretation of his second premise. He should be claiming only that women need protection against being left unsupported – which need not mean actually keeping the man around, though that could be one way of doing it.

That is likely to make a difference to the progress of the argument as a whole. However, with that problem noted, we can continue to assess the individual arguments as they stand. The next one is:

Women must be protected from desertion by their husbands.
_____

Therefore marriage should be permanent.

This can work only if it is regarded as incomplete, so we have the familiar question of what premise could be added to make it valid. The most obvious completion would presumably be:

Women must be protected from desertion by their husbands.
The only way to prevent desertion by husbands is to make marriage permanent.
_____

Therefore marriage should be permanent.

But is the second premise true? If you want to protect women from desertion, *one* way of doing this is indeed to make marriage permanent – that would be a sufficient condition of their not being deserted. But it is not a necessary condition. If desertion by the man is the worry, the only thing needed is the specification that he should not be able to escape *without the woman's agreement*. It gives no reason for saying the *woman* should not escape if she wanted to, or why she should not be able to give the man permission to go if he made appropriate arrangements. So once again the conclusion is stronger than is justified by the premises.

You might weaken the implied premise to claim that the *best* way to protect women from desertion would be to make marriage permanent. But then you would need to argue, separately, that this would be better than alternatives such as the ones just suggested, and it would be difficult to do this on grounds of the interests of the women.

So the argument is already beginning to creak a little. However, now consider the next part, once again without challenging the first premise:

Marriage should be permanent.
A contract of equals cannot be permanent.
_____

Therefore marriage should be a contract of unequals.

That looks valid; but is the second premise plausible? Stephen justifies it by saying that a contract of equals can be dissolved at will; but there are at least two decisive objections to that assertion.

First, whether a contract of equals can be dissolved at will depends on the legal and social context in which it is made. Laws and circumstances can make some contracts binding, irrespective of the wishes of the contracting parties. Marriage was pretty well like that in Stephen's time, and Catholic marriage still (officially) is. The law could easily allow for a contract of equals that neither side could dissolve.

And second, a contract of equals, even when dissoluble at the will of the parties, is never one that *one* side can break. Can a business partner unilaterally break a contract with another? It is a remarkable idea; in fact it makes nonsense of the whole idea of a contract. And since a contract of equals cannot be unilaterally broken, there is nothing wrong with a contract of equals from the point of view of protecting the wife from desertion. Note the slip from 'may be dissolved at pleasure' to 'whenever he pleased', which is a straightforward, and blatant, fallacy of equivocation. The pleasure of the consenting parties is not by any means the same as what pleases *one* of them.

This premise, then, is simply absurd. And since the argument really has fallen apart here, there seems little point in going on to the final claim about women's being so unsuited to the superior position that nobody would think of giving it to them. But perhaps it is worth noting in passing that Stephen nowhere justifies the assumption that the superior must always be either the wife or the husband. Even given his claim about the need for inequality, that could allow for the wife to be superior in some cases and the husband in others.

This is, in other words, a pretty bad argument, even if you grant Stephen all his claims about the weak position of women.

A wider view

Stephen's argument offers only one possible way to bridge the gap between his premises about the differences between the sexes and his conservative conclusion about the nature of marriage, so the fact that it runs into disaster in this way leaves open the theoretical possibility that someone else might make a better job of it. But it seems to me that this possibility is not worth exploring, because the problem here goes far deeper than the mistakes of this particular argument, and it is this more general point that is most important for the implications of sociobiology.

Think of the way the argument goes. It depends on the idea that women are at a natural disadvantage to men, and therefore need special protection. Many of the familiar arguments to justify the traditional position of women make similar claims: women are weak and need protection by the strong; women are vulnerable when childbearing, and need support, and so on.

Now try a thought experiment. First, list the main differences between the traditional legal and conventional situations of women and men from the point of view of sex and marriage. Obviously the details have varied enormously between different societies, but all that is needed here is a broad picture of women's traditional position. Think of social pressures as well as laws and institutions, and social situation as well as property and legal power.

Now, referring to that list, imagine yourself a benevolent dictator, recognizing the natural vulnerability of women and their children, and wanting to set up laws and institutions to protect them as much as possible. What kinds of thing would you do? Think about this as far as possible completely from scratch, rather than defending any existing political position. If it helps, think of yourself as a visiting hermaphrodite Martian, with no special connection with either sex.

Finally, compare these two lists. You should find the comparison quite striking.

First, what has the traditional position of women been? At the time when Stephen was writing, we know that women were subordinate to their husbands in marriage (legally, to quite an extreme degree), and it was extremely difficult for them to escape. Their property became their husband's, and the children were legally his. Even if the partners separated, and even if the fault was clearly the husband's, he could prevent his wife from seeing their children, and her money – including her earnings – remained legally his. Women were also excluded from higher education and the professions, and therefore from all respectable ways of supporting themselves. They could not vote, and therefore could not change the law. And, of course, they were subject to fierce sexual constraints: any sexual lapse in women incurred severe social penalties. Young women had to be chaperoned, to guarantee their virtue; erring wives, unmarried mothers and illegitimate children were outcasts. (For an account of the legal position at the time, see Mill's *The Subjection of Women* (in Mill (1991 edn)).

That was the actual situation. How does that compare with the arrangements you would make if you were a benevolent dictator, determined to protect women?

Here is what I wrote on the subject some years ago:

Consider … what you would do if you were really setting out in an unprejudiced way to arrange for the protection of the weak. You would probably start by trying to make the weak stronger, or by giving them extra powers to defend themselves. You might also try to lessen the power of the strong, or impose restrictions to prevent their getting out of hand. The very last thing you would do is systematically deprive the weak of all other options in order to force them into dependency on the very people from whom they might be presumed most to need protection, and then provide social and legal powers to make the strong stronger still, as has been the case with women and men. The idea that the weak can be protected by being abandoned to the power of the strong involves as remarkable a piece of twisted reasoning as can ever have been devised.

Much the same goes for arguments about the needs of childbearing women. If you were really concerned about the well-being of women and children, and also thought that women needed men to help them, you would hardly think of rules making it difficult for women to escape from men since, according to your hypothesis, women would be anxious to hold on to them anyway. What you would need would be rules to keep *men* in order. You might reasonably insist on the chaperoning of men, to make sure they did not go around idly begetting children without committing themselves to their support, and on men's being subject to social ostracism if they were found to have eluded this vigilance and *fallen*. And given that your concern was for the protection of women and children, you would also want to make sure that they were left as well off as possible whenever men did try to evade their responsibilities, perhaps by making it harder for men to divorce women than the other way round, or putting a straying man's possessions into the control of the deserted woman. You would also be anxious to see that women were sufficiently well educated and employable to fend for themselves if all else failed. Nothing could be further from this than the traditional arrangements, which not only allowed men to scatter their maker's image through the land without suffering much in the way of social consequences, but also systematically deprived women of any adequate means of supporting themselves independently of men, and made matters even worse by heaping ferocious social penalties on unsupported women and unauthorized children. … Feminists need hardly bother to dispute traditional premises while traditionalist logic is in such a state.

(Radcliffe Richards (1994), pp. 369–70)

Stephen obviously thinks of men in general as solidly upstanding citizens who can be relied upon to look after their wives with benevolent paternalism: people who arrive 'deliberately' at decisions which the wives ought to respect, and who are 'of all fools the greatest' if they do not avail themselves of their wives' good advice; but as Mill also pointed out (Mill (1991 edn), p. 507), when you are making laws you must allow for the fact that many women will find themselves married to such fools, and worse. Good men will treat women properly whatever the laws say; the only people who benefit from the powers given to men are therefore the men who will abuse them.

What this shows, I think, is that the problem with Stephen's argument lies not in the details, but in the general principle. It is just not possible to start with premises claiming that women are vulnerable by nature and should be protected, and construct anything resembling a sound argument to the conclusion that they should be placed in a state of legal or conventional subjection to their husbands.

Another way of thinking of this is to look at the matter from the other direction, and consider whether there is any kind of argument at all that could *validly* link Stephen's premise and conclusion:

> Women are at many natural disadvantages to men.
> _____
> Therefore the marriage contract should be one in which the wife is legally and socially subordinate to the husband.

In view of what has just been said this may seem impossible, but in fact it could probably be done quite easily if, instead of putting in a premise about the need to consider the interests of the weak, you put in something like:

> The weak should be treated as the slaves of the strong.

or

> We should follow the will of God, which is to advance the interests of men as far as possible.

or

> The strong should be made even stronger, and the weak made even weaker.

Not many people would be willing to do that, however; not, at least, in public.

Fundamental and derived values

The overall purpose of this long discussion has been to investigate a claim of Kitcher's about the implications of sociobiology: that if its claims are true, we shall have to abandon our ideals of political justice. It is this that underpins his contention that it should be presumed false until proved true.

It is clear that the ideals he is referring to are of a left-wing kind, and it is true that sociobiology is often presumed to have right-wing political implications. However, we have just been testing this idea by looking at an argument that claimed to derive decidedly right-wing conclusions about the appropriate relationship of the sexes from premises that sound very like some of the things sociobiologists claim about men and women. But the argument does not work even if you accept the premises – which shows, if nothing else, that you should no more take your political opponents' word for the *implications* of their claims about human nature than for the claims themselves.

Of course the failure of one particular argument does not in itself dispose of all claims about right-wing implications. But in fact the analysis of Stephen's argument does also show, indirectly, that particular sociobiological theories cannot undermine egalitarian – or indeed any other – fundamental ideals. The point is that the structure of the argument we have been considering shows two different *levels* of ideal. One ideal, expressed in the conclusion of the argument, is about the laws and conventions that should define the relationship between the sexes; but that is an ideal Stephen purports to *derive* from a more fundamental ideal of protecting the weak. According to the argument, therefore, his *fundamental* ideal is of protecting the weak. And *that* has nothing to do with his theories about the nature of men and women. Those theories are relevant only to what might be called his *derived* or *applied* or *practical* ideals: the ones he derives – or rather claims to derive – from the application of the fundamental ideals to what he regards as the facts of a particular case. So the fundamental ideals are quite independent of any claims about men and women; and even the derived/practical ideals are not derived from the claims about men and women alone, but from those claims *in conjunction with* the more fundamental ideals.

So what can be said about Kitcher and the idea that evolutionary psychology is a threat to his ideals? If the question is about *fundamental* ideals, then, whatever his ideals are, it seems that there can be no threat. If one of his fundamental ideals of justice is, for instance, that the well-being of men and women should be regarded as equally important, that concern is quite untouched by whether the blank-paper or the gene-machine view of the natures of the sexes is right. Of course he may also hold a particular set of *derived* or *practical* ideals, based on the application of his fundamental ideals to beliefs about what the sexes (to continue this example) are like; and if he changes those beliefs, he may have to change those practical ideals *in order to* keep to his fundamental ideals. In that sense a change from a blank-paper to a gene-machine view might involve a change of ideals (though it might not, and it might be no more likely to involve such a change than would a change of theory *within* one of these broad approaches; everything would depend on the details). But someone who really holds a particular set of fundamental ideals should welcome any evidence that shows more accurate ways of applying them.

Kitcher's argument is based on the claim that in contexts where we are using our scientific theories about human nature as a basis for action, 'close methodological scrutiny is appropriate precisely because of the consequences for social policies and individual lives if we turn out to be mistaken'. That is obviously right; but it provides no reason at all for saying that the mistake of presuming sociobiological ideas true if they are false is worse than that of presuming them false if they are true. According to this argument, a mistake is potentially bad either way. It may often be possible in particular cases to decide that a risk in one direction is better than a risk in the other, but no reason has been given for taking the default presumption to be against sociobiology in general.

So it seems to me that Kitcher is just wrong about this matter. The only values that might be threatened by the truth of evolutionary psychology are the derived ones that result from combining the fundamental ones with particular empirical beliefs. Of course people are often strongly attached to the details of their beliefs about values at the practical level, probably in practice more strongly than to the fundamental values in terms of which they try to justify them. Stephen is obviously attached to his ideas about the appropriate relationship between the sexes, and so, probably, are many left-wing critics of sociobiology to their views of what a good society would look like. But if they really hold the fundamental values they profess to hold, they should be eager to change the derived values if the need arises.

It is also worth adding to this conclusion another moral to be drawn from the Stephen analysis: that the relationship between the two levels of ideal may not be at all obvious. When people are wedded to particular habits of mind at the derived, practical level (as Stephen is to his beliefs about how marriage should be organized) but are also committed – at least in theory – to benevolent general principles such as that of protecting the weak, they automatically try to justify one in terms of the other. But in doing so they may well entangle themselves in logical confusions that would have been immediately obvious if they had not already been so committed to their practical conclusion. So, even though the pursuit of your fundamental values should make you willing to change your derived, practical values in the light of new evidence about matters of fact, you certainly should not take your opponents' word for the need to do this. Feminists need not resist Stephen's premise about the sexes in order to resist his conclusion about marriage, because even if the premise is true, the conclusion does not follow. All that can be inferred from his premises is something diametrically opposed to the situation he is trying to defend. And you will find, if you analyse them, that this is true of nearly all traditional arguments about the position of women.

Exercise 9.2

What kind of moral presupposition ('ought' statement) is implied by the following claims?

(i)   [Social Darwinism] Evolution works by eliminating the unfit, so we should not support socially incompetent people.
(ii)   [Eugenics] There is a strong hereditary component in intelligence, so we need social policies that encourage intelligent people to have more children.
(iii) Men are naturally inclined to philander, and as this makes women unhappy it should be punishable by law.
(iv)   It would be wrong to do medical experiments on unconsenting people even if we were sure those experiments would prevent enormous suffering elsewhere.

(v)   Sadomasochistic practices between consenting adults should be completely legal.

(vi)   More people would enjoy the ascent of Everest if there were a railway, so we should build one.

(Answers on pp. 286–7)

Ethics and the natural order

According to the previous arguments, the only values and ideals threatened by changes in our understanding of our nature are the practical, derived ones, while the fundamental ones remain intact. In other words, the 'is'/'ought' distinction remains intact.

But is this obviously true? Many people express doubts about Hume's distinction, and a great many more – who do not think to put the matter that way – clearly do, in practice, make the assumption that conclusions about what ought to happen *can* be derived directly from an understanding of the nature of things. And, interestingly, I think there is evidence that this is the idea that really underlies Stephen's attitude. His official argument is based on the need to protect the weak; but there are in his text indications of a quite different kind of reasoning about the positions of the sexes, which makes a much more direct connection between their natures and their appropriate situations. Here, for instance, is a passage that comes just before the extract we have been considering …

> Government … ought to fit society as a man's clothes fit him. To establish by law rights and duties which assume that people are equal when they are not is like trying to make clumsy feet look handsome by the help of tight boots. No doubt it may be necessary to legislate in such a manner as to correct the vices of society or to protect it against special dangers or diseases to which it is liable. Law in this case is analogous to surgery, and the rights and duties imposed by it might be compared to the irons which are sometimes contrived for the purpose of supporting a weak limb or keeping it in some particular position. As a rule, however, it is otherwise … Rights and duties should be so moulded as to clothe, protect and sustain society in the position which it naturally assumes.
>
> (Stephen, ibid., p. 192)

Similar ideas are also suggested at various points in the extract we have just been discussing. For instance, Stephen says of the differences between men and women that 'this general truth, which has been observed under all sorts of circumstances and in every age and country, has also in every age and country led to a division of labour between men and women, the general outline of which is as familiar and as universal as the general outline of the differences between them', and that anyone who says their functions should be the same 'has got into the region at which argument is useless'. The differences between the sexes and the implications of those differences for the way they should be treated seem to him as obvious as each other.

In other words, Stephen clearly believes that there are arrangements into which society naturally falls, and the only business of the law and institutions is to reinforce these natural arrangements, by correcting aberrations in the way that you would try to correct deformities and diseases in bodies. They should certainly not themselves do anything to *produce* such distortions and deformities, by going against the natural course of things. To understand the nature of men and women, therefore, is to recognize how society should organize their relationships.

This is still a widely held idea. It often seems to be taken for granted that the question of whether or not some characteristic is deep in evolved human nature is *directly* relevant to the question of how we should respond to it and its manifestations, rather than just evidence that we should take into account along with other evidence. Many responses to the kinds of claim made by genetic researchers and evolutionary psychologists show an automatic presumption that if some characteristic can be shown to be deep in human nature, we should not be trying to control or prevent or suppress it; and, conversely, that if we do want to suppress whatever it is, we need to show that the characteristic is not deep in our nature, but socially induced: a kind of deformity, such as might be caused by ill-fitting shoes.

One familiar illustration of this comes in the arguments about homosexuality, and the debate about whether people are born gay. On the face of it, it seems most unlikely that homosexuality could be an evolved characteristic, since you would expect a genetic preference for your own sex to be eliminated by natural selection the moment it appeared; but people do propose sociobiological theories to explain it, and there are much-publicized claims about discoveries of gay genes and the like. These theories and purported discoveries, however, are not generally treated just as interesting scientific hypotheses, to be tested in a spirit of objective enquiry; they are obviously regarded as directly – not indirectly – relevant to the debate about how homosexuals should be treated. There is a high correlation between the demand for unconditional social acceptance of homosexuality and the insistence that it is innate, and there is a virtually universal correlation between demands for restriction and the claim that it is an unnatural, socially induced corruption, to which impressionable children should on no account be exposed.

This pattern of thinking is repeated in innumerable contexts. It is strongly connected with every single debate about sex. Whenever there are claims from evolutionary psychologists about evolved tendencies of men to philander, or rape, or prefer younger women, or seek status, or fight each other, or of women to be much more closely tied to their children than men or to long for the protection of high-status men, those claims are instantly taken by one side of the political debate to imply that all these things should be condoned or encouraged, while the other side takes it for granted that if that condoning or encouraging is to be resisted, the claims themselves must be denied. In other words, the defenders on *both* sides of such political controversies are presupposing that if something is deep in evolved human nature, its manifestations must be regarded as positively desirable or at least not wrong. The same happens with ideas about natural tendencies to establish hierarchies, or to respond with suspicion to foreigners, or to engage in hunting or warfare. The presupposition is that to know our nature is not just to know how to set about applying ideals that exist independently of that knowledge, but to know directly how we should behave.

There seems little doubt that ideas of this kind – which see 'ought' and 'is' as intimately connected – lie at the root of much of the anxiety about evolutionary psychology. They may even be the real source of Kitcher's conclusion that evolutionary psychology should be presumed false until proved true; they certainly would, if justified, offer a possible line of argument to his conclusion. But are they justified? The idea that any discoveries about human nature should be treated as moral guides is one that needs to be addressed directly.

This was a subject raised and then set aside in Chapter 6, in the discussion of responsibility and blame. It was pointed out there (p. 129) that there were two distinct questions about whether people should be blamed for acting according to impulses that were deep in their natures: one about their *responsibility* for such actions, and the other about their *wrongness*. Blame is inappropriate unless there is both responsibility and wrongness. The discussion in Chapter 6 was specifically about whether the truth of the gene-machine view would preclude philandering men's being genuinely *responsible* for their actions; here the question is whether its truth would show that their actions were not *wrong*, and should therefore not be criticized.

Keeping to this specific example – though of course any other candidate would do as well – this means we need to consider the truth of the conditional:

> If polygynous inclinations are deep in the evolved nature of men, then we should not criticize/punish/try to prevent male philandering.

This gives the outline argument:

> Polygynous inclinations are deep in the evolved nature of men.
> ───────
> Therefore we should not criticize/punish/try to prevent male philan-dering.

And since the idea we are considering is that acting according to our deepest nature is positively right, or at least not wrong, the argument needs to be completed along these lines:

> Polygynous inclinations are deep in the evolved nature of men.
> *We should not prevent people from acting according to their natures.*
> ───────
> Therefore we should not criticize/punish/try to prevent male philan-dering.

The problem now is to assess the added premise. As usual, there is no obvious limit to the kinds of argument that might be offered in support of it, but there seem to be two main ideas around. One is that nature is harmonious, and should not be disrupted; the other is that evolution is progress, and should not be held back. Consider those in turn.

Nature as harmonious

The first of these ideas is another that lies in the background of the Stephen passage, which makes it clear not only *that* he sees nature is a guide to what we should do, but also *why* he thinks so. He clearly has a view of the world as a place where if you follow the natural order of things, all will generally go well; and if you do not, you will run into trouble. This shows in the similes of well-fitting clothes and tight shoes; a society that tries to force people into places they do not naturally fit will cause distortion and misery. It is also suggested in the same paragraph by the idea that laws are needed to correct what goes wrong. We know what properly functioning legs are supposed to do, so we know when to apply irons to straighten or support them. Then, at the end of the earlier extract, he refers to the *common* interests of 'the two great divisions of mankind', and specifically says that men and women can no more have conflicting interests than different members of the same body. The natural arrangement is what is best for both of them. The same thing is also implied, I think, in the idea that an insubordinate woman is *mutinous* – rebellious against the established order – in trying to subvert the arrangements that are in place for the good of both parties, even though on some particular occasion she may have better judgement than her husband.

What all this suggests is that Stephen's world view is of a broadly Aristotelian kind, in which everything has a natural place, and in which, when everything is where it should be, there is harmony. Once you understand the nature of something you know what its place is, and you understand that when it is taken out of that place there will be turmoil until it returns.

According to this way of thinking, then, we can consider the justification of the second premise as going something like this:

> *If everything acts according to its nature/occupies its natural place, the world is best for everyone.*
> *We should make the world best for everyone.*
> _____
> Therefore we should not prevent people from acting according to their natures.

(It may be worth noting in passing that even this way of setting things out makes the fundamental value independent of the facts; you might not want to make the world best for everyone. But since the details of the 'is'/'ought' distinction are less important than the general idea about nature and order, I shall not discuss it further.)

Now of course the question about whether the world is actually of this kind, where there is a natural and harmonious order, is a substantive one: it is part of the debate about Mind First views of the world. But we are at the moment concerned not with substantive questions of which view of the world is right, but with the *implications* of the different views; and the question at the moment is about the implications of the gene-machine view. So what we have to ask is whether *given* that view of human nature – a materialist, cranes-only view – we should accept the idea that nature is harmonious, and that to know the natures of human beings is to know how they should act and be treated.

And to that the simple answer is that, in a materialist Darwinian universe, there is no natural order of this kind at all. Things do not have proper places which result in overall harmony. There are arrangements we take for granted because they are what we are used to – or what we used to be used to, or what we think people used to be used to before some selected disapproved-of innovation appeared – and to which we give names like 'the balance of nature', but in Darwinian nature what we are used to is just a passing phase in a universe that has been in a state of turmoil since it began. Objectively, according to the materialist view, none of the possible or actual states of the universe is any more natural or proper than any other; all states are equally natural. There is nothing that counts even as a state of rest or balance, let alone one that could be expected to produce peace and harmony of the kind human beings value. In fact you can turn Stephen's simile back to front. He says that the sexes can no more have conflicting interests than different parts of the same body; Darwinian biologists are increasingly claiming that different parts of the same body are in just as much conflict as are men and women. Within bodies, as between the sexes, remarkable accommodations are made, but this is not because of an overall, underlying harmony. It is just because anything that could not make such compromises would not survive.

From this it follows that understanding the evolved nature of Darwinian organisms, including ourselves, shows nothing at all about the position they *should* be in, because there is no such position. To understand them is only to understand another series of conditionals: *if* this is done, the effect will be this; *if* that is done, the effect will be something else. If you want to produce as much harmony and happiness as possible you need to know what all these things are like, so that you have a thorough grasp of your raw materials. But that is only the beginning of the work. Organisms do not carry implicit instructions about how they are to be moved towards that state, let alone guarantees that they can be got there.

Perhaps the simplest and most effective way to express all this is to understand the familiar inference from Darwinian nature to political and moral conclusions as involving equivocation with different, and opposed, conceptions of nature. If we add the argument about a harmonious universe, above, to the earlier argument (p. 244) about philandering, we get a composite like this:

> If everything acts according to its nature/occupies its natural place, the world is best for everyone.
> We should make the world best for everyone.
> _____
> Therefore we should not prevent people from acting according to their natures.
> Polygynous inclinations are deep in the evolved nature of men.
> _____
> Therefore we should not criticize/punish/try to prevent male philandering.

Is that argument valid? If it is to be interpreted in a way that makes it valid, 'nature' and 'natural' must have consistent meanings throughout. But the first premise presupposes an ordered, Aristotelian-type world, while the claim about evolved polygynous inclinations presupposes an incompatible gene-machine world. The conception of nature changes, so the argument is a fallacy of equivocation.

Alternatively, if you interpret it as being valid, by taking the first premise to refer to materialist Darwinian nature, that premise is false. The first premise is true only if 'according to their nature' means something quite different from the characteristics produced by Darwinian evolution.

My suspicion is that this conflation of two incompatible ideas about nature lies at the root of most of the resistance to evolutionary psychology. The claims of evolutionary psychology can be accepted only on the basis of a belief that the universe is not naturally ordered and harmonious, and therefore that the claims about what is natural in that sense have no normative force at all. They tell you what the raw materials are, which you need to know if you are to implement your values, but give no indication of what you should be doing with them.

This general point is also of much wider importance if, as I suspect, the confusion infuses nearly all our social and moral thinking, and most current debates about scientific and environmental matters. But that needs a book to itself.

Evolution as progress

We have been considering the second premise of the argument:

> Polygynous inclinations are deep in the evolved nature of men.
> *We should not prevent people from acting according to their natures.*
> _____
> Therefore we should not criticize/punish/try to prevent male philandering.

The last section was a discussion of *one particular possible defence* of that claim: the idea that following nature was the best route to harmony. But even if the second premise cannot be defended in that way, it may be possible to find another argument. Quite often the rejection of one particular line of defence has the effect of clarifying others; and this discussion may have brought to mind a quite different idea about natural behaviour, which is explicitly evolutionary and seems devoid of all ideas of quasi-Aristotelian ordered universes. This is the idea that if you try to thwart the characteristics that have been bred into us by evolution, you damage evolutionary progress.

A justification of the second premise along these lines might go something like this:

> *Evolution by natural selection works by replacing less good designs by better ones.*
> *The characteristics bred into us by evolution are the ones that have made us succeed in the evolutionary competition.*
> *We should not interfere with the onwards and upwards progress of evolution.*
> ⎯⎯⎯⎯⎯
> Therefore we should not prevent people from acting according to their natures.

This is rather vague (for reasons that will become clear later), but it is recognizable, and it gives a different kind of reason for not interfering with natural characteristics. There is no expectation of harmony here. Evolution is seen as perpetual competition, and the argument depends on taking not harmony, but continuing upward progress, as the overriding value.

This is a familiar idea of evolution. It is the one that is caught by the expression 'the survival of the fittest', and which sees natural selection as steadily replacing substandard designs with better ones. Variations arise by chance and are of all kinds, but natural selection, on this view, ensures that only the best survive. The result has been the steady progress from the very simplest organisms to us. We have superseded the dinosaurs and other obsolete creatures, and, according to this line of thought, if we want to make sure this progress continues, or even maintain evolutionary achievement at its present level, we must not interfere with the exercise of the characteristics by which nature has ensured these marvels.

It is ideas like these that underlie the use of 'dinosaur' for anything that has been overtaken by new and by better things, and also the familiar, linear picture of human evolution, which starts with a monkey and leads through hominids of gradually increasing and upright stature to us. They are also recognizable as the roots of Social Darwinism, with its belief that if you prop up the unfit, you damage the progress of the human race by not letting the substandard die off as nature intends. The idea that we should not curtail characteristics that are deep in our evolved nature is the Social Darwinist idea viewed from the other side.

Still, in spite of the persistence of this image, it is quite wrong as a representation of Darwinian evolution, for several reasons.

To start with, the centrepiece of the picture dissolves under even the most cursory consideration. It is obviously false that we are here because we have replaced lesser things, because many of those lesser things are still here, in numbers and quantities that leave us insignificant. Although we are (presumably) cleverer than dinosaurs, that is obviously not the explanation of why we are here and they are not, since bacteria and nematode worms, which developed long before the dinosaurs, are still here; as are crocodiles and coelacanths, which are dinosaur contemporaries. And this is because the 'fitness' selected for by evolution is *nothing but* success at leaving descendants. The evolutionary competition is not about increasing cleverness, or increasing anything else, except incidentally to the extent that these characteristics help the creatures that have them to pass on their genes. Although we have obviously found intelligence useful, most creatures get on with the business of passing on their genes perfectly well without it.

In fact, since evolution is not forward-looking, it is not even true that the creatures produced get better and better at surviving. Survival happens in particular contexts, and although natural selection quickly weeds out the no-hopers, it can let all kinds of rather precarious creatures (like flightless birds) carry on for ages if suitable predators do not appear; and, conversely, wonderful bits of design can be eliminated by floods or asteroids.

So the first element of this idea, that evolution works by letting superior things like us replace the primitive ones lower down the scale, is just false. This means that if we want evolution to take an upward direction, we cannot just refrain from intervening and let nature get on with its course – which is why Social Darwinism was superseded by eugenics. *Whatever* we think the human race should be trying to achieve, there is bound to be indefinite scope for improving on nature.

Perhaps, however, this does not seem to undermine completely the idea of evolution as progress. Surely, it may be said, the fact that the lesser creatures remain around doesn't alter the fact that evolution has obviously been a steady forward progress? If we try to impede nature by curtailing our ingrained impulses, we may stop that forward movement.

This claim does look plausible at first glance. There were originally only very simple creatures, but gradually more complex ones developed, and now we have the pinnacle of achievement (so far) in ourselves. Nevertheless, there must be something badly wrong somewhere in this argument, since if the upward progress of evolution does not work by the replacement of the inferior by the superior, how is it supposed to work?

This was the problem faced by early ideas of evolution, such as those held by Erasmus Darwin. It certainly looked as though evolution was a progression from simple to complex, since that was what the fossil record seemed to show, but the problem was to find a mechanism by which this could come about. Charles Darwin eventually solved the problem by finding a mechanism by which evolution could work – but in doing so he completely overturned the early conception of evolution as steady onward progress. Darwinian evolution does not take the form of steady progress up the Great Chain of Being, as the earlier ideas of evolution had imagined.

This is a point that evolutionary biologists keep trying to explain, though they do not seem to have had much effect on the deep perception of evolution as progress. But here is one succinct account, which seems to make the point with admirable clarity – as well as reinforcing the previous point about replacement:

> Evolution is diversification in all directions, but there are more options available in some directions than others. Organisms started out small and short-lived and couldn't get much smaller, but they could always get larger and more long-lived. For the smallest organisms, the resources that can be devoted to internal representations of the world are limited … But the upper end of the range of information-handling abilities was not similarly bounded, and so the difference between the low end and the upper end of this range has increased over the hundreds of million years of animal evolution as part of this diversification. Nevertheless, the number of small-brained creatures has not diminished because of competition with those with big brains, and the no-brainers – all the plants and single-celled organisms – vastly outnumber the rest of us.
>
> (Deacon, 1997, p. 30)

The point is easily understood if you concentrate on some simple characteristic like size. Diversification meant that bigger and bigger organisms could be produced; but we know that increase in size was not straightforward, uninterrupted progress, because the biggest (land) animals there have been no longer exist. Large animals must be preceded by smaller ones, but that does not mean that small animals cannot follow larger ones. There is nothing to stop evolutionary change from being (in this sense) backwards, because the bigger animals get, the more niches are created in the smallness direction.

There is also no reason to presume that things must be different in the case of what we particularly value, our intelligence. For all we know there may have been in the past people more intelligent than any alive now; we really haven't the faintest idea. We certainly have no reason to think that our most intelligent forebears must have left the most children. Stone-age Newtons and Einsteins would probably have been eaten by bears while their minds were otherwise occupied, and anyway would have been unlikely to stand much chance, with females, against impressive providers of food and protection.

The impression of Darwinian evolution as pushing relentlessly forward is an illusion caused by the fact that organisms must be small and simple before they can be large and complex, and, perhaps, also by the necessary truth that some currently existing creature is going to be the extreme representative of any characteristic at all. So we certainly cannot presume that it would, left to itself, produce a steady increase in human intelligence, or any other capacities we value.

These two points are enough to dispose completely of the case against interference with evolutionarily produced inclinations; but it is worth mentioning, as well, what is perhaps an even more fundamental point: the fact that in a Darwinian world there can be no such thing as *interference*. You cannot interfere with something that has no underlying purpose to be interfered with, and Darwinian evolution has none. Evolution is just what happens, not what is in any sense trying to happen, and this means that everything is part of the evolutionary process.

The significance of this point lies in the suggestion, at the beginning of this section, that this way of defending the claim that nature should not be impeded was entirely Darwinian, and did not – like the harmony defence – depend on quasi-Aristotelian ideas of a planned and ordered universe. But this is wrong, because the whole idea of interference depends on the assumption of an ordered universe. On a Mind First view it makes sense to claim that human beings can choose to act in a way that is out of line with the way ordained by nature, and that it is this improper, unnatural behaviour that is sending things awry. But in a world of Darwinian materialism there is nothing to interfere with.

And, in fact, the whole idea of general onward and upward progress depends on the same non-Darwinian assumptions. It is only against the background of a universe with a natural order – something like the Great Chain of Being – that the idea of all-purpose progress makes sense. Without that assumption, you can ask only about *particular kinds* of progress: increasing speed, or resistance to cold, or length of life, or whatever. There is no all-purpose measure for progress in general.

So this line of defence of the idea of leaving things to nature, which seems to appeal only to ideas of Darwinian evolution, is really as dependent on imported ideas of a non-Darwinian ordered universe as the previous one. Evolution in an ordered universe might have an onwards and upwards progress which could be interfered with; Darwinian evolution has not. And once again if you mix the two, you commit fallacies of equivocation as before.

Actually, the whole idea of evolution as progress is so confused that it is difficult to construct an argument that looks valid even before you start pointing out equivocations – which is why the argument at the beginning of this section looked so vague. (This is one reason why it is good to try to put things like this in argument form: you may reach the root of the problem quickly by discovering that it cannot be done.) But if you were not too critical, you might think something like this looked plausible:

> Evolution is an onwards and upwards process.
> We should not interfere with that process.
> Evolution has made men polygynous.
> ———
> Therefore we should not try to prevent male philandering.

But even if you were sufficiently off guard to take that as structurally valid, there would still be a fallacy of equivocation. The idea of evolution as an onwards and upwards process is a variant on the ordered universe; the claim about male polygyny presupposes a Darwinian universe in which there is no such onwards and upwards progress. The argument depends on a shift from one to the other.

So the conclusion remains, on this argument as on the previous one. A Darwinian understanding of evolved characteristics cannot on its own offer any guide to what we ought to be doing. It can give us the information that may be relevant to the achieving of our ends, whatever those are, but it cannot specify the ends. There is no natural goal any more than there is natural harmony. In a Darwinian world values remain obdurately separate from the facts, and we have to decide what to try to achieve on the basis of the understanding we have.

And once that is clear, it also becomes clear that even if the idea of leaving things to nature in a Darwinian world made any sense – which it doesn't, since we are part of nature and everything we do is part of the evolutionary process – it would be the *least* reliable way of trying to achieve anything we wanted to achieve. Natural selection does not select for anything except survival, so it has no mechanism by which it could systematically produce whatever we thought of as valuable. And even if it could, it would still have as its raw materials only chance variations piled on top of QWERTY phenomena. Our own plans are saddled with the QWERTY phenomena too, but at least we can do something to control the variations available, and make the selections ourselves. It may not seem a very reliable way to achieve our ends, but it is beyond measure more reliable than standing back and trying to let Darwinian nature take an Aristotelian course.

Hopes and disappointments

Finally, consider one other way in which the claims of evolutionary psychology might seem a threat to our aspirations to better things. It might be thought that even though the truth of its theories would not dictate the social arrangements we should make, it would nevertheless constrain the kind of success we might hope to achieve.

The concern here is that if evolutionary psychologists are right, then no matter how we manipulate our social institutions, human nature will set limits to how much real change we can bring about. If women are by nature less driven and ambitious than men, for instance, and their attention more easily distracted from their careers by the needs of their families, then women will remain in low professional positions no matter how much effort we put into removing institutional glass ceilings. If women's nature induces them to want men long after men are programmed to find them attractive, then no matter how independent and self-sufficient women are made, they will always be vulnerable to desertion. If men are by nature ambitious for status and influence in the public world, we shall never be able to make men share equally in domestic life; if we are all innately xenophobic then we shall never end racism. And so on. And this may also seem to offer yet another possible way to justify Kitcher's conclusion that we should presume evolutionary psychology false until it has been proved true. If the truth of evolutionary psychology would make our hopes of a just society unfulfillable, it might seem better to act on the basis of the standard social science view, just in the hope that this might work.

So is it really true that if the gene-machine view of human nature is true there is no chance of our changing the familiar facts of life such as the pattern of interaction between the sexes, while if the blank-paper view is right change is possible? Once again, answering this question is a matter of assessing a pair of conditionals:

> If the gene-machine view is true, change in sexual relationships is impossible.
> If the blank-paper view is true, change in sexual relationships is possible.

But here there is no need to go further and set the conditionals out as arguments, because this issue has already been analysed in Chapter 5 (p. 117). The idea that the blank-paper view allows for radical change, while the gene-machine view does not, depends in turn on the idea that characteristics induced by social conditioning can be changed or prevented, while characteristics explainable in terms of evolutionary origins are fixed. But if the arguments of Chapter 5 are right, there is no reason at all to regard this as generally true. Whether something is easy or difficult to change depends on the state of our knowledge, and on our ability to control circumstances. Even if a change in social values and organization could, in principle, alter any of the familiar characteristics we regard as unwelcome, that is not of the slightest practical use unless we both know how they are caused and have the power to make the necessary changes. People with blank-paper views of human nature and ideals of sex equality are only too well aware of how far we are from achieving those ideals; and if they are convinced their underlying theory about social causes is right, they must also accept that making the necessary changes cannot be easy.

Conversely, an evolutionary explanation of the emotional gulf would not preclude the possibility of our finding means to lessen it. Even if, as Gould says, characteristics produced in us by natural selection could not be removed 'either by will, education, or culture', an ingenious and technologically minded species may well be able to find other ways of improving the situation. Women may have as yet no idea how to remove the male preference for younger women, but they have for as long as anyone knows been trying to outmanoeuvre it by manipulating what are now understood as visual clues to age – lightening their hair, pulling in their waists, and enlarging their eyes – and that was even before the Joan Collins possibilities of cosmetic surgery. Techniques to counteract the appearance and other symptoms of ageing are bound to go on developing. And there are all kinds of other directions from which the problem of sexual mismatch might be approached. Researchers already claim to have isolated, and are marketing, both male and female pheromones, intended to cause sexual attraction even when the visual signals are less than ideal. Mind-affecting drugs are being discovered all the time, so maybe it will not be all that long before someone comes up with that gyno-Prozac, to make women unconcerned about male interest, or with something on the lines of a traditional love potion that men could take to fix their affections on a particular woman and leave them immune to the traditional temptations of variety and youth. The possibilities are endless, and only moderately fanciful.

Such possibilities, of course, immediately raise another objection – also mentioned in Chapter 5 but then set aside for later discussion – which is that whatever we may be *able* to do, we *should* not interfere with nature in such radical ways. Even where change of deeply rooted human characteristics does not seem impossible, it seems to be widely taken for granted that if troublesome differences between the sexes – or any other human woes – are produced by social values and pressures, we are *justified* in trying to eliminate them; if, on the other hand, they are deep in human nature, and changeable only by artificial interventions, they must be accepted whether we like it or not.

But it is probably already obvious that the answer to this has already been given, by implication, in the last two sections. There is nothing about Darwinian nature to make either kind of action intrinsically more legitimate than the other. The idea that if unwelcome characteristics can be put right by social arrangements it is legitimate to do it, but not if they they need changes of a pharmacological or genetic kind, again seems to be rooted in assumptions of a naturally ordered universe. Against that background it would make sense to distinguish between social and other kinds of change, because if things were awry that would show that our arrangements were the cause of the trouble and should be remedied, whereas interventions of other kinds would be meddling in the nature of things, playing God, and generally inviting the kind of retribution that has traditionally been visited on hubris. But against a background of Darwinian nature there can be no such distinction. Each case for each kind of intervention must be considered individually.

This may seem obvious in theory. Materialist Darwinians are not likely to invoke ideas of universal harmony when they justify their resistance to interventions of these radical kinds. But even if such ideas are not there explicitly, they may be lurking in the background, distorting arguments that seem to be presented in other terms – as with Stephen's attempts to justify his deep convictions about the natural place of women in terms of their need for protection. And in the light of this, it is always worth working in critical detail through arguments that seem to provide a justification for avoiding such unnatural activities, because even though the traditional reasons may no longer be given, the traditional presuppositions may still be in the background, doing the same work.

If you want to test this, look at the details of any case where people are arguing against some interference with nature (GM crops, pharmacological approaches to psychological problems) and see whether the arguments would persuade anyone who did not already believe on other grounds that the intervention in question was wrong. Or consider some invented case as a thought experiment, perhaps imagining that someone had come up with that gyno-

Prozac, or the male fidelity drug. Start by clearing the case of extraneous clutter by assuming such a drug has gone through the usual run of safety tests, and that nobody is being forced to take it. Would there be any good reason for objecting to its being made available?

The starting point of the analysis in cases like this must be the potential for *good*. If women are made miserable by philandering men, for instance, or non-philandering men made miserable by desires to philander where their opportunities or principles do not allow them to do so, there is something presumptively good about a means of suppressing these desires. Any man who took the hypothetical fidelity drug would no longer be tempted by variety and youth, and would remain contentedly with his ageing woman, to the satisfaction (let us suppose) of both. The burden of proof is therefore on anyone who objects, to say what the ground of that objection is. Are there any objections good enough to overcome the presumption on the other side? What suggestions might there be?

One might be that if you suppressed the instincts that had kept the human race going, there would be a threat to its survival. But that does not work. To start with, the number of children born is determined by reproductive capacities of women, not men; for another, there is no suggestion in this experiment that the men will not breed. The effect would only be the same as if the men who took the drug kept to the monogamy enjoined anyway by many religions and social codes, so from this point of view there is no difference between social and pharmacological interventions – except that the drug makes fidelity easier and more pleasant.

Well, then, it might be said, the children born would have different fathers from the ones they otherwise would have had. The men who take the drug will be less sexually, and therefore less reproductively, successful. But there are several replies to this, too.

First, the drug would make no difference at all to most men's sexual success. For one thing, some men are monogamous on principle; the drug would make no difference to their activities. More fundamentally, it would be quite impossible for all men to fulfil their natural desires unless a large proportion of women had and could indulge comparable desires. The very existence of prostitution as a profession shows how far this is from the case. If evolutionary psychologists are right, women in general are not emotionally inclined to great sexual variety, and their partners are also likely to take a dim view of infidelity; but whether or not that is the reason, most male desire for sexual variety goes unmet. The men who were going to fail anyway would have nothing to lose but their frustrations – and, perhaps, their wives' anxieties.

Second, sexual success does not, anyway, translate into reproductive success. Even if you get more than your fair share of sex, that certainly does not in itself imply more than your share of children. In many parts of the world there is probably already very little correlation between success in achieving sexual variety and the kind of success the genes might be said to be interested in; contraception and feminism are seeing to that. The general point here is, once again, that evolution by natural selection is never forward-looking. If male tendencies to philander are deep in the genes, as evolutionary psychologists think, that is because those tendencies *have been* successful in our evolutionary history; but characteristics that have led to reproductive success in the past may not do so in the future. In fact if they did, there would never be evolutionary change. Success depends on environment as well as the intrinsic characteristics of organisms, and environments are changing all the time. For this reason, as well, there is no reason to think that a suppressor of male desires for variety need have much effect on any man's reproductive rate.

But finally, suppose all that were not true, and that men who otherwise would have had more than their fair share of children had fewer. What harm would that do? It may seem that the best specimens of manhood would fail to leave as many children as they otherwise would. But in what sense are they the best? As already established, success in reproduction does not in itself imply being best at anything else at all, let alone at anything we particularly value. (Are the most reproductively successful people you know the best in other ways?) If the men that would have been successful cease to be so, that only means that others will be successful instead. And if we are concerned about which men have children – because we are concerned about making the race as good as possible – we should start by deciding what characteristics to select for. Most people will shudder at the thought, since that amounts to eugenics. But there is certainly no reason to think that letting the natural desires of men continue on their course will do the job for us.

What other objections might be raised to the availability of a male fidelity drug? There is, of course, the commonest of all objections to all innovations about which people feel uncomfortable: the possibility that the drug might have unforeseen side-effects. And of course it might, but so might any intervention whatever, including social and political ones, and so, equally, might *refraining* from using this drug. The trouble with unknown effects is that, just because they are unknown, they apply equally in all directions. Unknown effects are another universal acid; and when people start to use them selectively it shows, as much in this case as in others, that they have run out of proper arguments. Once the case against intervention reaches this stage, it does look as though what is doing the real work is pre-Darwinian presuppositions, grafted on to premises drawn from Darwinian nature.

I am not suggesting that this is all there is to be said here; in any particular case, of course, there might be particular arguments against allowing such a drug. But when the immediate response to the refutation of any objection is to seek out another objection, it is a sign that other considerations are in the background. There is a good deal of evidence, from all kinds of contexts, that the Mind First view continues to influence the reasoning of people who have officially rejected it. Without such presuppositions, there is no reason to think that our social ideals are more difficult to achieve on the blank-paper view than the gene-machine view. Once again, there is no difference between the implications of the two.

Overview

The purpose of this long chapter – in case its overall argument has by now been lost in the detail – has been to compare the implications of the blank-paper and gene-machine views of human nature from the point of view of political ideals and hopes for a better world, and in particular to consider the familiar idea that gene-machinery has right-wing implications. This is the basis of Kitcher's claim that sociobiology should be presumed false until proved true. But *fundamental* values lie beyond the territory of the Darwin wars; and derived, practical values are not derived from the facts alone but from facts in conjunction with fundamental values. And the implications of the facts – even with values conjoined – do not depend on the general question of whether gene machinery or the standard social science view is on the right track, but on the details of what is claimed in either case. Once again, there is no difference of implication between the two views.

Dennett thinks of standard social science opponents of evolutionary psychology as materialists who are still hankering after skyhooks. I don't think that is true: there seems no doubt that they are thoroughgoing materialists. To the extent that they are hankering, it seems to be after particular political programmes. But on the basis of the foregoing analysis, it does seem that the hostility may stem largely from carrying skyhook habits of mind to the materialist side of the divide, and taking it for granted that to discover what is deep in our Darwinian nature is to prescribe the way we ought to live. It is difficult not to do this; the skyhook way of thinking is so deep in our tradition that it pervades all our habits of thought, even when officially renounced. It is probably one of the main reasons for there being so many misunderstandings about the implications of the more radical forms of Darwinism.

The problem about much familiar reasoning in these contexts is that there are many ways in which we have not yet appreciated how radical, when it goes far enough to provide a foundation for materialism, the Darwinian revolution really is. People who theoretically accept the materialist version still often take for granted many of the presuppositions that belong to earlier views of the world. For instance, it does seem to be widely taken for granted, even among people who left religion behind long ago, that the sexes are designed to suit each other in a harmonious pairing, and that all we need to do is find what that design is and keep to it. This could not be further from the gene-machine view, that what determines the natures of males and females is not some overall plan. It is just a struggle between genes that happens to have resulted in some good and harmonious elements, but also in a great deal that is not in the least harmonious. In Wright's terms, the puppeteer – natural selection – has zero regard for the feelings of the puppets. And since natural selection is just a matter of the survival of some genes and the disappearance of others, there is not the slightest reason to expect the sexes to be well designed to make each other happy. This does not mean that it designs them to make each other miserable; it just doesn't design them at all. On a materialist view, any design is going to have to come from us.

There is a widespread belief that if the claims of evolutionary psychology were true, this would provide a justification for right-wing political programmes. This is not so. The idea results from a range of mistakes: failure to distinguish between fundamental and derived values, failure to notice mistakes of logic in traditional conservative arguments, and, of particular significance, importing quasi-Aristotelian presuppositions into Darwinian reasoning. Fundamental values of a left-wing kind cannot justify resistance to evolutionary psychology, or even claims that it should carry the burden of proof. The rival theories of materialist Darwinians have on their own no moral or political implications. Once again, a supposed difference of implication between two degrees of Darwinism turns out not to exist.

10 The real differences

So far all fears about the implications of deepening Darwinism seem to have been misguided, but one major question has not yet been discussed: the implications of the materialism boundary for ideals, hopes and the way we lead our lives. Here the differences are potentially enormous. A materialist Darwinian cannot have any of the most fundamental hopes of religious believers, and this must lead to a radically different approach to life.

Nevertheless, the fact remains that most other familiar assumptions about the implications of Darwinism seem to be wrong, so the question arises of why there should be such far-reaching implications in some contexts but none in others, and why it is that there are so many mistaken ideas about which are which. There is a range of reasons, but all involve a failure to recognize the limits to what can and cannot be changed by the advance of science, and the place of philosophical analysis in understanding ourselves and our situation.

It is obviously important to understand the facts about our situation as far as possible, since mistakes will prevent our making the best judgements about how to lead our lives. But mistakes in making inferences from those facts are just as serious. For understanding our nature and situation, the philosophical work is at least as important as the science.

Darwinians come in dyes of differing depth, and it seems to be widely thought that the deeper your dye, the more you are forced to abandon in the way of traditional ideas about ourselves and our situation, and of deeply held moral and political ideals. If the arguments so far have been right, however, this impression is mistaken. For all the issues so far discussed, no difference is made by crossing the boundary from Mind First, typically dualist, views into materialism, or from standard social science theories to evolutionary psychology.

But this is surely puzzling. What becomes of Simpson's claim, quoted at the beginning of the book, that all ideas of human nature before 1859 were worthless, and should be abandoned? What becomes of Dennett's idea of Darwinism as a universal acid, dissolving everything it touches? It is obviously true that Darwinism, at least in its radical forms, turns upside down traditional accounts of our nature and our place in the scheme of things. How can such a radical change make so little difference to so much of our everyday thinking about ourselves?

There are two answers to this. The obvious one is that we have not yet come to the end of the investigation. We still have not considered the implications of the materialism boundary for hopes, ideals and the way we lead our lives. This is, indeed, the point at which the pattern breaks. From this point of view, the differences of implication between the two sides are potentially enormous.

The other answer is more complex. In outline, it is that Darwinism is a scientific theory that seeks to explain how things work, and to give an understanding of the origins of the world as we know it. But many ideas and problems about ourselves and our situation are of a kind that cannot be affected by scientific change; and others, which in principle may be so affected, are contingently unaffected by this one. Sorting out which ideas come into which category is a philosophical task, which is why philosophical analysis is essential for understanding the implications of Darwinism.

The next sections deal with these two issues in turn.

The implications of materialism

The materialism boundary effectively coincides with the difference between religious and secular views of the world, and here no amount of analysis can dislodge the intuitively obvious conclusion that the differences of implication for our lives and how we live them can be enormous.

It is important to stress the 'can be'. How much difference would be made by a particular transition from a religious to a secular view, or vice versa, would depend on which version of each was at issue. From the point of view of implications for life and hope there may be more differences between two religions than between some religions and some secular views: a religious person's world view could be as thoroughly changed by conversion to belief in a different kind of God, with a different plan for the universe, as by the abandoning of religion altogether. Nevertheless, there is still a general question about how many possibilities *allowed for* by the Mind First, dualist view of the world would be ruled out by any form of materialism, and therefore would involve a loss for anyone who hoped for these things but was forced to cross over to the materialist side.

This investigation really needs to be pursued in the same kind of detail as the previous ones, by the formulation and testing of candidate conditionals, since in this context, as in all the others, it turns out that many ideas usually associated with Mind First, dualist views, are entirely compatible with materialism. For instance, it often seems to be assumed that if you do not believe in souls or spirits that are distinct from matter you cannot have spiritual values and must be entirely materialistic in outlook. But if by having spiritual values is meant caring about other things than power and possessions – such as beauty, or nature, or love, or the experiences that are commonly (but question-beggingly) described as religious – then they are compatible with materialism. Materialism as a metaphysical view has no connection at all with materialism as a set of values.

However, although it is important to be ready for the appearance of mistakes of this kind, it seems more important here to concentrate on the differences of implication that are not illusory, and really do exist between the two sides of the materialist divide.

This divide, to recapitulate, is the one whose connection with Darwinism Dennett catches so vividly in his skyhook/cranes distinction: the difference between top-down and bottom-up accounts of why things are the way they are. And, as discussed in Chapter 3, it has two important aspects for our understanding of the world and our place in it.

The first of these has to do with what Dennett describes as the belief that cranes-only explanation can go *all the way down*: the position you accept when you abandon the Mind First view and think that the appearance of design in the universe can be explained without any invocation of consciousness and design in the foundations of things. The second, which is strongly connected in practice with the Mind First view, whether or not it need be in principle, is the idea that what makes the difference between human beings and other things, animate and inanimate, is the possession of a rational soul. This is the other aspect of a skyhook view of the world: the dualist idea that minds are distinct from matter, and are needed to account for our being so different from other material things. There have been many variations on this idea – ideas about Life Forces, or about different kinds of soul in different kinds of living being – but the prevailing idea among religious people is that the essence of a human being is an immaterial soul. This seems to be the idea Dennett is contrasting with the materialist idea of cranes' going *all the way up*, and consciousness and rationality as emergent properties of matter. Materialism has no place for a soul.

If these are the main differences between materialists and their opponents, what familiar ideas about life and purpose are necessarily lost in the transition from the conservative to the radical side of the divide? As might be expected, there seem to be two striking implications, corresponding to the two aspects of skyhooklessness.

The first of these is immediately obvious: the implication of the absence of souls in a materialist universe for hopes of personal immortality. Not all religions have clear ideas about immortality, but many do, and if we are ultimately nothing but complex configurations of matter, without any extra, independently existing ingredient, the implication must be that when that configuration falls apart, that is the end of us as individuals. Personal survival seems impossible without a separate element that is the essence of the person, and capable either of independent existence, or of re-embodiment through resurrection or transmigration. If your aspirations are directed towards a life beyond this one, therefore, the truth of materialism seems to cut them off at the foundations.

The other great difference of implication is connected with the Mind First aspect of traditional religion, and the idea that the universe is underlain by a divine order. Of course there is some sense in which materialism sees the world as orderly, since without a background of regularity it would not be possible for us to live, let alone do science. But the difference between this and a typical Mind First universe lies in the idea that an underpinning of teleology allows for there being a *moral* order as well as a physical one. Nearly all ideas that put a creator at the beginning of the world involve the incorporation of a moral order in which everything has an ordained place and function, and if everything is ultimately under moral control, that gives reason to hope that eventually all manner of things will be well. But for materialist views – for any Matter First conception of the universe – there can be no such reasonable hope. The kind of order and complexity produced by evolution has nothing to do with the right or the good. Moral ideas cannot be part of the scheme until evolution produces creatures like us; and we, being accidental offshoots of the universe, have no power over the whole and very little within it. Even if we all agreed about what would be best, and put all our knowledge and efforts into achieving it, there would be very little we could achieve. If there are no separate souls there is no reasonable hope of heaven; if there is no Mind at the root of things there is equally little hope of heaven on earth.

Both these differences between the opposing sides of the materialism boundary, furthermore, have inevitable implications for the process of making decisions about how to live. Few people could fail to be strongly influenced by a serious belief that what happened in this life might have eternal consequences in another, since the possibility of eternal bliss or suffering must weigh very heavily – not to say infinitely heavily, as Pascal recognized – in any rational calculation. Such beliefs must also be highly relevant to what you regard as the right treatment of other people. If you are bent on saving souls you are likely to act in quite different ways from people who are motivated by the aim of making minds and bodies comfortable. If you believe that a population is in danger of being led into eternal flames unless you burn a few heretics or stone adulteresses *pour encourager les autres,* that is presumably what elementary compassion demands that you should do.

This does not mean that people with and without eternal life in view must necessarily reach different *conclusions* about how to lead their lives, since, once again, such conclusions depend not only on beliefs about whether or not there is anything beyond this life, but also on the details of the beliefs in question. There may be little difference between some kinds of secular morality and the requirements of some religions, and a suitably motivated atheist might do very well by the standards of the more humanly reasonable accounts of God; and, on the other hand, devout followers of one religion might find themselves in serious trouble if someone else's turned out to be true. (This is why Pascal's Wager does not work.) But whatever the conclusion you reach, belief or not in a life after death must enormously influence the way you approach the question of how to lead this life.

Even more significant from this point of view is whether or not you hold a Mind First view of the world. Religions that see the world as founded on a moral order generally take the view that the duty of human beings is to try to understand their own place in God's plan and to go along with it. This usually turns out, in fact, to be the real belief of people who claim that God is essential for the existence of moral values – and is one reason why it is so essential to distinguish between fundamental and derived values. Most religious believers find when pressed that they answer the Euthyphro question by saying that God chooses what is good, rather than that what is good is so because God chooses it. What they really understand by the claim that without God there can be no morality is that since we can see only through a glass darkly what God understands in its entirety, we are not in a position to see for ourselves what we should do. Our duty, therefore, is to discover the will of God, and follow that.

For the materialist, on the other hand, there is no question of finding out by looking at the universe how things ought to be, because the universe has in itself no moral order. Understanding the workings of the world gives you an understanding of the raw materials, but tells you nothing about what to do with them. A secular view of the world allows for no short cuts: traditional moral codes cannot be regarded as having been worked out by God for the long-term good of all, so despite inevitable and overwhelming ignorance about the long-term effects of our actions and arragements, we have to make our own decisions. So, once again, a quite different set of procedures is involved in trying to determine and do what is right or good in the Mind First and materialist worlds.

And in fact the difference between religious and secular approaches to life may at this point be even greater than is often realized, because so many habits of mind taken over from the skyhook tradition persist among materialists. There is still a strong tendency for non-religious people to think of nature as taking the place of God in specifying how the world should be, and of evolution as producing progress of all kinds. But materialist Darwinism demands recognizing the world as unplanned, and therefore without any *proper* place for anything to be, or any course of nature that can be *interfered* with. When the difference is fully recognized, there is hardly any coincidence between traditional religious and secular moral reasoning, even though the two paths may often lead to overlapping conclusions.

There is one kind of solace available to materialists, though it may seem slight in comparison with what religion has to offer. If the world really is Darwinian down to the roots, there is a limit to the extent to which we can be held responsible for the moral chaos that surrounds us. You cannot expect a Darwinian world to be anything other than a moral mess. The traditional world was seen as ordered and good until creatures with free will, like us and the fallen angels, sinfully chose to go against the divine plan, and in such a world everything bad about human society can be seen as resulting from sin and its punishment. In the world of Darwinian materialism the fact that so much is bad needs no special explanation, and what we represent is – as far as we yet know – the only hope of making any moral improvement at all.

This may seem a pretty feeble kind of hope, given our record, but our evolutionary background and the general confusion of the world do give us a great deal to contend with. Quite apart from the turbulence of our emotions and the limits of our intellectual abilities, there is the fact that in a Darwinian world the sum of individually well-motivated actions cannot be expected to produce overall harmony. As yet we have no idea what the best moral principles for a world of Darwinian materialism would be, and we cannot live according to them until we know what they are. But although this is in some ways a pessimistic view of our situation, at least it allows us to see ourselves as trying to rise above unpromising origins, rather than as having spoilt everything in a fall from grace. And although it is a view that seems to show that there are limits to what we can possibly achieve, it still allows the adopting of a secular equivalent of the ancient Norse view that although the forces of darkness would eventually engulf the world, it was still better to be on the side of the gods and go down fighting. It is a dark view, but not an ignoble one.

Still, it could hardly be more different from the Mind First view of things. The materialism boundary is indeed the point at which Darwinism turns the world upside down. On this subject, the question of which side is right is – as Hume might have said – of the last consequence.

The unchanged elements

Even though the implications of crossing the materialism boundary are in these respects so great, the fact nevertheless remains that this is the first difference of implications between two degrees of Darwinism to have emerged from this enquiry. No important differences of implication at all have appeared on the evolutionary psychology boundary, and none other than this – enormous as it is – even on the materialism boundary. All the other prevalent ideas about the sinister implications of deepening Darwinism have turned out, if the arguments of this book have been right, to be unfounded.

The reasons for reaching these conclusions were given as the discussion went along; but even if the details of the individual arguments seemed right, there may still be something puzzling about the wider view. How can such a huge change in ideas about human nature and origins and destiny leave unaffected so many familiar ways of thinking about ourselves? What makes the difference between the things that do and the things that do not change with deepening Darwinism? And if so much is left unchanged, why are so many mistakes made about the matter?

The answer seems to be something like this. One aspect of each of the steps of deepening Darwinism is its denying the existence of something believed in by the more conservative position. This is most striking in the transition to materialism, where separately existing minds disappear altogether; but the transition to evolutionary psychology can also be thought of in this way, in its denial of standard social science beliefs about the extent to which cultural and social change can change familiar human characteristics. Now if some traditionally accepted characteristic of ourselves or our situation (for instance our capacity for responsibility) is generally associated with an element of one theory that a more radical theory eliminates (for instance the soul), it may be easy to presume that the radical theory (in denying the existence of the soul) must involve denying the existence of the corresponding characteristic (capacity for responsibility).

And, indeed, this is just the situation described in the previous section. Traditional hopes of immortality depended on an immaterial soul, and hopes of the eventual triumph of good depended on a universe ultimately founded on Mind and a moral order. Materialism, in eliminating both those things, destroys the hopes on which they depend. But although that is what happens in this particular case, there are all kinds of context in which an inference along the same lines would be mistaken.

Such mistakes are the ones the arguments of this book have been claiming to expose. In spite of appearances, there is in fact no connection between the matters over which the Darwin wars are being fought and the traditional idea about ourselves whose prospective loss causes so much concern. These issues do not *turn on* the existence of the element eliminated by the more radical theory.

For instance, to take the example used a moment ago, capacity for responsibility – free will – was traditionally regarded as an attribute of the soul. It might easily be presumed, therefore, that any scheme of things that eliminated souls could not allow for responsibility; and this impression seems confirmed by the idea that a wholly material world must be one that moves along in an inexorable series of causes and effects. In such a world, it seems, we cannot really choose, or be responsible for, anything. Free will without souls is therefore impossible.

But what the earlier arguments showed (I hope) is that this impression changes when you look in more detail, and start by sorting out just what is meant by a capacity for responsibility. In ordinary life – and in law – we distinguish between people who have and have not the capacity to control their actions, make choices and interact with other people in reliable ways. But none of the three degrees of Darwinism gives any reason to regard this distinction as mistaken; and the reason is that this is, as it were, a *surface* distinction, between people *as they are*. It is unconnected with underlying accounts of how they came to be that way, which is what the competing degrees of Darwinism are about.

That is one way in which people may be mistaken in thinking that the existence of some characteristic turns on which Darwinian theory is right. If the characteristic at issue is descriptive of people *as we experience them*, rather than part of some scientific explanation, then it will necessarily be unaffected by competing underlying explanations. As argued earlier, the truth of current theories in evolutionary psychology would not show that all men were in a state of uncontrollable sexual frenzy.

But, it may be said, this kind of surface distinction between responsible and non-responsible people is not the important issue. When we ask about the capacity for responsibility, we are asking whether the people who pass this first test, and are not in a state of diminished responsibility, are *really* responsible for what they do. And – it might be insisted – the answer to this question does depend on which theory is right. The capacity for *ultimate* responsibility – what usually goes by the name of free will, and is the basis of retributivist ideas of punishment – is something given by God, and an attribute of the soul.

But this raises the opposite problem. It is true that materialism does not allow for what might be called ultimate (as opposed to ordinary) responsibility; but then neither does non-materialism. Souls do not help here, because the impossibility of ultimate responsibility in materialism is not, as it were, a shortcoming of materialism; it is a shortcoming of the concept of ultimate responsibility itself. As usually imagined it is incoherent, and could not exist in any possible world.

So that is a second way in which the question of whether we have some characteristic does not turn on which version of Darwinism is true. The concept in question may be incoherent, and impossible under any circumstances. Before you can ask a positive question about whether a capacity for genuine responsibility is possible in a dualist universe but not a materialist one, you have to start by making sure you have a coherent concept, and then showing that it fits one set of possibilities but not the other.

A similiar pair of conclusions also emerged from the arguments about altruism, which is another characteristic traditionally associated with souls and divinely inspired conscience. The distinction between altruistic and non-altruistic actions is between actions which are and are not against the interests of the agent, and these are characteristics of actions as they *are*. Altruism, like the capacity for responsibility, is a surface phenomenon – not in the sense of being instantly recognizable on the surface of actions (you may have to do a good deal of investigation of motives to find out whether some case of apparent altruism is genuine), but in the sense of being independent of which theory of its origins is true. If you want to find out whether some apparently altruistic person is genuinely so you do not need to know about souls or evolutionary psychology. You just look closely at the way the person acts in a range of circumstances, and try to see whether there are hidden motives.

Alternatively, if you claim that people who are altruistic by this ordinary criterion are not *truly* altruistic, because they are still acting according to their own desires and therefore just being selfish at a more fundamental level, you are making genuine altruism, like ultimate responsibility, a logical impossibility. Materialism does not allow for it, but souls cannot help either.

Once the conceptual disentangling has been done in cases like these, and surface characteristics and incoherent concepts are recognized for what they are, there is no difficulty in understanding why ordinary responsibility and altruism must exist irrespective of which version of Darwinism is true, and why ultimate responsibility, and the kind of altruism that involves going against all-things-considered desires, cannot. But it is in the disentangling that the difficulty lies. It may look easy and obvious once it has been done, but it is not at all easy or obvious when you are actually struggling in the confusion; and unless you are used to this kind of philosophical investigation it will probably not even occur to you that there is any confusion. This is why questions about responsibility and altruism may seem to turn on the differences between different scientific and religious views when in fact they do not.

A different way in which important aspects of our lives may be mistakenly connected with particular explanatory theories is illustrated by the idea that if you lose God you lose all moral standards. God is traditionally regarded as the source of moral standards, so it is easy to presume that a world without God is one in which anything goes. But most theists find, when they do the appropriate thought experiments, that they do not really believe any such thing. They believe that God wills the good because it is good or right, not that the will of God is the criterion for the good and the right.

Once again, the confusion is caused by the running together of different ideas. The real belief is usually the one described in the previous section: that since God has the universe under control and understands its overall purpose, he alone can know how human beings should fit into that plan. God is, in other words, regarded as the setter of *derived* standards, not fundamental ones. Different theories about the world are bound to have different implications for derived standards, as discussed in the last chapter, because derived standards involve implementing fundamental standards in the world as it is. The illusion that God is essential for the existence of moral standards can be preserved only because of philosophical confusion of these different issues.

This shows a third way in which ideas about ourselves and our place in things may float free of any particular scientific theory. Some things we believe about ourselves, such as our capacity to recognize moral values, may traditionally be associated with a Mind First view of the world, and therefore thought to depend on whether God exists. But the question of whether there can be moral truths is a philosophical one, about which philosophers may (and do) disagree; its answer is as unaffected by scientific evidence as are questions about the status of mathematical truths. How moral (and mathematical) ideas can be *applied* depends on the world as it is, and different scientific theories will give different answers. But they do not affect the ideas themselves.

In all these cases, then, the mistakes are made because ideas traditionally associated with one particular understanding of the world turn out to have no such connection. Questions about our capacities for responsibility and altruism, about our ordinary capacities for responsibility, and about whether there are such things as objective moral standards, are not of a kind to be affected by changes in scientific theory, which is why Darwinism has no implications for them.

A final set of mistakes is of a different kind. These are ones in which the implications of the radical theories are simply misunderstood; and the misunderstanding seems to be rooted in a failure to recognize how radical they are. The familiar inferences seem to depend on presuppositions drawn from incompatible conservative theories.

The clearest case of this is the one discussed at the end of the last chapter: the widespread belief that the claims of evolutionary psychology have direct normative implications. But I suspect other mistakes that come into this category include the idea that the gene-machine thesis entails genetic determinism, and perhaps that materialism implies the impossibility of moral understanding and improvement.

Consider, for instance, the idea discussed in Chapter 5 and elsewhere, that if the claims of evolutionary psychology are true, it is impossible for us to do anything about various aspects of our character that we may not like – such as deep differences between the sexes. This is not true. Apart from the fact that evolutionary psychology does not for a moment deny the influence of environment (the claim is only that our evolutionary background can provide an understanding of how that influence works), there is also the possibility – indeed the likelihood – that we may be able to achieve all kinds of change by genetic or pharmacological means. Why, then, is the allegation made?

There seem to be two possibilities. First, someone approaching evolutionary psychology from the direction of standard social science theory, with its belief that just about any characteristic may be induced in human beings by social and cultural means, is likely to be particularly struck by the fact that evolutionary psychologists deny this. It may, therefore, seem that they are denying that change can be made *by any means at all*. (Consider the slip made by Gould, discussed on p. 117, from the idea of characteristics' being unchangeable by *will, education or culture* to their being *ineluctable*.) To reason in this way seems to involve thinking of your opponents as holding your own theory *minus one particular element* – the element responsible for the development of character – rather than as having a different theory of their own, which allows for the possibility of change in quite different ways.

Alternatively, the mistake may come through simply discounting the possibility of change by genetic and pharmacological means because of an assumption that only changes made through social and cultural means can be justified at all. But if so, the mistake is deeper still. The idea that it must be wrong to interfere with the deep workings of nature depends on the Mind First idea of the universe, which is incompatible not only with evolutionary psychology, but with the standard social science theory as well. Without that assumption, there is nothing to *interfere* with, and no reason whatever to think that nature as a whole is arranged for the good of anything. It would take some proving, but my suspicion is that a great many claims about the implications of evolutionary psychology – made not only by standard social science theorists but by many evolutionary psychologists themselves – depend on such failures to recognize how radical Darwinian materialism is.

It is possible that a similar kind of mistake is made by people (again on both sides of the divide) who think that the transition from Mind First views to materialism means that it becomes impossible for there to be objective moral standards – that without God, everything is permitted – which seems to depend on the idea that the disappearance of a particular source of moral information entails there being no source at all. It may also be involved in ideas that without God and souls we must be incapable of moral improvement.

However, the diagnosis of these mistakes is complex, and a different subject. All that is needed here is to point out the possibility of their existence, and to emphasize, in general, the importance of working through the alleged implications of the different views in detail, rather than presuming that they are obvious. They are not; and the more closely you look, the more pitfalls and confusions become apparent. For understanding the implications of Darwinism in its different degrees the close analysis of conditionals, and the recognition of philosophical problems for what they are, is indispensable.

Conclusion

As Kitcher says, the debate over sociobiology is of great importance because your beliefs about it are not just of abstract intellectual interest, but have enormous effects on the way you reason about yourself and other people, and consequently on how you act. The same is true of the debate over materialism; and, of course, of all the debates within each category. This is simply because if you are mistaken in the beliefs you use as the premises in your practical reasoning, you are likely to reach the wrong conclusions about what to do, no matter how far beyond reproach your values may be. Carelessness with facts, in such contexts, is moral carelessness.

But if you are concerned about reaching the best practical conclusions, facts are not the only things to worry about. If your reasoning from premises about facts to conclusions about actions goes wrong because of muddle, or equivocation, or mistakes of logic, then your practical conclusions will be just as unreliable as if you get the facts wrong. This means that the dangers of mistaken reasoning are potentially just as great as the dangers of mistaken facts.

Everyone knows that the disagreement between evolutionary psychologists and standard social scientists is important because which side you believe will affect how you try to investigate and influence the world. If evolutionary psychologists are right but you act on the basis of standard social science assumptions, or vice versa, your social planning is likely to go seriously awry. But what happens if you believe – from either side of the evolutionary psychology divide – that direct inferences can be made from premises given by evolutionary psychology to political and moral conclusions? What happens, for instance, if you think that the truth of evolutionary psychology would imply that men were right to try to control women sexually and to philander or rape, or that people were right to press their own relatives' interests ahead of everyone else's, or that it was right to make war against other societies or species? Such mistaken inferences have a greater potential for danger than many false beliefs about facts. One such danger is that people who are appalled by the conclusions will think it essential to attack evolutionary psychology whatever the evidence for it, and in doing so lessen the chances of our getting the matter *right* (itself a matter of moral importance). Or, even worse, people who do accept evolutionary psychology will think they have a justification for adopting these moral views, and may persuade others likewise. There is greater danger here in the mistaken inference than in the mistaken premises, if they are mistaken.

The same applies on the materialism boundary. It matters a great deal if we are wrong about the nature of ourselves and the universe, and plan as though there were no after life and no underlying moral order if these things in fact exist (though it should not be forgotten that this may be no worse than being on the Mind First side but following the wrong religion). But an equally – or at least seriously – dangerous mistake would be a belief that the non-existence of God, or the truth of evolution, supported the conclusion that moral standards did not exist, and that we had no reason to pursue moral goodness. Again, this would be dangerous for two reasons. It would lead people who were convinced that morality was important to think they must defend religion, and in doing so recommend an approach to moral reasoning that might be radically misguided. Or it might lead people who were convinced of materialism to persist in the kind of confused semi-relativism that pervades so much current moral controversy, and in so doing to allow all kinds of morally dubious activities to seem justified.

Sorting out the implications of competing scientific claims can be as difficult as deciding between the claims themselves, but that is just why it is essential to recognize the enquiries as distinct. If we mistakenly assume the implications of Darwinism are obvious, and that all the problems are about the facts, we may inadvertently thwart our own purposes – whatever God or evolution has made us, and whatever we hope to make of ourselves.

The arguments of this book have claimed, in one context after another, that the different depths of Darwinism have in themselves no implications for most ideas about ourselves and our situation. The great exception comes in the difference between materialist and non-materialist views, from the point of view of hopes for better things and the way we approach the problems of trying to bring them about. Here there is no escaping the conclusion that there are radical differences between the two sides of the divide. A materialist view of things seems to preclude both personal immortality and a morally ordered universe.

This is an enormous difference; but it is nevertheless the only one that has appeared. All the other supposed implications of deepening Darwinism have turned out to be mistaken; and the reason is that many familiar ideas about ourselves are not of a kind to be affected by the advance of science. Some are about ourselves as we now are, irrespective of origins; others present problems that are philosophical rather than scientific and may turn out to be incoherent. Distinguishing these problems from the ones that are affected by the truth of Darwinian theories is crucial for making the best of human nature, whatever the truth about its nature and origins.

Notes

1 I shall use 'materialism' throughout to refer to the metaphysical view that the most fundamental entities in the universe are material (non-conscious), and that mind is dependent on matter in the sense that if all matter disappeared, so would all mind. This is not the only meaning of 'materialism' used by philosophers, but it is the one I shall keep to here.

2 This argument may seem to support Popper's falsification thesis. But that thesis depends on an *asymmetry* between confirmation and falsification; and in this argument, the two necessarily go together. The reason for being confident that Ptolemy's account is false is the discovery that incompatible beliefs are certainly true.

3 See, for example, Ferris (1997), Chapter 7 and Deutsch (1997), Chapter 14.

4 See Nesse and Williams (1995).

5 Terms originally intended as abusive often become established as neutral, as in the cases of 'baroque', 'rococo' and 'impressionist'.

6 A substance, philosophically speaking, is something that does not depend on other things for its existence.

7 Social Darwinism is, roughly, the idea that everyone is naturally in competition and we should encourage the course of evolution by letting the weak go to the wall, thus helping to ensure the survival of the fittest. This is discussed further in Chapter 9 (pp. 221–2).

8 The naturalistic fallacy involves deducing conclusions about the way things ought to be from the way they are: deducing 'ought' from 'is'. This is discussed further in Chapter 9 (pp. 242ff.).

9 In Glover (1984).

10 See, for example, H. A. Orr, 'Darwin v. Intelligent Design (Again)', *Boston Review*, December/January 1996–97.

11 Notice, however, that if the antecedent were true and the consequent false that would show the conditional to be false.

12 This must not be confused with the quite different claim that everything we want to say could in principle be translated without loss into claims about matter.

13 The appearance given by many of the exercises in this book that their author is obsessed by animal rights, the devastation of landscapes and – perhaps more surprisingly – boxing, is another of the book's design fossils (see Introduction). In its original form and context the book followed three others, dealing with political freedom (with a case study of freedom to harm yourself, as in boxing), animals, and environmental ethics. The exercises could have been changed, but Darwinians are rather fond of design fossils.

14 It would be more accurate to say that she needed to investigate the same consequents, in the expectation that the new antecedent would make the conditionals false. But it is slightly easier, and not too inaccurate, to do it this way.

15 It is perhaps worth mentioning that there are various kinds of problem. One is a philosophical problem of what grounds there are for thinking that uncaused events do not exist. It is no good arguing that they could not possibly exist because there is nothing to produce them, because that begs the question. There are also problems about how we would recognize them if they did occur, since it is not clear how we would distinguish them from caused or determined events.

16 Or, more accurately, 'It is not the case that the world is a disc supported by four elephants', and in some contexts the accuracy is important. But the simpler version will do for our purposes here, since it is only an illustration.

17 Compare this with the earlier discussion of science. Scientists usually regard themselves as conducting investigations to discover the truth about the world, and have debates and disagreements about whether some theory is true or not. But if they do this, they are presupposing that there is such a thing as scientific truth to be found.

The question of whether there is such a truth is at a higher level of abstraction, and comes into the areas of philosophy of science and epistemology, rather than science. The opinions you have about answers to questions at that level will determine what you think you are doing at the level of scientific investigation, and perhaps whether you think it worth doing at all.

18   i.e. of the greatest importance.

Answers to exercises

Exercise 1.1

1   At the time there was no reason to accept the theory: it was contrary to common sense and ordinary observation in all respects. The reason for its acceptance later was partly the increased accuracy of observation, which showed large problems with the old cosmology; but also, to a greater extent, the development of a quite new kind of mechanics which made the arrangement seem possible, and which made all the elements fit.

2   Because astrological ideas had been based on a cosmology which made the heavens different in kind from the earth, and there was now no reason to believe that they could have this kind of influence.

3   Because, even though it had broken down the traditional distinction between the earth and the heavens, it did not in itself threaten the distinction between mind and matter, and body and soul, which were the most important bases of religion.

Exercise 1.2

1   Too many offspring were produced for all to survive; there would inevitably be shortages of food and resources as long as people produced as many offspring as they did.

2   Darwin's addition was that since there was variation among individuals and offspring resembled parents, characteristics that helped survival in the competition would spread throughout the population.

Exercise 1.3

1   That there must be a purpose at the root of things.

2   (a), (d), (g) and (j) are teleological. In each case, the question is whether the explanation looks forward to what the person was trying to achieve (the *telos*, or end), or whether it looks back to how the result came about.

3   (a) and (d) are competing explanations; (b), (c) and (e) are compatible. It is important to realize that explanations of a single happening or state of affairs can be different without being in competition, and to recognize which are which. This will be significant later in the book.

4   (a) If there were a lot of seeds around, the birds with stronger beaks did well in finding food and were able to rear a great many offspring, who in turn had beaks that enabled them to do well by their own offspring. The ones with weaker, pointed beaks produced far fewer offspring and eventually died out; but on other islands, where there were more insects, they produced more offspring than the birds with the blunt beaks.

   (b) The light brown forms of the peppered moth used to be well camouflaged against the trunks of trees, and since they were not easily seen by predators they tended to survive and produce offspring better than more conspicuous moths. But when pollution changed the colour of the tree trunks they became more easily seen and caught by predators, and the ones that happened to be darker survived more readily to reproduce.

   (c) Some flowers happened to develop into forms that resembled particular insects, and that attracted insects (who mistook the flowers for potential mates). Because these forms were more efficiently pollinated than the flowers that did not attract so many insects, the insect-like forms became increasingly common and the less successful variants eventually died out.

Exercise 2.1

1   (ii), (iii) and (iv) are radically sceptical.

2   For example:

   (i)   You can't be sure, you haven't checked the brakes.
          You can't prove that the laws of nature won't change without warning.

   (ii) I know they haven't got a central nervous system, but isn't there some evidence that they react to trauma?
          You can't tell; they may be suffering agonies without anything to show for it.

   (iii) But they have threatened a rail strike, and you have no other way of getting here.
          You can't be sure; the universe may suddenly come to an end.

3   It means that accepting its truth is the only (or perhaps best) way to achieve success, if success is achievable at all.

4   What you need is another matrix with payoffs. There are two possible situations – animal pain is real or illusory – and two possible courses of action – treat them as though their pain is real, treat them as though it is illusory. If their pain is real and you treat them as though it is real, you will treat them properly; if you treat them as though it is not, you will cause great suffering. If their pain is not real and you treat them as though it is, you will be wasting the time and effort spent of being considerate. So the question is whether it is worse to risk causing great suffering, or wasting some effort. Given the great importance of pain, anyone who cares about suffering in others will regard it as methodologically rational to treat animals as though they are capable of suffering.

Exercise 2.2

1   For example:

   B: Nonsense – the only evidence you have for that is that she is very attractive. There is good evidence that her behaviour was perfectly proper.
   A: But his genetic constitution makes him naturally prone to strong desires; he cannot be blamed for his genetic constitution.

2   For example:

   B: She knows perfectly well I have no money. She was helping me with my accounts only last week.
   A: Well, she just gets her pleasure out of looking after people. So it's all selfishness, not altruism, anyway.

Exercise 3.1

1   Something that is capable of producing copies of itself, either directly, or indirectly by producing a negative which then produces more of the original.

2   By reference to the enormous length of time in which it could have happened: as the saying goes, in the long run the improbable will probably happen. And, as he also points out, it only had to happen once. Immediately after that, Darwinian processes could take over.

3   They are the result of copying errors. Most erroneous copies are not viable, but occasionally they are, and may even have advantages over the original.

Exercise 3.2

1   The males whose deep inclinations are to prefer a lot of promiscuous sex to eating and sleeping will leave more descendants than the ones whose preferences are the other way round.

2   (i)   (c). (a) and (b) are wrong because evolution usually doesn't give desires about the propagation of genes – for almost all of human history we didn't even know about genes. The idea is that it gave various desires that had that effect. (d) is wrong because evolution has no eye on the future. The men who have the strongest sexual desires may be efficient users of contraceptives, or have strong moral commitments to monogamy.
    (ii) (d). (a) is wrong because evolutionary psychology doesn't say anything about all men, only about tendencies. (c) is wrong because evolutionary psychology doesn't say anything about the effect on numbers of offspring now; only about the characteristics that would have been significant for evolutionary success in our past. (b), (e) and (f) are wrong because they all carry implications about what ought to be, and evolutionary psychology is purely descriptive, about causes and effects. The question about what the moral implications are, if any, is separate. This subject will be discussed in Chapter 9.
    (iii) (b). (a) is wrong because the claims of evolutionary psychology are not about what anyone does, let alone what all men do. They are about emotional drives, and these are often resisted. (c) is wrong because, once again, evolutionary psychology is about our evolutionary past, not about what will be successful in the future.

3   (i)   It is what happens when the male desire for sexual variety finds itself in a present day urban environment, with contraceptive technology.
    (ii) Genetically speaking, when they have an opportunity to improve the genes of their offspring while still retaining the support of a reliable husband. What that means in practice is that they are attracted to men who are of higher status, or more sexually attractive, than their husbands.
    (iii) Almost any.
    (iv) Because they have non-identical genetic interests; each is trying to exploit the other, and although this is sometimes to their mutual advantage this is not always the case.
    (v)   Because women want their mates to be reliable providers, and courtship gifts are both resources in themselves and an indication of an ability and willingness to give more.
    (vi) No. Evolutionary psychology is about the emotions induced by genes, not by

individual calculations about offspring. You would expect the attraction to remain.

Exercise 3.3

1 (i) Stated or implied claims about people: Sociobiological writers (unspecified) say they reject Social Darwinist egoism and give reasons for rejecting it, but in fact take the idea of competitiveness for granted and treat it as part of science. The cause of this (note that this is still a claim about the writers) is that they take their own competitive culture for granted. (So there are several kinds of claim: about their official beliefs, their real beliefs that show through, and the causes of their holding these beliefs.) There is also an implied claim about the original Social Darwinists: that they had a 'competitive attitude'.

Stated or implied claims about issues: it is implied that Social Darwinist egoism is quite wrong: one of the 'quasi-scientific superstitions' around. It has been refuted (because the writers rehearse 'familiar refutations' – 'refutation' is a success word). It is also dangerous (as shown by the term 'alarming').

   (ii) Stated or implied claims about people: Glover's tone is reasonable and moderate (unlike those of other writers in the field). But he has faith in technology. He sees several dangers in Nozick's genetic supermarket, but not all the problems. There is also a claim about what Nozick says; and the claim about idiocy and amazingness seems to apply as much to the person as the theory.

About issues: Nozick's proposal is idiotic, and it is 'amazing' that he proposed it, but we can't tell on the basis of this extract what the idiocy consists of. Glover is disapproved of for being carried away on waves of undiagnosed faith in technology, but we can't tell from this passage which claims attract this criticism. So from this passage we know, roughly, why Midgley disapproves of Glover's ideas, but not what they are, and which of Nozick's ideas she disapproves of, but not why.

Remember that all that this is doing is distinguishing claims about ideas and issues from claims about people. This does not involve any criticism of Midgley. To do that you would have to start deciding whether she was right in these various claims.

2 (i) This is about people, and doesn't give you any direct reason to think that the theory is false; but if you are relying on the word of these people, it does cast doubt on your reasons for thinking it is true. You will need to look directly at the evidence instead of taking their word for it, or get someone scientifically competent to assess it.

   (ii) This is also about people, and is even less directly relevant to the question of whether the theory is true. It is possible to hope something is true without thereby becoming incapable of assessing the evidence. (You can hope that your home pregnancy test will be negative – or positive – without being in any danger of misreading the result.) Some people are better at avoiding wishful thinking than others. If you are trying to decide whether to believe the evidence offered by these people, the knowledge that they have these hopes may make you cautious, but what you really need to know is how good and honest they are as scientists – and if they are good, what they personally hope for is neither here nor there. The truth of this statement doesn't even begin to give positive evidence that the claims they are making are false. (Do you think the truth of these ideas of evolutionary psychology would justify male philandering? This question will be discussed in Chapter 9.)

(iii) Completely irrelevant to the question of truth. Not, however, necessarily irrelevant to the question of which way to guess in case of doubt. This, and the question of whether the claim is true, will be discussed in Chapter 9.

Exercise 4.1

1   (i)   If there is water on Mars, we shall be able to live there.
    (ii) If there is no water on Mars, we shall not be able to live there.
    (iii) If there were no books in their home during childhood, adults never learn to enjoy reading.
    (iv) If you don't practise for at least four hours a day, you won't become a concert pianist.
    (v)   If materialism is true, there is no free will.
    (vi) If Dawkins's selfish-gene theory is true, we are entirely selfish.

2   (i)   Not clear; it depends how easy each is to find out. If you are at some distance from your new house, and you can't just ask someone, it is probably easier to look up the requirements of rhododendrons first.
    (ii) Given your concerns and your not thinking you know the answer to either question, you should probably try to settle the conditional first. It's much easier to find out what the Bible says about Hell than to find out whether the Bible is the word of God.
    (iii) Again, I'd certainly go for the conditional first, on grounds of its being easier. You might think it easier to settle the question of whether male dominance was actually natural and eradicable, but if so you may change your mind by the end of the book.

Exercise 4.2

1   (i)   Valid.
    (ii)   Invalid; it commits the fallacy of affirming the consequent (see p. 000), as you can see by rearranging it: All earwigs are about two inches long, that is two inches long, therefore that is an earwig.
    (iii) Valid.
    (iv)   Incomplete. You need to link floating upwards and helium in such a way that helium is the only candidate. One filling that would do the job (for validity, not soundness) is 'Helium is the only gas that is lighter than air; balloons do not float upwards unless they contain a gas that is lighter than air'.
    (v)   Incomplete. The gap is between 'men' and 'unfaithful'. The argument could be made valid by 'Only men are unfaithful to their spouses'.
    (vi)   Invalid; it commits the fallacy of denying the antecedent (see p. 000).
    (vii) Invalid: affirming the consequent again.
    (viii) Valid. (You can add, if you want, that abortion is the deliberate taking of human life, but I am taking that to be part of the definition. If you think the extra premise needs to be added, you can say the argument is incomplete as it stands.)
    (ix)   Invalid (unless you go in for fancy explanations about step-grandmothers and the like). The two elements contain a contradiction.
    (x)   Incomplete. You need to add a statement linking causing harm and the justifiability of prevention, such as 'nothing should be prevented unless it does harm'.

2   (i) For example:
Sentient beings are capable of suffering, the processes of farming and slaughter cause suffering, it is not necessary for us to eat meat, we should not associate ourselves in any way with anything that causes unnecessary suffering.

Or:

Sentient beings taste horrible, we should not eat anything that tastes horrible.

(ii) For example:

Dangerous sports should be banned.

Or:

Dangerous sports please the public, the public should not be pleased.

(iii) For example:

We should not damage what is magnificent, a railway would damage the mountain.

Or:

Magnificent things should have only the most magnificent form of transport going up them, motorways are much more magnificent than railways.

3   Set it out in argument form:

Women's inclination to put their families ahead of careers is genetic.

Therefore there is no hope of changing it.

Then see whether it is possible to construct a sound inference from premise to conclusion by completing a valid argument with true premises. (This kind of question is discussed in the next chapter.)

Exercise 5.1

1   For example:

(i)   Only rational beings have rights to life.
Animals are not rational beings.

Therefore animals do not have a right to life.

Animals do not have a right to life.
It is morally acceptable to eat anything that has no right to life.

——————
Therefore it is morally acceptable to eat animals.

(ii) Boxing is dangerous.
Anything dangerous should be forbidden by law.

——————
Therefore boxing should be forbidden by law.

Boxing should be forbidden by law.
It is wrong to do anything forbidden by law.

——————
Therefore it is wrong to box.

2 (i) The castaway devastated the island before he died.
There were no sentient beings on the island.

——————
Therefore the castaway did not harm any sentient beings.

The castaway did not harm any sentient beings.
The only thing that matters is harm to sentient beings.

——————
Therefore what the castaway did did not matter.

(ii) We arose entirely as a result of the laws of physics and natural selection.
The laws of physics and natural selection can produce only automata.

——————
Therefore we are only automata.

We are only automata.
Automata are of no moral importance.

——————
Therefore we are of no moral importance.

Exercise 5.2

1 A fallacy of equivocation occurs when the meaning of a crucial term changes during the course of an apparently valid argument. If you rewrite the argument making the change of meaning clear, the argument is obviously invalid.

2 (i) Valid only if you interpret the first premise as meaning 'all men'; but then the premise is manifestly false. The premise is plausible only if it means something like 'the average man'; but then the argument is not valid. The apparent soundness of the argument depends on equivocation: making the premise sound plausible, but then changing its meaning to make the argument seem valid. (In this case, of course, the slip is obvious, but in other arguments about men and women the same mistake often goes unnoticed.)
(ii) Valid if you take the premise to be about the average man and the average woman, because you can reach conclusions about probabilities on the basis of averages. This does seem the most plausible interpretation of the premise.
(iii) Valid only if you interpret the scientists as meaning that smoking (how much?) always causes cancer. This is obviously not what they mean, and therefore not a plausible interpretation of the premise.

(iv) Valid only if the claim is interpreted as meaning that all New Yorkers are richer than all Londoners. This is a manifestly implausible interpretation.

3   For example:

(i) Therefore it is likely that I can lift heavier weights than you.
(ii) n/a
(iii) Therefore scientists would regard my grandfather as lucky
(iv) Andy is likely to be richer than Bruce.

4   For example:

If it is April there will be rain
It is April

———————

Therefore there will be rain   (valid)

If it is April there will be rain
It is not April

———————

Therefore there will not be rain   (denying the antecedent)

If it is April there will be rain
There will be rain

———————

Therefore it is April   (affirming the consequent)

Exercise 5.3

1   (i) (a); (ii) (b); (iii) (a); (iv) (a); (v) (a); (vi) (b)

2   None of them does; all of them turn on the details of particular theories, not on the general approach.

Exercise 6.1

1   (i) (a); (ii) (b); (iii) (b); (iv) (a)

2   (i) (c); (ii) (b); (iii) probably (b), although if the fear were well enough founded it might count as (a); (iv) (a); (v) (c); (vi) (a); (vii) (c).

Exercise 6.2

1   (i), (ii)   No. Nothing has been said about the truth of either determinism or inde-terminism. All the questions being asked here are of conditional form: 'If this is true, *then* is this … ?'

(iii), (iv) No. These are widely believed, but neither is obviously true and both have been left open here.

(v)   Yes – though it was argued mainly in the previous section rather than this one.

(vi)   Yes.

(vii)   No see (iii) above.

(viii)   No. Since the argument has been that even if we are not determined we are not free, our not being free is not because we are determined.

(ix)   No. This has been explicitly argued against.

(x)   Yes.

(xi)   No. Freedom of the will is as incompatible with conservative as with radical Darwinism.

(xii)   No.

2   Because the question of whether we have free will does not *turn on* the question of whether the world is deterministic or not. Either way (if these arguments are right), free will does not exist.

3   It is a false opposition. The question presupposes that we must be one or the other; according to these arguments we are not free even if we are not determined.

Exercise 6.3

1   Contradictories are pairs of statements that are mutually exclusive and jointly exhaustive: they cannot both be true and they cannot both be false. Contraries are mutually exclusive but not jointly exhaustive: they can both be false.

2   Contradictories:

(i)   There are such things as blue tulips (i.e. at least one blue tulip exists).

(ii)   None of the houses in this street is four stories high.

(iii)   Some cats eat lettuce (i.e. at least one cat …).

Contraries (for example):

(i)   All tulips are blue.

(ii)   All the houses in this street are three stories high.

(iii)   My cat eats lettuce.

3   For example:

(i)   Half the tulips in the world are blue; mine are the only blue tulips in the world; only three people in this town grow tulips that are not blue.

(ii)   The houses in this street are all either three or four stories high; the houses in this street are all bungalows; the only four-storey house in this street was demolished last year.

(iii)   Yours is the only cat I know that eats lettuce; my cat is the only cat that doesn't eat lettuce; all lettuce-eating cats live in Outer Mongolia.

Check whatever answers you have given to make sure they are incompatible with both the original statement in the exercise, and the one you gave as a contrary in the previous answer.

4   That whether it exists or not depends on the way the world is. It might exist if the world were different, but as it happens it does not.

5   For example:
Contingently nonexistent: unicorns, the tooth fairy, Aristotle's crystalline spheres, phlogiston, means of transport faster than the speed of light, the Elixir of Youth.

Necessarily nonexistent: Round squares, hills in comparison with which other hills are valleys, married bachelors, the Sunday between last Tuesday and last Thursday, a pink attitude, someone who had been knocked into the middle of next week.

6   She should say that you had failed to specify a wish at all, because anything that met one part of your specification would necessarily fail to meet the other.

Exercise 6.4

(i) intrinsic; (ii) instrumental – what is intrinsically desirable is not getting into trouble; (iii) intrinsic; (iv) instrumental – in this argument what is intrinsically important is keeping them for later, rather than (as in the previous one) avoiding them because they just aren't worth eating; (v) instrumental – the various aims to be achieved are the intrinsically valuable things; (vi) instrumental – the aim is to avoid parking problems; (vii) intrinsic.

Exercise 7.1

For example:

(i)   If people leave before midnight they always catch the one o'clock train.
(ii) If a cat remains in one house, he can't unravel knitting in another.
(iii) If the Bible says something it is true.
(iv) If a characteristic is genetic, it can't be changed.
(v)   If you have a genetic tendency to do something, you can't be blamed for doing it.

Exercise 7.2

(i)   For example: Sometimes genes that have the effect of making organisms less directly competitive, or less effective as reproducers, will be more successfully transmitted than genes that produce direct competition in organisms.

(ii)   For example: Genes may induce in organisms characteristics that are bad for the organism if those characteristics help to transmit copies of those genes to the next generation.

(iii) For example: The genes that survive and spread through populations are the ones whose combination with other genes produces organisms that are effective propagators of those genes.

(iv)   For example: As the hedgehog's body was developing by natural selection, so were its emotions/psychology. Chance would throw up hedgehogs with varying kinds of temperament. But in the days when the main environmental threat was predators, the hedgehogs born with an inclination to run would not be very successful, because most of their predators could outrun them. But when chance threw up hedgehogs who combined the development of spikes with an inclination to curl up, those would survive more often, because their predators had sensitive noses and mouths. However, the environment has now changed, with the result that these curling up hedgehogs are getting killed in their thousands, and the odd, accidental hedgehogs born with an inclination to run are reproducing and filling the hedgehog niche. So running genes are spreading through the population, and curling up genes becoming less frequent – at least in some areas. (If areas with cars and areas without became separated for long enough, presumably two different species would eventually develop.)

(v)   For example: On the whole, genes that cause competitiveness and sexual eagerness when they are in male bodies will leave more copies of themselves than ones that do not.

(vi) For example: Genes that contribute to producing in female mammals a strong disposition to care for their young will on the whole be more effectively transmitted to future generations than ones that do not.

(vii) For example: In a sexual species, a gene that has different effects in male and female bodies will often be transmitted more effectively than one that does not.

(viii) For example: The genes that spread through populations are the ones that leave more copies of themselves than do rival genes.

Exercise 7.3

1   The real interests of the animals has nothing to do with the metaphorical interests of their genes.

2   Something on the lines of: Our dispositions, emotions, inclinations and so on are the way they are because ancestors with these characteristics have tended to survive better than others. The successful survival of genes has nothing whatever to do with the happiness of the organisms they construct; if what makes them perpetuate their genes also makes them happy, that is entirely a matter of chance.

Exercise 7.4

1   (i) (a); (ii) (b); (iii) (b); (iv) (c); (v) (b); (vi) (a); (vii) (a); (viii) (b); (ix) (c).

2   (i)   Yes
      (ii)   Not clear: it depends on how long the 'temporary' is, and what the speaker means by 'really love'. If 'temporary' is taken to mean several years, the claim looks like an explanation of feelings of love, rather than a claim that the profession is mistaken.
      (iii) Yes
      (iv)   Yes
      (v)   No
      (vi)   No
      (vii) Yes
      (viii) No. (Probably, but it may depend on context. If you are explaining what solidity is to a non-scientist you may be using 'really solid' to refer to that person's intuitive idea of what it is.)
      (ix)   Yes
      (x)   No

3   (i)   This depends on the mistake of implying that if you can give a causal explanation of a belief or opinion, you have somehow shown it to be spurious. You could, in principle, give a causal explanation of how some good person came to be good, or how a mathematician – or electronic calculator – reached the correct answer to a problem, but that would not undermine either the goodness or the correctness. Would the politician have made a remark about their origins if the audience had agreed with him? There is a shift of level here; and since you can always – in principle – give a causal explanation of any opinion, this is another case of the selective use of a universal acid.
      (ii)   Once again, a spurious rebuttal of the original claim. The remark about electical impulses is presented as if it showed the pain to be illusory, when it was only an explanation at a different level.

Exercise 8.1

1   (i)   (c)
    (ii)   probably (b)
    (iii)   (c)
    (iv)   probably (c), maybe (a)
    (v)   probably (d), possibly (b)
    (vi)   probably (b), possibly (a)
    (vii)   probably (a), possibly (b)
    (viii)   (c)
    (ix)   (d)
    (x)   (c)
    (xi)   (a)

2   (i)   normative
    (ii) normative
    (iii) metaethics
    (iv) normative
    (v)   metaethics
    (vi) normative

3   (i)   science
    (ii) epistemology and philosophy of science
    (iii) epistemology and philosophy of science
    (iv) science
    (v)   science

Exercise 8.2

(i)   No. Nothing has been said about whether there are objective moral truths. The argument has been only that their existence does not depend on the existence of God. But maybe there aren't any anyway, for other reasons. (In the previous chapter it was argued that freedom of the will did not depend on indeterminism. But that was not because it existed independently of indeterminism. The claim of the chapter was that it did not exist anyway, whether the world was deterministic or indeterministic.)

(ii)   No. This claim is really identical to the previous one.

(iii)   Yes.

(iv)   No. The only thing that has been shown is (v). There may be other arguments to show that the issue does turn on the truth of materialist Darwinism. All we have shown is that this argument doesn't show it. It is, in general, crucial to distinguish between proving something false and failing to prove that it is true. (Think of the BSE crisis. The scientists failed to prove that BSE was transmitted from animals to humans, but that was not enough to show that it wasn't.)

(v)   Yes; this is just what has been shown.

(vi)   Yes.

(vii)   Yes. This is really a restatement of (v).

(viii) Yes.

(ix)   No.

(x)   Yes.

Exercise 8.3

1 (i) Liberal.
   (ii) Liberal (because this is just about tastes, not moral principles).
   (iii) Self-defeating relativist. The claim is incoherent. What else could you judge them by? Even if you tried to judge them by their own values, you would still be using your own values in saying that was how they should be judged. And the speaker is making a judgement in expressing the claim.
   (iv) Incoherent. What about the value of the opinion that other opinions are not equally valuable?
   (v) Liberal.
   (vi) Self-defeating relativist.

2 (i) Principle: e.g. 'Killing to prevent murder isn't murder', or 'People who murder deserve to lose their own lives'.
       Disagreement with principle: e.g. extra-judicial killing of other human beings is never justified.
       Disagreement with application: abortion isn't murder.
   (ii) Principle as stated: There should be limits to freedom of speech, and this is one of them.
       Disagreement with principle: e.g. Freedom of speech should be unlimited.
       Disagreement with application: This demonstration wouldn't have stirred up racial hatred.
   (iii) Principle: The only thing that can make killing illegitimate is the possession of rights.
       Disagreement with principle: There are other grounds on which it can be wrong to kill.
       Disagreement with application: Animals fulfil the necessary criteria for the possession of rights.

Exercise 9.1

1 For example:

	Travel	Don't travel
Crash	Dead; daughter distraught	Huge relief all round, outweighing missing of wedding
No crash	Wonderful	Great disappointment on all sides, perhaps some resentment

Given the usual safety of flying, you would probably take the risk anyway for something so important. But presumably you would think it definitely all right in the case of (ii).

2   Your examples should be appropriate adaptations of the matrix in (1).

3   (i)   AIDS

For example:

	Medicine available	**Medicine unavailable**
Effective	Wonderful	Death; remorse because it could have been prevented
Harmful	Not much harm done; that person was dying anyway	No harm done

In that case, it seems rational to go for the medicine.

(ii)   Morning sickness

For example:

	Medicine available	**Medicine unavailable**
Effective and harmless to child	No maternal sickness No harm to child	Maternal sickness No harm to child
Effective but harmful to child	No maternal sickness Harm to child	Maternal sickness No harm to child

In that case, it seems clear that the medicine should not be available.

Exercise 9.2

There are many acceptable variations here. Possible answers are:

(i)   Socially incompetent people should not be born.
(ii)   We should encourage the birth of the intelligent and discourage that of the unintelligent.
(iii)   The law should be aimed at preventing suffering (in women?).

(iv)   People have an absolute right not to be experimented on without their consent.

(v)   People should not be prevented from doing what they want to do, even for their own good; the good of others provides the only legitimate justification.

(vi)   It is more important to increase access to beautiful things than to preserve their beauty intact.

Revision questions

Answers on pp. 299–303.

Chapter 1

1 Which of these traditional ideas about ourselves and the universe were changed by the Copernican/Newtonian revolution?

    (a) The universe is enclosed and finite.
    (b) We are in a physical situation that reflects our position in the great chain of being, just below the angels.
    (c) We are partly material and partly spiritual.
    (d) The heavens and earth are of radically different kinds of substance.
    (e) The soul is distinct from the body.
    (f) The soul is superior to the body.
    (g) Mind must underlie all existence and order (the Mind First view).

2 What does Dennett mean by explanations involving cranes and skyhooks? Why are these terms useful in explaining the difference between Darwinian and traditional kinds of explanation?

3 What does Dennett mean by his claim that Darwinism is a universal acid?

4 What is a teleological explanation? Give a non-teleological and a teleological explanation of some event, for instance, the slamming of a door.

5 Which of the following explanations are (as they stand) teleological?

    (a) The accident happened because his neighbour had cut through the brake cables of his car.
    (b) He cut through the brake cables because he wanted to kill his neighbour.
    (c) The brakes failed because he had not bothered to have the car serviced.
    (d) People got the idea of flight by watching birds and insects.
    (e) He spent his life working on aeroplane designs because he envied the birds their ability to fly.
    (f) I expect I shall go out this afternoon; the children will nag me until I do.
    (g) I expect I shall decide to go out; I do want to hear that lecture.
    (h) *Parsifal* is wonderful, so we shall certainly go to see the new production.
    (i) He was driven out of the house by his hostile neighbours.
    (j) His neighbours drove him out because they didn't like him.
    (k) He went because he didn't feel he could contend any longer with his hostile neighbours.

6   Translate the following into non-teleological Darwinian language:

(a) The peacock developed his tail to attract females.
(b) Giraffes have long necks so that they can reach the food on high branches.

7   Say whether the following express monist or dualist views. In the case of monism, say whether it is materialist (taking matter as fundamental) or idealist (taking mind as fundamental).

(a) Matter is, literally, something we construct out of our sensations. What we mean by a tree is a collection of tree-like sensations.
(b) Thoughts are just neurons firing in the brain.
(c) Minds and emotions are the result of natural selection, just as body parts are.
(d) After death the soul goes into another body.
(e) At the round world's imagined corners blow
     Your trumpets, angels, and arise, arise
     From death, you numberless infinities
     Of souls, and to your scattered bodies go ...
                                        (John Donne)
(f) The whole world is an idea in the mind of God.

Chapter 2

1   Which of the following claims express ordinary scientific doubt, and which radical scepticism?

(a) I know it hasn't rained there for over a hundred years, but that doesn't prove anything; no matter what has happened in the past, anything can happen in the future.
(b) I know it hasn't rained there for over a hundred years, but there have been some odd climate changes recently, and they may affect that area.
(c) It's absurd to make such a fuss about animals. We can only see their behaviour, so we have no idea whether they are suffering.
(d) It is impossible to tell when the world began, because whenever it was created it would have borne the traces of an illusory past.
(e) We may be completely wrong about the information coming from Mars; there may be some kind of magnetic band that distorts the signals.

2   What was wrong with Gosse's rebuttal of geologists' claims about the age of the earth?

(a) He believed the Genesis account was true, when in fact it was false.
(b) He did not understand how much evidence the scientists had.

(c) He thought that however much evidence scientists collected, there was always a possibility that they could be wrong.

(d) His own empirical evidence was faulty.

(e) He was making a metaphysical claim in reply to a scientific one, so his reply was irrelevant.

Chapter 3

1   The diagram on p. 54 shows differences of opinion about:

(a) Whether Darwinism is true.
(b) Whether we are entirely material.
(c) The scope of Darwinian explanation.
(d) The nature of Darwinian explanation.

2   The three lines on the band of deepening Darwinism mark the thresholds of: (i) Darwinism; (ii) materialism; (iii) evolutionary psychology. Which would be most likely to separate people who disagreed about:

(a) The existence of God.
(b) Whether radically changed social conditions could produce significant changes in human nature.
(c) The truth of the Bible.
(d) Whether the mind and body were distinct entities, capable of separate existence.
(e) Whether creationism should be taught in schools.
(f) Whether men and women would be psychologically similar if they were brought up in similar ways.
(g) Whether there is a hope of life after death.
(h) Whether the disappearance of matter would mean the disappearance of everything.

3   The central (materialism) division on the band marks a distinction between people who do and do not believe that (tick one):

(a) There are no such things as minds.
(b) Consciousness does not really exist; we are just collections of inanimate material working according to physical laws.
(c) All life and consciousness originated from inanimate matter, working according to the laws of physics and without any other intervention.

4   The right-hand division on the band marks a distinction between people who do and do not believe that (tick one):

(a) Everything about our characters is produced by our cultural environment.

(b) An understanding of our evolutionary origins can throw light on human nature.

(c) Most of the differences between people are genetic.

(d) Everything about our characters is produced by our genes.

(e) Most characteristics of people result from environmental influences.

5   Many of Mill's contemporaries claimed that the sexes were by nature 'in nothing alike'. What was his reply?

(a) There is no natural difference between the sexes; all the differences are produced by social conditioning.

(b) There are some natural differences, but social conditioning produces a great many more.

(c) It is impossible to tell, because the sexes are brought up in systematically different environments, which makes it imposible to disentangle the different elements.

6   Evolutionary psychologists think that male and female natures are bound to be different on average because (tick one):

(a) Their different reproductive systems would make different emotional characteristics evolutionarily successful.

(b) Women have always been tied to children, and so would originally have learned different skills.

(c) The evolutionary success of the human race depends on a difference of function between the sexes.

(d) Mothers and fathers have importantly different roles in the successful rearing of children.

(e) Men and women differ from each other in 2 per cent of their genes.

7   Evolutionary psychologists believe that (tick one):

(a) Individuals of both sexes want to have as many children as possible.

(b) Individuals of both sexes do everything they can to ensure the survival of their genes.

(c) The emotions bred into the sexes by evolution are ones that will do most to ensure the survival of their genes.

(d) The emotions bred into the sexes by evolution are ones that have been successful in bringing about the survival of their genes.

(e) Most men will have far more offspring than most women.

8   Are the following claims about people or about issues or about both?

(a) The evidence given by X in his book does nothing to support the conclusion he draws from that evidence.

(b) Most of the evidence given by X has been shown by Y's research to be illusory.
(c) Y's research is all motivated by a wish to defend his political conclusions.
(d) If Y is right, the political implications are appalling.
(e) Y's research is distorted by his political loyalties.
(f) Y is a careless researcher whose views are not to be trusted.
(g) The evidence Y gives is interesting, but it doesn't deal with the problems raised by X.

Chapter 4

1   Are the following claims made, or at least strongly implied, in the text? (Yes or no to each.)

(a) Once we know the truth about Darwinism, the implications are obvious.
(b) There is no point in finding out whether a Darwinian claim is true until we have investigated its implications.
(c) There is no point in investigating the implications of a Darwinian claim until we know whether it is true.
(d) The truth and the implications of a Darwinian claim need separate investigation.
(e) People often presume that the implications of a view are clear, when really they are not.
(f) It is generally better to investigate the truth of a claim first, and its implications afterwards.
(g) It is generally better to investigate the implications of a claim first, and its truth afterwards.
(h) Whether it is better to investigate the truth of a claim or its implications first depends on circumstances.
(i) When the truth of a claim is difficult to establish, it is often worthwhile to investigate its implications, to find out how much turns on its truth.

2   What is presupposed by each of the following? (There is more than one possible answer in each case. Remember that this is only about what is presupposed, not whether the presupposition is true.)

(a) Darwin proved that we have no soul by showing that we have evolved by natural selection from ape-like ancestors.
(b) Our character is determined by our social environment, not our genes, so we may eventually be able to bring about a just society.
(c) We can't expect to be happy in our present society; we evolved under quite different circumstances.
(d) Of course we are all fundamentally selfish. We have evolved as a result of natural selection.

3   A conditional statement *if p then q* is true when (tick one):

   (a) *p* is true.
   (b) *q* is true.
   (c) Either *p* or *q* is true.
   (d) *p* and *q* are both true.
   (e) The truth of *p* is a sufficient condition of the truth of *q*.
   (f) The truth of *p* is a necessary condition of the truth of *q*.
   (g) The truth of *p* is necessary and sufficient for the truth of *q*.

4   Show the steps involved in testing these conditionals:

   (a) If we are entirely material, we cannot be responsible for our actions.
   (b) If evolution has bred polygynous tendencies into men, women will always be made miserable by male philandering.

Chapter 5

1   When evolutionary psychologists claim that natural selection has produced certain characteristics in men and women, that should be understood as meaning or implying (yes or no to each):

   (a) All men have the male characteristics and all women the female ones.
   (b) The average man and the average woman have different emotions.
   (c) If males and females are given the same formative environment, they will turn out differently on average.
   (d) Those characteristics cannot be modified by the environment.
   (e) People who have those characteristics are bound to act according to them.
   (f) These characteristics will result in strong tendencies to different behaviour in the sexes.
   (g) It is impossible to eliminate them by any means.
   (h) Acting according to those characteristics will result in genetic success.

2   If characteristic differences of temperament between the sexes are caused by different environments, must it be easy (a) to eliminate those differences in adults, and (b) to prevent their becoming ingrained in children? Explain.

Chapter 6

1   For each of the following excuses for murder, say whether the idea is to remove blame on the grounds (i) that the defendant had few options or no choice at all, or (ii) that he was not capable of choosing rationally between the options that were available:

    (a) He killed his lover because he was so crazed with misery when she left him for another man.

    (b) He killed her because it was the only way he could stop her from taking the children away.

    (c) He was never taught to control his temper; once he loses it, he has no control at all.

    (d) He was on hallucinogenic drugs, and thought God was telling him to do it.

    (e) He killed her because he knew of no other way to end her suffering.

2   If you want to find out whether something exists (unicorns, life on Mars, free will, a highest prime number), or could exist under certain circumstances, what is the first thing you need to do?

3   Which of the following are necessarily nonexistent, and which contingently nonexistent? (If you find any of the answers unclear, try to work out why.)

    (a) The Elixir of Youth.
    (b) The Earth's second moon.
    (c) A spherical cube.
    (d) A vegetarian carnivore.
    (e) Your dream partner.
    (f) Flying cats.
    (g) A prime number between 8 and 10.
    (h) A planet between Mars and Jupiter.
    (i) Deciduous trees that never shed their leaves.

4   A deterministic state of affairs is one in which everything that happens is entirely caused by what went before. An indeterministic state of affairs is one in which (tick one):

    (a) At least some things are caused.
    (b) At least some things are not caused.
    (c) Everything is uncaused.

5   What are contraries and contradictories?

6   Give the contradictory and two contraries of the following:

    (a) This is a black raven.
    (b) All ravens are black.
    (c) There's no smoke without fire.

7   Why is determinism usually thought to rule out free will (genuine choice and responsibility)?

8   What problem arises with the idea that indeterminism could allow for genuine responsibility?

9   What is meant in this chapter by:

(a) Ordinary responsibility?
(b) Ultimate responsibility?

10 Does any of the three degrees of Darwinism preclude ordinary responsibility? Does any allow for ultimate responsibility?

Chapter 7

1   Why did altruism present a problem for classical Darwinism? (Start by saying what altruism is, and then saying why Darwinism would seem to rule it out.)

2   What is neo-Darwinism?

3   How did neo-Darwinism solve the problem of altruism? (tick one)

(a) By showing that the sacrifice of the individual worked for the good of the group or the species.
(b) By abandoning the idea of natural selection.
(c) By showing that altruism in organisms could, under certain circumstances, propagate particular genes more effectively than selfishness could.

4   Translate into non-teleological, Darwinian language:

Worker bees help their mothers to reproduce rather than having offspring of their own so that they can get more of their genes into future generations.

5   Barash claims that the kinds of altruism identified by Trivers and Hamilton are not true altruism because:

(a) Reciprocal altruism involves doing favours only in the expectation of return.
(b) Parental altruism is a matter of trying to get genes into the next generation, and therefore selfish.

How should Trivers and Hamilton reply?

6   One way of clarifying and assessing an author's argument is to try to write

it out just as it appears in the text. The method used in this chapter, for reconstructing Barash's arguments, works differently. It is useful whenever the form of the argument is at all unclear, and is a good way of finding the best way to interpret the argument anyone puts forward. Briefly, what are the steps involved? (Make a list.)

7 Is acting according to your desires the same as acting in your interests? Explain and illustrate.

8 In which of the following statements are the second parts inappropriate? Why?

   (a) He thinks the house is haunted, but it's only the noises of the heating system.
   (b) She thinks she's dying of a deadly disease, but it's only a bad cold.
   (c) She thinks she's dying of a deadly disease, but all that's happening is that some micro-organisms are multiplying in her bloodstream.
   (d) She's not really being altruistic; she's only doing it because she hopes to inherit a lot of money.
   (e) She's not really unselfish; helping people is what gives her pleasure.
   (f) He didn't really choose to jump; he was pushed.
   (g) He didn't really choose to jump; it was just those neurones firing in his brain.

Chapter 8

1 Do the following questions belong to the area of normative ethics or metaethics?

   (a) Are there any objective moral truths?
   (b) Is lying always wrong?
   (c) Are moral judgments anything more than expressions of emotion?
   (d) Is it wrong to eat animals?
   (e) Are we ever justified in suppressing freedom of speech?
   (f) Can we ever be justified in saying that our moral opinions are better than other people's?
   (g) Can genetic survival devices indicate real moral truth?

2 Can someone who believes in the Divine Command theory of ethics recognize the Problem of Evil? Explain.

3 Which of the following express liberal principles, and which self-refuting relativism?

   (a) Everyone should be allowed to say whatever they believe.

(b) Everyone should be allowed to follow their own principles without interference.

(c) Everyone should be allowed to follow the dictates of their own religion.

(d) People should not be prevented from doing what harms only themselves.

(e) We should be tolerant of all customs that do no harm to others.

(f) Everyone's opinions are as valuable as everyone else's.

4 Are there any objective ways of testing our moral intuitions?

Chapter 9

1 What is presupposed by Kitcher's claim that the theories of sociobiology should be rejected until there is strong evidence in their favour?

2 Why does Kitcher think we should take politics into account when deciding how much evidence we should expect in favour of a theory?

(a) Because we should resist any theory that has unwelcome political implications.

(b) Because political implications are relevant to our assessment of the seriousness of taking different risks.

(c) Because when people have strong political commitments they need strong evidence to dislodge their opinions.

3 Why does Kitcher think sociobiology should be assumed false until there is strong evidence in its favour?

4 What is the naturalistic fallacy?

5 What is the point of discussing, in this chapter, the arguments of James Fitzjames Stephen? How are they relevant to this issue?

6 James Fitzjames Stephen argues that women should be subordinate to their husbands in marriage. What claim about matters of fact forms his main premise? What is his implied value premise?

7 Stephen's argument runs into serious mistakes of detail, but there is a broader problem as well. What is the general difficulty about reaching his conclusion from his premises?

8 What kind of value premise might allow for a valid argument from Stephen's first premise to his conclusion?

9 How should we respond, in general, when anyone claims that a particular scientific theory has objectionable political implications?

10 What is presupposed by the claim that we should not be interfering with the course of nature?

11 What problems are there with the idea that if we try to change the characteristics evolution has put into us, we are bound to do harm? List three, if possible.

12 What are QWERTY phenomena?

Chapter 10

1 According to the arguments given here, what two aspects of disagreement between materialists and their opponents have the greatest potential to influence our hopes and actions? What are the relevant differences of implication?

Answers to revision questions

Chapter 1

1 (a), (b) and (d) changed. The others remained intact.
2 Skyhooks come down from above to lift what cannot rise by its own efforts; cranes lift while remaining rooted to the ground. Traditional explanations were of the skyhook form, and explained the lower/less powerful in terms of the higher/more powerful. Minds are traditionally more powerful than matter, and this gave rise to the traditional Mind First view. Darwinian explanation reverses this, and explains the higher and more complex in terms of the lower and simpler.
3 He means that explanations of a Darwinian (cranes-only) kind are potentially relevant to a huge range of phenomena; and because they reverse the traditional order of explanation, they have profound effects on our understanding of everything about ourselves and the world.
4 A teleological explanation is one that explains in terms of ends, or purposes, rather than mechanical causes; e.g. She slammed the door to demonstrate her anger (teleological); The door slammed because she gave it a sudden push (non-teleological).
5 Teleological: (b), (e), (g), (h), (j), (k).
6 (a) Males with large tails were attractive to peahens, so they left more offspring than smaller-tailed males. The genes for large tails in males passed (along with the genes for preferring large tails in females) into the offspring, and tails gradually increased in size.
   (b) Among ancestral giraffes, the ones who could reach higher leaves had an advantage over the others when there was a shortage of food. The animals with these genes were more successful in reproduction than the short-necked animals (perhaps just because they survived, perhaps because females liked the look of well-fed males), and the genes for long necks spread through the population.
7 (a) Monist (idealist)
   (b) Monist (materialist)
   (c) Monist (materialist)
   (d) Dualist
   (e) Dualist
   (f) Monist (idealist)

Chapter 2

1 Radical scepticism: (a), (c), (d).
2 (e)

Chapter 3

1 (c)
2 (a) (ii); (b) (iii); (c) (i); (d) (ii); (e) (i); (f) (iii); (g) (ii); (h) (ii).
3 (c)
4 (b)
5 (c)
6 (a)
7 (d)

8   (a) issues; (b) issues; (c) people; (d) issues; (e) people – but also issues if you take 'research' to refer to the finished product (a report containing distortions) as opposed to the activity; (f) people; (g) issues.

Chapter 4

1   (a) no; (b) no; (c) no; (d) yes; (e) yes; (f) no; (g) no; (h) yes; (i) yes.
2   Possible answers:
    (a) Evolution by natural selection from ape-like creatures cannot result in creatures with souls.
    (b) If character is determined by genes a just society is impossible.
    (c) If creatures evolve under one set of circumstances they are likely to be unhappy in others.
    (d) Natural selection cannot produce genuine altruism.
3   (e)
4   Start by turning the conditionals into argument form:

    We are entirely material
    ――――
    Therefore we cannot be responsible for our actions

    Evolution has bred polygynous tendencies into men and possessive ones into women
    ――――
    Therefore women will always be made miserable by male philandering.

    Complete the arguments to make them valid, using the most plausible premises you can think of, e.g.
    For the first argument:
    Material things cannot have free will.
    Free will is essential for responsibility
    For the second argument:
    Tendencies bred by evolution cannot be removed.

    Then assess the truth of the added premises. If a sound argument cannot be constructed that way, see if other added premises might fare better.

Chapter 5

1   (a) no; (b) yes; (c) yes; (d) no; (e) no; (f) yes; (g) no; (h) no.
2   (a) Knowing how something was caused does not generally imply knowing how to undo the effect. Even if we knew the details of how these characteristics were produced, we might have no idea how to undo them.
    (b) Even if something is environmentally rather than genetically caused, we may have no idea which aspects of the environment are causing it; and even if we do know, we may have no power to change it.

Chapter 6

1   Too few options: (b) and (e)
    Incapable of rational choice: (a), (c) and (d).
2   Make sure you know what you mean by the term in question; what state of affairs

you would count as one in which the thing did exist. You need to know what you mean by a unicorn before you can go out to find out whether they exist. (How would you respond if someone asked you whether snarks existed?) You must also check that your specification is coherent. If what you specify is a unicorn with two horns, what you are thinking of is necessarily nonexistent.

3   Necessarily nonexistent: (c), (d), (g) and (i);
    Contingently nonexistent: (a), (b), (f) and (h). You may not regard (e) as nonexistent; if you do, it may not be clear whether your standards are impossibly (self-contradictorily) high, or just high.

4   (b)

5   Contraries are statements that are mutually exclusive (they cannot both be true together), but not jointly exhaustive (they do not exhaust the possibilities, and so can be false together). Contradictories are both mutually exclusive and jointly exhaustive.

6   Contradictory followed by possible contrary:

    (a)   This is not a black raven (more accurately: it is not the case that this is a black raven).

          This is a yellow raven; this is a pink panther.

    (b)   It is not the case that all ravens are black; i.e. (more or less) at least some ravens are not black.

          No ravens are black; all ravens are yellow with blue spots.

    (c)   There can be smoke without fire.

          There is never fire with smoke; smoke can happen without fire when the temperature is below freezing.

7   Because if the course of events is fixed before you exist, it doesn't look as though you can be genuinely responsible for it.

8   If an event is literally uncaused, nobody can be responsible for it.

9   (a) Being competent to make choices in the familiar sense – i.e. not being insane, under the influence of drugs, in a state of diminished responsibility, of too low intelligence, too young, etc.
    (b) Being responsible for being the person you are, making the choices you do.

10 If these arguments have been right, the answer to both questions is no.

Chapter 7

1   Altruism is (roughly) attending to the interests of others at cost to yourself. But if you divert resources away from yourself (or your offspring) you are lessening your chances of leaving offspring.

2   The account of Darwinian evolution that takes account of the genetic revolution, and in particular sees natural selection as working at the level of the gene, rather than the organism.

3   (c)

4   Something like:
    Because female bees are more closely related to their sisters than their offspring, bees that accidentally developed an inclination to care for their mother's offspring

rather than having their own were more successful in passing their genes into the next generation. That inclination therefore spread throughout the population.

5   They should say:

(a)   This reply mistakes the nature of the theory. Barash's claim is true of the arrangements between selfish individuals, but Trivers's theory works at the genetic level. The genes have as-it-were done the calculating, and instilled into the phenotypes a capacity for genuine (though necessarily limited) altruism.

(b)   This depends on the assumption (i) that the emotions that have on the whole been genetically successful in the past still are genetically successful, and are so for all individuals; (ii) that the interests of the genes are the same as the interests of the individual. Neither of these is true.

6   The procedure is flexible, but it works along these lines:

(a)   Identify the conclusion.

(b)   See whether there are any kinds of premise that are essential to an argument leading to that conclusion. (E.g. if the conclusion is that something is not true altruism, one of the premises must say what true altruism is.) See whether the author says or implies anything of the kind; if not, note that a presupposition is being made.

(c)   See what other elements can be found to complete the argument. Can it be made valid? Does it contain fallacies that prevent it from working at all? If it is incomplete, what further premises would complete it?

(d)   When the argument seems valid, test it for soundness: see whether the premises seem true, and check for equivocation.

If it doesn't work, see whether the text suggests any better way of producing an argument to that conclusion.

7   No, because whenever you choose to do anything (or not do anything) you are necessarily acting according to your all-things-considered desires. Your desires may be to act against your interests and in favour of someone else's. If the two are taken to be identical, altruism is impossible by definition (nonexistent in all possible worlds).

8   Inappropriate: (c), (e) and (g). The others give a rival account of what is going on, showing that these things are not what they seem to be – hence the use of 'but', 'only' and 'really'. This is what (c), (e) and (g) purport to be doing, but in fact they give an explanation at a different level, which does not compete with the original description.

Chapter 8

1   Normative ethics: (b), (d) and (e).
    Metaethics: (a), (c), (f) and (g).

2   The Divine Command theory is the view that whatever God wills is, by definition, right. The traditional Problem of Evil is the difficulty of reconciling the idea of a good and omnipotent God with the evil in the world. But if whatever God wills is good, and God is omnipotent, nothing in the world can be evil.

3   Liberal: (a), (d) and (e).
    Self-refuting relativist: (b), (c) and (f).

4   We can at the very least test them for consistency. If we have contradictory principles, we know they cannot both be right as they stand.

Chapter 9

1   That it would be worse to act as though sociobiology were true, if it was in fact false, than the other way round.

2 (b)
3 Because he thinks it has implications that are opposed to our ideals of social justice. It is widely believed that the ideas of sociobiology have right-wing implications.
4 The idea that conclusions about what ought to happen can be deduced from premises stating nothing but facts about the natural world. Or, in other words, the idea that 'ought' can be derived from 'is'. If an argument to an 'ought' conclusion does not contain an explicit value premise, it is important to work out what is implied and make it explicit.
5 Stephen starts with a claim about the natures and situations of men and women – some aspects of which sound like the ideas of present-day evolutionary psychologists – and reaches a decidedly right-wing conclusion. The details of his argument may help to show how premises about deep aspects of human nature are claimed to support conclusions of this kind, and put us in a position to assess whether they really do. In this case, as in many others, the premises do not support the conclusion.
6 The claim about matters of fact is that women are at many natural disadvantages to men. The implied value premise is that the weak need protection.
7 That if you want to protect a weak group, the last thing you do is put it into the legal and conventional power of a stronger group.
8 Perhaps a claim that the weak did not matter and could be treated as slaves by the strong; or that we should let the strong get all they could.
9 That you can't reach any conclusions about what ought to happen on the basis of factual claims alone. You need value premises as well (or you will be committing the naturalistic fallacy). It is here that political ideals come in, not in the factual claims.
   When someone does put a value premise into the argument (as Stephen does), check carefully that the argument works. Arguments are often fudged to make it seem that unwelcome conclusions follow from benevolent premises about such things as protecting the weak.
10 That nature has a course to interfere with. Interference can only be with some plan or scheme; the essence of Darwinian evolution (in its materialist forms) is that it has none. You can't interfere with the course of evolution, because whatever happens is part of the course of evolution.
11 (i) The characteristics we now have are the result of genetic success in the past; there is no reason to think they are the best for present genetic purposes. (ii) Genetic success is, anyway, not necessarily connected with anything else we regard as good. (iii) Whatever purposes we want to fulfil, evolution is most unlikely to have made the best possible job of it. It is plagued with QWERTY phenomena, and has no foresight.
12 Fossils of past functions, which form a basis from which it is difficult or impossible to reach what would be best under present circumstances.

Chapter 10

1 Dualism and the Mind First view. These beliefs allow, respectively, for the possibility of life after death and for a morally ordered universe. Neither of these seems possible with Darwinian materialism.

Suggestions for further reading

Chapters 1 and 2

The Copernican Revolution, by Thomas Kuhn, is by now quite an old book, but it gives a wonderful sense of how people standing on the surface of the earth, looking at points of light in the sky, could move from that position to the understanding that the earth was the same kind of thing.

Darwin: A life in Science, by Michael White and John Gribbin, one of many biographies of Darwin, also contains a fascinating account of the surprisingly long history of pre-Darwinian speculations about evolution.

Created from Animals: The Moral Implications of Darwinism, by James Rachels, is an excellent, well argued and accessible introduction to Darwinism and philosophy, dealing with religion, animals and ethics in general.

Darwin's Dangerous Idea, by Daniel Dennett, another philosophical introduction to Darwinian matters, is extensively trailed in this book, and needs little further introduction. Dennett is in the thick of Darwinian controversy and therefore has his opponents, but even they would probably admit that the book was a real *tour de force*, with a wonderful scientific and philosophical sweep.

Evidence and Enquiry: Towards Reconstruction in Epistemology, by Susan Haack, is a recent analysis of questions about knowledge and evidence. It is serious philosophy – not a light read – but a first-rate study of some of the questions introduced in Chapter 2.

The Flamingo's Smile: Reflections in Natural History, in which the essay on Gosse appears, is one of Stephen Jay Gould's many collections of essays on Darwinian and related matters. Gould is one of the best-known combatants in the Darwin wars, but even people who disagree with many of his views would probably agree that his essays are delightful reading and full of interest. Ideal bedtime reading for newcomers to this terrain.

Chapters 3 and 4

The Moral Animal, by Robert Wright, is an immensely good read and an excellent popular introduction to evolutionary psychology.

The Red Queen: Sex and the Evolution of Human Nature, by Matt Ridley, is also very good. It is quite difficult in the first half, but becomes easier later, and connects well with the material of Chapter 3.

Richard Dawkins has written dozens of books. *The Selfish Gene* is a classic, as is *The Blind Watchmaker: Why the Evidence of Evolution Reveals a Universe Without Design*. If after reading those you still find it almost impossible to believe that the complexity of the living world could have arisen by natural selection from simple beginnings, try his *Climbing Mount Improbable*.

The Darwin Wars, by Andrew Brown – published after most of this book had been written – gives the newcomer an introduction to Darwinian hostilities of a different kind from the one offered here: one that goes into personalities as well as issues, and is more descriptive than analytic. It is a good read, and provides the kind of information that is useful when you are browsing in bookshops and need to know which authors come where in the debate.

Abusing Science: The Case against Creationism, by Philip Kitcher, is a critical account of the ideas of American creationism. It is an oldish book, but still relevant; the subject has not changed much.

Chapters 5 and 6

For a much fuller discussion of problems of free will and responsbility see Galen Strawson's 1986 book *Freedom and Belief*, and his 1994 article 'The impossibility of moral responsibility'.

For another accessible introduction to the problem, which reaches similar conclusions but for different reasons, see *How Free are you?: The Determinism Problem*, by Ted Honderich. This also discusses how we should respond, personally, to the conclusion that free will as traditionally conceived does not exist.

How the Mind Works, by Stephen Pinker, is a different kind of discussion of issues raised in these chapters and elsewhere in this book, by an author in the thick of current controversies.

Chapters 7 and 8

The Moral Animal, by Robert Wright, already mentioned, provides a very good introduction to ideas about altruism in current Darwinian thinking.

The Ant and the Peacock: Altruism and Sexual Selection from Darwin to Today, by Helena Cronin, is a much more scholarly and analytic, but still very readable, account of the development of Darwinian ideas about altruism, and is an ideal antidote to the crude simplifications offered in this book and in many other popular accounts.

Chapter 9

Plan and Purpose in Nature, by George C. Williams, belies its title by being an account of Darwinian nature as totally unplanned, and full of design flaws. It is a quite delightful account of what the author calls the adaptationist program in evolutionary thinking; an ideal introduction to the world through Darwinian eyes. It contains a brief introduction to Darwinian medicine, which may lead you to *Evolution and Healing: The New Science of Darwinian Medicine*, by Nesse and Williams.

A Darwinian Left, by Peter Singer (published after this book was written) is another set of arguments against the idea that evolutionary psychology has right-wing implications.

This book is one of the Weidenfeld & Nicolson series *Darwinism Today*, edited by Helena Cronin and Oliver Curry: a series of short books introducing a range of Darwinian issues.

Bibliography

Axelrod, R. (1984) *The Evolution of Co-operation*, Penguin Books.

Barash, D. (1979) *Sociobiology: The Whisperings Within*, Fontana/Collins.

Behe, M.J. (1996) *Darwin's Black Box: The Biochemical Challenge to Evolution*, Free Press.

Brown, A. (1999) *The Darwin Wars*, Simon & Schuster.

Cronin, H. (1991) *The Ant and the Peacock: Altruism and Sexual Selection from Darwin to Today*, Cambridge University Press.

Darwin, C. (1859) *On the Origin of Species by Means of Natural Selection*, Murray.

Darwin, C. (1871) *The Descent of Man, and Selection in Relation to Sex*, 2nd edn, Murray.

Dawkins, R. (1976) *The Selfish Gene*, Oxford University Press.

Dawkins, R. (1982) *The Extended Phenotype*, Oxford University Press.

Dawkins, R. (1986) *The Blind Watchmaker: Why the Evidence of Evolution Reveals a Universe Without Design*, Norton.

Dawkins, R. (1995) *River out of Eden*, Weidenfeld & Nicolson.

Dawkins, R. (1997) *Climbing Mount Improbable*, Penguin Books.

Deacon, T. (1997) *The Symbolic Species: The Co-evolution of Language and the Human Brain*, Penguin Books.

Dennett, D. C. (1995) *Darwin's Dangerous Idea: Evolution and the Meanings of Life*, Penguin Books.

Deutsch, D. (1997) *The Fabric of Reality*, Penguin Books.

Ferris, T. (1997) *The Whole Shebang: A State-of-the-universe(s) Report*, Weidenfeld & Nicolson.

Glover, J. (1984) *What Sort of People Should There Be?*, Penguin Books.

Gosse, P.H. (1857) *Omphalos: An Attempt to Untie the Geological Knot*, John Van Doorst.

Gould, S. J. (1978) *Ever Since Darwin*, Burnett.

Gould, S. J. (1985) *The Flamingo's Smile: Reflections in Natural History*, Norton.

Gould, S. J. (1997) *Life's Grandeur: The Spread of Excellence from Plato to Darwin*, Penguin Books.

Haack, S. (1993) *Evidence and Enquiry: Towards Reconstruction in Epistemology*, Blackwell.

Hamilton, W. D. (1964) 'The genetical evolution of social behaviour', *Journal of Theoretical Biology* 7: 1–16, 17–52.

Honderich, T. (1993) *How Free Are You?: The Determinism Problem*, Oxford University Press.

Hume, D. (1978 edn) *A Treatise of Human Nature*, Oxford University Press.

Kitcher, P. (1983) *Abusing Science: The Case against Creationism*, Open Univiversity Press.

Kitcher, P. (1985) *Vaulting Ambition: Sociobiology and the Quest for Human Nature*, The MIT Press.

Kuhn, T. (1957) *The Copernican Revolution*, Harvard University Press.

Locke, J. (1964 edn) *An Essay Concerning Human Understanding*, ed. J. W. Yolton, Dent.

Locke, J. (1976 abridged edn) *An Essay Concerning Human Understanding*, ed. J. W. Yolton, Dent.

Maynard Smith, J. (1974) 'The theory of games and the evolution of animal conflicts', *Journal of Theoretical Biology* 47: 209–21.

Maynard Smith, J. (1988) *Games, Sex and Evolution*, Harvester (also published as *Did Darwin get it Right?*).

Midgley, M. (1986) *Evolution as a Religion*, Routledge.

Mill, J. S. (1991 edn) *On Liberty and Other Essays*, ed. J. Gray, Oxford University Press (World's Classics).

Moore, G. E. (1903) *Principia Ethica*, Cambridge University Press.

Nesse, R. M. and Williams, G. C. (1995) *Evolution and Healing: The New Science of Darwinian Medicine*, Weidenfeld & Nicolson.

Orr, H. A. (1997) 'Intelligent design (again)', *Boston Review* December/January 1997.

Pinker, S. (1998) *How the Mind Works*, Penguin Books.

Rachels, J. (1999) *Created from Animals: The Moral Implications of Darwinism*, Oxford University Press.

Radcliffe Richards, J. (1994) *The Sceptical Feminist*, 2nd edn, Penguin Books. (First published 1980.)

Ridley, Matt (1994) *The Red Queen: Sex and the Evolution of Human Nature*, Penguin Books.

Rose, S. (1978) 'Pre-Copernican sociobiology?', *New Scientist* 80: 45–6.

Rose, S. (1997) *Lifelines: Biology beyond Determinism*, Oxford University Press.

Ruskin, J. (1974 edn) *Sesame and Lilies*, Dent.

Schuster, P. and Sigmund, K. (1981) 'Coyness, philandering and stable strategies', *Animal Behaviour* 29: 186–92.

Simpson, G. G. (1966) 'The biological nature of man', *Science* 152: 472–8.

Singer, P. (1999) *A Darwinian Left*, Weidenfeld & Nicolson.

Stephen, J. Fitzjames (1991 edn) *Liberty, Equality, Fraternity*, University of Chicago Press.

Strawson, G. (1986) *Freedom and Belief*, Oxford University Press.

Strawson, G. (1994) 'The impossibility of moral responsibility', *Philosophical Studies* Vol. 74.

Trivers, R.L. (1971) 'The evolution of reciprocal altruism', *Quarterly Review of Biology* 46.

Trivers, R.L. (1972) 'Parental investment and sexual selection' in Campbell, B. (ed.) *Sexual Selection and the Descent of Man 1871–1971*, Heinemann.

White, M. and Gribbin, J. (1995) *Darwin: A life in Science*, Simon & Schuster.

Williams, G. C. (1996) *Plan and Purpose in Nature*, Weidenfeld & Nicolson.

Wilson, E. O. (1975) *Sociobiology: The New Synthesis*, Harvard University Press.

Wilson, E. O. (1978) *On Human Nature*, Harvard University Press.

Wright, R. (1994) *The Moral Animal*, Abacus.

Index